D1480382

THE GREATEST TRAITOR

Ian Mortimer was educated at Eastbourne College, Exeter University and University College London. He has worked for several archival and historical research organisations, including Devon Record Office, Reading University, the Historical Manuscripts Commission and Exeter University. He is married with three children and lives on the edge of Dartmoor. He was elected a Fellow of the Royal Historical Society in 1998. He is not descended from Sir Roger Mortimer, the subject of this book.

THE GREATEST TRAITOR

The Greatest Traitor
The Life of Sir Roger Mortimer,
Ruler of England: 1327–1330

———

IAN MORTIMER

Thomas Dunne Books
St. Martin's Press
New York

Maps by Reginald Piggott

www.stmartins.com

Library of Congress Cataloging-in-Publication Data

ISBN 0-312-34941-6
EAN 978-0-312-34941-7

First published in Great Britain by Jonathan Cape under the title
The Greatest Traitor: The Life of Sir Roger Mortimer,
1st Earl of March, Ruler of England, 1327–1330

First Edition: March 2006

10 9 8 7 6 5 4 3 2 1

This book is gratefully dedicated to the memory of my father
JOHN STEPHEN MORTIMER
who took me to Wigmore Castle as a child,
told me not to climb on the walls (but let me do so anyway),
and always encouraged me to explore my fascination with the past.

CONTENTS

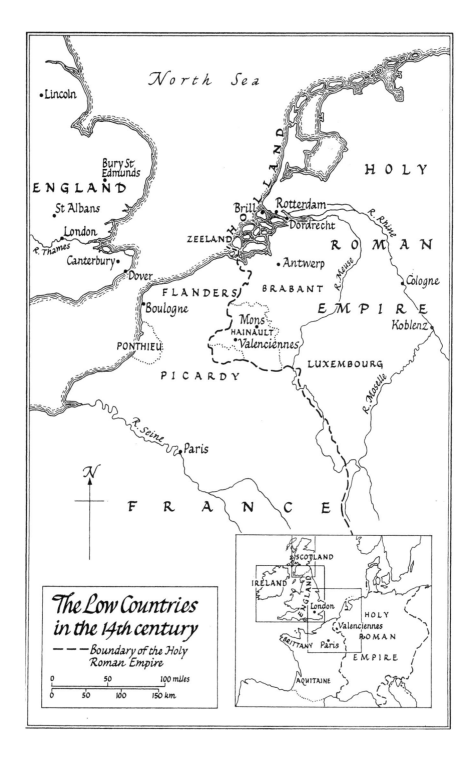

North Sea

•Lincoln

E N G L A N D

Bury St
Edmunds

St Albans•

London•

R. Thames

Canterbury•

Dover•

ZEELAND

Brill• •Rotterdam
         •Dordrecht

H O L L A N D

•Antwerp

FLANDERS

BRABANT

Boulogne•

Mons•
HAINAULT
•Valenciennes

PONTHIEU

P I C A R D Y

H O L Y

R O M A N

E M P I R E

R. Rhine

•Cologne

R. Meuse

•Koblenz

LUXEMBOURG

R. Moselle

R. Seine

•Paris

N

F R A N C E

The Low Countries in the 14th century

— — — *Boundary of the Holy Roman Empire*

0   50   100 miles

0   50   100   150 km

SCOTLAND

IRELAND

ENGLAND

•London

HOLY

•Valenciennes

ROMAN

BRITTANY   •Paris

EMPIRE

AQUITAINE

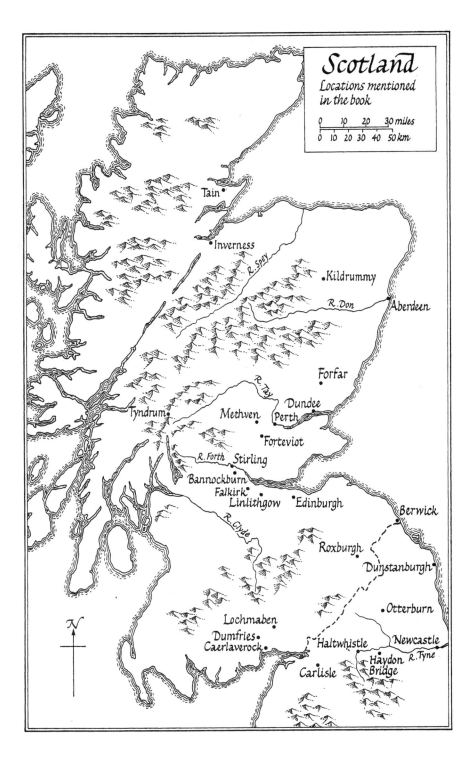

Scotland
Locations mentioned in the book

0   10   20   30 miles
0 10 20 30 40 50 km

Tain

Inverness

R. Spey

Kildrummy

R. Don

Aberdeen

Forfar

R. Tay

Dundee
Perth

Tyndrum

Methven

Forteviot

R. Forth

Stirling

Bannockburn
Falkirk
Linlithgow

Edinburgh

Berwick

R. Clyde

Roxburgh

Dunstanburgh

Otterburn

Lochmaben

Dumfries
Caerlaverock

Haltwhistle

Newcastle

Carlisle

Haydon
Bridge

R. Tyne

N

ATLANTIC

OCEAN

Rathlin Island

Coleraine

R. Bann

Olderfleet
(Larne)

Carrickfergus

Lough Neagh

IRISH

SEA

Dundalk

Nobber • Ardee
R. Dee
Kells • Slane
Navan • Drogheda
Athboy • Duleek
R. Boyne • Trim

Roscommon •

Granard •

Athlone •

R. Shannon

R. Liffey

Naas • Dublin

Kildare •

Dunamase •

Ardscull

Wicklow

Glendalough

R. Nore

R. Barrow

Limerick •

Kilkenny •

Cashel • Thomastown •

Clonmel •

Wexford

R. Blackwater Fermoy •

R. Lee Cork •

Waterford

Youghal

Haverford •

N

Ireland

Showing locations mentioned
in the book

0 10 20 30 40 50 miles

0   50   100 km

Tintagel •

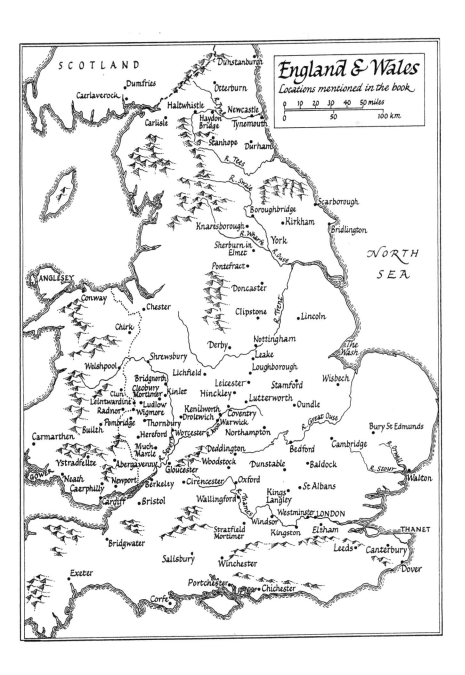

AUTHOR'S NOTE

The early fourteenth century is a particularly difficult period for the systematic application of naming styles. Many of the individuals in this book were noblemen and knights whose hereditary surnames were originally derived from a placename, and thus included the prefix 'de' as a part of the name itself. For example: Roger appears in contemporary documents as Roger de Mortemer (French) or Rogerus de Mortuo Mari (Latin), although his family had their castle at Mortemer (in Normandy) confiscated before 1066. Many of the lower classes, on the other hand, had not adopted hereditary surnames by 1300, and so documents which prefix their second names with 'de' are in fact recording the places where they lived or were born. Historians have usually treated the former separately to the latter, maintaining the French 'de' only for hereditary surnames and using 'of' for geographical epithets: for example, Adam 'of Orleton' is often described thus by historians because he was (rightly or wrongly) believed to have come from Orleton in Herefordshire. A similar surname/epithet problem attends names incorporating the element 'fitz' (son of). The Earls of Arundel continued to use the name FitzAlan throughout the period without changing it, while the Earls of Kildare continued to use 'fitz' as meaning 'son of'; hence Thomas FitzJohn was the son of John FitzThomas, Earl of Kildare, who was the son of Thomas FitzMaurice. A third complication arises in the fact that some characters have become better known by their surnames than their titles, e.g. Simon de Montfort (rather than the Earl of Leicester), while other names are better known in a French or hybrid form, for example Piers Gaveston (not Peter de Gaveston or Gabaston). A last complication is that most standard reference works drop the prefix 'de' (but not 'fitz') when listing titles.

As a result of all this complexity, inconsistency and confusion I have chosen to adopt the following naming system. Firstly, I have normally used the best-known version of the name of a well-known historical personality. Thus I refer to Roger as 'Roger Mortimer' not 'Roger de Mortemer', 'Isabella' not 'Isabelle', etc. Secondly, as 'de'-prefixed surnames in this book are normally hereditary, I have tended to retain 'de' (rather than 'of'), only making exceptions for those individuals for whom 'de' would be inappropriate, such as earls and counts (e.g. Thomas of Lancaster, Donald of Mar, William of Hainault), members of the royal family (e.g.

Edmund of Woodstock), and those who appear under their first name in the old *DNB* (e.g. Adam of Orleton). In a few cases, such as Hugh Audley, the inconsistently applied prefix has been dropped from the surname. Thirdly, all 'Fitz' names have been written as one word, whether hereditary or not. Fourthly, where baronial titles based on surnames have been used – for example, Lord Badlesmere – the 'de' prefix has been dropped, following the practice of the *Complete Peerage*. Where a nobleman is referred to by a single name, it is normally his unprefixed title which is intended (e.g. 'Gloucester' for Gilbert de Clare, Earl of Gloucester, or 'Badlesmere' for Sir Bartholomew de Badlesmere, Lord Badlesmere). Where a nobleman's family is mentioned, however, the full prefixed surname is used.

ACKNOWLEDGEMENTS

I hope readers will not begrudge me using this page to express gratitude to the following individuals. Firstly my wife, Sophie, for her patience and understanding, and my children Alexander and Elizabeth, despite their lack of both. Secondly my agent, James Gill, for deciding this book was worth writing, Will Sulkin, for agreeing with him, and Jörg Hensgen, for helping to bring the book to its final form. Thirdly Paul Dryburgh for sharing some of his research findings on Roger Mortimer, and for discussing various historical points, and Barbara Wright for her many valuable suggestions and corrections, especially with regard to the Wigmore inventories. Fourthly Brian and Jay Hammond for their advice, help and encouragement. Fifthly Zak Reddan and Mary Fawcett for putting up with the family on research trips to London, and for the consequent damage to their possessions and their home. And lastly my wife Sophie again, for continuing to smile at me, and for giving the ever-grinning face of adversity a good smack on the nose.

Storys to rede ar delitabill,
Suppos that they be nocht bot fabill;
Than suld storys that suthfast wer,
And thai war said on gud maner,
hawe doubill plesance in heryng.
The fyrst plesance is the carpyng,
And the tothir the suthfastnes.

(The stories we read delight us,
but suppose they be nothing but fable?
Then should stories which are true
and which are masterfully told
have double the pleasure in being heard.
The first pleasure lies in the telling,
and the other in the truth.)

John Barbour (ed. Walter Skeat), *The Bruce, part 1*,
Early English Text Society extra series XI (1870), p. 1.

INTRODUCTION

On 1 August 1323 a thirty-six-year-old man lay in a chamber high up within the Tower of London. He was a nobleman, the lord of Wigmore, Radnor and Ludlow castles, and the lord of many manors throughout England. He held half the county of Meath and the castle and lordship of Trim in Ireland, and had twice been the governor of that country. He was one of the most experienced battle leaders alive, having fought campaigns in England, Scotland, Wales and Ireland. But he was also King Edward II's prisoner, sentenced to life imprisonment for having taken part in a rebellion two years earlier.

The man's name was Sir Roger Mortimer, Lord Mortimer of Wigmore. That he was a prisoner was not particularly remarkable: a great many noblemen in the early fourteenth century found themselves captive at some point in their careers. What was remarkable was that he was still alive. Nearly all of the other noblemen who had taken part in the recent rebellion against King Edward were dead, most hanged or beheaded at the king's order; and those who were still above ground, such as his sixty-seven-year-old grizzled war veteran of an uncle, were imprisoned without hope of release. With the hated son of the Earl of Winchester, Hugh Despenser, whispering policy into the king's ear one moment and acting as if he himself were king the next, to be a prisoner was to be at the mercy not only of the executioner but also the assassin, the 'smiler with the knife'.

Tension was high. Shortly after their surrender, Sir Roger Mortimer and his uncle had been condemned to death as traitors. Then they had been reprieved, but there was still a danger that they would be condemned to death again, in secret. Eighteen months had passed in this grim uncertainty. In that year and a half the king and Hugh Despenser had ruled without restraint. To many observers, the government was out of control, spiralling into tyranny, as the king and his manipulative friend indulged themselves in an unchecked exploitation of royal power, delighting in the humiliation and destruction of those who questioned their authority. Only one man was considered a serious threat to them – Sir Roger Mortimer – even though he was their prisoner. As opinion in the country hardened against their regime, Despenser convinced the king that they should take this opportunity to destroy him. Thus in the summer of 1323 they agreed to have Roger killed. The date was set for the beginning of August.

The morning of 1 August began like any other for those in the Tower. The afternoon too was not unusual. The early evening meal, however, was to be special. It was the feast of St Peter ad Vincula – St Peter in Chains – whose chapel occupied a corner of the Tower and whose mystical presence watched over those within its walls. The feasting in the hall of the castle was accompanied by much drinking: the drinking continued after the eating had finished, and soon the majority of the guards were drunk. Not only were they drunk, they were sinking increasingly into a soporific state induced by the sub-lieutenant, Gerard d'Alspaye. He had arranged for the kitchen staff to administer drugged wine to the garrison. As the men fell asleep or stumbled about, d'Alspaye hastened to the chamber in which Sir Roger Mortimer waited with a fellow prisoner, a squire, Richard de Monmouth. A short while afterwards they heard the scraping of iron against stone as d'Alspaye prised stones from his cell wall with a crowbar. Soon the soft mortar gave way, the stones tumbled free, and they scrambled through a ragged hole in the wall.

Loose within the castle, Roger and his two companions hurried to the kitchen. The cook, who held domain over his kitchen staff as if they were his feudal subjects, silenced the boys and servants present and guarded the escape as the three men climbed into a wide chimney and up into the twilight air. They crossed the roofs of the palace, climbing on to the wall walk and down into the inner bailey, then up on to the outer curtain wall of the castle, by St Thomas's Tower, near Traitor's Gate, using rope ladders. From the top of the wall they let themselves down to the marshy banks of the river. A little way downstream they were met by two Londoners, who armed them and rowed them across the river. At Greenwich, on the south bank, four men-at-arms were ready with extra horses on which they fled in the darkness down the road south, dodging the pursuing king's men by taking the byways to Portchester, finding the hidden rowing boat waiting to take them to a ship bound for France.

*

Sir Roger Mortimer remains to this day one of the very few prisoners to have escaped from the Tower, and in his own time perhaps was only the second to accomplish the feat. His freedom was not merely of personal significance. As a result of it he became the widely acknowledged leader of the resistance to the king and the hated government of Hugh Despenser. Three years later, together with Queen Isabella, he invaded England and took control of the country, thereby completing the first successful invasion since 1066. While the nature of his invasion was very different from that of William the Conqueror, the results had a huge impact on the political state of the nation. Just as at Hastings, the reigning monarch was soon removed from office, his government destroyed, and his favoured retainers stripped of their power and lands. But more importantly, for the first time in English history the king's deposition was agreed in Parliament, not on the battlefield. It was one of the most significant events of medieval European history.

Extraordinary though it may seem, no one has written a full-length biography of Sir Roger Mortimer. One would have thought that the life of a man who ruled the country for almost four years deserves further examination. But even his name is barely known, except as the lover of Queen Isabella. As far as the literary legacies of front-rank English political leaders go, his is one of the slightest: a couple of early plays, a couple of political satires on eighteenth-century statesmen, a minor nineteenth-century romantic novel, and the odd chapter here and there in a few collective biographies.[1] Even with regard to academic study Roger Mortimer has been much ignored, being the subject of only one higher degree thesis and the part-subject (on his rule with Isabella) of two others.[2] Few academic articles have been published on his role, or his possible importance. His current reputation among scholars may be summed up as a brief, elusive, unsavoury shadow in between the reigns of Edward II and Edward III.

What are the reasons for this absence of a legacy? One might say that it is because there are more engaging personalities who steal the early fourteenth-century limelight, most notably Piers Gaveston and Edward II himself. Yet Gaveston's relationship with the king was no more remarkable than Mortimer's with the queen. One was probably homosexual in nature, the other adulterous: both were outrageous aspects of royal behaviour in the early fourteenth century. A more likely explanation of the absence of a biography of Lord Mortimer lies in the fact that it is very difficult to bring medieval personalities to life: we simply do not know enough about their driving forces, their hatreds and loves, to be able to build portraits of characters as opposed to uninspired, armour-clad drones following patterns of feudal behaviour. Alison Weir draws attention to the challenge faced by medieval biographers in the preface to her book on Eleanor of Aquitaine, referring to this lack of first-hand personal detail as the greatest obstacle to creating a credible portrait of her subject.

There is another reason why Lord Mortimer has not been written about before. He has had a bad press. As the man who partnered a queen – the notorious 'She-wolf of France' – in adultery, he has received no sympathy from those moralists down the years who deplore such behaviour in a woman, especially a beautiful and powerful one. In none of the dramatic works which touch upon him is he viewed with any sympathy, and in recent interpretations of Marlowe's *Edward II* he is portrayed as an unflinching, testosterone-exuding military man. Such a two-dimensional representation is neither supported nor denied by academic historians, who place Lord Mortimer and his contemporaries into parties of political leverage rather than presenting them as personalities. Yet if we know anything of the period we know that its politics were intensely personal. Wars were sometimes lost because of one pig-headed lord's refusal to fight alongside a man he did not like. Edward II might not have lost his throne if he had not been so intense in his friendships with men who had equally intense enemies.

Another reason for the bad press Roger has received is the fact that he was condemned as a traitor by Edward III, one of the few monarchs to be as well-thought of by contemporaries and historians as the universally adored Queen Elizabeth I. There was much to lose and nothing to gain from writing well of Lord Mortimer, or even reminding the king and his court of the man's past existence. Shortly after his death there was a deliberate attempt to destroy his reputation and the memory of his popularity by dragging his appointed officers through the courts. Even when the sentence of treason on him was reversed in 1354, twenty-four years after his execution, Edward still had another twenty-three years to reign; and by the time one of Roger's descendants stood in line for the throne, sixty years later, he himself had largely been forgotten. There is thus a considerable amount of 'politeness' behind his failure to stand tall in history. This blanking of the man's positive attributes differs from deliberate propaganda or bias, but it still remains a long way adrift of the historical facts.

This brings us to the key question: is our picture of Roger Mortimer as a crooked, selfish, adulterous, military traitor deserved? All such labels are, of course, relative, especially when reflecting on an age so different from our own. But if we can sympathise with the reasons why a man does something, we might understand even his worst 'crimes'. For example, if he had no choice but to order the king to be killed, on account of the political risk of his being released from prison, his order was not necessarily a cold-hearted one, even if it was cold-blooded. But as will be shown, Roger Mortimer emerges as a far more interesting character than a mere royal murderer. He was one of the very few important lords who remained totally loyal to the king and Piers Gaveston in their most severe troubles. There is evidence to suggest that, although one of the most experienced soldiers of his age, with a particular penchant for the joust, he was as sophisticated in his tastes for *objets d'art*, comfortable architecture and exotica as he was in his war machines. He was certainly not ignorant of history, nor of its importance. He was a literate man, trusted as an emissary by the king, loved by the queen, and respected by the citizens of London. Even the chronicler Froissart notes his popularity. Finally he planned and carried out the most daring and complicated plot in British medieval history, which has remained secret right up until the present day. As a historical figure he stands in three camps: firstly, as one of the great fourteenth-century aristocrats and secular patrons; secondly, as a baronial warlord of an earlier period; and, thirdly, as one of those remarkable people whose misdeeds set them apart from their contemporaries, forever defying categorisation.

So, before we try to reconcile Roger Mortimer with the pantheon of English history's maligned political leaders, we must remind ourselves that society then, as now, judges men and women on their single worst deed or crime, and in Roger's case we are talking about a man who deposed Edward II and ruled in his stead for three years, who adulterously slept with the queen, who arranged the judicial murder of the king's uncle, the Earl of Kent, and who greedily gathered to himself vast estates throughout Britain and Ireland. As the last chapters of this book will reveal, the extent to which he undermined the English monarchy is truly astounding. By the standards of his own time – the only ones by which a man can be judged – he was most certainly the greatest traitor of his age. It is perhaps significant that, in a reign when many men turned traitor and were killed, only three executions dramatically altered the course of events – those of Piers Gaveston (1312), the Earl of Lancaster (1322) and Roger Mortimer (1330), and only the last brought peace to the kingdom.

This book does not answer all the questions about the character of Roger Mortimer. Ultimately, as with any medieval man, we may only know him by his recorded deeds, and we will never be sure that we understand his personality when he left no personal written testimony of his character. Even his deeds are in doubt: unlike virtually every other ruler in history his obsession was in being seen *not* to rule, to govern invisibly, and to leave little or no trace of his unofficial dictatorship in the official records of government. Thus there are a few points in this book which, owing to lack of evidence, can only be loosely associated with Roger Mortimer. However, with the important exception of Chapter 12 and the final chapter (Chapter 12 Revisited), this book is not a series of academic arguments as to the strengths and reliability of individual pieces of evidence; it is an attempt to illustrate the vast chessboard on which Roger Mortimer and his eminent contemporaries played out their ambitions – kings, queens, bishops, knights, custodians of castles – and to trace his career, his loves, struggles, ambitions, power structures and defeats. Even if one cannot fully understand the personality of a man who lived and died more than twenty generations ago, to see his personal struggle framed by the age in which he lived is a start to understanding his thinking. That age was one of unbridled personal ambition and bloodshed; it saw enough betrayal, corruption, greed and murder for it to merit the description 'the Age of Treason'. And yet it was also full of piety, chivalry and patriotic fervour. It was a society in which all its leading participants struggled to survive. In this light one can begin to sympathise with the actions of Roger Mortimer, and gauge for him what is perhaps the most important element of any historical personality: his integrity.

ONE

Inheritance

The roots of betrayal lie in friendship; those of treason lie in loyalty.

It would be easy to begin an account of the life of Roger Mortimer with the simple statement that he was born on 25 April 1287, the eldest son of Edmund Mortimer, Lord of Wigmore, and Margaret de Fiennes.[1] But though a life begins with a birth, a life story often begins much earlier. History, genealogy, geography and social situation all have their part to play. Roger himself would have acknowledged this, as his tournaments often alluded to the deeds of his grandfather, one of Henry III's most trusted advisers, and he described himself as 'the king's cousin', recalling one relationship going back several generations on his mother's side, and another through his grandfather going back to King John. Thus this story begins not with the Roger Mortimer who is the subject of this book, but with another Roger Mortimer, the man after whom he was named: his grandfather.[2]

The elder Roger Mortimer was a heroic figure, famous throughout England, and feared throughout Wales. He was a knight of the first rank, a military commander and a champion tournament fighter. But what distinguished him from many of his contemporaries was his loyalty to the Crown. In the wars between King Henry III and Simon de Montfort, Lord Mortimer fought for the king, and continued to fight against de Montfort even after the king's defeat and capture. This loyalty almost cost him his life at the Battle of Lewes in 1264, but a year later Roger rescued the king's son, Prince Edward (later King Edward I), and thus rejuvenated the royal cause. He formed a pact with the prince and the Earl of Gloucester to defeat de Montfort and restore the royal family to power. Thus it was Lord Mortimer who set in motion the chain of events which led to de Montfort's last battle.

On 3 August 1265, Prince Edward, Lord Mortimer and Lord Gloucester marched westward from Worcester towards Dunnington with ten thousand men. De Montfort and his army were south of the River Avon, but he turned north towards Evesham to stay that night, crossing the bridge at Bengeworth. He and his men had unwittingly walked into a trap. At Evesham they were surrounded by the river on three sides, and on the fourth by the royalist army. The bridge at Bengeworth was their only possible escape. Lord Mortimer knew this and accordingly forced his men to march through the night and wade across the river at a ford a few miles away so they could take the bridge from the south. Next morning de Montfort's scouts reported that their way north was barred by the royal army, and, as a result of the night manoeuvre, the bridge behind them was blocked by the azure and gold banners of Lord Mortimer. De Montfort ascended the tower of Evesham Abbey. 'Let us commend our souls to God,' he said solemnly, 'for our bodies are theirs.'

What followed was one of the most devastating scenes of carnage on English soil. With storm clouds racing above their heads, and rain falling heavily, the ground was soon a sea of mud and blood. The Welshmen sent by Llywelyn of Wales refused to fight for de Montfort, and tried to flee across the river. But Lord Mortimer was there and too full of anger towards Llywelyn, his cousin and longstanding enemy, to let them pass. Rain dripping down their faces, swords in the air, yelling their war cries, this was the revenge which all the royalists had dreamed of for so many years. De Montfort desperately tried to line his men up to punch a hole through the combined armies of Lord Gloucester and Prince Edward, but failed to break through. The royalists rushed in on all sides, Lord Mortimer's men holding the bridge, and Lord Mortimer himself advancing through the fray with his knights, cutting down the de Montfort men, seeking out his adversaries. There he found Hugh Despenser whom he killed with his own hands. And there was Simon de Montfort himself. Men rushed at him and tore him from his horse, and pulled him to the ground. They hacked at his head and limbs as the storm crashed around them. The helmet off, a knight cut through the neck and held the head up in the rain for all to see, to ecstatic cheers. Prince Edward looked at the corpse and ordered the hands and feet also to be cut off as a mark of dishonour. Then de Montfort's testicles were cut off and draped over his nose. With the army laughing,[3] Prince Edward gave the dead man's adorned head to Lord Mortimer, as a trophy of war. Later he sent it to Wigmore Castle, to be presented to Lady Mortimer.

The consequences of this battle were far-reaching. For a start, the death of Hugh Despenser would have the most calamitous repercussions more than fifty years later, almost ending in Roger's own death. After the death of de Montfort, the Mortimers were drawn closer to the royal family, to the point where Lord Mortimer later became joint Regent of England. But for young Roger, born twenty-two years later, the most significant consequence was a vivid display of the family tradition of military service, an example of a loyal knight fighting for his king despite having the odds stacked against him, and eventually overcoming his lord's enemy in complete fulfilment of his knightly duty.

We do not know whether de Montfort's skull still hung in the treasury at Wigmore Castle when Roger and his brother and sisters were growing up there in the 1290s, but even if not there were still plenty of reminders of the family's glorious past to remind the young heir of his illustrious forbears. The castle was adorned with old armour and other relics of bygone conquests. Old chronicles remained in Wigmore Abbey, where five generations of the family were buried, which spoke of the deeds of the warlords from whom Roger was descended. Before his illustrious grandfather there had been a long line of barons who had fought the native Welsh with an ongoing and bitter savagery. One, his great-grandfather, had married the daughter of Llywelyn the Great, but this had been merely an attempt to stave off the worst excesses of the Anglo-Welsh conflict. Nor was it just Welshmen they attacked. In the twelfth century Roger's ancestors had fought their rival English lords as regularly as they had defended the Welsh border. Those they captured were sometimes blinded in their prison cells to prevent them fighting again. A small insight into the brutality of the world into which Roger was born may be gained from the epitaph on his grandfather's tomb in Wigmore Abbey, written just five years before his birth:

Here lies buried, glittering with praise,
Roger the pure, Roger Mortimer the second,
called Lord of Wigmore by those who held him dear.
While he lived all Wales feared his power,
and given as a gift to him, all Wales remained his.
It knew his campaigns, he subjected it to torment.[4]

This was Roger's real inheritance, not just land and castles but the tradition of royal service and military victory, the will to win glory and a physical and mental aptitude for war. And yet it was more than this too, for medieval family traditions were not static, unchanging tales of the past but growing, changing concepts. Many of the family stories with which Roger was familiar linked his family's history with its destiny. Such stories had a life of their own. For example, Roger's descent from Llywelyn the Great and the ancient Princes of Wales carried with it a legendary descent from King Arthur. One of the popular 'prophecies of Merlin' recited throughout England and Wales at the time was that a descendant of this line would become King of England. 'When English money is made round, a Welsh prince in London shall be crowned.' This story was enlarged upon and commemorated by Roger's grandfather, who had held a great Round Table tournament at Kenilworth in 1279. Kenilworth had been the great castle of de Montfort, and thus Lord Mortimer had held his last great tournament in the castle of his vanquished enemy. King Edward and Queen Eleanor had both attended, confirming the old knight's greatness, and providing the royal presence necessary for a tournament to be referred to as a 'Round Table', in emulation of the court of King Arthur. But the real significance of the event was to remind everyone of the Mortimers' Arthurian ancestry. Roger was not just descended from glorious warriors, he was part of a living and growing tradition. One day one of his kin would rule all England and Wales.

*

On the death of Lord Mortimer in 1282, the family estates passed to his second son, Edmund, Roger's father. Edmund's elder brother, Sir Ralph, had been an impressive knight, but he had died young, in 1276. Thus Edmund was thrust into the position of heir, and, in 1282, had to take on the mantle of Lord Mortimer of Wigmore.

Edmund was not groomed for lordship. As a younger son he was educated as a clerk and promised an official position. King Henry granted him this in 1265 when he made him nominal Treasurer of York, removing Simon de Montfort's son Almeric from the position. Edmund was then aged about fifteen, and went off to Oxford University. In 1268, while his elder brother Sir Ralph was showing off his martial prowess in tournaments up and down the country, he was studying theology, living at the house of the Archbishop of York in Oxford. Such luxury as the archbishop's house offered was supplemented with the odd gift of deer from the king, but it was still a far cry from the glories of the tournament. Despite this Edmund seems to have taken to studying, for he remained in Oxford even after the death of his elder brother, by which he became heir to Wigmore Castle and the other Mortimer estates. On the death of his father he could no longer continue with learning. He was required to put away his goose quill and parchment and take up the sword.

Within a few weeks Edmund was leading a party of men-at-arms towards Builth in Wales. With him were his brothers – Roger, a captain in the king's army, Geoffrey and William – and other Marcher lords, including Roger Lestrange and John Giffard. Llywelyn ap Gruffydd, Prince of Wales and grandson of Llywelyn the Great, had re-established his control of North Wales, and had broken out of a siege to come south and rouse his fellow Welshmen in the Marches. Edmund, in an attempt to entrap Llywelyn, sent him a message saying that he was marching to his aid, and wanted to meet with him. Llywelyn came with his army through Radnorshire, keeping to the hills. Then he made a fatal mistake. He left his army to meet the Mortimers, supposing that, if it were a trap, his men guarding Orewin Bridge would be able to hold it and protect his retreat. The Mortimer brothers, however, had heard of a ford across the river and, as Llywelyn came to meet Edmund, they sent men across to attack the bridge from the rear. Soon they had taken it, killing Llywelyn's guards, and allowing the whole Marcher army to advance towards the Welsh position. Not knowing what to do, and not wanting to desert their posts, the Welsh gave battle then and there. Their efforts were in vain. As they broke ranks and fled, Llywelyn, without his armour, hastened back to take charge of the situation. Unrecognised, he was stopped by the English, and run through with a sword by Stephen de Frankton, who did not stop to look more closely at his victim. Only later, when the dead bodies were being stripped of their weapons and other belongings, was Llywelyn's corpse noticed. Edmund Mortimer himself confirmed it was his father's cousin, and, to the great delight of the English, Edmund's younger brother Roger set out for Rhuddlan Castle with Llywelyn's head to show to King Edward. With Llywelyn's only child being a daughter in Edward's custody, Wales was finally conquered.

Thus the scholar Edmund Mortimer became a soldier. He was knighted by the king at Winchester.[5] From then on his life was that of a baron and a warrior, attending Parliament and being summoned to fight in King Edward's campaigns in Scotland and Gascony. The year after Llywelyn's death he was summoned to do military service in Wales again, to crush the last vestiges of revolt. Then in September 1285 he did something which would never have happened if he had remained at Oxford. He married. His bride was Margaret de Fiennes, daughter of William de Fiennes, the second cousin of Queen Eleanor of Castile, wife of Edward I.[6] Roger Mortimer, eighth Lord of Wigmore, was born eighteen months later.

*

The formal education of a baron's son in the late thirteenth century began at the age of seven. Roger remained at Wigmore until he had reached this age, with his younger brother John and four sisters, in the care of the women of the castle, principally his mother and grandmother. Not that his mother, Lady Mortimer, was always present; she spent most of the year travelling around the country with her husband. Thus young Roger probably spent much of his early life in the company of his grandmother, Maud, the widow of the great Lord Mortimer, his famous grandfather. Young Roger was no doubt enthralled by the stories of his grandfather's exploits, yet his grandmother also had stories of her own worth hearing. Her father, William de Braose, had been hanged by Llywelyn the Great on suspicion of adultery with his wife. But that was nothing compared with her mother, who was of truly distinguished stock, she being Eva, the daughter of William Marshal, the greatest knight in Christendom. His name was spoken everywhere with a sense of awe. He had won success in every tournament he had entered, and, when confronted by his adversaries at court, had challenged them all to single combat. None had dared face him. On the death of Henry, second son of Henry II, to whom he was a friend, guardian and mentor, William was charged by the king with carrying out his dying son's request, of carrying his cross to Jerusalem. His prowess there was such that the crusaders who hung on to the last shreds of Christian rule in Syria were loath to let him return to Europe, he having won as many battles in one year as they had in seven. When fighting broke out between France and England, he suggested that the war should be decided by four champions on each side fighting in single combat, and volunteered to head the list for England. Again, no one dared face him. In the war between Henry II and his son Richard the Lionheart, Marshal was the man who defended the king's retreat and thus came face to face in battle with the Lionheart himself. 'God's feet, Marshal,' shouted Richard. 'Slay me not!' Marshal replied: 'The Devil slay you, for I will not,' as he plunged his spear into Richard's horse. Richard recognised Marshal's valour and loyalty when he became king, and Marshal in return proved just as steadfast a supporter of King Richard as he had of Henry II. He carried the gold spurs at Richard's coronation, and even in advanced years was spoken of as the most feared soldier in Richard's army. For young Roger, to know that the one man feared in battle by Richard the Lionheart was his great-great-grandfather was a treasure in itself.

At about the age of seven Roger was sent away to be taught the rudiments of knighthood in a fellow nobleman's household. It is not known to whom he was sent. There are several possibilities, the most probable being the important lords related to the Mortimers, such as the Earls of Surrey and Hereford, or the young Prince of Wales. Another possibility is that he was sent to his more humble but more violent uncle, another Roger Mortimer, most easily distinguished as Lord Mortimer of Chirk.

It is worth pausing to consider Roger's uncle here, as in later years the two men were close, and acted almost as a two-headed lord of a single huge lordship in North Wales and the Marches. In 1282, when Edmund Mortimer and his brothers had found Llywelyn dead on the hillside above Orewin Bridge, it had been this Roger Mortimer who had taken Llywelyn's head to King Edward at Rhuddlan. This was not a random choice of head-bearer: his rise to prominence had begun some years earlier. By far the most soldierly of the Mortimer brothers, he had earned his lordship through bitter and cruel fighting in the king's army in Wales. When the Lord of North Powys died in 1277 leaving two small boys as his heirs, this Roger Mortimer was appointed their guardian. Then, in mysterious circumstances, he took their inheritance. Some claimed he had drowned the boys in the Dee. Although this now appears doubtful, such a deed would not have been uncharacteristic of the man. In 1282 he was confirmed as lord of their lands, and thus became Lord Mortimer of Chirk, warrior lord of a lawless country. He was something of a throwback to the old members of the family, the warlords who had hacked their neighbours – and especially the Welsh – to pieces in the twelfth century. Children and Welshmen were not his only targets. He was at one point accused of adultery with Margaret, the wife of Roger of Radnor, and 'with many other women'. Given the misogynism of the time, one should not suppose these were romantic affairs. The priest sent to remonstrate with him in the matter was thrown into a deep cell at Chirk Castle. Those who today see the extant dungeon there might shudder to think of the experience: it is a rock-cut chamber eighteen feet beneath one of the towers of the castle, dank when not flooded, almost totally dark, and very cold.

*

To the north-east of Wigmore, a couple of hours away by horse, is Ludlow Castle and its town. In 1300 the castle and a large portion of the town were in the hands of the family of de Geneville. The head of this family, Sir Geoffrey de Geneville, had come to England in about 1250, and had married Maud de Lacy, a co-heiress of the great family of de Lacy, and thus had acquired not only Ludlow and other lands in England and Wales but also extensive properties in Ireland, including half of the county of Meath, and Trim, the great castle and town at its heart. On the death of their son and heir in 1283, they gave all their estates in England and Wales to their second son, Peter de Geneville. To these lands Peter added extensive lands in Gascony through his marriage with Joan, the daughter of the Count of La Marche and Angoulême. However, when Peter died in 1292 leaving only three daughters, Sir Geoffrey and his wife knew that their line was facing extinction. It was likely that their estates would be divided three ways between the husbands of their three grand-daughters. Rather than let this happen, they agreed to settle all their estates on the eldest, Joan, and to place the other two, Beatrice and Maud, in Aconbury Priory.[7] They then offered Joan, their sole heiress, to the Mortimer family as a bride for Roger.

Roger and Joan were probably betrothed in 1299 or 1300. The reason for suggesting this date is the evidence of a financial arrangement between the houses of Mortimer and Geneville. Maintaining the various Mortimer castles – Wigmore in Herefordshire, Bridgewater in Somerset, and Cefnllys, Radnor, Dinbaud and Knucklas in Radnorshire (then Herefordshire) was a costly business. In May 1300 Edmund Mortimer turned to Geoffrey de Geneville for a loan, and mortgaged several of his English manors to him, promising to repay the debt in eight annual instalments of £120.[8] Large financial agreements were often accompanied by a statement of affiliation between two families. If this was the case, Roger and Joan were betrothed to one another for sixteen months. They were married at the Mortimer family manor of Pembridge on the eve of the feast of St Matthew the Apostle 1301 (20 September).[9] The night after the feast a comet appeared, which lasted for the following seven nights.

Most medieval aristocratic marriages were largely statements of intent, rather than of immediate physical bonding, in which the young – sometimes very young – bride and bridegroom lived apart until ready to begin their lives together. Given Roger's and Joan's ages – fourteen and a half and fifteen and a half – they probably began to live their lives as a married couple from the time of their marriage. Their union immediately proved fruitful: within three years the couple had had two children.[10] From this we can safely say that, although we cannot be sure where Roger was, or in whose household he had been brought up, one of his close companions of his early years was his wife.

Roger's other companions of his youth are harder to identify. Most can only be guessed at from later evidence, which is discussed below, but one name must be mentioned here: that of his distant cousin, Prince Edward of Carnarvon, the future King Edward II.

In all probability Roger had had first-hand knowledge of the prince at least from the time of the siege of Caerlaverock Castle in 1300. In that year Roger's uncle had been one of the half-dozen knights appointed to watch over the prince and to guide him in military matters.[11] The prince was then sixteen years old, a robust, tall young man, with shoulder-length blond hair: the very image of his warrior father in youth. He was spiritually minded – at Bury St Edmunds he had refused to accept more food than the monks received – and he was an excellent horseman, an essential requirement of a warrior. On occasion he had shown he could be courageous, and his friends and companions (including several members of the de Fiennes family, Roger's relations) showed themselves keen soldiers and altogether good company for a future king.

In the spring of 1303, when Prince Edward was nearly nineteen and

Roger himself nearly sixteen, the prince's company was becoming more exotic and attractive. His love of jewellery was famous, and the whole country knew about his generous gift of a great ruby and gold ring to his stepmother, the young Queen Margaret of France, of whom he was very fond. He made similar gifts to his friend and companion, Piers Gaveston, a young Gascon knight, of whom he was even fonder. But Piers was only the foremost of a number of esquires who lived life to the full in the prince's company. Together these young men wanted to liven up the court, to escape its dull seriousness arising from the king's old age and obsession with politics. They preferred jousting and music to politics and war. The prince, as the centre of this band of youths, delighted them by travelling with a lion, which he kept chained up with its own cart and keeper. He acquired a camel, which he kept at his manor of Kings Langley. Minstrels accompanied him from castle to castle, playing drums, rebecs and viols in all the halls where he and his entourage feasted. Fools amused him and travelled in his company, and he was not averse to engaging with them in playfights. Dicing was another of the prince's pleasures, and Roger no doubt gambled a game or two with him. Indeed the two men had a lot in common: love of fine jewellery, costumes and ornaments, carpets and metalwork, exotic animals (peacocks in Roger's case), and even books.[12] There is no direct evidence which indicates the level of friendship between Roger and the prince from the last years of the reign of King Edward I, but if later evidence may be taken as an indication of their relationship, it is probable that Roger was one of the prince's group of young men who brightened up the somewhat stuffy court.

There was a more serious side to the prince, which was apparent in his religious zeal. He attended masses with great frequency, was often in the company of his personal priests, and was assiduous in his alms-giving. This apparent double-faced character, of simultaneous religiosity and frivolity, was certainly contradictory but nevertheless is not in doubt. The prince was a complex, thoughtful individual. Strange forces moved the consciences of thirteenth- and early fourteenth-century monarchs. Seeing his father haunted by death, and living out a sort of existential life, in which the king was defined by his martial exploits, the young prince could not help but be affected. His mother had died when he was only six, depriving him of the affection enjoyed by many of his contemporaries: an affection which even his closeness with his stepmother could not replace. And then there was the legacy of his birth. His father had made him Prince of Wales in an attempt to forestall the prophecy of Merlin; but this had a double edge, for such an obviously contrived political solution to a prophecy might fail to appease the forces that worked it. On top of all this there was the matter of his birthday. Edward was haunted by the date: 25 April. This day – the feast of St Mark – was a day of bad omen, for on this day people dressed in black and, with their crosses also veiled in black, prayed in processions that the year ahead would be one of abundance. One prophecy, noted by the writer Jean de Joinville, stated that the birth of King Louis of France on 25 April had been a sign that many would die in the forthcoming crusades.[13] Similar things were said about Prince Edward, and, even if he did not believe such prophecies, they cannot have eased the sense of foreboding.

Roger Mortimer, three years younger than the prince, no doubt heard these poor omens of Edward's birth and considered them carefully. For his birthday was also 25 April. He was only too aware of the evil portents of the day, and the prophecy of the deaths of King Louis's subjects in particular, for Jean de Joinville was the elder brother of Geoffrey de Geneville, or de Joinville, his wife's grandfather.

These then were the shadows and lights which filled Roger Mortimer's mind as he passed his seventeenth birthday in the year 1304. He longed for a life of martial glory, and felt himself bound to serve his king through family tradition, a spiritual sense of knightly service, and the sense of political duty engendered by ruling a border country. Such martial glory would fulfil his dreams of emulating the knights at the court of King Arthur, his ancestor. His family had hereditary allies and enemies: allies in the king, enemies in the family of Hugh Despenser. There were prophecies indicating possible future greatness, and comets predicting personal glory. And finally, his future was bound up with that of the prince. If the date of 25 April had evil forebodings about it, then it would be a fate they shared.

Before any evil could befall either of them, however, a messenger rode to Wigmore Castle with news which hurled into despair all those who heard it. Edmund Mortimer had been injured in a skirmish near Builth and was being brought back in a litter. A bed was made ready, physicians and surgeons were summoned. But after Edmund had entered the castle, and he had been carried to his chamber, there was nothing more anyone could do. On 17 July 1304 he died,[14] and the two great weights of personal ambition and his ancestors' tradition came to rest on Roger's shoulders.

TWO

Youth

If an animal died in medieval England, its death affected no one but those who were planning to feed off it. If a peasant died, even a rich one, his death affected no one but those whom he supported: his family and his servants. If a nobleman died, however, it affected his family, his retainers, his bailiffs, his servants, the clergy he employed, his manorial and borough officials, monastic communities which held land from him, the rest of the nobility and everyone who knew him, and all those who depended on the authentication of his seal. It caused wrenches in loyalties and allegiances, in reclaiming debts and payments of wages, and it could trigger huge upheavals in local and national administration. With regard to border lord-ships and the greatest territorial magnates, it could even jeopardise the defence or stability of the realm. In a society almost totally dependent on personal affiliation, a lord's death could affect the whole country.

Within days the news of the death of Edmund Mortimer reached Scotland, where the king and court were engaged on a campaign. As with all crises in medieval England, control reverted to the Crown, which now took the income and direction of the estates. It also took responsibility for Roger in person. Although we cannot be sure whether Roger's education had begun in the king's household, alongside Prince Edward and Piers Gaveston, we can be sure that, from 1304, that was where it was completed.

This is probably the most important single aspect of Roger's early life, and it is crucial to understanding his later political position. Throughout his life Prince Edward surrounded himself with, and favoured, his friends from his youth. These men were well-educated, intelligent and literate, like him.[1] Favouring these educated young men caused mistrust amongst his generally illiterate barons, but this inarticulate opposition only served to strengthen the bonds between members of his entourage. Thus the prince's cherished friends from his youth – such as Piers Gaveston, the Earl of Gloucester, Ingelard de Warley, Guy de Ferre, John de Charlton and Robert de Clifford – were also Roger's friends. Such bonds meant that, for Roger, opposition to his king would be a harder route to follow than for a man with few connections to the court, and one only to be pursued in the most extreme situation.

The evidence for Roger being a royal ward is unfortunately only conclusive for the year 1304–5. The principle source is a document, an 'ordinary', which makes provision for both Roger Mortimer and John de Warenne as wards in the king's household, on the respective deaths of their father and grandfather.[2] The ordinary mentions four household officials including John Benstead, the Controller of the Household, thus allowing it to be dated to the period from 25 September 1304 (the death of Lord Warenne) to 25 September 1305 (the date of Benstead's replacement). Because the document mentions the higher ranking John de Warenne *before* Roger, Roger must have still been entertained as a royal ward after 25 September 1304. It is, of course, entirely possible that Roger was with the court before this. The fact that Prince Edward begged his father to grant custody of the Mortimer lands to his friend Piers Gaveston, when such a grant would normally have been awarded to someone of much higher status, and the fact that the king agreed, suggests Gaveston and Roger were already acquainted.[3] Also the presence of some of Roger's cousins in the prince's household inclines one to believe that Roger was at court before 1304, and thus one of the prince's group of established companions along with Gaveston.[4]

Gaveston was hardly any older than Roger himself. Chroniclers described him and the prince as contemporaries. Since the prince was born in 1284, it is unlikely that Gaveston was born any earlier than 1281. Thus he was probably no more than twenty-four, and possibly as young as twenty-one, when he became guardian to the seventeen-year-old Roger Mortimer. He was of considerably lower rank than the young heir. He was the son of a knight called Arnaud from Gabaston in Gascony, southern France, who had fought for Edward I and who had been used as a hostage by him on two occasions. On the second of these Arnaud had escaped captivity and had fled to England, bringing with him his son Piers, who had also entered the royal household. So well behaved and virtuous did the young Gaveston appear to the king that he declared him an example for his own son to follow, and made him a member of Prince Edward's household in 1300.

As soon as Gaveston and Edward met they became great friends. The prince, overshadowed by his father the king, was yearning to break free and to be his own man. Gaveston was witty, rude and enormously entertaining, with a Gascon accent and moreover a healthy disregard for all things old-fashioned, English and traditional. He delighted the prince, and more importantly gave him confidence, and in his company the prince grew to discover his own character. Hence the lion and the camel, the jewels and the horsemanship. The emergent frivolity of the prince in the last years of his father's life can be put down to the liberating influence of Gaveston. The prince declared that he loved Gaveston 'like a brother'. His real half-brothers, Thomas and Edmund, were mere babies at this time, and unable to provide him with the close companionship he craved. Gaveston, having also lost his mother at a young age, was the perfect 'brother'. Their shared interests gave them further common ground. That Gaveston could express his disdain for the old-fashioned nobles, insult them, and still ride out in armour and hold his own in the joust with the best of them, made Edward proud to call Gaveston his friend.

The reason why Gaveston's name has remained famous to this day is not the extent to which the prince admired him but the nature of their relationship. Were they merely close friends or were they lovers? Did they experience physical desire for one another as well as close friendship? We do not know for certain. We do know that Edward fathered four legitimate children and at least one illegitimate son, and therefore was not repelled by heterosexual coupling. Nor was Gaveston, whose wife bore him a daughter just before he died. In addition, the present-day tendency to define sexuality largely through physical acts makes it harder to assess the erotic degree of emotional relationships in the fourteenth century. The very categorisation of Edward's and Gaveston's relationship is a problem, since all the chroniclers agree that theirs was a unique friendship, comparable only with that of Jonathan and David in the Bible. The problem is compounded by the fact that physical homosexual acts were socially unacceptable and thus would not have been mentioned by most chroniclers. Suffice to say that Gaveston was Edward's best friend, the love of his life, and, in many respects, his hero.[5]

In 1304, when Roger's wardship was granted to Gaveston, England had yet to make up its mind about the Gascon knight. From Roger's point of view, Gaveston was a fine tournament fighter, and an admirable companion, but Roger wanted his freedom to enjoy his own property. The ordinary made for him and Warenne gave him some level of distinction – for example, that he could have three valets to serve him, each entitled to three changes of robes each year, and that he could maintain his favourite four horses – but this was still a far cry from his own castles, retinues of men-at-arms and authority.[6] Thus it was decided between him and his family that he should buy his way out of his wardship.

The question was merely one of money. The lands to which Roger was directly heir (just his father's and grandmother's estates, since his mother and Joan's grandfather and mother were all still alive and in possession of their lands) amounted to about £700 per year, less the £120 mortgaged to Geoffrey de Geneville. That left Gaveston with the remaining £580 for at least another three years while Roger was under twenty-one, a staggeringly large income for a man who was not even a knight. Thus Gaveston was unlikely to relinquish the wardship cheaply. He settled for 2,500 marks, or £1,666 13s 8d, probably the equivalent of the family income (excepting the mortgage) over three years.[7] The amount is put into perspective by the fact that at this time the daily allowance of a knight on active service was just 1s, a skilled carpenter might earn 4d, and an unskilled labourer earned no more than 2d per day. If we are right in saying that the 2,500 marks was the rough equivalent of three years of Roger's income, we can assume that it was paid before much of those three years had elapsed. Possibly it was paid before the end of December 1304, when Roger was granted the right to pay back his father's debts to the Exchequer at the rate of £20 per year.[8] Roger would have come of age in March 1308, and so it is likely that the period of approximately three years on which the fine paid to Gaveston was assessed fell at some point in early 1305 at the latest. It must have been paid before 16 May 1305, as Roger's guardian and the executor of his father's will, Walter de Thornbury, granted some land in Stratfield Mortimer on his behalf on that date, with no reference to Gaveston.[9] It was not until the following year, however, that he was given full control over his estates.

By the time he bought his freedom to enjoy his inheritance, Roger had been married for about three years. He had a son and heir, Edmund, named after his own father in accordance with the family custom, and a daughter, Margaret, named after his mother.[10] More children – in fact at least ten more – followed.[11] This fact alone suggests the marriage was a highly satisfactory one: in order to remain regularly pregnant by her husband, Joan would have needed frequently to travel with Roger when he was summoned to attend Parliament, or to attend the king, only remaining behind in times of actual combat. This represents a high level of companionship sustained over many years, a situation by no means universal in the early fourteenth century. It is likely that Joan returned to the family estates as each confinement drew near, but, even so, the fact that they had twelve surviving children in less than twenty years, and that she travelled with her husband at least twice to lawless Ireland, points to a relationship which was much closer than most among the medieval nobility. No previous generation of the family had managed to produce such a brood. It suggests that they are an example of that rarity – a mutually beneficial, secure medieval partnership.[12]

We do not know for certain where Roger was at any point in 1305, but given the evidence of the ordinary for his accommodation as a royal ward, he was still probably in the king's household at the beginning of the year, watched over by Walter de Thornbury. Since over subsequent years Roger would show a greater enthusiasm for being at court than on his own estates, there is every likelihood that he remained with the king throughout the year. Walter de Thornbury showed a similar propensity for remaining at court. Either way, there is one assumption which is safe to make about Roger at this time, and that is that he took part in tournaments. Within a short while he had risen to prominence as a tournament fighter, and this was the one sure way of attracting the king's attention.[13] For the early four-teenth-century tournament was not the mere chivalric parade it came to be in later years; then, it still resembled the original show battles of the thirteenth century, in which men very often died. In 1241 more than eighty knights had been killed in a single tournament. The Round Table tour-nament which Roger's grandfather had held at Kenilworth and the king's Round Table tournament in 1284 were pitched fights in which, although edged weapons were blunted, men fought all the more viciously to conquer their opponents. Several of Roger's family had been killed tourneying, including one lord of Wigmore in 1227. In addition to the wounds wrought by weapons, men were trampled to death, crushed, suffocated or broke their necks. But champion knights could make themselves famous and comparatively wealthy, paying only a few marks to enter and display their skills to the audience and judges. It was probably in this way that Roger drew attention to himself as a fighter and convinced the king that he deserved to come into his inheritance sooner rather than later.

Although he was not quite nineteen, on 9 April 1306 Roger was endowed with full possession of all the estates he inherited from his father and which he held directly from the king.[14] He thus became Lord Mortimer of Wigmore and inherited the barony of Wigmore, with its castle, manors, towns and estates. He also inherited the castle, town and barony of Radnor, the castle and one third of the town of Bridgewater in Somerset, three castles in the Welsh cantred of Maelienydd, and the town of Presteigne in Wales. He became lord or overlord of hundreds of manors and estates scattered across the counties of Bedfordshire, Berkshire, Buckinghamshire, Cambridgeshire, Cornwall, Devon, Dorset, Gloucestershire, Hampshire, Herefordshire, Huntingdonshire, Leicestershire, Northamptonshire, Nottinghamshire, Oxfordshire, Shropshire, Somerset, Suffolk, Wiltshire, Worcestershire and Yorkshire.[15] Added to these lands and titles, he stood to inherit through Joan her estates in Gascony, the barony of Meath and the Liberty of Trim in Ireland, including Trim Castle, and half the lord-ship of the town of Ludlow. Last but by no means least he stood to gain possession of Ludlow Castle. This was the grandest castle on the Welsh Marches, only a few miles from his own seat at Wigmore. Joan's Irish estates would in time be added to the Irish lands of his grandmother, who had died in 1301, and which he now also inherited. These included the lordship of the honour of Dunamase. He might not have been an earl, but his ancestry, background and estates placed him in the front rank of the baronage, and his marriage made him as wealthy as several men of higher rank.

The first purpose of the baronage, however, was not to amass wealth but to fight. On the very day that Roger came into his inheritance he received a summons to serve in the king's army in Scotland, and for this purpose to assemble his men at Carlisle on 8 July. The time of war, to which he had been bred and trained, had come.

*

Not long after the summons was issued, a second writ from the king was sent out announcing that all those who had not yet received the honour of knighthood, and who were the holders of a knight's fee (a feudal estate normally worth £40 or more a year), were to come to London to be knighted on Whitsunday, 22 May. For Roger, the opportunity to receive such an honour so early in his career was not to be missed, especially as chivalric displays were relatively uncommon and the number of men actually dubbed was small. Even his warrior uncle, battle-scarred after thirty years' fighting, had not yet been dubbed. Thus both Roger and his uncle set out for Westminster at the beginning of May 1306.

A huge number of men had responded to the announcement, of which 267 were accepted. The excitement was great indeed; never in England had so many knights been dubbed at a single occasion. It seemed these new knights would form the basis of a war band, a new court of the Round Table. They were treated with great respect, being allowed to camp in the grounds of the Temple church, the London centre of the Knights Templar. When the precinct of the Templars' house was full of tents and pavilions, the order was given to pull down the precinct wall and to cut down all the fruit trees in the adjacent gardens. Fifty carpenters set up huge canvas pavilions for the lords and ladies to sleep in and other tents to act as bathing and robing chambers. All their provisions were supplied from the prince's household. The old guard was making way for the new. Roger's generation of knights was about to come of age.

On the 22nd a huge crowd gathered along the way from the Temple to Westminster Abbey, cheering and waving, all hoping to see the new knights of England as they passed to the ceremony. So many struggled to get a view that people had to clamber on each other's shoulders or climb on to garden walls. At the same time the prince, wearing full armour, knelt in the secure silence of the palace chapel. The king, watched solemnly by a few of his oldest and most trusted lords, touched the royal sword to Prince Edward's shoulders. When he stood up, his father girded him with his sword and belt, and the old Earl of Lincoln and the war-scarred Earl of Hereford knelt down to fasten his spurs. He was thus made a knight, and given the lordship of the Duchy of Aquitaine. It was a solemn moment, but it preceded an occasion of even greater gravity: the prince was now to go to the abbey and convey the honour of knighthood to the new chivalry of England.

Such was the noise, chaos and crowding in the abbey church that no one could silence the lords and their men. Eventually war horses were brought in to drive a path to the altar. Then the ceremony began. A mass was sung by the abbey monks, and two by two the knights were called forward from the throng. After about thirty names the clerks called for *Rogerus de Mortuo Mari de Wigmore* and *Rogerus de Mortuo Mari de Chirk*, as they were called in Latin. They went forward, washed their hands in silver bowls, and were sprinkled with holy water by attendant priests. Solemnly they made their vows of knighthood: to uphold the Church, the Crown and the order of knighthood itself, to spare the life of a vanquished enemy who pleaded for mercy, to respect women and to live chastely. Then each was touched by Prince Edward with the royal sword, was girded with a belt and sword, and received his spurs. Before that moment they had merely served their king; now they were knights with a higher purpose.

Besides Prince Edward and his intimate friend, Piers Gaveston, there were many men at the May 1306 knighting who would prove important in Roger's life.[16] John Maltravers was there, a man who would not only fight in Ireland and Scotland with Roger but who would become one of his most trusted captains in later years. Lord Berkeley was there with his son Maurice, representatives of the ancient lordship of Berkeley in Gloucestershire and cousins of the Mortimer family. Bartholomew de Badlesmere was present, known as Badlesmere the Rich, lord of Leeds Castle in Kent. He was one of the greatest examples of how dutiful service could raise a man up from the mere fringes of nobility to a position at the very heart of the court. And of course there were many lords of the Welsh Marches knighted, most of them in some way connected to the Mortimer family and together presenting one huge faction of powerful lords and knights. That day Prince Edward knighted men who would serve him and men who would denounce him, men who would betray him and take up arms against him, men whom he would put to death and men who would ultimately overthrow him. In Roger Mortimer he knighted the man who, in more than twenty years' time, would force him to abdicate.

But all that was far off. The present was full of joy, celebration and thoughts of the war in Scotland which lay ahead.

After the mass knighting the newly created knights and their retainers filed out of the abbey to walk the short distance to the great hall of Westminster Palace. As the feast began, eighty minstrels (many picked specially by the prince and Gaveston) played exciting rhythms and tunes around the hall in small groups on drums or tambourines, English bagpipes, flutes, harps and rebecs. They stamped and danced, sang and laughed. Course after course, each one consisting of many different dishes, was brought for the lords and knights to pick at and savour as they talked and listened. Then, much later, the music died down. The last few murmurs of conversation gave way to astonished gasps as some of the musicians reappeared with a huge silver salver on which there were two motionless white swans apparently swimming in a net of gold. Slowly the swans were paraded around the hall and brought before the king. People waited as the old sovereign, now white-haired and bearded, and dressed in white, rose to his feet.

The king's speech was the centre of the whole occasion. He spoke of knighthood's virtues and purpose, and he spoke of the band of warriors now before him. And he spoke of Scotland.

No one in the hall needed reminding about Scotland. King Edward had been proclaimed overlord of that country in 1291, in an attempt to pacify rival factions for the Scottish throne, and had eventually chosen John Balliol to be king under him rather than Balliol's rival, Robert Bruce of Annandale. When Balliol refused to act as Edward's puppet, Bruce and a number of other Scottish lords successfully sought Edward's support against Balliol, and forced his removal. When William Wallace raised the question of Scottish independence, and was executed in its cause, the grandson of Bruce, another Robert Bruce, Earl of Carrick, met with his rival claimant to the throne, John Comyn, in the Greyfriars' church at Dumfries. These men were supposedly discussing respect for one another's property after the death of the aged King of England. But what happened next shocked the Christian world. In front of the altar of the church, Robert Bruce drew a knife and stabbed John Comyn. As Comyn lay stricken and shrieking, his uncle Robert Comyn lunged forward and attacked Bruce. Seeing his lord under threat, Bruce's brother-in-law Christopher Seton threw himself into the line of attack and killed Robert Comyn. Bruce then ordered his esquires to silence John Comyn for ever, which they did. A claimant to the throne of Scotland had been murdered in church, in blessed sanctuary, on holy ground. Nothing as shocking and as abhorrent to the laws of knighthood had happened since the murder of Archbishop Thomas Becket before the altar of his own cathedral, over 130 years earlier.

That had been Robert Bruce's offence to Christian humanity. His offence to King Edward had been just as extreme. Immediately upon killing Comyn, Bruce had seized control of Dumfries Castle and imprisoned the English judges gathered there. He had then set about obtaining the Kingdom of Scotland for himself. On 25 March he had himself crowned at Scone Abbey in the presence of the Bishop of Glasgow, the Bishop of St Andrews, the Earl of Atholl, the Earl of Lennox, and his mistress, Isabel of Fife, Countess of Buchan. It was a calculated and deliberate challenge to the King of England, a declaration of independence.

It was with this horror in mind, and the knowledge that the English army must go north to fight Bruce, that the new knights watched the old king step forward. 'By the God of Heaven and these swans!' he cried, 'I will avenge the death of John Comyn and have vengeance on the perfidious Scots!' Then turning to his son and his chief nobles, still standing at the high table, he demanded, 'As soon as I have accomplished this task, and revenged the injuries done by Bruce to God and to the Church, I will go to the Holy Land and there end my days fighting the Infidel. But swear to me this: that if I die before the task is finished, you will carry my bones with the army and not bury them until full vengeance has been wrought on the Scots!'[17]

Immediately the hall was filled with shouts of assent and wrath against Bruce and his men. The Earl of Lincoln, one of the king's oldest and most loyal knights, immediately went down on his knee and swore to fight beside the king for the remaining years of his life. The prince, swept up in the fervour of the moment, swore before all that he would not sleep two nights under the same roof until he reached Scotland to help his father fulfil his vow. Many other lords stepped forward and promised to do likewise. The hall was awash with solemn oaths and calls for the destruction of Robert Bruce.

The king was no doubt satisfied for the time being, but the support, however ecstatic, was merely what he had anticipated. The main force had already been ordered to march north. Aymer de Valence and Henry Percy, each in charge of an army, had already secured the border, and a few days before the Feast of the Swans the king had given de Valence overall command and ordered him to attack. What Edward was doing back in Westminster Hall was putting in place the army which would not fight Bruce this year, nor necessarily the next, but which would ultimately conquer Scotland, even if it should not happen in his lifetime. He was in effect planning a military conquest to take place after his death.

*

After leaving London in early June, the royal army proceeded north slowly. Roger and the other men knighted at Westminster were still in England when they heard the news that Aymer de Valence had met Robert Bruce in battle on 26 June at Methven and inflicted a heavy defeat on the Scots. On 8 July, when de Valence established his headquarters at Perth, the royal army was at Carlisle. Over the subsequent days the prince's advisers, such as Lord Mortimer of Chirk and the Earl of Hereford, guided the army up the western side of Scotland and brought them across the lowlands to back up de Valence's advance. This took them to Lochmaben Castle, the birthplace of Robert Bruce, a target significant much more for its symbolism than its military strength. To the great delight of the prince, the castle garrison surrendered without a struggle on 11 July. The royal army accepted the surrender, and straightaway pushed on north towards Perth, ransacking and burning the villages in its path. They reached Forteviot on 1 August.

King Edward was not with the army. By the time the prince set off from Carlisle, the appointed mustering place, his father had only reached Nottingham. The old man was ill, and could only travel in a litter, but this did not mean that he played no part in the campaign. At Methven, Aymer de Valence had captured the Abbot of Scone and the Bishops of Glasgow and St Andrews, all of whom had attended Bruce's coronation. These prisoners – and many others over the subsequent weeks – were sent to King Edward in irons. From his litter Edward provided not only the impetus for the campaign but also the justice to be inflicted on the Scottish rebels.

At Perth Aymer de Valence rode out to meet the prince, and to welcome the royal army. To young Roger it served further to cement him into the front rank of the nobility. Here he was with the prince, his distant cousin, and de Valence, another relation. His company could hardly be more eminent. De Valence's career had been one of outstanding service: he had fought with the king from 1297, he was an internationally important aristocrat, known and respected throughout northern Europe, and capable of leading the most important diplomatic missions. Besides this, he was a first cousin of Edward I. Although de Valence knelt at the prince's feet at their meeting, there was no doubt that it was he, not the prince, who was in charge.

The command of an experienced warrior like de Valence was an essential element of any campaign, and particularly one which was about to advance deep into Scotland. While the English were still at Perth, John McDougall of Argyll led a locally raised army against Bruce and met him in battle at Dalry, near Tyndrum, on the western border of Perthshire.

Bruce was again defeated, and this time his army was scattered. He sent his womenfolk, including his sister and mistress, northward with his brother Sir Neil Bruce, to Kildrummy Castle. The mission for de Valence and the prince was clear: to take Kildrummy and its precious occupants.

Leading the English army so far into Scotland, however, was a daunting task, especially with Bruce still at large. At any time their supply lines could be cut from behind, and the king would not have known where to send replenishments by sea. Also that summer was hot, and forcing the troops to march in arms over seventy miles of enemy highland was a significant challenge, requiring careful use of water and food supplies. It is to the credit of its commanders that the army entered Aberdeenshire without incident.

At Kildrummy itself they faced a problem. The castle was situated at the top of a ravine and very strongly defended, with curtain towers and high battlements. Being set on rock, the walls could not be destroyed by mining beneath the foundations, which was normally the most effective way of attacking a castle. Any siege would be dangerously protracted, as the castle was well stocked with provisions. To storm it would require siege engines to be built on-site, a lengthy and complicated process. It was the sort of castle which could well hold up an army at the very limit of its supply lines that little bit too long, until Bruce managed to raise an army and cut them off.

De Valence was an able strategist, however. First he secured his position by sending miners to undermine the walls of Dunaverty Castle, where Bruce was sheltering, driving him to seek shelter on the island of Rathlin. Simultaneously he sought a quick – if unchivalrous – solution to the siege of Kildrummy. It was found in the person of the castle blacksmith. He was prevailed upon to set light to the castle granary. With his food supply destroyed, Sir Neil Bruce had no option but to surrender. He did so thinking his brother's womenfolk were safe, for in fact they were no longer at Kildrummy but had escaped north, to the sanctuary of St Duthus at Tain. Soon, however, the English had the women in their custody, despatched to them by the loyal Earl of Ross, in chains.

By mid-September the campaign in Scotland was effectively over. The king, now at Lanercost Priory, near Carlisle, had every reason to be well pleased. He had not captured Robert Bruce himself but he had in his custody the man's wife, mistress, brother, sisters and daughter, as well as the major churchmen who had supported the rebellion and other notables such as Christopher Seton, Sir Simon Fraser and the Earl of Atholl. It was more than he had dared to hope for at the outset. Even during the campaign he had been plagued by worry that he would not live to see its conclusion. His health and the war were increasingly becoming one and the same in his mind: his fight was as much against the forces of death as the Scots. But now, the range of prisoners allowed him his choice of punishments. Twelve knights captured at Methven were hanged at Berwick. Sir Simon Fraser and the Earl of Atholl were sent to London to die in the same way that William Wallace had, being drawn to the gallows, hanged and quartered, their parts being distributed around the realm. Christopher Seton, Bruce's brother-in-law, who had killed Robert Comyn at Dumfries, was sent back there to be hanged and dismembered, along with Neil Bruce. His wife, Christina Seton, Bruce's sister, was sent to England to be imprisoned, along with another sister, Elizabeth Siward, and his daughter. The three notable clergymen of the rebellion were all sent to England in fetters to begin lengthy terms in separate prisons. The most vindictive punishments of all were reserved for Bruce's sister, Mary, and his mistress, Isabel, Countess of Buchan. These two women were incarcerated publicly in wooden cages at Roxburgh Castle and Berwick Castle respectively. The only privacy they were afforded was a toilet, a concession to decency which the king only begrudgingly allowed. Both women endured this for more than three years. The only person honourably treated was Bruce's wife, Elizabeth, who did not approve of her husband's rebellion. In her words, they had been 'like children, playing at being kings and queens'.

*

With the end of the campaign, the English army began to break up. Quite unofficially a few of the younger knights decided they would leave the royal command and head off to find some fighting at a tournament in France. Few of those eager young knights who had come north with Edward had seen much close action, and they and their boredom could be contained no longer. Despite the king's orders to the contrary, twenty-two of the best-connected and most accomplished young tournament fighters deserted the army. Among them were Sir Piers Gaveston and Sir Roger Mortimer of Wigmore.[18]

The king was furious. Despite his frailty and age he raged against the deserters, and declared their estates forfeit. He issued orders for the men themselves to be arrested and to be declared traitors. Thus Roger found himself suddenly landless for the second time. Faced with such reproach there was nothing to be done except to make amends, and accordingly he and his fellow knights went to the prince at Wetheral Priory, near Carlisle, to ask him to intercede on their behalf with the king. The prince sought the best intercession he could, through his stepmother, the youthful and kind Queen Margaret, who pleaded with her husband to forgive the young men. For Roger, as for most of the twenty-two, that forgiveness and the restoration of his estates was forthcoming the following January. To Piers Gaveston it was not.

The prince's sympathies were entirely with his young friends. In order to try to reduce the outrage, he himself suggested that he should hold a tournament at Wark, but the king would have none of it. The king had learnt of a secret compact between the prince and Gaveston which went far beyond the desertion of a few knights. It turned out that they were sworn together as brothers-in-arms: that they would fight together as brothers and protect each other against all other men, sharing all their possessions![19] It was outrageous. Although an admiration for Gaveston's excellent knightly qualities was understandable, a liaison which threatened to share the government of the realm with a provincial knight was unthinkable.

Roger Mortimer had no objection to the prince having a brother-in-arms, and no problem with the chosen man being Gaveston. It was a knightly and courtly thing to do, and besides, Roger liked Piers Gaveston, and respected his skills in the tournament. But nothing could have prepared him and the other lords for the king's next quarrel with his son. The occasion was a request by the prince. Having decided that, if Gaveston was too low-born to be his companion, he would give him one of his own counties, the prince sent the Treasurer, Walter Langton, to the king. On his knees, Langton said: 'My lord king, I am sent on behalf of my lord the prince, your son, though as God lives, unwillingly, to seek in his name your licence to promote his knight Piers Gaveston to the rank of Count of Ponthieu.' The king could not believe what he was hearing. To Langton he shouted back: 'Who are you who dares to ask such things? As God lives, if not for fear of the Lord and because you said at the outset that you undertook this business unwillingly, you would not escape my hands! Now, however, I shall see what he who sent you has to say, while you wait here.' The prince was summoned, and stood before his white-haired father. 'On what business did you send this man?' demanded the king. The prince stoically replied: 'That with your consent I might give the county of Ponthieu to Sir Piers Gaveston.' On hearing these words, spoken by the prince himself, the king flew into a rage, exclaiming, 'You wretched son of a whore! Do you want to give away lands now? You who have never gained any? As God lives, if not for fear of breaking up the kingdom, I would never let you enjoy your inheritance!' As he spoke the king seized hold of the prince's head by the hair and tore handfuls of hair out, then threw the prince to the floor and kicked him repeatedly until he was exhausted.[20]

When the king had recovered he summoned the lords who were gathering for the parliament at Carlisle and before them declared Gaveston banished. It was a punishment upon his son more than on Gaveston, and since Gaveston's conduct had been irreproachable he gave him a pension to be enjoyed while abroad. He also forced Gaveston and the prince both to swear an oath never to see each other again without his permission. The prince, facing the prospect of life at court without his beloved companion, travelled south with him to Dover, showering him along the way with presents of jewellery, gold and exotic clothes, including two velvet jousting suits, one in red and the other in green, with silver and pearls on the sleeves. Then he was gone.

*

The prince, bereft of his 'brother Perrot', must have felt in the spring of 1307 that only one obstacle lay between him and his happiness: his father. Most of those now at court were younger men, and a change of monarch was long overdue. Young noblemen, bred on stories of great deeds, needed a king who offered them opportunities to match their ambitions, not a sixty-seven-year-old man obsessed with the political vicissitudes of Scotland. The king himself knew this, and knew his strength was ebbing. But with all the world against him, he would not give in. He waited in the north, ready for war. The reprisals against his treatment of Bruce's family would not be long coming, and he wanted to be there to meet them.

Most men, after more than half a century of military service, might have been content to retire to a monastery and there end their days in quiet contemplation. Not King Edward. Driven by the furies against first the Welsh and then the Scots, he had made war an integral part of his life. It was not that he was a vicious man – although he showed moments of vindictiveness, as in his treatment of the Countess of Buchan – but he had defined his own qualities in terms of military leadership. In his own mind, if he did not carry the fight against England's enemies, England would be at their mercy. Therefore his country needed him, he believed, and his right to rule depended on his military judgement and leadership in war.

In March 1307 the king moved to Carlisle in anticipation of the parliament he had called to take place there. Roger and his uncle, together with the rest of the English host, were summoned to attend. The Scots had apparently taken heart with the revival of another old prophecy of Merlin's: that after the death of the Covetous King, the Scots and Welsh would unite and have everything their own way. Robert Bruce had returned to the mainland and, although his brothers Thomas and Alexander Bruce were captured and executed on their arrival in the west of the country, Bruce himself was stronger than ever before. On 10 May he defeated Aymer de Valence at Loudon Hill, and a few days later he outwitted another English force under Ralph de Monthermer, and drove them back to Ayr Castle. Edward, by contrast, was sicker than ever, and did not appear in public. As the English army assembled at Carlisle, rumours spread that he was already dead.

No challenge, not even that of death, held any fears for the old king. When he heard that people were saying he was dead he forced himself out of his bed and once more set out towards Scotland. He did not know how much further he could go, but now the English army was with him, and thousands of men behind him. He was riding against all his enemies. On 3 July he managed two miles. Through a supreme force of will he pushed himself to go another two miles the next day. Worn out, on the next day he rested. The following day, however, he pressed on again, and made it to Burgh by Sands, with the waves crashing on the shore in the distance and the estuary between England and Scotland in sight. On 7 July he decided he would rest a little more. That afternoon, at about three o'clock, when his esquires lifted him up in his bed to take a little food, he fell back dead in their arms.

It was time for Prince Edward and his brother-in-arms to take power.

THREE

The King's Friend

The death of a member of the royal family is an unsettling event even in modern times; the death of a medieval monarch was much more so. When that monarch had reigned for most people's lifetime, and had become, for each and every one, a crucial part of how society operated, in terms of justice, law, security and religious observance, the effect was traumatic. So it was with Edward I. Most people could not remember the death of the previous king, thirty-five years earlier. Of the lords, knights and prelates who could, very few were old enough to have been at court at the time. Thus, as the country struggled to come to terms with the fact that the only king they had ever known or served was dead, they did the only thing which they were sure was right: they welcomed his son to the throne with open arms, and conferred on him all the powers of his father.

The realisation of his freedom burst on Edward like a ray of light. Immediately he recalled Gaveston from exile, and within a month the two men were again laughing together as they had done in the early days of their friendship. No more, it seemed, could old kings and proud earls challenge their relationship. And neither could they prevent Edward advancing Gaveston to the front rank of power. On 6 August 1306 at Dumfries, still a day short of a month since his father had died, he endowed Gaveston with one of the richest earldoms in the country, that of Cornwall, worth approximately £4,000 a year. The earldom had been intended for the late king's second son, Thomas of Brotherton, but Edward disregarded his young half-brother's interest. Even more alarming to the lords, who were just recovering from the shock of losing their old king, Edward proposed making Gaveston a member of the royal family. He planned to do this by allowing him to marry his niece, Margaret de Clare, sister of Gilbert de Clare, Earl of Gloucester, and daughter of his own sister, Joan. For the great lords it was like seeing a servant taken up from the kitchen and sat at the king's high table.

Gilbert de Clare, the sixteen-year-old Earl of Gloucester, was one of the few who saw no problem in the king's raising Gaveston to high rank. He had grown up with the king and Gaveston, and understood their friendship. Roger Mortimer, who had been at court for at least the last four years, similarly saw Gaveston's promotion as breaking new ground for the new generation. Now twenty years old, and firmly at the heart of the new administration, Roger stood to benefit from the change of monarch. Other men, like Hugh Audley, Roger Damory and John de Charlton had no doubt that their interests lay in supporting the king. Only slightly more distant were older royal advisers, such as Bartholomew de Badlesmere, Lord Mortimer of Chirk, and the elder Hugh Despenser, men whom Edward valued for their counsel and their loyalty. For all these lords opportunities beckoned, as long as they remained on the right side of Gaveston.

This was the sticking point for many of the older men, especially those who were not friends of the prince. Remaining on the right side of Gaveston was very difficult. He was not just an entertainer, he was ambitious and manipulative too. He took full advantage of his relationship with Edward, seeking opportunities for preferment for his tenants and dependants, and wilfully controlling the lords' access to Edward.[1] The great earls saw no reason why they should play second fiddle to the wishes of a Gascon commoner, and several of them soon wished they had not been so hasty in confirming his advancement to an earldom. To them and many others it was clear that their ancient lineage and noble titles – so hard won by their ancestors – counted for little when marks of profound dignity and distinction could be showered on Gaveston, who had yet to prove himself of benefit to anyone but the king.

Roger Mortimer was firmly in the king's camp, and as one of the king's young knights he was enjoying his new-found association with power. With the summer of 1307 drifting past aimlessly, the campaign in Scotland was called off, and Roger accompanied the rest of the court back to Westminster. There they spent a month preparing for the burial of Edward I and the marriage of Gaveston to Margaret de Clare. The funeral took place in Westminster Abbey on 22 October, fifteen weeks after the king's death.[2] After seeing his father safely into his tomb, Edward set out for Berkhamsted, the manor of his widowed stepmother, Queen Margaret, where Gaveston's wedding was to take place.

For Edward and Gaveston and their friends, the gathering of the court was little more than an excuse to drink, feast, joust, hunt and be merry. After a stay at Berkhamsted they moved on to the manor of Kings Langley in Hertfordshire where they spent most of November. The king's cousin Thomas of Lancaster was with them, by far the most powerful man in the country after the king, with four earldoms and a colossal income.[3] The Earl of Pembroke (Aymer de Valence had recently been confirmed in succession to this earldom) and the Earl of Gloucester were also in the royal party, as well as the Mortimers. On 26 November Roger's name appears next to that of Gaveston's in a small group of witnesses of a grant to the king by John FitzReginald.[4] At the end of the month they set out again, this time for Wallingford.

The tournament held in honour of Gaveston by the king on 2 December 1307 was a turning point in the reign. For a start, Wallingford had previously been a royal residence and so the two hundred or so assembled knights all saw for themselves how splendid was the gift Edward had given his dear Perrot. But that was nothing besides the tournament itself. Gaveston, a renowned champion fighter, led the knights on one side, while those on the other were led by the Earls of Warenne, Hereford, and Arundel. To the fury of the earls, and to the delight of the king and Gaveston, the young talented knights on Gaveston's side, with the benefit of their youth and strength, ran rings around the older earls' men. The earls were unceremoniously defeated and humiliated. Earl Warenne bitterly turned against Gaveston from that moment, and never forgave him. His violent declaration against the king's favourite only slightly exceeded the anger and frustration of the other two earls. This upstart had not only been raised above them, he could defeat them in battle too. Worst of all he publicly crowed over their fallen status, laughing at their humbling as they tumbled from their horses into the Berkshire mud. To the frustration of the earls, the king laughed also.

A tide of hatred against Gaveston swept across the country in the wake of the tournament, but those who had sided with the king and his beloved Perrot reaped their rewards. Among them were Roger and his uncle. The Justiciar of Ireland was ordered to restore all Roger's lands there due to him, and letters of protection were drawn up for him to accompany the king to France for his marriage to Princess Isabella.[5] Geoffrey de Geneville, Joan's octogenarian grandfather, was given permission to pass to Roger and Joan all the lands and estates in Ireland which they stood to inherit on his death. At the same time it seems that Roger was proposed for the position of Seneschal of Gascony, which would have made him governor of the Duchy of Aquitaine.[6] Shortly afterwards, Roger's uncle was made Justiciar of Wales, with enormous powers across the principality. For some reason Roger did not take up his position in Gascony; perhaps on account of his youth the earls persuaded Edward that it was a premature appointment. But whatever the reason, it is clear that the Mortimers both stood high in the king's favour as they accompanied him down the coast road to Dover in January 1308.[7]

While the appointment of Lord Mortimer of Chirk as Justiciar of Wales seems to have been considered entirely suitable by the earls and barons, Edward's appointment of Gaveston as sole Regent of England during his forthcoming absence from the realm shocked them profoundly. Edward clearly saw no difference between his adopted brother and a real brother. His real half-brothers – young though they were – would have both been considered acceptable, but again he ignored them. In putting Gaveston in nominal control of the country he was showing exactly how sincere he was in his wish to share power with his brother-in-arms. This was an act more outrageous than anything Gaveston himself had ever done or said. Ironically, it is through this very appointment that one can see how reliant Gaveston was on the king's wholehearted support. Left to rule the country for two weeks he did nothing controversial.[8] Indeed, one suspects he found himself somewhat out of his depth. It is true that he adopted a proud bearing towards those who came into his presence, and it is said that he forced the earls to kneel before him.[9] But in this one can see Gaveston brazening out his awkward position as head of the administration. The man was sweating in his king's absence, merely keeping up appearances. It seems that Gaveston needed the reassurance of Edward's distinguished lineage as much as Edward needed the reassurance of Gaveston's friendship. Between them they made up for aspects of character which each of them lacked.

For Roger, the importance of this extraordinary promotion of Gaveston was that, rightly or wrongly, he and his uncle had pledged themselves to the support of a partnership which was heading for confrontation, if not disaster. Even in France the earls with the king perceived that the king's affection for Gaveston was dangerously out of control. He was mixing his personal life and his public role so closely that the country was threatened. The antidote to this potentially lethal cocktail was to separate the two sides of kingship, to distinguish the king from the Crown.

It was at Boulogne, in the two weeks that Gaveston was ruler of England, that the Earls of Lincoln, Surrey, Pembroke and Hereford, together with the Bishop of Durham and five barons, drew up a declaration that they would act to protect the honour of the king and the rights of the Crown.[10] The idea quickly spread: that a lord's oath of fealty necessitated his loyalty to the Crown, but if the king himself was disloyal, then the lords' loyalty was due to the Crown, not to the king. Over the coming months this idea developed further. Men became convinced that, if the king did not act in the interests of the nation, those loyal to the Crown would be obliged to correct him. And since the king was personally above the law, there would be only one way to effect this correction: force.

Roger did not apply his seal to the Boulogne declaration. Two things may have motivated him: friendship for Edward and Gaveston, and personal ambition. With regard to the latter, Roger would have been aware of men like Bartholomew de Badlesmere, who had risen dramatically over the years through devoted, obsequious, service. And he realised that if he opposed the king in the name of justice he might only open the way for great earls like Lancaster to increase their power. A principled stand would not help lesser lords such as Roger. On the other hand, if he remained completely loyal to the king – and that was no crime in anybody's eyes – he stood to be richly rewarded.

On 25 January 1308 Edward was married to Isabella the Fair, the only daughter of King Philip of France, in Boulogne. If Roger was at the ceremony, as is believed, he would have seen the future queen of England for the first time at about the same moment as Edward himself. She was still very young, only twelve years old, but already noted for her good looks. And she was clever too. Writers in later centuries may have given her the title of 'She-wolf', especially referring to their disapproval of her immoral behaviour in the last years of her husband's reign, but contemporaries repeatedly focus on the same two qualities when describing her: beauty and wisdom. While most royal brides across the ages have been described as beautiful, there seems undoubtedly to have been something special about Isabella. Geoffrey of Paris carefully stated that, at that time, Isabella was the 'beauty of beauties . . . in the kingdom if not in all Europe'. With reference to her intelligence, to describe free-thinking females, even royal ones, as 'very wise' (*sapientissima*) was far from conventional.[11] Then, of course, there is the matter of heredity: her father was not known as Philip the Fair on account of his equitable nature but for his extraordinary good looks, which Isabella and her brother Charles seem to have inherited. As for her clothes, the preservation of her wedding dress – a 'tunic with a mantle of red, lined with yellow sindon' – until the day she died, indicates its fineness.[12] Thus on his wedding day Edward set his eyes on a girl who had every desirable attribute, and for whose face every man in England would have launched at least one ship, if not the full thousand.

Every man in England, that is, except Edward. The king had thoughts only for Gaveston. As soon as he landed back in Dover, he singled out Gaveston among the lords assembled there and ran to him and flung his arms around him, repeatedly kissing him while the onlookers shifted uncomfortably. London had been bedecked with decorations, banners and flags to welcome Isabella to England, and the crowds turned out in their thousands to catch a glimpse of the young queen; but it was clear that this poor girl was not receiving the attention she deserved from the one man who mattered – her new husband – and that her future happiness was anything but assured.

King Philip had not let his daughter travel to England alone. With her came her two uncles, Charles de Valois and Louis d'Evreux, and most importantly, the youngest of her three brothers, Prince Charles, the future Charles IV of France. A number of continental dukes and lords came too. Also there were the French ladies at court who were married to English lords, one such being Joan, Roger's wife, and another Margaret, his mother.[13] But nevertheless it must have been with great trepidation that Isabella prepared to take part in her first official function: her husband's coronation.

The coronation had been planned for 18 February, and invitations had been sent out on 18 January bearing this date. The event was delayed by a week, possibly owing to a dispute over protocol with the Archbishop of Canterbury, but more probably because of a disagreement over the role Gaveston was to perform at the ceremony. Edward's affection for his friend was now more intense than ever. He was not blind to the fact that he was angering a number of the nobles through his favouritism, but their anger only strengthened his resolve, for he was convinced they had no right to question his authority. He was absolutely determined that England should see him and his adoptive brother as partners in government. In this he was as bloody-minded as his father had been in subduing Scotland.

The previous October the king had ordered tapestries bearing his coat of arms and Gaveston's to be prepared for the coronation.[14] Now he demanded that Gaveston be allowed to carry the crown of St Edward the Confessor in procession before him: the most important secular role in the ceremony apart from that of the king himself. The earls, in conjunction with the outraged French princes, protested. On the day of the intended coronation they gave Edward an ultimatum: either banish Gaveston or face the consequences. Edward disparagingly opted for the latter, and thus a week passed with all the tension of a dozen knives being silently drawn around the king. Before the earls would consent to the ceremony going ahead with Gaveston carrying the crown, they insisted that Edward agree to sanction whatever policies the forthcoming parliament introduced. In addition, he had to add a fourth clause to the traditional coronation oaths, to 'uphold and defend the laws and righteous customs which the community of the realm shall determine'. Uncrowned, and with so many powerful men ranged against him, Edward had no choice but to acquiesce on the political matter. On the subject of Gaveston, however, he refused to give in. The earls, confident that they could remove Gaveston at a later date, let the ceremony go ahead.

On 25 February 1308 Edward II was crowned King of England, Wales and Ireland before the great altar of Westminster Abbey by the Bishop of Winchester. So many Londoners turned out to watch the spectacle that a wall collapsed along the route taken by the guests, and a knight was crushed to death. Edward himself avoided the crowds, being steered into the abbey through a back door. In the ceremonial procession, William Marshal, a descendant of the famous warrior-statesman, carried the great gilt spurs, followed by the Earl of Hereford carrying the sceptre, who was in turn followed by Henry of Lancaster, brother of the Earl of Lancaster, carrying the royal staff. These men were followed by the Earls of Lancaster, Lincoln and Warwick carrying the three swords of state, the one carried by Lancaster being Curtana, the sword of St Edward the Confessor. These three earls had been selected on account of their status, rather than how close they were personally to Edward, but the next group, none of whom was an earl, were clearly present because of personal association with the king. Hugh Despenser, Thomas de Vere, Edmund FitzAlan and Roger carried between them a large, fine chequered cloth on which lay the royal robes. All four of these men had spent at least part of their youth at court, and it seems reasonable to suppose they formed an outer ring of Edward's close friends. Two were cousins of Roger's (de Vere and FitzAlan). After this group came the two great officers of state: the Treasurer and the Chancellor. The last figure to enter the abbey before the king, and thus the most important, was Gaveston, carrying the crown.

The ceremony itself passed without incident. The banquet afterwards in Westminster Hall did not.

As an earl, Gaveston had the right to wear cloth-of-gold in the king's presence. To the dismay of all, he appeared wearing imperial purple trimmed with pearls. He sought to show off as much as he could, and the king enthusiastically encouraged him. Edward ignored his young bride, despite the fact that her uncles and brothers were official guests at the coronation. Rather than sit next to her, he sat next to Gaveston. Together they laughed, ate, joked, and paid no attention to anyone else. It was revealed that Edward had given all the gold and jewellery he had received as wedding presents, including those from the King of France, to Gaveston.[15] Outraged and insulted, the French princes stood up, shouted their disgust, and left the hall there and then, to the embarrassment of all but the king.

Two days later, at a parliament held in the same hall, the old Earl of Lincoln sternly demanded that the king should confirm in a charter what he had promised before the coronation, that is to assent to the will of the lords in Parliament, whether he agreed with them or not. Only one earl openly defended the king's rights: his cousin, Thomas of Lancaster. With the help of Hugh Despenser he managed to persuade the Earl of Lincoln to delay his demand, but no sooner had they left the hall than the lords began to prepare for a possible conflict. It was clearly the only way of controlling royal authority. The king himself was alert to the danger, and replaced any custodians of royal castles connected with his opponents with men loyal to himself. If it took a civil war to show his determination to rule as his own man, Edward was ready.

Roger Mortimer was also ready, and he was prepared to defend the king. The very fact that he remained at court at this time, when so many were preparing for conflict, is evidence of his loyalty.[16] On 17 March he went a step further and made a clear statement of his friendship for Gaveston, when he jointly made a request with him for a gift of land to John de Boltesham.[17] Before this, no secular lord had ever acted publicly in conjunction with Gaveston. To associate himself openly with him at this juncture reveals the extent of Roger's royalist sympathies, and his friendship with both the king and Gaveston.

By the end of March the mood was tense. Castles were fortified, men were summoned and equipped, messengers were despatched around the country, hastily coordinating plans. King Philip of France sent money to the earls to help rid England of Gaveston. The days passed. Only the Earls of Lancaster and Richmond declared they would defend the king in battle. Even the Earl of Gloucester would not commit himself. Few other lords besides the Mortimers remained faithful.[18] The Earl of Lincoln was determinedly for war, and behind him were Pembroke, Arundel, Warwick, Surrey and the majority of the country. The situation for the king and his favourite looked bleak.

Temporary respite came in the form of a parliament, held at Westminster at the end of April. The rebel lords came armed with their retinues. As a show of force it was persuasive, and their demands were just as emphatic. The Earl of Lincoln announced their purpose. Firstly he repeated the well-rehearsed argument that the king was not synonymous with the Crown, to which each lord owed a higher allegiance. Secondly, Gaveston should be banished, for his treason to the Crown, which took the form of appropriating Crown lands to himself. Thirdly, that the people, whose will the king had sworn to accept, had already judged Gaveston, and found him guilty. The only thing remaining to be discussed was whether the king also stood to be accused.

Edward could not defend himself, but he tried to defend Gaveston. Incredibly, for three weeks he refused to accept the lords' demands. But the situation was too serious and the lords did not back down. On 18 May Edward finally agreed to Gaveston's banishment. Distraught at the prospect of once more being separated from his beloved Perrot, and furious at such pressure being brought to bear upon him by the earls, he searched for a way to spite them. The appointment of a new Lieutenant in Ireland gave him an idea. By making Gaveston Lord Lieutenant of Ireland he could offer him considerable authority, much dignity, and a good deal of honour. He could also kick sand in the earls' faces. It was an excellent strategy: if he had to lose Perrot, he would give him Ireland.

By this time Roger seems to have left court. He probably departed soon after Parliament broke up, as his name is not among those who witnessed various letters in favour of Gaveston in mid-June.[19] Probably he accompanied his wife and mother back to Wigmore, or another of their demesne manors. It marks the end of the first period of his attendance at Edward II's court, which had probably lasted the whole year, and in which he had shown himself, like his uncle, unswervingly loyal to the king.

*

The following autumn Roger and Joan followed Gaveston and his wife to Ireland. Their main reasons for going were to meet Joan's grandfather, to take possession of Meath and to attend a court to answer a case concerning their manor of Duleek, over a dispute about tolls exacted on their behalf which had rumbled on in their absence since January 1306.[20] It is quite possible that Roger also wanted to meet Gaveston, and the evidence touching upon his stay in Ireland certainly tallies with this. Perhaps Roger would have sailed with Gaveston but for the fact that on 21 June a summons was issued for him to muster his forces for a campaign in Scotland. Although this campaign did not go ahead, it may well have delayed him.

Ireland was nominally under English rule, but English rule amounted to very little rule in practice. The country was a land of communities living in dire poverty, with an empty treasury, and a great absence of major lords, none of whom wished to risk their lives in such a lawless and impoverished place. And that accounted only for the parts conquered by the English. Considerably more than half the island was still ruled by continually warring native Irish clans. The English lords were constantly defending themselves against the Irish, and attacking them, and fighting amongst each other. Indeed, over the last century the English lords had become partly Irish themselves, so it is more accurate to say that part-English and part-Irish warlords ruled nearly the whole country. War, with all its terror, had swallowed Ireland whole and was spitting out the bodies.

Some measure of how cruel the land was, and the bloodiness of daily life, even to the point of brothers attacking and killing each other, can be gleaned from the *Annals of the Kingdom of Ireland*, the principal chronicle of the native Irish, written in Gaelic.[21] Almost every entry relates to some small band of warriors attacking another: Irish attacking Irish, Irish attacking English, and English attacking Irish in a swirling mass of Gaelic and Anglo-Norman names and fire, destruction and bloodshed. The English perspective, given in a series of annals written in Latin in a Dublin monastery, is equally horrific.[22] Every year there are multiple references to villages being burnt, and the English defeating – or being defeated by – gangs of Irish warriors. Thus whichever point of view you take, the country to which Roger and Joan had come was a bloody one. By implication, the position which Edward had conferred on Gaveston was no sinecure. The land most closely resembled the Marcher lordships of the twelfth century, with the wars between Gaelic-speaking clans and Englishmen, with groups of men murdering wayfarers, burning villages, killing their enemies' cattle, ambushing messengers. For men like Roger and Gaveston, with everything to prove and eager for military experience, this meant Ireland was not a place to avoid but a land of opportunity.

Trim, at the heart of the de Geneville estates, was the first place to which Roger and Joan went, to meet Lord Geoffrey de Geneville, now aged eighty-two. Having resided at Trim Castle since 1254, he could remember most of the history of the English in Ireland: who were his most loyal retainers, which English family had married into which Irish tribe, and who had killed whom and burnt what. For three years in the 1270s he had governed Ireland, holding the position of Justiciar. As for the castle, it had stood like a bastion of English rule throughout. It was the largest and probably the strongest castle in Ireland, with its colossal Norman keep and high stone curtain walls, further defended on the north side by the River Boyne. But once it had been at the centre of a peaceful palatinate; now it was a frontier castle again.

We do not know a great deal about the role played by Gaveston in Ireland, and even less about that played by Roger. Clearly the most marked aspect of their stay was military activity and, unfortunately, soldiers in the field very rarely leave written evidence of their deeds. We cannot even be sure that Roger and Gaveston were acting together. However, there is some evidence that they were. They were in the same small part of Ireland at the same time, and their previous close alliance in England has already been noted. A further strong indicator is the number of friends they had in common in Ireland. One of the men who had sailed with Gaveston was John de Charlton, a yeoman of Gaveston's household and a friend of both the king and Roger.[23] Another man present was Walter de Thornbury, Roger's guardian, who was appointed Chancellor of Ireland on Gaveston's recommendation.[24] A third common companion – and probably the closest to both men – was John de Hothum, who, having left Ireland at the time Gaveston arrived, returned early in 1309 and was, with Gaveston's help, made Chancellor of the Irish Exchequer, a post previously held by Walter de Thornbury.[25] A fourth close mutual companion was John de Sapy, who served in both Roger's household and Gaveston's.[26] Thus, with at least four of Roger's closest associates being among Gaveston's closest associates, one may safely say that the companionship hinted at by Roger's defection from the royal army with Gaveston in October 1306 had not weakened, and may well have grown stronger.

Roger and Gaveston were certainly both together in Dublin in April 1309,[27] and in the light of this fact there is every reason to suppose Roger assisted Gaveston in his spring campaign. This took the form of an expedition through Leinster, defeating the rebel Irish and Anglo-Irish, and once more securing the region under English control. The Wicklow Mountains south of Dublin, centred on Castle Kevin, were exactly where Geoffrey de Geneville had been defeated by the native Irish forty years earlier. Roger may have learnt from his grandfather-in-law, or men then in his employment, how difficult it was to fight a traditional pitched battle with mounted knights in those parts. One had to use guerrilla tactics, as used in the mountains of Wales, and to centralise forces on a strong, defendable castle: in this case Castle Kevin. These were the tactics employed now by Gaveston. Whether or not there was any direct link between de Geneville's experiences in the 1270s and Gaveston's strategy is of course entirely conjectural; either way, it was probably in this part of Ireland, under Gaveston's command, that Roger had his first experiences of helping to form military strategy.

By the summer of 1309 Gaveston had gained a reputation as a sound military administrator in Ireland. Not only had the English forces under his orders achieved the destruction of Dermot O'Dempsey, a rebellious Irish lord, he had secured Leinster, defeated the equally rebellious O'Byrne clan, and refortified key strongholds such as Newcastle McKynegan and Castle Kevin. He had built a road leading through the mountains from Castle Kevin to Glendalough to secure these achievements. All this work strengthened the capital, Dublin, and provided a firm base for the English to rule more effectively. If the way was cleared for him to return to England, he could hold his head high.

Back in England, ever since Gaveston's departure King Edward had been doing all in his power to pave the way for his beloved's return. In order to gain the approval of the earls he offered each of them grants of land and persuaded them, one by one, to return to the fold of loyalty. Once he had convinced the most sympathetic lords, he despatched them to Avignon to consult the Pope, and subsequently presented the pontiff with jewellery. He bribed the Pope also by making grants of lands to his family in Gascony. In addition he persuaded the King of France to drop his opposition by making large grants to Isabella for her maintenance. By the spring of 1309 he was ready to demand that Gaveston be allowed to return.

Edward had shown himself to be a shrewd manipulator in his dealings over Gaveston. Exactly how shrewd was shown even more clearly over the next two months. At the Westminster parliament in late April and early May, Edward had requested that he be granted leave to levy a tax and that Gaveston be allowed back into England. He was granted the tax on certain conditions, but Gaveston's return was flatly refused. Edward's next move was cunning: he offered to accept all the conditions attached to the tax in return for Gaveston's return. In this he was eventually successful, playing off the earls against each other. Although not formally summoned, Gaveston left Ireland on or just before 23 June,[28] returning to England surreptitiously, by way of Tintagel Castle in Cornwall, and appearing openly beside the king at the parliament held at Stamford in late July.

Roger returned to England at about the same time. Given his Arthurian interests, from his ancestry and his later chivalric displays, it is tempting to speculate that he was with Gaveston at Tintagel Castle, and saw the low ruins of the legendary birthplace of the ancient British king. One might also speculate that the reason why Gaveston was able to travel across England without arousing suspicion was that he was travelling in Roger's company. By 20 July Roger had reached the court, as on that day the king favoured him by issuing a mandate to the Justiciar of Ireland to restore to him rights formerly enjoyed by his predecessors in Trim. It is thus possible that Gaveston was secretly with Edward from this point onwards. Roger subsequently attended the Stamford parliament at which Gaveston made a surprise public appearance, and at which Edward renewed his grant of the earldom of Cornwall on his favourite. The days of Roger's closeness with Gaveston were, however, numbered.

The problem was, once again, Gaveston's lack of respect for the earls. He was unable to contain his spitefulness towards those who had forced his exile. He gave them all nicknames, which he used openly at court. He called the Earl of Warwick 'the Black Hound of Arden', and the Earl of Lancaster 'the Fiddler'. Most importantly, he alienated the moderate Earl of Pembroke, whom he called 'Joseph the Jew'. He regarded his enemies' failure to keep him in exile as a sign of their weakness, and mocked them accordingly. He finally pushed his luck too far when he demanded the king dismiss one of the Earl of Lancaster's retainers, which of course Edward did. The earl swore to destroy Gaveston, and there were many who would have gladly offered assistance.

Roger remained with the court for the remainder of 1309. In all probability he spent Christmas with the king and Gaveston. The gravity of the situation regarding Gaveston could not be ignored, however, and in February 1310 matters came to a head. The Earls of Lancaster, Hereford, Warwick, Oxford and Arundel demanded that he be banished for a second time. As a precaution, the king did as he had done in 1308: he appointed his faithful retainers to positions in charge of vital castles. Roger, for example, received the constableship of Builth Castle. But it was slight protection for the king against the combined wrath of the key military earls and the Archbishop of Canterbury. Only three of the earls remained loyal, and one of them, Surrey, was of dubious worth, having declared his everlasting hatred of Gaveston. As a safeguard, Gaveston was sent north. Edward was forced to accept the appointment of a committee of twenty-one Lords Ordainers drawn from the earls, barons and bishops, who would draw up a series of articles limiting royal power.

By this time, the king had become adept at elusive political manoeuvring. He decided to answer those of his critics who had complained about his neglect of Scotland by announcing a campaign, and his intention to shift the whole government to York. On 18 June a writ was issued summoning Roger to appear with the other lords and their retinues to march against the Scots, mustering at Berwick on 8 September. At the same time a second writ requested Roger to allow one hundred men to be raised from his lordship of Ewyas, held jointly with his kinsman, Theobald de Verdon, and a third writ requested that two hundred men be raised from three of his Welsh lordships.[29] Roger himself, however, had obtained permission from the king to go to Ireland just two days earlier, and this remained steadfastly his intent.[30] He returned to Wigmore to organise the despatch of the men from his Welsh lands to assist the king, and set out for Ireland through Wales.[31] On 2 August a desperate last-minute call from the king was sent to Roger 'earnestly requesting' him to attend the muster at Berwick. It was in vain. Shortly after the appointed date of 8 September, Roger landed in Ireland.[32]

*

Lords with extensive land holdings, when travelling abroad, appointed lawyers to represent them in their absence. From the official enrolment of such appointments we know that among the English knights in Ireland with Roger in October 1310 were William de Adforton, John de Stratfield, Hugh de Croft, Hugh de Kynardsleigh, William de Thornbury, William de Cleobury and Hugh de Turpington. Of these, the last named would stand by Roger to his dying day. The others all came from Mortimer heartlands, most of them from Mortimer-held manors within a few miles of Wigmore. Also with Roger was one Master John le Keu de la Rook, who, holding a degree and yet being of sufficient status to need to appoint attorneys in England, was possibly Roger's chaplain and secretary. And last but by no means least of those who accompanied Roger on his expedition of 1310 was his wife, Joan.[33]

It might seem surprising that a military commander heading to a war zone and expecting to do battle should take his wife with him, but he had good reasons. Joan was herself an Irish heiress, and there may have been some legal technicality requiring her to go in person, to take possession of lands, for example, or to answer a case in court. More probably, travelling with Roger was simply her practice. Judging from the number of children they produced, Roger wanted his wife to be with him in Ireland (as in England) as a sexual companion, especially as he would be there for months if not years. But there is also the fact that the lady of a household was second in command after her lord. If anything should happen to Roger, Joan was the ideal person to hold the lines of feudal duty together and to take command, she being the heiress of Meath in her own right.

Upon landing Roger and Joan found that Meath, like most of Ireland, was in turmoil. The previous year John FitzThomas had gone to war with Roger's vassals, the brothers Hugh and Walter de Lacy, and Roger had obtained pardons for manslaughters committed by those of his men who had resisted the attack.[34] There is also evidence that the native Irish had attacked deep into West Meath in 1310, and had been repulsed. The Annals of Clonmacnoise record that in 1310 'Geoffrey O'Farell, with the forces of the Annaly, came to Donover, in Kyneleagh, to take the spoils and prey of that country, but the natives and inhabitants defended their country so well that they killed Donnell MacHugh Oge O'Farell, Hugh MacMoylissa and Geoffrey MacMortagh'.[35] This 'Donover' probably relates to Donore in the barony of Moycashel, close to Roger's lands. These enemies may have been politically unimportant in England, and had too few retainers to make a major impact upon Ireland as a whole, but it did not take many men to terrorise a neighbourhood, or to burn a granary, or to steal a few dozen head of cattle. Such acts could destroy a community, a manor, and accordingly destroy the income of the lord. The lands of absentee lords like Roger were especially at risk.

Worryingly for the absentee Irish lords, these attacks were not isolated incidents. Throughout English-held Ireland incursions were being made into English rights. What was happening was more than just a rebellion: the entire existence of the English in Ireland was under threat from a move to reintroduce Gaelic law and customs to Ireland, to Gaelicise the country.

English lords saw opportunities this way; they could become petty princes by marrying Irish heiresses and switching between Irish and English allegiances as they found fit. Indeed, some had done this from the mid-thirteenth century and spoke Irish as naturally as French, the language of the English aristocracy. Just as worrying for the English lords was the fact that the Irish Exchequer revenues had collapsed, and there was pitifully little money for raising troops now: between a third and a half of the revenue available in the reign of Edward I.[36] And then there was the succession question. Certain lords, especially those who were part-Irish, from mixed marriages, held that Irish inheritance laws applied to their lordships. These varied from tribe to tribe, but in some cases women were altogether debarred from inheriting. If such laws were taken into account, Roger and Joan should not have inherited Meath through Joan's grandmother, Maud de Lacy, and Roger should not have inherited his grandmother's estate at Dunamase. It is thus important to see Roger's ambitions in Ireland in this light: he had to fight to retain his lordships, and to retain the loyalty of his tenant lords, otherwise he would lose his lordships in Ireland altogether.

We know little of what direct action Roger took in Ireland over the course of the next year. In April and September 1311 he was firmly stationed at his great fortress of Trim, probably protecting his inheritance through force of arms and negotiation. Ironically, the most important thing about this period of his life is what he was *not* doing. He had so far supported Gaveston and the king completely. Now his powerful and respected kinsman, the Earl of Pembroke, had broken with the king and sided with the other earls. This altered things. Gaveston was clearly hell-bent on antagonising Lancaster and Warwick, and he would drag down with him many who supported him. Perhaps Pembroke warned Roger to keep clear of Gaveston. Roger's Irish campaign was undertaken for military reasons, but it helped remove him from the company of Gaveston, and thus protected him from later events. Never again did Roger put himself in a position of risk for the sake of helping the king's favourite.

*

While Roger was facing the turmoil of Ireland, Edward was struggling in Scotland. The campaign started badly when, of the ten earls besides Gaveston, only Gloucester and Surrey accompanied him on the expedition. In October they reached Linlithgow, but failed to meet Bruce in battle. Bruce was far too wise to risk venturing an attack on a better equipped army which would sooner or later retire to England, as it always did. Instead he hid battalions of men ready in defence. On one occasion, a number of Scotsmen hidden in a cave above a narrow valley road saw an opportunity too good to miss, and took advantage of the higher ground, massacring the English footsoldiers below them. By the time the English knights were on the scene, and able to rally the men and to order a systematic advance on the position, the Scots had disappeared, leaving three hundred dead and many wounded.[37] Thus the English campaign failed in all its objectives, including its main one: to distract the English earls from the impeachment of Gaveston.

It was the summer of 1311 by the time Edward came south. He ordered Gaveston to remain in the safety of Bamburgh Castle, and summoned a parliament for 8 August. Roger was also summoned, but, in all probability, ignored the writ, as he habitually did when in Ireland. The rest of the lords came with a purpose: to present Edward with the Ordinances, and to force him to accept them all.

There were forty-one Ordinances. These included six which had been issued directly on the appointment of the Lords Ordainers the previous year, which included general statements about the rights of the Church, the keeping of the king's peace throughout the realm, and the keeping of Magna Carta. The thirty-five new Ordinances touched upon such subjects as the king's right to declare war without the consent of his lords (as Edward had recently done with regard to Scotland), and the removal of royal officials especially close to Gaveston, among them John de Charlton, John de Hothum and John de Sapy. Interestingly, the sixteenth Ordinance stressed that the lands of Ireland, Gascony and Scotland were at risk of being lost unless capable and efficient ministers could be appointed as their keepers. But Edward cared only about one Ordinance: the twentieth. This stated that Gaveston had to leave the realm by 1 November, for the crime of having misled and poorly advised the king. In case of any doubt, the lords stressed that by 'the realm' they meant England, Scotland, Ireland and Wales, and all the other dominions of King Edward. There would be no new appointments for Gaveston.

Edward could do nothing. He offered to accept all the Ordinances except the twentieth, but he underestimated the gravity with which the Lords Ordainers viewed the situation. He delayed as long as he could, squirming under the attack on his authority. Eventually, in October, he agreed to all the Ordinances, and prepared to say goodbye to his beloved once more. The following month, Gaveston embarked on a ship at a London quayside, and sailed down the Thames and away from England.

*

The Lords Ordainers had observed that Gascony, Scotland and Ireland might be lost because of inefficient government, but they conspicuously did not mention Wales. There Lord Mortimer of Chirk was governing the principality with efficient ruthlessness. He had demonstrated this quality in his youth, and even now at the age of fifty-six he was just as uncompromising. By the beginning of 1312 he had successfully exercised the office of Justiciar for four years. When Edward had secured the Welsh royal castles by granting them out to his loyal retainers, Lord Mortimer of Chirk received the constableships of Blaenllyfni and Dinas, in addition to those already in his keeping, which included several of the most strategic Welsh castles. Numerous small grants came his way with regularity over the subsequent years. In effect he ruled Wales as a surrogate prince.

Like Roger in Ireland, Lord Mortimer of Chirk avoided being drawn into the worsening situation surrounding Gaveston. While the rest of the country was nervously preparing for a conflict over the king's favourite, the elder Mortimer prepared for an attack on Griffin de la Pole, the repercussions of which were to prove far-reaching. Three years earlier the heir to the lordship of Welshpool had died while a royal ward.[38] Lord Mortimer of Chirk, as Justiciar of Wales, had been ordered to take custody of the lordship, which he had done. An inquiry had found that the rightful heir was the dead heir's sister Hawise, who was married to John de Charlton, the King's Chamberlain, and a friend of Roger and Gaveston. The lordship was accordingly delivered to John de Charlton. But Griffin de la Pole, the brother of the late lord and Hawise's uncle, had complained, insisting that according to Welsh custom the inheritance was rightfully his. To further his claim, he sought a commission of inquiry to determine whether the lordship was held according to Welsh or English law. Edward had prohibited this from being held, hoping that the question would end there. It did not. Griffin de la Pole attacked John de Charlton in early 1312, besieging him and his wife in Welshpool Castle.

If Griffin de la Pole had been acting completely independently, the matter would have been over quickly and soon forgotten. But he had sought and obtained the support of the Earl of Lancaster, who, as the king's cousin, had decided his role was to lead the opposition to Edward's personal style of government and, in particular, his acts of favouritism. There is little doubt that Edward had not been fair in his appointment and suppression of the inquiry. As for the Earl of Lancaster, to take de la Pole under his wing only contributed further to his status. Now that he had inherited a fifth earldom – that of Lincoln, after the death of Henry de Lacy in 1311 – he lurked like a fat black spider at the centre of his huge web of estates in the north, pulling together the threads of feudal obligation, and international and national political disaffection. So great was his power, and so extensive his influence, that one did not go to war with an ally of his without good reason.

For Lord Mortimer of Chirk, the reason for war was simple: the king ordered him to break up the siege of Welshpool Castle by force.[39] He raised an army, encamped near Welshpool, and waited. He offered de la Pole recourse to the law courts, but the man refused. The king wrote, offering to recompense de la Pole, sending the Steward of the Royal Household, John de Cromwell, to pacify him.[40] But still de la Pole held out. It took several weeks to persuade him that the Earl of Lancaster was not going to ride to his rescue, and that his cause was best fought diplomatically. In the mean time de la Pole had found another supporter in the Earl of Arundel, a cousin of the Mortimers. Arundel gave shelter to de la Pole's men as they ransacked the countryside. This was a personal betrayal, as well as treason. Lord Mortimer of Chirk eventually broke the siege, rescued John de Charlton and his wife, restored order, and arrested de la Pole. But in the eyes of the Earl of Lancaster, who was an impetuous and spoilt man, with little sense of duty and a commensurate inability to appreciate others' dutifulness, he had sworn enmity. Early the following year, when Lord Mortimer of Chirk was appointed to sit on the commission to investigate the debacle, the Earl of Lancaster objected to his presence. An estrangement between the two men resulted, which would ultimately lead to the destruction of both of them. In the meantime it meant the breakdown of trust between the Earl of Lancaster and Roger too, for the two Mortimers invariably acted as one in political matters.

For the time being, however, Roger remained in Ireland. In April and May 1312 he was in Dublin. A distant kinsman, Robert de Verdon, had started a rebellion in Louth during Lent, and, as the younger brother of the heir to the de Verdon half of Meath, it had swept up a number of Mortimer and de Verdon followers in its fury.[41] They rode over the baronies of Ferrard and Ardee, and so desecrated that of Louth that John Wogan, the Justiciar, was forced to take it into his own hands. Wogan then collected an army to put down the revolt, and, having sent men to Ardee to defend that barony, he marched to Drogheda. There the people asked that they might themselves defend their lands with an army commanded by another two of the de Verdon brothers, Miles and Nicholas. Rather than remain loyal to their elder brother, who was in England, they simply joined Robert. Under the guise of King Edward's banner, the de Verdons together attacked the force at Ardee and defeated them. As the local lord and the brother-in-law of Theobald, Roger was bound to intervene, even before this last outrage became known. After Wogan had raised a second army, and had again been 'miserably defeated' by the de Verdons, Roger took control of the situation, and forced them to surrender and to appear in court in return for their lives.[42] At the end of May 1312 he handed over forty of the ringleaders to the Justiciar to be imprisoned.

By the end of the summer of 1312, Roger had fully come of age. He was twenty-five years old, had witnessed political decision-making at the heart of government, and had spent the previous two years coming to terms with the brutal circumstances of Ireland. He had tackled armies composed of Irishmen and Englishmen, and rabbles of Anglo-Irish rioters. He had observed the inability of some administrators to deal with insurrection, and he had also seen the enormous prizes which could be won by those who remained loyal to King Edward. He had a well-connected and devoted wife, and a growing number of children. He was in a position to return to England and take a role at the front rank of English politics.

But then occurred one of those deaths which rocked society to its foundations. Gaveston, the Earl of Cornwall, had returned from exile in early 1312, and aroused such hostility that he was forced to give himself up to the Earl of Pembroke. The earl had sworn an oath to surrender his lands and titles to protect the man's life. But the Earls of Lancaster, Arundel and Warwick did not care what the Earl of Pembroke had sworn or stood to lose. In June they kidnapped the king's brother-in-arms while he was in the earl's protection.

And they killed him.

FOUR

Bannockburn and Kells

Gaveston's murder tore the country in two. Even those who had been most opposed to the man were horrified. The three earls had killed the king's dearest friend. Bloody retribution seemed inevitable. Those responsible stood to lose their lands, their titles and their lives.

The Earl of Lancaster made no attempt to shift the blame from himself. From the moment Gaveston had arrived back in England Lancaster had hounded the king and his brother-in-arms. Gaveston had joined the king at York in February, where they remained until Margaret de Clare, Gaveston's wife and Edward's niece, gave birth to a daughter, Joan. In March, with the baronage and earls convinced now that war was certain, Thomas of Lancaster had openly assumed the leadership of the opposition to Gaveston, and gave the Earls of Pembroke and Surrey the task of leading an army to capture him. Gaveston knew the risk he was taking by remaining in the country, not least because he had been excommunicated by the Archbishop of Canterbury on his return. But he decided nevertheless to stay in England. He chose to remain with Edward despite all the dangers. Edward, joyful that his beloved would not leave him, joined him at Newcastle at the end of March.

Edward and Gaveston may have thought that the opposition they would face would be unorganised, slow to muster and reluctant to start a civil war. Despite many harsh words, no one had yet actually taken up arms against them. But this time things were different. The Earl of Lancaster – the man whom Gaveston had mocked with the title of 'the Fiddler' – now used his authority to gather his own feudal army. He marched north, hiding his army by day and moving by night in order to escape notice. On 4 May he approached Newcastle. Edward and Gaveston were taken wholly by surprise and had to flee suddenly by ship to Scarborough Castle. In so doing they left everything behind: jewels, money, horses, soldiers and arms. Lancaster took the lot.

For the time being Edward and Gaveston were safe. But then Edward made a fatal mistake: he left Gaveston in Scarborough Castle while he went south to raise an army. The Earl of Lancaster quickly moved to place his forces between the king and the favourite, thereby separating Gaveston from all hope of aid. On 19 May, Gaveston, fearing the Earl of Lancaster would kill him, agreed to submit to Henry Percy and the Earls of Pembroke and Surrey. The Earl of Pembroke took responsibility for escorting Gaveston back to London. But at Deddington in Oxfordshire, Gaveston was kidnapped by the Earl of Warwick and taken to Warwick Castle. For the next nine days he was held there until the Earl of Lancaster arrived. Lancaster's advice as to what to do next was the cold-hearted sentence Gaveston so feared: 'While he lives there will be no safe place in the realm of England.'[1] On 19 June Gaveston was taken to Blacklow Hill, land belonging to the Earl of Lancaster, and two Welshmen killed him. One ran him through the body with a sword, then the other hacked off his head as he lay dying on the grass.

The country went into shock. Every lord and knight throughout the realm readied for war. The Earl of Pembroke was beside himself, having sworn an oath to protect Gaveston's life on penalty of forfeiting his lands and titles. In the days between Gaveston's capture and murder Pembroke desperately tried to raise an army to free him, even appealing to the University of Oxford, who, besides not being known for their military strength, were not remotely concerned with Gaveston's wellbeing or the earl's plight. The country was not prepared to fight to save Gaveston, who had done nothing to make himself popular with the common people.

Edward's own reaction to the murder was utter rage, which very quickly became cold fury.[2] On hearing of Gaveston's death he remarked, 'By God's soul, he acted as a fool. If he had taken my advice he never would have fallen into the hands of the earls. This is what I always told him not to do. For I guessed that what has now happened would occur.'[3] But his remonstrance of his dead friend masked a depth of grief which would never leave him, and which was compounded by his sense of betrayal at the hands of his cousin, Lancaster, who was now far beyond forgiveness. His mind became focused on the destruction of the earls who had acted against him, and, given strength through grief, he thought and acted more clearly. With Gaveston dead, there was nothing more for the vast majority of the rebels to gain from opposing him. He stopped the earls marching on London by forewarning the city, shutting the gates against all comers, and defending its hinterland. The rebel earls, unable to seize the initiative, lingered at Ware, in Hertfordshire, their position growing weaker by the day. Edward meanwhile received help from all quarters. The Pope sent an embassy, as did the King of France, and lords and bishops came to his assistance to give him counsel and, if necessary, force of arms.

We do not know exactly when Roger returned from Ireland, and it could have been as late as January 1313; but there is every reason to suppose that he was brought back by news of Gaveston's death. Not only was he a loyal lord, he was also experienced in battle. If the king himself did not summon him back, no doubt his kinsman, the Earl of Pembroke, did. By mid-July Lord Pembroke was advising the king to declare war on the rebel earls, a policy which necessitated the return from Ireland of as many loyal men as were available. Also, since the Earl of Lancaster had set himself against Lord Mortimer of Chirk, Roger and his uncle needed to be in England to defend their estates from the armies of the rebel earls and their allies.

War did not break out immediately. Edward was in no hurry, for the longer he waited, the stronger he became. The earls too were reluctant to declare war on the king, an act for which they would undoubtedly lose their lives if defeated. While the earls demanded that they be pardoned for the death of Gaveston, on account of his illegal return from exile, the king made agreements and alliances with others. In November his position was greatly strengthened by the birth of a son and heir, Edward. This removed Thomas of Lancaster even further from the succession, and provoked an outbreak of patriotism in the country. The best that the earls could do was to negotiate, and hope that the king's resolve would weaken.

Roger played no part in the negotiations which began in September 1312. Indeed it is difficult to determine what exactly he was doing at this period. The only piece of evidence so far to have come to light is a reference to a payment to Roger of £100 ordered on 2 April 1313 at Westminster, 'for his expenses in Gascony'.[4] There are a number of possible explanations for this. One is his undertaking some personal service for the king. He could have been returning something or someone of Gaveston's household to Gascony. However, Gascony at this time suddenly flared up in a conflict between Amanieu d'Albret and the English seneschal, John de Ferrers, and it is more likely that Roger was sent to deal with this. De Ferrers had abused his position in 1312 to attack d'Albret with an army of four thousand men. D'Albret had appealed to King Philip, and the king had judged in his favour, sentencing King Edward to pay a large sum in compensation. De Ferrers died, possibly as a result of poison, in September 1312. A third possibility is that Roger acted on behalf of his kinsman, the Earl of Pembroke, in some business connected with the Count of Foix in Gascony, which the king had asked Pembroke to attend to in January 1313.[5] In considering these three possibilities, it is worth bearing in mind that Amanieu d'Albret was a relative of Roger's wife, Joan, and the man appointed to replace de Ferrers as Seneschal of Gascony, Amaury de Craon, was also a relative of Joan.[6] Whatever the reason, it is clear that

Roger was wholly loyal at this time, and actively so, being trusted with overseas royal business.

*

If there was one single measure of how the government of the country weakened during the first six years of Edward's reign, it was his policy failure in Scotland. No doubt he associated war in Scotland with his father, the 'Hammer of the Scots', and there was probably a personal element in his reluctance to continue his father's campaigns there. But each year Robert Bruce had made incursions into English territory, and Edward had done little to stop him. Bruce, who had learnt his hard craft of resistance against Edward I, one of the most formidable practitioners of the art of war, now showed how well he had learnt from his years of opposition. He did not have the numbers to defeat the English in open battle, so he and his men harried them, and terrorised the garrisons, and laid waste all they could in the hope that Edward would decide Scotland was simply too great a problem and withdraw. Such a strategy was unchivalrous, perhaps, but effective. And its effectiveness was increased by Edward's reluctance to launch a Scottish campaign. Indeed, during Gaveston's lifetime, he only organised Scottish campaigns in order to deflect attention from his polit-ical problems in England.

Bruce knew that the key to controlling Scotland was to control the castles. The Scottish forces could ransack manors held by men loyal to the English king, but, unless they held the castles, theirs would only be a tempo-rary grip on the land. Thus, one by one, Bruce attacked the English garrisons. Castle after castle fell to the Scottish grappling irons. Had this happened in Edward I's time, efforts would have been made to retake them, but in his son's reign fallen castles were not recaptured. Edward II saw the taking of a castle as a symbolic act, largely undertaken to improve his political position in England. He understood little of the strategy neces-sary to maintain control of an unquiet country, and cared for it even less.

By 1312 more than the symbolic recapturing of a few castles was required. Robert Bruce and his brother Edward had systematically attacked English fortifications with a will and an audacity which had won them the love as well as the loyalty of their fellow men. After Dundee fell in spring 1312, Perth was the only fortress left in English hands north of the Forth. In the summer of that year Edward Bruce attacked the minor strongholds of Forfar, Dalswinton and Caerlaverock, with some success. In the winter Robert Bruce himself commanded an extremely audacious attack on Berwick, the castle nearest to England. He was thwarted, but his method of attack was new, effective and ingeniously simple. Rather than attach ropes to grappling irons to scale the castle walls, the Scots attached rope ladders. These had the advantage over wooden ladders in that they could be carried by one man for long distances on horseback, and were better than mere ropes for they permitted a far swifter ascent, and allowed the assailants to use their weapons more freely. They also allowed far swifter escape: at Berwick Bruce would have surprised the garrison but for a dog which heard the rattle of the grappling irons and barked, so that the garrison awoke and the alarm was raised. On that occasion the Scots fled, leaving their rope ladders dangling from the walls.

While Edward II was ranting against the earls for the murder of Gaveston, Bruce moved straight on to his next attack. From Berwick on the English border he took his men to the most northern point of English control: the great castle at Perth. He laid siege to the castle openly, but during the nights of the siege his men discovered the shallowest point in the town moat. After a few days they withdrew. To the garrison it appeared that the Scots had decided against attacking the castle, and they relaxed their guard. But a week later, on the particularly dark night of 8 January 1313, Bruce returned with his men and their rope ladders. That night Bruce himself slipped into the dark, icy water up to his neck, and waded forward. A few moments later, he pulled himself out of the water and rapidly climbed his ladder. Once inside, with the advantage of surprise, his men quickly overcame resistance.

Had it been Edward II who had captured the castle, he would have spent a week feasting to celebrate his success. Bruce hardly paused for a moment. He knew that the more he could conquer now, the stronger he would be when the next English army came north. After taking Perth, Bruce took his men to Dumfries; within a month he had managed to starve the castle and town into submission. It was probably soon after news of this disaster reached the king at London that men began to urge on him the importance of a Scottish campaign, and Roger secured the release of the de Verdon rebels to that end. But still Edward did not act. And then Robert Bruce sent his brother against Stirling Castle, the most strategically important of them all.

Edward Bruce was a competent soldier, and no fool, but he was not a military genius like his brother. There was little chance of him forcing Stirling Castle into surrender: it was so strongly defended, so well supplied and so shrewdly commanded by Sir Philip de Mowbray that his army might have waited many months outside the walls. But when de Mowbray (a Scotsman loyal to Edward) observed the lack of English determination to relieve him, he suggested the following terms: if the English had not come within three miles of the castle with a relieving army within a year, he would freely hand over the castle to the Scottish king. Edward Bruce accepted.

Robert Bruce was furious when he discovered the terms to which his brother had agreed. The current run of Scottish success was entirely due to the failure of the English to bring a large army into Scotland. Now his brother had ensured that the English would advance within twelve months. Just as it was nearing completion, with only a few castles left to capture, Bruce's strategy of piecemeal conquest had been undermined by his own brother.

That was how Bruce read the situation in the summer of 1313. But Edward still refused to countenance a Scottish campaign. His mind was totally set upon his personal battle with the rebel earls; considerations of the wider affairs of state did not interest him. He was waiting for the moment when he could force the Earls of Lancaster, Warwick, Hereford and Arundel to kneel before him and ask for his pardon. This finally occurred, after lengthy negotiations, in October 1313. The following month he finally gave orders for preparations for a Scottish campaign. But even then it was with no particular regard for Scotland. Edward was using the Scottish threat as an excuse for raising an army to destroy not just the Scots but the rebel earls as well. Their begging for pardon was not enough. He hoped to lead an army into the north of England to crush Lord Lancaster and take revenge for the death of his beloved Gaveston, whose body still remained embalmed and unburied at a friary in Oxford.

In December 1313 ninety-five English earls and barons, including Roger and his uncle, were summoned to assemble with their retinues at Berwick-on-Tweed to relieve Stirling Castle. The date of the muster was to be 10 June, which gave the army a full six months to prepare. It also gave the Scots time to continue their onslaught on the English castles. Not that they had paused while Edward had dithered over the question of war. In September a Scottish carter named William Binnock had been hired to bring in the hay cut for Linlithgow Castle. He carefully chose a time when some of the garrison were out helping with the harvest. With eight armed Scotsmen concealed within his haywain, he drove towards the open gate and stopped it just across the drawbridge. The men leapt out and killed the porter. Binnock's boy, sitting on top of the cart, uncovered his axe and cut the ropes by which the drawbridge could be raised. As the portcullis came down, the cart was only partly crushed, and it allowed the rest of the Scots waiting nearby to gain entry. After a short fight, the castle was taken. The remainder of the garrison returned from the fields to find their own castle held against them.

On the dark night of Shrove Tuesday 1314 James Douglas and a band of knights, with their armour covered in black surcoats, crept on their hands and knees towards Roxburgh Castle. Using their trusted rope ladders the Scots were soon on the walls. The watchman at the top was silenced. Few of the garrison, celebrating Shrove Tuesday with the overindulgence traditionally expected, lived to regret it on Ash Wednesday. Not to be outdone by this bold manoeuvre, another Scottish knight, Sir Thomas Randolph, led a party to Edinburgh, an even more strongly defended castle, being built high above the town on volcanic rock. There he enlisted the help of William Francis, who had grown up in the castle. As a young man, Francis had been in the habit of visiting a woman in the town, and had learnt how to scale the rock face. On 14 March, another moonless night, the main Scottish force threw themselves at the east gate. As they fought in vain against the great defences of the castle, William Francis and a handful of knights silently crept up the huge rock. At the top they again used their rope ladders and entered the castle, killing the guards they found in the dark corridors within and making their way to the gate to welcome in their compatriots. With the exception of the border fortress of Berwick, the English were left with only three castles in Scotland: Bothwell, Dunbar and Stirling.

English military preparations continued while the Scots seized the fortresses. In March Roger was ordered to find three hundred footsoldiers in his lands in South Wales. Lord Mortimer of Chirk, in his capacity of Justiciar of Wales, was ordered to find three thousand fighting men from the principality. Every port was ordered to provide ships and sailors; every county to provide large numbers of men. Edward was taking no chances; his campaign was going to be the largest and best equipped the island had yet seen. In all 21,640 men were summoned, not including a significant contingent from Ireland, and although not all of these arrived, the vast majority did, and their numbers were supplemented with men from Gascony, Germany, France, Brittany, Poitou and Guienne.[7]

Gathering the men and forcing the march north was a huge effort. The footmen mustering at Wark and the nobles at Berwick all had to converge on Stirling before 24 June. Huge amounts of food were needed, requiring wagons which, had they all been put in a single row, would, it was said, have stretched for twenty miles.[8] On 27 May Lord Mortimer of Chirk was ordered to hasten the arrival of his men from South Wales. Gradually the army drew together. On 17 June the huge force set out from Berwick and Wark along the old Roman road north-west through Lauderdale, towards Edinburgh, which the leaders reached over the course of 19–20 June. At Edinburgh they waited for the rest of the army to gather, and then, on the morning of Saturday 22 June, they pushed on.

It was full midsummer heat. In order to keep on schedule to arrive by Midsummer's Day the footsoldiers had to cover the twenty miles to Falkirk. Many were tired, having arrived late, and twenty miles had been the distance which many had had to march each day for the past week or more. The sheer numbers contributed to the extra effort; one fit man can easily walk twenty miles but an army of twenty thousand men, lurching forward and then brought to a standstill, carrying armour and weapons, forced to strike camp and then to set up camp again, is another matter. The supplies required to feed that many men, and their carthorses, pack animals and the knights' destriers (specially bred war horses) added to the logistic problem. Moving all these men, animals, tents, armour and supplies in a coordinated fashion, so that the whole army was equipped and fed, greatly slowed the army. Thus, on the night of the 22nd, as the men settled under their blankets for a short night's sleep before the last fourteen miles to Stirling, they were very tired indeed. One commentator noted that 'brief were the halts for sleep, briefer still for food; hence horses, horsemen and infantry were worn out with toil and hunger . . .'[9]

On the 23rd the mounted men began to come within sight of Stirling Castle. The Earls of Hereford and Gloucester led the first wave, the vanguard. The road led down a slight slope and then ran through a wood called the New Park. Here Bruce had assembled his army of about eight thousand men. Hidden by the trees, the Scots were in fact amassed in one great ambushing party. Hereford and Gloucester led the way towards the wood ignorant of the dangers.

Riding some way behind the vanguard, the Earl of Pembroke looked at the road ahead and recalled his battle with Bruce seven years earlier, at Loudon Hill. On that occasion the self-proclaimed Scottish king had occupied a road lying across boggy ground, made impassable to mounted knights by earthworks and holes in the road. But although Pembroke was the most experienced leader in his army, Edward did not put him in command. The king was so confident that he regarded the credit for victory as a gift within his power, and placed his nephew, the Earl of Gloucester, in charge of the army. Gloucester was inexperienced in battle. He was a proven tournament champion, it was true, but war was a different matter. The appointment not only disappointed Pembroke, it outraged the Earl of Hereford, the hereditary constable of England, who claimed his hereditary right was being overlooked. As the first footsoldiers trudged into sight of the castle, sweating with their efforts, the huge array of knights before them shifted and seethed like the surf on a beach, uncertain of their next move.

At this point Philip de Mowbray rode out from Stirling under a pass of safe conduct from the Scots. The king had already relieved the siege, de

Mowbray announced to Edward and his assembled magnates. The army had come within three miles of Stirling by the appointed day. There was thus no need to engage with Bruce on such difficult ground. And it was very difficult ground, he informed them. Bruce had blocked every narrow path through the woods. The road had been undermined and covered with caltrops (small iron balls with four evenly spaced spikes), to break any charge of knights. To go to the left of the wood was not feasible owing to the raised ground, which only left the English the option of fighting their way through the trees on foot or trying to manoeuvre through the ground to the right, which was low-lying marsh ground, criss-crossed by brooks and rivulets running into the River Forth.

While de Mowbray was speaking to the king's companions, the knights in the vanguard noticed some Scotsmen running at the entrance to the wood, and pursued them, believing them to be in flight. Hidden by the trees, the Scottish battalion at that end of the wood, commanded by Bruce in person, had not expected the English knights to attack before their foot-soldiers had arrived. As the English knights came riding through the wood, Bruce, who was mounted on a palfrey and armed only with a hand-axe, turned to see Sir Henry de Bohun, nephew of the Earl of Hereford, levelling his lance and charging him down. De Bohun had recognised Bruce from his crown. There was no avoiding a confrontation. The young knight came on, doubtless with visions of his moment of glory. Bruce readied himself, and, at the last moment, swerved out of the way of the lance point and, raising himself up to his full height in the stirrups, brought his axe hard down on the knight's helmet. The axe blade broke the metal, and cleaved into his skull. As de Bohun fell dead, Bruce's astonished followers and the equally astonished English found themselves gawping at the broken haft of the axe still in Bruce's hand.

Suddenly the vanguard and the Scots found themselves face to face, committed to battle. With a cry each side rushed forward and the fighting began. The Earl of Gloucester was pulled from his horse, but supported by his fellow knights he got to his feet and fought himself free of the enemy's clutches. In the close confinement of the woodland road, the English could not easily turn their back on their enemy and ride to safety, nor could they charge them down. Many men fell before they broke free from the trees, pursued for a short distance by the exultant Scots.

While this fight was taking place, another large contingent of English knights set off to ride around the wood, through the marshland across which the Bannockburn flowed. Their purpose was to see whether the English could surround the wood, and so attack the whole Scottish army on all sides at once. They too were in for a surprise. Groups of men in close-drawn clusters, called *schiltroms*, bristling with pikes up to sixteen feet long, advanced from the woods towards them, blocking their way. As the heavily armoured knights rode towards these *schiltroms*, the Scots held their ground. The technique for breaking up such a dense thicket of pikes was to use archers to open up gaps, but the English knights had no archers. Their archers in fact were still dusting themselves off after their march or still traipsing over the hills several miles away. After a frustrating skirmish, in which the Scots undoubtedly came off best, the English withdrew.

Now the lack of English strategic thinking began to show. Men were still arriving, and it was impossible to march on without them, for the Scots would simply emerge from the wood and kill them and take their baggage train. Thus the English could neither move on, nor could they remain where they were, in a weak position. They could neither attack nor easily defend themselves. After much debate, Edward decided to advance a little, across the Bannockburn, and to form up there, ready in case the Scots should attack by night, and not beyond reach of the arriving men and wagons.

It was a catastrophic decision, probably the worst tactical move in English military history. The English footsoldiers, already exhausted, now had to spend the night without sleep as they found ways to cross the streams of the low-lying land around the village of Bannockburn. The village itself, abandoned in the face of the English advance, was pulled to pieces as men took doors and whatever wood they could find to make bridges and paths across the mud. But the army was too big to manoeuvre into such a small area in the darkness. All night men splashed around, hungry, tired and shouting with frustration, completely demoralised.

The principal reason underlying the English decision to camp in such a poor location was an assumption. They did not imagine for a moment that the Scots would attack *them*, and thus they did not imagine they would have to fight a battle on that very awkward site. They were aware of the possibility of a night attack, but they were sure that next morning they would be safe. Bruce himself was not certain he wanted to attack the English; his security lay in his position in the wood, not in the strength of his army, and his skill lay in his well-planned surprise attacks. Only when, after dark, Sir Alexander Seton and his men crept away from the English force to meet Bruce and tell him that the English were disorganised and demoralised, and that this was his one chance to defeat them in pitched battle, did Bruce put the question to his fellow band of captains. Their answer was unanimous.

In the early hours of Monday 24 June 1314, as first light spread, the English saw the Scottish army proceed out of the wood towards them.

Edward Bruce led one battalion of men out, followed by James Douglas leading another, who in turn was followed by Thomas Randolph with another. 'What?' exclaimed King Edward as he gazed across the land towards the massed Scottish forces, 'Do they mean to fight?' Then as he watched, he saw the Scottish army, to a man, go down on their knees. 'Look!' he laughed. 'They are begging for mercy!' 'Yes,' replied Sir Ingram d'Umphraville, 'but not from you. They are asking God for forgiveness, for their trespass against Him. For those men will either win or die.'[10]

D'Umphraville was not the only one who reckoned that the English army was not properly prepared. The Earl of Gloucester also considered that a day's wait would be to their advantage. Even now, as archers on either side began to loose their arrows off against one another, they did not need to join battle. But the king, who was becoming unnerved by his captains' hesitancy, accused Lord Gloucester of treachery and deceit. Gloucester, having had to suffer comments on his inexperience as a military leader, had had enough. 'Today it will be clear that I am neither a traitor nor a deceiver!' he shouted at the king, and at once he prepared his knights to ride forward. With trumpets blaring, shouts filling the air, and the massed praying of frightened men and the whinnying of terrified horses, the Earl of Gloucester and his five hundred horsemen galloped towards the ranks of James Douglas. Other groups followed him in unco-ordinated attacks, until within seconds the situation had slipped from the control of any commander.

The king saw that there was now nothing to do but fight. With the heroic-to-the-point-of-legendary knight Sir Giles d'Argentein on one side and the experienced Earl of Pembroke on the other, his helmet was strapped on, and his weapons handed to him. Although no sources record the whereabouts of either Mortimer at this stage, it is very likely that they were with the king, also readying themselves for the charge.[11] But as they waited, on the brink of attacking, they saw a group of Scotsmen rush forward. To their horror, amidst the clanging of weapons on armour and the screams of dying men and horses, the Earl of Gloucester's great war horse was skewered by a pikeman and, rearing up in panic, unseated the earl in its dying throes. The onlookers willed his men to push forward and save him, but, at the very moment when he could have been saved, the Scots rushed forward with a great cry. His men could only watch astonished as he was hacked to death. The second greatest lord of the kingdom, second only to the Earl of Lancaster, died at the hands of Scottish soldiers in the churned up mud of Bannockburn.

Now the charge began in earnest, the horses galloping forward as Sir Giles d'Argentein led the rush to where the earl had been struck down.

Riderless horses which had been wounded on the pikes rushed here and there, creating confusion. Knights' armoured destriers charged on to the pikes, so that the air was filled with the sounds of pike shafts splintering and cracking as well as the screams of dying horses and men, and the war cries of both sides. At one stage Edward Bruce was struck down, but Thomas Randolph saw the danger in which the king's brother found himself and launched his men forward, his banner before him, and swept over the place to bring Edward Bruce to safety. The English redoubled their efforts, but Randolph held his ground, and, despite another English onslaught, remained steady.

If Edward had had an opportunity to talk through his strategy with his commanders, they would have counselled him to break up the Scottish lines using his archers. But as the overconfident English had not expected the Scots to attack them in the open, their archers were stationed on the ground furthest from the front. Only now did they come to the fore, to unleash a volley of arrows on the Scotsmen. But their ability to break the Scottish line was limited. Moreover, Bruce had a few hundred horsemen in hand for just such a purpose as this, and he ordered this contingent to charge into the archers. The archers broke ranks and fled, leaving the knights on the field to fight out the hand-to-hand battle unaided, while the Scottish archers rained down arrows on the English.

It was now that the real weakness of the English position became clear. So narrow was the place they had chosen that they blocked themselves from moving forward and encircling the Scots. Men waited at the rear while the knights perished on the Scottish pikes, unable to force their way forward. Thus the English superiority in numbers was rendered meaningless. At one point King Edward's horse was killed beneath him. Down he went, with a great cry from both sides as the Scots tried to push forward to capture him and the English fought even harder to save him. In the desperate scuffle which followed, the king had his shield struck from his grasp, and looked as if he was lost, but at the critical moment, as the Scots advanced, they were met by Sir Giles d'Argentein, charging furiously to the fore, through the thrusting spears and swinging axes of the Scots infantry, to rescue him.

The shock of their king being unhorsed was catastrophic to the English; the scent of victory to the Scottish was euphoric. Bruce's men fought like madmen, raining axe blows on the English shields and helmets with all the justification of men whose families had been hanged and whose houses had been burnt. So hideous were the sounds of weapons on armour, the grunts as spears were thrust forward, and the screams, cries, groans and shouts of men in battle that many ran from the place. Those who continued to fight trampled on dead bodies, their shields so covered in blood that their heraldic devices could not be made out, the horses of the dead galloping in blind panic here and there, colliding with men stumbling with exhaustion from the effort, the heat and the lack of sleep.

And then the trumpeters in the English vanguard sounded the retreat.

'On them! On them! On them! They fail!' yelled the Scots triumphantly, pushing forward with their pikes against the few knights still mounted. At the shout the Scottish camp attendants, noncombatants, appeared on the ridge where the wood descended to the battlefield. To the English in their panic, it seemed as if a new, fresh Scottish army was approaching. The English footsoldiers completely lost heart. John Barbour, the Scottish clergyman who so carefully chronicled the events in his long poem, *The Bruce*, drawing from eyewitness accounts, recorded that some of the English stood firm even now, and would not give way. But all was lost, the army out of control, in flight, in panic. In the River Forth, behind them, men were drowning as they tried to escape. Men were being struck down as they tried to cross back across the Bannockburn towards the wagons. Men too heavily armed for flight were trying to strip off their mail in order to run. Already the Scots were killing the boys watching the packhorses and wagons, helping themselves to whatever they found.

The Earl of Pembroke, seeing the king uncertain what to do next, grabbed the reins of Edward's horse and determined to lead a charge towards the castle to the north. It was the only way out. But Sir Giles d'Argentein shouted to the king as he saw the earl drag him away. 'Sire, seeing that it is so, farewell! I am not accustomed to fleeing a battle, and I choose here to bide and die rather than shamefully flee!' And with that the king's most trusted warrior turned his war horse about, levelled his lance for one last time, and charged into the Scots, crying 'Argentein! Argentein!' It was only a matter of minutes before the Scottish spears killed his war horse, and an axe blow gave him the final chivalric immortality he craved.

Now the deepest ties of loyalty came into play, as five hundred mounted knights gathered around their king, with no other purpose than to protect his life like a swarm of bees protecting their queen. None of them had ever been in a situation such as this, and it was behaviour beyond any logical or planned strategy. They rode madly towards the castle, a fast-moving impenetrable wall of steel-clad men, scattering the Scottish footsoldiers on the periphery of the battle. But not all the mounted knights fled. When he was sure that the king was safe from the pursuing Scots, the Earl of Pembroke and some of his personal knights reined in their horses and turned to stand their ground and hold back the Scots. From what little evidence we have, it seems that Roger Mortimer was among them.[12]

This rearguard action was the most dangerous part of the whole battle, save the suicidal attacks of the Earl of Gloucester and Sir Giles d'Argentein. Many of Lord Pembroke's men were killed as they resisted the Scottish onslaught.[13] When the time came the men had to fight as they retreated. The earl himself lost his horse and only just managed to escape from the battlefield on foot. Roger was not so lucky. He was surrounded, disarmed and taken captive.

We do not know what happened next, but conjecture is possible. Roger was a third cousin of Robert Bruce, through the same connection as the dead Earl of Gloucester.[14] He was also a close ally of the Earl of Ulster, to whose daughter Bruce was married. Thus he was taken to the Scottish king and treated with dignity. He was not ransomed. Instead he was given the duty of taking King Edward's privy seal and the royal shield, both of which had been found on the battlefield, to the king at Berwick, with the corpses of the Earl of Gloucester and Robert Clifford. To him fell not the penury of ransom, nor the pain of death, but rather the embarrassment of bearing the tokens of the Scottish king's magnanimity to the English king.[15]

*

Bannockburn shocked the English in a most profound way. Never could such a defeat have been envisaged. It had destroyed the last vestiges of English rule in Scotland, and had opened up the north of England to Scottish raids. It had also taken the pressure off the Earls of Lancaster and Warwick. They now had the authority to demand changes in the royal household. They claimed the king had openly disregarded the Ordinances in the two years since Gaveston's death, that he had appointed men to office who did not deserve high honours, and that he had forgiven debts which were not within his power to forgive. It was feared by some that Edward's flouting of the Ordinances had in particular incurred divine wrath,[16] as the Archbishop of Canterbury had threatened with excommunication all those who did not obey their provisions, resulting in the rout of the English army at Bannockburn. Parliament was summoned to address these matters, meeting at York in early September.

The fact that Edward did not suffer greatly in this parliament was due to his loyal supporters, like Pembroke and Roger: men who could not simply be disregarded as royal hangers-on, and who wielded considerable political authority. Roger's retainers represented Herefordshire and Shropshire as knights, and it seems he was flexing whatever political authority he had at every opportunity. The proceedings of the 1314 parliament confirmed this. The Chancellor and the Treasurer were removed from office, but the men who replaced them were no enemies of the king, and one certainly was a friend of Roger.[17] It was the same with the lesser officers. While there had been calls for John de Charlton to be exiled from court, the York parliament confirmed him in his position as Chamberlain of the royal household. William de Melton, another man later chosen by the king along with Roger to reform the royal household, was appointed Keeper of the Wardrobe. Despite the renewed calls from Lancaster for his men to be appointed to office, in almost all respects the York parliament saw courtiers favourable to Roger, his uncle, and the Earl of Pembroke reinstated or promoted. There was one notable exception: the continued presence of Sir Hugh Despenser the younger.

Despenser, who was married to the king's niece, had been moving into the king's favour ever since the death of Gaveston. Though the king trusted the advice of men such as the Earl of Pembroke, and, after he had gone down on his knees to beg forgiveness for his part in the Gaveston affair, the Earl of Hereford, he longed for a special companion to help him in his government. In an age when, among the nobles, friendships were defined by blood ties, marriage ties, political alliances and strategic military considerations, Edward wanted a real friend, a personal friend to support him in the way that Gaveston had. Although the right age, Roger was clearly not a candidate, being too much of a warrior, too interested in Ireland, and quite probably too fond of his wife's embraces. What was becoming clear by 1314, and what the Mortimers truly feared, was that the right man was Hugh Despenser, the man who had sworn to destroy them by way of revenge for the death of his grandfather at the hands of Roger's grandfather at the Battle of Evesham, fifty years earlier.

Roger remained at court for the remainder of 1314, travelling south in late October and November. In all probability he was with the king when, on 2 January, the corpse of Piers Gaveston was finally buried at Edward's favourite manor of King's Langley. The Earls of Pembroke and Hereford were present, as were four bishops, an archbishop, thirteen abbots and more than fifty knights.[18] No doubt it was a poignant moment for the king. His two closest boyhood companions, the Earls of Cornwall and Gloucester, were both dead, and he himself had only just turned thirty.

*

Scottish authority had not simply received a boost at Bannockburn, it had received final confirmation of the independence for which Bruce had fought since 1306. In all that time he had learnt never to rest on his laurels. Accordingly King Robert now planned to send his brother Edward to carve out a kingdom in Ireland. The two brothers would both be kings, one either side of the Irish Sea. In confirmation of his brother's royal blood, Robert settled the inheritance of the throne of Scotland on his brother if he died leaving no male heir.

The Scots managed to keep their plans of invasion very quiet. John de Hothum, who was in Ireland from 5 September to the end of November 1314 on official business, did not hear of anything suspicious. But as soon as a rumour of the invasion reached Westminster, Roger acted. Indeed, his sudden decision to go to Ireland is the first indication we have that the English court had heard of the imminent invasion. On 14 March he appointed attorneys to act on his behalf in Ireland for two years, clearly not anticipating a journey there for some while. On 26 April, however, he changed his mind, and appointed attorneys to act on his behalf in England, and obtained royal letters of protection for himself and Robert FitzElys to go to Ireland. After clearing his remaining business in Westminster, which included making a grant of rents to his brother John Mortimer, a yeoman in the king's household, a grant of £40 per year for life to his faithful retainer Robert de Harley, and a request for his faithful retainer Hugh de Turpington to be given the constableship of the castle of Kildare, he made his way westward through the rain-sodden country, and took ship in Wales for Dublin.[19]

How did Roger know about the Scottish invasion so early? This is an interesting question, as clearly the rest of the English court were unaware: even after Bruce had landed, plans were being laid to take Irish troops to fight in Scotland. The explanation must lie in Roger's intelligence-gathering contacts. We know from later evidence that he used spies, and indeed his accounts for Ireland as governor record that he himself sent clergymen and others to England with secret information for the king which he did not want committed to parchment.[20] More specifically, in 1317 Roger accused two of his own vassals of inviting Bruce to Ireland in the first place. We know that Robert Bruce was initially very wary about letting his brother attack Ireland, but if Roger's accusation was true, it may explain why Roger changed his plans and obtained protection to go to Ireland a full month before the invasion took place. It is possible that a spy in Ireland let him know that such a message had been sent. However, this would beg the question why he allowed men whom he suspected to be traitors to continue to act within his army. It is more likely that Roger heard word from a contact among the native Irish that the Scots were planning to attack, as Bruce wrote to them in advance, asking for their support. It was thus with only the scantiest information that Roger set off to Ireland.

Edward Bruce landed at Olderfleet, now Larne, in County Antrim, on 26 May 1315. The English lords of the country seem to have been less well-informed than Roger, and were taken wholly by surprise. The native Irish were not much better prepared, despite being sounded out by Bruce in advance. But the change in the weather played into Edward Bruce's hands. Arriving while the torrential rains of 1315 were threatening to wipe out the harvest, he was able to convince the native lords to adopt a radical solution to their plight. He carried with him copies of a letter from his brother Robert, addressed 'to all the kings of Ireland, to the prelates and clergy, and to the inhabitants of all Ireland, his friends':

> . . . [since] our people and your people, free since ancient times, share the same national ancestry and are urged to come together more eagerly and joyfully in friendship by a common language and by common custom, we have sent over to you our beloved kinsmen, the bearers of this letter, to negotiate with you in our name about permanently strengthening and maintaining inviolate the special friendship between us and you, so that with God's will our nation may be able to recover her ancient liberty.[21]

Robert Bruce hoped the Irish would help his brother win a kingdom but this was not his sole aim, or even his primary one. His real intention was to spread the frontier on which the English had to defend themselves, thus lessening the chances of Edward sending an army to seek revenge for Bannockburn. The native Irish for their part saw the Scots offering themselves as military assistants in their struggles, precisely at a time when many clans were having difficulty finding enough to eat, and several of them gladly gave Edward Bruce their support.

Edward Bruce had come with no mean force of men. With him were the renowned Sir Thomas Randolph, conqueror of Edinburgh Castle, Sir John de Soulis, Sir John de Stewart, Sir Fergus d'Ardrossan and the shrewd Sir Philip de Mowbray, constable of Stirling, now a fully fledged Scottish patriot. They were joined by Donnell O'Neill, king of Tir Eoghain, and lords O'Cahan, O'Hanlon, MacGilmurry, MacCartan and O'Hagan. The Earl of Ulster was at this time in Connacht, too far away to organise any resistance, and those Ulster lords who decided against immediately joining the Scots made little or no immediate attempt to resist them. A few Irish lords, unhappy with O'Neill's confederacy, and suspecting that the Scots would impose taxation and tribute of their own, decided to resist. They gathered at the Moyry pass, but were crushed by the Scots army as Edward

Bruce and his fellow lords set about their first object: the subjugation of the land nearest Scotland.

On 29 June 1315 Edward Bruce came to Dundalk. Until now he had wooed and coerced the local Irish into helping him, and had divided them amongst themselves so that he could more easily defeat them in battle. As he and his advisers knew well, the only way the Scots would conquer Ireland completely would be if they gained the support of the Irish lords. But now at Dundalk he employed another tactic: terror. The Anglo-Irish gathered in the town had slept poorly the night before the battle, with Bruce encamped at their gates. The following morning, scouts were sent out to assess the size of Bruce's army. 'They are nothing; they're half-a-dinner,' they reported, and the townsfolk armed and sent forth their men. The battle, however, was hard, and victory was in doubt until the Scots forced the men of Dundalk back into the town. The Irish lords fighting alongside them fled, leaving the Dundalk men to be slaughtered. The mud of the streets turned red with blood. The Scots started looting and killing indiscriminately. They found large stores of wine, and the soldiers went on a continuous drunken rampage, and their lords let them, until the town was destroyed and most of its men and a great number of its women and children had been hacked to death. It was a message to all other unde-cided Irishmen: turn to Bruce, or the fate which befell the people of Dundalk will also befall you.

Roger was probably at Trim when news of the massacre at Dundalk reached him. It did not spur him to join the army the Justiciar had raised, which met at Greencastle. Nor does it seem that he joined the separate army of the Earl of Ulster, who had summoned the men of Connacht and the vassals of the powerful Irish lord, Felim O'Connor. This is possibly due to a parliament which may have been held at Kilkenny in early July.[22] Either way, it seems that it was agreed that Roger's forces would act as a rearguard, ready to supply reinforcements if necessary. The earl's army marched through the north of Meath to Athlone, and then north, meeting up with the Justiciar's army just south of Ardee on 22 July. After a few skirmishes, in which they forced Bruce to withdraw, it was agreed that the earl would proceed alone against the Scots. The Justiciar's army returned south, as food supplies were short, and apparently a second army was no longer needed. The earl marched north to Coleraine, but Edward Bruce retreated across the deep and fast-flowing River Bann, and destroyed the bridge over it, making a full confrontation between the two armies impos-sible. Minor skirmishing continued, and the two sides left the country either side of the river devastated. 'Both armies left neither wood nor plain, nor field nor corn crop, nor residence, nor barn, nor church, without burning and wholly destroying', as one chronicler put it.[23] Together with the rain, the devastation was terrible. All that was not sodden or rotten already was burnt.

Edward Bruce was not a great strategist, but he did have men with him who were, and he and his advisers saw a way to break up the army massed against them on the other side of the river. To Felim O'Connor Edward Bruce secretly offered the lordship of all Connacht if he would desert the earl. To Felim's rival, Rory O'Connor, who came to him separately, he promised assistance in his own war over Connacht, as long as he protected Felim's land. Rory, an old rival of Felim's, then returned to Connacht and ransacked and burnt all the principal towns in the region, including Felim's estates. Felim left the earl to return to Connacht to defend his territory, was defeated by Rory, and forced to accept his overlordship. Without having to fight at all Edward Bruce had destroyed most of Connacht, killed hundreds of its men, and had drastically reduced the army at the disposal of the Earl of Ulster on the other side of the Bann.

At this point questions were being raised in England about the loyalty of the Irish. On 10 July Edward had written to all the Irish lords, including Roger and a number of the Mortimer tenants in Ireland, asking for a confirmation of their loyalty to the English Crown. This was probably discussed in common among the lords in the Justiciar's army, for many of the extant answers, all of which protest loyalty, are couched in similar language.[24] Also it is noticeable that none of the replies is from Roger's knights, and Roger himself sent no reply to the king. This may well signify that he personally took responsibility for the loyalty of his men, showing a great confidence in them.

On 1 September Parliament met at Lincoln and decided to send John de Hothum to Ireland, to keep the king informed about events there. But before he even set out things turned disastrously for the worse. On 10 September the Earl of Ulster and Edward Bruce met in battle at Connor. It seems that, as at Bannockburn, the earl had not expected to be attacked, and that in fact he was retreating to join Felim O'Connor; but the Scots gave chase to the earl's army, and forced the battle. For the earl it was a disaster. His cousin, William de Burgh, was captured, as were several other lords and heirs, and his army fled to Carrickfergus Castle, where the pursuing Scots immediately set about besieging them. The earl himself slipped away from the battle, joining Felim O'Connor in Connacht, while the remaining English accused him of betrayal behind his back. He was, after all, father-in-law to Robert Bruce. He had not only lost his position as a leader of men, he was suspected of treason.

Roger, along with the other nobles in Ireland, was summoned to a parliament to meet at Dublin at the end of October. Its purpose was for John de Hothum to coordinate resistance. But the Scottish naval captain, Thomas Dun, maintaining his sway on the high seas, prevented de Hothum setting sail in time, and he did not arrive until 5 November. By then Roger and his fellow lords had left Dublin and abandoned the parliament. There was no time to discuss strategy: almost every town in Connacht was ablaze and under destruction from warring Irish tribes and Scottish plunderers. It was only a matter of time before the destruction came over the border to Meath.

It is not entirely clear what happened over the next month. No chronicler followed Roger as he organised his men on the north border of Meath. The most detailed account of the Scottish campaign, written by a Scottish clergyman back in Scotland several decades later, probably confuses parts of the forthcoming onslaught with the earlier Battle of Connor, at which the Earl of Ulster was defeated. What we do know for certain is that on or about 13 November Thomas Randolph returned from a short visit to Scotland with five hundred fresh, experienced soldiers, and that he and Edward Bruce then began to march south from Carrickfergus, leaving a besieging party there. Cautious about advancing straight into Roger's territory of Meath, they left a reserve contingent at Nobber, about ten miles north-east of Kells. On 30 November they crossed the River Dee and headed for the River Blackwater.

A week later the two armies met at the town of Kells. Roger had stocked the castle, removed the cattle from the outlying districts, and had placed the gates and walls of the town in a readily defensible state. This was not a preparation for a siege, but to sustain him in the field, for it appears that it was Roger's choice to fight here, on the north border of Meath, to try to keep the Scots away from his own lands. Details are very scanty, but it seems that, in order to bring the Scots to where he wanted them, he sent two of his vassals, Hugh and Walter de Lacy, to lure Bruce towards Kells.[25] Their bait may have been the loyalty of Lord O'Dempsey, an Irish king from Offaly, who had supposedly decided to swear fealty to the Bruce.[26] As both sides knew, such promises were Bruce's only hope of subjugating Ireland. And so he came.

Given that Edward Bruce had left reinforcements at Nobber, on the main road south to Navan, he may have originally planned to bypass Kells altogether. But in the event he came straight to Roger's army. The outcome was a catastrophe. The Scots began to burn the town. The one chronicler to describe the battle (the annalist of St Mary's Abbey, Dublin) attributes the defeat to treachery on the part of Hugh and Walter de Lacy, who had deserted Roger 'at the third hour'. This could mean at the third hour of the battle, or the third hour of the day, i.e. about 9 a.m. It is possible they feigned withdrawal from the battlefield, for the chronicler states they 'turned their shields', perhaps implying that they trapped Roger's army between them and the Scots.[27] But this is unlikely, given that several of Roger's leading vassals later acquitted the de Lacy brothers of directly dealing with the Scots, and these vassals would have been unlikely to support them if they had turned against them on the battlefield.[28] A more likely suggestion is that the de Lacys simply fled after three hours of battle, leaving Roger to fight on against a greater force.[29] Whatever the cause, Roger was soon in a desperate situation. The chronicler goes on to add that 'Roger alone with a few others' survived the battle. It is likely that he withdrew into the town, which was burnt around him, and that he was forced to fight his way out through the Scots, who, to judge from their past strategies, would have held the town gates. For a handful of experienced fighting knights in full armour and on horseback, such a bold manoeuvre was dangerous but well within their capabilities. The end result was that Roger broke free from the carnage at Kells with a handful of knights, and rode towards Dublin. But his army was utterly destroyed, Kells was burnt, and Meath was now, like all Ireland, open to the Scots invaders.

In Dublin Roger met John de Hothum. It was decided that Roger should return to England to report on the recent calamities. The country was all but lost. Only a few castles remained in English hands. English government in Ireland was in tatters. At Christmas 1315, Robert and Edward Bruce could fairly say that they had wrested overlordship of more than one third of the British Isles from the King of England within two years. But while English rule had been obliterated in Scotland, Ireland was not yet wholly defeated; and there were many, like Roger Mortimer, who were determined that the fight should go on.

FIVE

The King's Lieutenant

The rains continued. The harvest of 1314, which should have been taken in by the men who had fought at Bannockburn, was crushed by the appalling weather and rotted black in the fields. The following year was even worse. Animals collapsed and died, and their sodden bodies were to be seen decomposing in the wide stretches of water which had once been lowland meadows. Prices of corn and other foodstuffs in the markets rose alarmingly, and all the chroniclers speak of a terrible famine spreading across England, Wales and Ireland. Society was ill equipped to deal with two harvest failures in a row. It had no means of organising relief for large numbers of people facing starvation. On the political side, it had no means of raising the revenue required to equip itself militarily in a time of dearth. The way of raising revenue for war – a direct taxation of a tenth, fifteenth or twentieth, levied on possessions – was designed to pay wages of soldiers and to buy supplies, not to alleviate suffering, and the families of men required to do the fighting suffered all the more if their menfolk were taken away from their villages. The king could only order that it was illegal to charge more than a certain amount for corn. The result was that people did not sell the corn they had, or sold it furtively. People began to die of starvation. Lords found they had to buy imported grain at high prices, whereas before it had simply been grown and threshed for them on their manors. Providing supplies for garrisons of castles became extremely difficult. At the same time the trade in wool collapsed. Many townsmen lost their livelihoods, and towns lost their revenue from customs and tolls. The terrible economic depression, which over the next five years would reduce the population of England by more than a tenth, had begun.

Despite the drastic reduction in royal revenues, King Edward was sympathetic to Roger's situation in Ireland. Just before his defeat at Kells, the king had ordered an inquisition into his debts to the Crown, freezing them until the following Easter. The king was not to know that his gesture came too late to help Roger in Ireland: he only learnt that when Roger himself returned to England and came to court, in January 1316.

Roger's purpose in returning was to report on the state of Ireland and to ask for military assistance. It was his intention to return straightaway and resume the fight against Bruce. In respect of this Edward issued a special writ to him on 17 January requesting he attend Parliament, but only 'if he had not yet returned to Ireland'.[1] Edward's reason for asking him to stay and attend was because of his need of support in England. Not just against the Earl of Lancaster, but against the many rebels taking arms now in this time of deprivation.

Roger obeyed the summons. He, with the earls, prelates and the king, met in a chamber of a house belonging to the Dean of Lincoln. Edward announced that he wished Parliament to conduct its proceedings speedily, so as to lessen the burden of providing food on the city and locality. But the Earl of Lancaster had not yet arrived. He did not do so until 12 February, two weeks late.

This delay had been costly. The important business of the parliament, as Lancaster well knew, was to discuss the state of the famine-struck country. People were starving to death. The Scots had torn apart the northern counties, so that manors were disappearing under the combined terrors of starvation and extortion. In the north even loyal English lords had taken to organised robbery to keep their retainers satisfied. If Robert Bruce could ravage the country and be allowed to get away with it, they reasoned, they might as well take what they could from their neighbours before Bruce did. In Wales the plight of the people was just as extreme. But there they had found a leader who not only inspired them, he inspired his enemies too. His name was Llywelyn Bren.

*

When the Earl of Gloucester had perished beneath the spears and axes of the Scots at Bannockburn, he left the country with a great problem. He had no heir, and, despite his wife desperately claiming she was pregnant, none was forthcoming. The dilemma lay in the fact that his earldom was the richest single lordship in the country, worth about £7,000 per annum, and his income was second only to that of the combined five earldoms of Thomas of Lancaster. Even after the dower lands had been counted off, and the lands which his father had granted as annuities or gifts to his men, there was still more than £4,000 per annum left to be partitioned between his three sisters and their husbands. For the people of Glamorgan, however, his death meant that their lands were taken into custody while negotiations for the ultimate dispersal of the estate took place. With no lord, with no local administration, the lordship of Clare, including the great Marcher lordship of Glamorgan, was left in the hands of a series of royal administrators. These could be cold men, like Ingelram de Berengar, who regarded his role as having to contain the Welsh of

Glamorgan through force of arms, or they could be more judicious lords, like Bartholomew de Badlesmere, whose policy was more sympathetic to local grievances. But in July 1315, when the animals started dying in the fields, and when the suffering of the people was greatly on the increase, Bartholomew de Badlesmere was removed from office and the administration of Glamorgan was placed in the hands of Payn de Turberville.

It was a decision which had terrible consequences. De Turberville's policy towards the suffering Welsh was to beat out of the people what money he could to swell the royal coffers. Bartholomew de Badlesmere's careful alliances and considerate grants were ignored. Most importantly, those middlemen who had effected de Badlesmere's policy were dismissed, and replaced with de Turberville's instruments. Any Welshmen holding office were also dismissed as a matter of course. The most prominent of these Welshmen was Llywelyn Bren.

Bren means 'royal'. The epithet was given to him as a mark of respect, not just as a mark of distinguished ancestry. His proper name was Llywelyn ap Gruffydd ap Rhys, his father being one of the warriors who fought in defence of Prince Llywelyn, the last free prince of Wales. Llywelyn Bren himself was lord of Senghennydd, and a favoured sub-lord of the dead Earl of Gloucester. Even the English chroniclers, normally biased, describe him with respect. 'A great man and powerful in his own country,' wrote one.[2] His greatness imparted a sense of duty to his people. In 1315, with de Turberville persecuting the Welsh of Glamorgan, and taking arms against the people of Senghennydd itself, he could not ignore his countrymen's plight. As a result, de Turberville accused him of sedition. Llywelyn did the only thing he could: he appealed to the king. He told Edward what troubles his people were suffering, and how they needed relief from the king's self-interested officer. But Edward was not in a mood to listen, and, with a stunning lack of consideration or forethought, ordered Llywelyn to appear before Parliament to face a charge of treason. Edward also promised him that, if de Turberville's charge was true, Llewelyn would be hanged. Shocked, Llywelyn took himself back to his estates to prepare for war.

On 28 January, as Parliament gathered in the chamber of the dean's house at Lincoln, the Sheriff of Glamorgan was attending a sitting of a court outside the walls of Caerphilly Castle. As the voices cut through the chill air, the sheriff and the court became aware that they were being surrounded. Gradually a huge number of armed Welshmen appeared around them. For those at the court it was too late. In vain they tried to retreat into the castle. Before they could do so the portcullises came down and the drawbridge was raised. The sheriff's men were slain in the outer bailey of the castle, which was then set alight. The inner castle itself, so well planned and constructed by the ancestors of the Earl of Gloucester, was impregnable, but the sheriff and the constable of the castle were both captured. Then started the chaotic looting and burning as Llywelyn's men rampaged through Caerphilly with swords drawn, under the direction of Llywelyn's five sons and his adopted son, Llywelyn ap Madoc ap Howel.

News of the attack reached Edward a few days later. His first reaction was to appoint William de Montagu and Hugh Audley, the husband of one of the three Gloucester co-heiresses, to recapture the castle. He then reconsidered and appointed the Earl of Hereford as commander in chief of the expedition to put down Llywelyn's revolt, and directed both Lords Mortimer to assist him. 'Go quickly and pursue this traitor, lest from delay worse befall us and all Wales rise against us' were his instructions to the Marcher lords.[3] Roger returned to Wigmore to coordinate the raising of his men. By the end of February the force was ready and had assembled in South Wales, and the attack was ready to begin.[4]

The campaign against Llywelyn was a demonstration of superior organisation and strength. The Lords Mortimer and the Earl of Hereford marched from the north, while from the south marched John Giffard of Brimpsfield. From the east, Henry of Lancaster (the younger brother of the Earl of Lancaster), William de Montagu and John de Hastings approached with a third contingent. On 12 March the eastern army joined Giffard at Cardiff. The whole of their force, numbering one hundred and fifty mounted men-at-arms and two thousand infantry, went north. They met little real resistance as they pushed on to Caerphilly, and in a short time the castle was relieved.

With the Earl of Hereford and the Mortimers in the north, and pressed from the south, Llywelyn fled north-westwards, taking his army towards the bleakness of Ystradfellte. Here, on the edge of the Great Forest, he and his men prepared to make one final stand. But on the morning of the final attack, 18 March, as the cold light dawned over the valley, Llywelyn declared to his companions that their deaths were futile. 'I started this conflict,' he said to them, 'and I will end it. I will hand myself over on behalf of all my people. It is better that one man should die than the whole race be exiled or perish by the sword.' His men tried to persuade him not to give himself up, and, inspired by his speech, they declared they were prepared to die alongside him. But his mind was made up. Alone, in full armour, he rode down from the mountain to meet the English. There he surrendered in the presence of the Earl of Hereford, Roger Mortimer of Wigmore, and John de Hastings.

Roger and the other English lords were impressed with the nobility of the man and his brave gesture. His rebellion was over, a hundred of his men were arrested by the English, but Roger saw no reason to exact revenge. He understood why the man had taken arms. Indeed, he and the earl agreed that they would speak to the king on his behalf.[5] They took Llywelyn to the earl's castle of Brecon, from which the earl wrote to Edward, urging him not to sentence Llywelyn until they had been able to discuss his fate. Then they rode with him and his family to London. Roger and Llywelyn, both being of princely Welsh blood, and both being literate, intelligent and military-minded men, became friends. The list of Llywelyn's possessions recovered by the English from Llandaff Cathedral includes seven books in French and Welsh, including a copy of the *Roman de la Rose*, and jewellery and armour, as well as his Welsh chairs and charters and muniments. A few years later, a similar, albeit more extensive, list would be compiled of Roger's possessions.

Roger and Hereford were at court by 21 April. He or the earl may well have been instrumental in having Payn de Turberville replaced by John Giffard of Brimpsfield. As for Llywelyn himself, both the earl and Roger did indeed speak to the king on his behalf, and they succeeded in causing the penalty of death, which in normal circumstances would certainly have been imposed, to be commuted to one of imprisonment in the Tower. Nor did Roger's assistance to the man and his family stop there. In November it was at Roger's request that the king ordered John Giffard to take action to protect Llywelyn ap Madoc ap Howel, adopted son of Llywelyn Bren, who was being attacked by Englishmen in reprisal for the war.[6] Roger, it seems, was a man who remained loyal to those who had earned his friendship. Just how loyal would be shown later.

*

The famine worsened. One clerk wrote of the conditions in 1316 in the following words:

> After Easter the dearth of corn increased. Such scarcity has not been seen in our time in England, nor heard of for a hundred years . . . a great famine appeared, and after the famine came a severe pestilence, of which many thousands died in various places. I have even heard it said by some that in Northumbria dogs and horses and other unclean things were eaten . . . Alas poor England! You who once helped other lands from your abundance, now poor and needy are forced to beg. Fruitful land is turned into a saltmarsh; the inclemency of the weather destroys the fatness of the land; corn is sown and tares are brought forth . . . Spare, O Lord, thy people![7]

As the country starved, tensions which had remained dormant for many years resurfaced. In Bristol, a long-running disagreement between the constable of the town, Bartholomew de Badlesmere, and the townsfolk once again erupted. The disagreement concerned the customs of Bristol. Fourteen merchants, including the mayor, claimed to have control of the customs of the town, on behalf of the constable, but this tradition was opposed by a growing number of merchants. The dispute was overseen by justices, men who were not from Bristol and who, it was suspected by the townsmen, were prejudiced in favour of the constable and the fourteen. In the words of the same chonicler who had bewailed the weather and the famine:

> The leaders of the community, seeing that their objections were ignored, and that their rights were set aside by prejudice rather than reason, were much distressed as they left the hall where judgements are given, and spoke to the people, saying 'Judges have come favourable to our opponents, and to our disadvantage admit strangers, from which our rights will be lost forever'. At these words the senseless crowd turned to rioting, and the whole populace trembled from fear of the disorder. Returning once more to the hall, they entered with a large following and there turned their right to wrong. For with fists and with sticks they began to attack those opposed to them, and nearly twenty men that day lost their lives for nothing. A very natural fear seized noble and commoner alike, so that many leaped out of top-storey windows into the street, and seriously injured their legs as they hit the ground.

About eighty men were indicted and were ordered to be taken to Gloucester. But the people of Bristol hid them. The culprits were ordered to be exiled for their non-appearance, but still the people of Bristol protected them. The king repeatedly summoned the people to present the wrongdoers, but they did not do so. They still had not done so by May 1316, more than two years after the original case had been heard.[8]

Events over the next two months demonstrate how closely the social life of the nobility and regional politics were meshed at this time. In 1316 Bartholomew de Badlesmere and Roger Mortimer were ordered to take action against the townsmen. At the same time, these two men were discussing an alliance between their families. The plan was that Roger's son and heir, Edmund, who was turning out to be a clever boy, if not a fighting knight, should marry Badlesmere's infant daughter, Elizabeth. Negotiations took place at Westminster in the spring and, in mid-May, Roger and his household, together with a number of important guests, made their way to Wigmore to celebrate the wedding. Badlesmere agreed to pay Roger the substantial sum of £2,000 for the marriage.[9] At the same time Roger made a settlement of his estates, granting to his executors John de Hothum (recently elected Bishop of Ely) and Philip de Kyme (his steward) the castle and manor of Wigmore, the land of Maelienydd with the castles of Cefnllys and Dinbaud, the land of Cydewain with the castle of Dolforwyn, and the land of Deuddwr, together with the reversion or inheritance of the estates which his mother then held as part of her dower, including Radnor Castle. These the executors were empowered to pass to Edmund. Roger also made the young man the heir to his (Roger's) mother's Somerset and Buckinghamshire estates, including Bridgewater Castle. After the business was agreed, it was time for the wedding party to go to the Welsh Marches to hold the ceremony.

At the same time, Roger and many of his wedding guests prepared to attack Bristol.

It is typical of Roger's character that he should combine in one journey his son's marriage and a military offensive. To see these as complementary events, as he clearly did, it is necessary to appreciate that he was not a man who hated war but one who saw war as his honourable duty, his 'profession' and a matter of pride. Unlike the lords who had avoided Ireland through its difficult years, he had voluntarily gone to defend his estates, and had taken part in the fighting. Like the warrior king, Edward I, his vision of himself was as a leader in arms. War was totally compatible with the diplomatic event of a wedding ceremony. The marriage of his heir had as much to do with estates acquisition as producing a new generation. Testimony to this is the fact that the bride was only three years old at the time of the wedding.[10] Marriage was also about military capacity, bringing within his influence a family whose wealth and power could be added to his own. He would henceforth be obliged to help and defend the de Badlesmere family, but he too would benefit from their help and strength. In this particular case, the advantages he would obtain from the marriage were not so much military as political, since Badlesmere had spent many years working his way into a position of great influence at court. In addition there was the £20,000. As early as 1308 Roger had had to acknowledge debts to the Bardi banking house of Florence (one of the principal banking houses of Europe), and had constantly borrowed from friends and family ever since. There was a sound reason why Badlesmere's was a suitable family to which to link the Mortimers: Bartholomew was not known as Badlesmere the Rich for nothing.

Edmund Mortimer, then aged about fourteen, was married to Elizabeth de Badlesmere in the chapel of the manor house of Ernwood, in Kinlet,

Shropshire, on 27 June 1316. At the door of the chapel the 'couple' received the manor of Ernwood itself, plus the manors of Cleobury Mortimer, Stratfield Mortimer, and the reversion of the manors of Arlegh in Staffordshire, then held by Hugh Audley, and Bisley in Gloucestershire, then held by Joan, the widow of Henry de Bohun (the knight killed at Bannockburn by Robert Bruce). Those witnessing the gift and present at the wedding included a number of close Mortimer allies. The full list of the witnesses includes, besides Roger himself, his uncle Lord Mortimer of Chirk, William de Montagu, William de la Zouche, lord of Ashby de la Zouche, Roger Damory, John de Charlton, Thomas Botetourt, Robert de Waterville, Thomas de Lovaigne, Thomas Roscelyn, Bartholomew de Burghersh (Badlesmere's nephew), Giles de Mompesson, John de Coleville, another Robert de Waterville, Robert de Harley, John de Sapy, Robert de Sapy, Edmund Hakelut, Philip ap Howel, Master John Walwayn, Master Richard de Clare, Henry de Burghersh and John de Chelmsford.[11] These were the close circle of Mortimer adherents. Interestingly their number included fanatical supporters as well as men who would betray him. Among them was one whose son would ultimately lead Roger to his death.

After the wedding the guests probably returned to Wigmore. This stay, from approximately the end of May to the end of August 1316 (with a couple of weeks away to besiege Bristol), was the longest period Roger would be at his ancestral seat for the rest of his life. At roughly this time the castle was almost totally rebuilt. No accounts survive, since the family archive was mostly destroyed in the late sixteenth or early seventeenth century,[12] but architectural historians have always ascribed the huge rebuilding programme to Roger's lifetime, and recent archaeological work has confirmed this theory. Roger inherited a largely defensive thirteenth-century fortress in 1306, but he constructed a grander, more luxurious castle on the same site. This served as his *caput* – his principal permanent residence, head office, armoury and treasury – for the rest of his life. Thus, it is quite possible that Roger treated his guests to a preview of the building works he planned at Wigmore, before advancing with them to attack Bristol.

Badlesmere had not been able to attend the wedding of his daughter at Ernwood as his presence was required at court. He remained with the king throughout June 1316, and left to go to Bristol to put down the revolt with the Earl of Pembroke and Lord Berkeley in early July. There they met with Roger and his army. The earl took the lead in demanding that the people of Bristol surrender the culprits. He spoke to the leaders in their hall:

> The king on hearing your cause has found you guilty, and he warns and
> commands you to obey the law. Hand over the killers and the guilty,

and you and your town shall remain in peace. I promise that if you do this, the king will not be hard but merciful towards you.

The reply from the Bristol townsmen was defiant:

We were not the authors of this wrong; we have not failed the king in anything. Certain men tried to take away our rights, and we, as was proper, tried to defend them. Therefore if the king will remit his penalties, if he will grant us life and limb, rents and property, we will obey him and do as he wishes; otherwise we shall continue as we have begun, and defend our liberties and privileges to the death.[13]

Having heard this, the Earl of Pembroke returned to the king to discuss his final judgement. It was, predictably, to effect a full siege of the town, if only as an example to other towns and cities that they should obey the law. Badlesmere was placed in charge of the attack, but as he himself was not a military leader, it is likely that Roger organised the setting up of the siege engines.[14] These machines, six of which were kept at Wigmore, were capable of projecting heavy stone shot or burning matter for many hundreds of yards. In this case, the purpose was to force the town into submission, so while the townsfolk were incarcerated within their walls without supplies, the siege engines sent huge stones flying into their buildings at five-or ten-minute intervals, flattening houses and crushing property and defences. Such constant crashing and crumbling of buildings invoked terrible fear, which was harder to endure than the lack of food. The townsfolk of Bristol held to a hope that the attackers would give up and go away, as the Earl of Gloucester had done in an earlier assault on the town, but Roger, Badlesmere and the others dutifully carried through their mission. Fearing the whole town would be destroyed, the people of Bristol surrendered on 26 July.[15]

*

Crushing the revolts of Llywelyn Bren and the Bristol merchants were marks of efficient leadership, but they were nothing compared with what was required in Ireland. That country had been driven into a state so appalling, so mutilated and starved under the weight of an occupying army that it was hardly recognisable as a part of Christendom. After Roger had left in December 1315, Edward Bruce had destroyed Kells and moved to Granard, taking what he could from the manor before burning it. This was to be his policy from now on: to take, plunder and destroy. He spent Christmas at Loughsewdy. His army killed any inhabitants who had not fled, took what they wanted and burnt the place behind them. Led by the de Lacy brothers, the Scots ransacked their way around the country, through Leinster to Tethmoy and then to Kildare.[16] Here Bruce attacked the castle, but was repulsed by a vigilant garrison. Unable to sustain supplies for his army for any length of time owing to the destruction wrought by his own men and the inclement weather, he could not lay siege to the castle, and moved on to Castledermot. Near here, at Ardscull, on 26 January 1316, he met Edmund Butler, the Justiciar, and other lords, including John FitzThomas and Arnold le Poer, in battle. It was a close conflict, and the Scots losses were heavier than the English, but again it was the English who were put to flight, although their army had been quite large enough to defeat the Scots, according to John de Hothum.[17] Once more the English lords had defeated themselves by their own internal divisions. Trim Castle still held out under Roger's vassal Walter de Cusack, but only because, like Kildare, it was strong enough to resist assault, and there was insufficient food in the vicinity to sustain a besieging army for any length of time. In April, having ransacked and despoiled the south of the country, the Scots returned to the north. On 1 May at Dundalk, Edward Bruce was crowned King of Ireland. And with the exception of Dublin and a few English castles, it was a justified title. It was even more so after the death of Felim O'Connor in August, and the fall of Carrickfergus Castle in September.

That autumn, as the Scots were celebrating their almost total success in Ireland, the Mortimers were once again very much in favour in England. Roger had shown himself to be a thoroughly competent commander by the capture of Llywelyn and the siege of Bristol. At the beginning of October, Lord Mortimer of Chirk was once again restored to his position as Justiciar of Wales, although only for the north part at first, from which he had been removed by adherents of the Earl of Lancaster in January 1315. At the same time he cleverly manipulated the return of the constableship of two royal castles which had been confiscated from him under the Ordinances, claiming that they had been rewards for good service as opposed to demonstrations of unwarranted royal favour. Thus it is not surprising that, although summoned in August to fight the Scots in Scotland, in November Roger convinced Edward to let him return to fight the Scots in Ireland.[18]

For more than a year the Scots had stretched English resources by fighting a war on two fronts. Roger now persuaded Edward that, by releasing more money and men to continue the war in Ireland, the situation there could be turned to the English advantage. Accordingly Edward gave Roger command of a royal army.[19] On 23 November Roger was officially appointed King's Lieutenant of Ireland[20] – Viceroy. It was the most important position a member of the family had held since his grand-father had been guardian of England during the absence of Edward I, forty-five years before. It was a position higher than that of Justiciar, the normal governor of the country. It was the same position that Edward had conferred upon Gaveston in the summer of 1308, when he had been trying to thwart the earls who had forced Gaveston into exile. Roger effec-tively embodied the government and the legal system of the country, or what there was left of it. Ten years of faithful service had finally reaped the reward of real power.

The next few months were occupied wholly with planning the invasion. Roger remained at court in the north until at least early December, receiving grants for his own benefit and to help him pay his expenses. He was given possession of all lands in Ireland conquered by the Scots. He was given power to remove officials and to receive and pardon felons as he saw fit. He was given authority to make covenants with those who had assisted the Scots, to remit debts due to the Exchequer, to sell or grant custodies of land, wardships of minors, marriages of unmarried lords' heirs: in other words, anything of value which might be due to the king. Pardons for crimes committed were granted to any men travelling to Ireland in Roger's company. Orders were given to the Bardi banking house to advance large sums of money to him. His kinsmen and vassals also bene-fited from his new-found favour. One in particular who later played a small but crucial role later in Roger's life, Robert de Fiennes, was created Seneschal of Ponthieu.

For those men of status travelling to Ireland with Roger, grants of protec-tion were given. From these we can see that his company included a number of his tried and trusted followers. Hugh de Turpington was in his company, one of many who had fought in Ireland with him in 1310–12 and 1315. Edmund Hakelut and William de la Zouche, who had attended the wedding of Edmund Mortimer, were also present. John Maltravers, who had been knighted with Roger in 1306, had fought with him at Bannockburn and would remain a friend to his dying day, was another. Others included Robert de Harley and Hugh de Croft, who had also both fought with Roger in Ireland in 1310–12, and Gilbert de Bohun, a distant cousin of Roger's and a relative of the Earl of Hereford. William de Fiennes, another cousin of Roger's on his mother's side, also went. John Wogan was of the company, a former Justiciar of Ireland. Many more knights accompanied him, along with one hundred and fifty men-at-arms and five hundred foot-soldiers. These numbers were swelled by the order on 4 January to all the lords of the realm who had lands in Ireland, except the Earl of Pembroke, to go in person 'or send sufficient people according to the quantity of their lands to stay on them for defence'.[21] All these men were to muster with their equipment and their horses at Haverford on 2 February 1317. Their writs attested to the fact that they were under the orders of 'the king's cousin, Sir Roger Mortimer of Wigmore'.[22]

As things turned out, it took longer than expected to assemble the army. A fleet had to be organised, with ships from Bristol and Haverford and the ports in between. Payment had to be arranged through the king's clerk for the men, for the supplies, and for the mariners ferrying the men across to Ireland. A new captain of the fleet had to be recruited. Sir John de Athy, fomerly a sheriff in Ireland, was appointed, and given orders that when Roger landed, he (de Athy) was to 'remain at sea for the defence of Ireland and the king's land of Scotland'. That inevitably meant a battle with the successful Scottish naval captain, Thomas Dun, who still lurked off the coast and patrolled the ports of Ireland. Negotiations began for a thousand Genoese soldiers in plate armour to be placed at Roger's disposal.[23] The schedule began to slip. On 28 January the fleet was still not ready, and the king had to issue a mandate 'to hasten the navy ordained for the passage of the king's cousin Sir Roger Mortimer of Wigmore to Ireland, so that it be ready at the day and place assigned and the voyage not be delayed'.[24]

As the delays continued, the news from Ireland was not good. Confident that the English were unable to stage a meaningful attack on Scotland, and that Ireland was the real frontier, Robert Bruce had gone to help his brother secure his kingdom against Roger's invasion. Robert Bruce landed in January, and straightaway set about a campaign to take the Scots into the central and southern parts of Ireland in one great effort to raise the tribes and the unfaithful Anglo-Irish lords against the English. With the hero of Scotland at their head, the Scots again marched south. On 16 February they were at Slane, in Meath, from where they marched straight through Roger's lands towards Dublin.[25] The Earl of Ulster ambushed them near his manor of Ratoath, but was defeated and forced to flee to Dublin, where the citizens arrested him on 21 February, and locked him up in the mistaken belief that he was a Scottish sympathiser.[26] Left with no other defence, the Dubliners made desperate preparations for a siege of their city. On 23 February they burnt the northern suburbs and built a new defensive wall along the quay.

Roger was now a month late, and still not much nearer to setting out. In March the brothers Bruce marched around Dublin and went into Kildare, desperately trying to rouse the native Irish and the Anglo-Irish into rebellion. In each village where they were not welcomed they killed the inhabitants, plundered the settlement and burnt the houses. But their rapacity was soon to come to a halt. At the end of the month the army reached the Shannon, at Castleconnell, near Limerick, and there they heard that Roger had landed with a large army at Youghal, on the south-east coast, on 7 April.

Roger had with him only six hundred and fifty men in the royal army, together with perhaps a hundred or so of his own men, and a few hundred supplied by the knights and lords with lands in Ireland. Even so, the Irish and Anglo-Irish considered this a fine display. Annalists stated that his army was fifteen thousand men strong; it was probably no more than a tenth of this number on landing, and no more than five thousand after gathering the local Irish levies and the army which was with the Justiciar, Edmund Butler, at Cork. But it was enough. Great joy spread through Ireland that the continual depradations of the Scots, the plundering and looting, had come to an end. Dublin, which had held out for so long, was ecstatic. The Scots, seeing that they had signally failed to win the hearts of the Irish, and knowing they were in no condition to fight a fresh army, retreated at speed and by night through Kildare and Trim.

Roger knew he did not have to fight the Scots straightaway. Nor, for that matter, would he have been able to do so. To follow them would mean his army having to live off the same land through which the Scots had already passed: a land of corpses, burnt-out cottages, plundered towns, despoiled fields and wide-eyed starving men, women and children, suffering from the extreme famine. Instead, by letting the Scots go, he was able to use the famine as a weapon. Since Bruce had failed to take the important castles in the south of Ireland, his army had no choice but to live off plunder. They had few places outside Ulster where they could build up reserves, or replenish their resources. However brave, the Scots were suffering from fatigue, malnutrition and disillusionment. They were, in effect, already beaten.

With the Scots on the run, Roger's responsibility was to secure the law of the land and to effect the king's law. Although the king had given him extensive powers with which to govern, he clearly wished to orchestrate events from a distance. On 23 April he sent instructions to Roger to inquire into the reasons for the incarceration of the Earl of Ulster.[27] Roger was to call together the king's council to discuss whether it would be 'to the king's honour and profit' if the earl were sent to the king in England or were detained longer in Dublin Castle. In another letter, dated 22 April, the king ordered Roger not to grant pardons for murder and other felonies 'unless the matters had been considered by him and such of the king's council of those parts as he shall think fit to govern, notwithstanding the fact that the king lately gave him power to receive felons and outlaws'.[28] A third letter, dated 27 April, asked him not to harass the people of Dublin for their arrest of Richard de Burgh, Gilbert de Burgh, Hubert de Burgh and Henry le Clerk. And so it went on. At the end of May he was again requested to inquire into the circumstances of the Earl of Ulster. The king's involvement in Roger's government in Ireland hints either at a lack of complete confidence or a growing lack of respect on the part of the king, as if Roger was liable to pursue his own course of justice. Clearly Edward realised that in Roger he had a competent and loyal subject, but an independently-minded one as well.

In Ireland, Roger was like a snarling dog suddenly unleashed. He ignored the king's commands and set himself as his first military objective the challenge which had been in his mind for the last fourteen months: revenge upon the de Lacys. They had deserted him at Kells, and, being a soldier, he was not a man to forgive men who failed in battle. After his defeat they had led Edward Bruce through Leinster, consorting with the Scots every step of the way. When Roger had been appointed King's Lieutenant in November 1316, he had ordered the Justiciar to prosecute them. But they made a show of loyalty and persuaded several of their countrymen to swear that they had only acted on Roger's orders. Roger was furious: his claims against them were being thrown back at him. And yet, as he understood the sequence of events, the de Lacys had responded to Bruce's initial letter to the Irish before the invasion with a promise of military aid if the Scots assisted them in ousting Roger. They had then 'turned their shields' on him at Kells, and they had led the Scots through Leinster. Any subsequent pretence of constant loyalty was an insult. An even greater insult was that, as soon as the court case was decided in their favour, they acted again as guides for the Scots, leading them from Slane through Meath, around Dublin, and assisting in looting and burning on the way to Kildare.

As a show of justifying his attack on the de Lacys, Roger called together the king's council of Ireland at Kilkenny in early May and there proclaimed his war against his rebellious vassals. Revenge was uppermost in his mind. On 11 May he was at Naas, seemingly on his way towards Dublin, but he avoided the city and headed straight for his own lands in Meath. On 22 May he and his army were at Trim Castle, making final preparations for the assault on the de Lacy brothers and their adherents. As a last gesture of conciliation he sent one of his most faithful knights, Sir Hugh de Croft, to the de Lacys. Sir Hugh, who had served in Roger's household in both England and Ireland, carried letters bearing the royal seal, which ordered the brothers to come and submit to the King's Lieutenant. Not only did they not obey, they killed Sir Hugh.

It was a shocking act, without the slightest justification. If it was done to impress the Scots, it was too little too late: they were not moved to come to the aid of the de Lacys, whose squabbles with Roger did not interest them. Robert Bruce had left Ireland with Thomas Randolph on 22 May, and Edward Bruce was not strong enough to leave Ulster. If the murder was meant to impress the other lords of Meath, it was a demonstration which failed. The lords of Meath were in no position to take up arms against their liege lord, with a royal army at his command, in favour of two disgruntled murderous local lords and their equally murderous but starving and distant Scots allies. Roger was in the ascendancy.

No chronicler recorded the battle which ensued on 3–4 June 1317 in any detail, and most of what is known comes from a court case in 1334.[29] It is not even known exactly where it took place. It seems Roger managed to surprise Walter de Lacy and his army, as Walter alone of his clan faced Roger on the first day. Roger came at Walter's army with the banners of the king unfurled, signifying that he came for war. Overwhelmed by a better equipped, more experienced and far larger army, it was not long before Walter's men were in flight, or dead, Walter's standard-bearer being among the corpses trampled into the ground. The following day, Walter again mustered his men and joined with the rest of the de Lacy clan in an attempted surprise attack on Roger's army. With him were Hugh de Lacy, his brother, Robert de Lacy, Almaric and Simon de Lacy (brothers), John de Lacy (illegitimate son of Hugh), John de Lacy (illegitimate son of Walter), Walter de Say, Walter le Blount, John de Kemerdyn and many others. The de Lacys mustered behind Hugh's banner, which was ranged against that of the king. They attacked, but their attack soon turned into flight. Meath was once more securely under Roger's control.

Like Bruce in Scotland, Roger had a sense of urgency. There was no time for celebration; there was still much to do to subdue the rest of the land. At the end of June he summoned the Irish Parliament to Dublin to attend to royal business, and agreed the terms under which the people of Dublin would set free the Earl of Ulster. On 2 July John de Athy, faithfully sailing off the coast of Ireland, met the feared Thomas Dun in battle, and defeated him. Thomas Dun and forty of his men were captured, and Dun's head was hacked off and sent to Roger in Dublin. In mid-July, in an ever-increasing position of power, Roger summoned the king's council to approve his judgement of the de Lacy brothers. On 20 July he declared them felons and outlaws, guilty of breaking their vows of allegiance to him and the Crown, and enemies of the king. He confiscated all their goods, chattels and lands, and banished them from Ireland. His authority had never been so great.

For the rest of 1317 Roger continued to sweep across southern Ireland, participating in a series of small-scale battles all ending with Irish and Anglo-Irish lords surrendering to his authority. From Dublin he set out for Drogheda, a town which had prevailed upon King Edward to grant it protection. In another one of his interfering commands, on 10 June Edward had ordered Roger not to allow men to be housed in the town, nor to take provisions from it. Roger carefully obeyed this command and was even considerate enough of the king's order to kill a number of Ulstermen as they came to attack the Drogheda region and to steal cattle. Those who were not killed were led to Dublin Castle.[30] Roger's next target was Lord O'Farrell of Annaly. Roger destroyed all his people's houses, and forced O'Farrell to sue for peace and to surrender hostages. Pausing briefly back at Dublin to accuse and sentence further supporters of the de Lacy family, and to arrest the Bishop of Ferns for complicity in the Scottish campaign,[31] he started out again. On 11 September he marched against the Irish of Imail, 'where more Irish were killed than English' at Okinselagh.[32] His next confrontation was with the O'Byrne clan, whose chief was forced to surrender and locked up in Dublin Castle. By the end of October, Roger had pacified any and all of those Irish and Anglo-Irish lords who had considered siding with the Scots. Although Edward Bruce still held Ulster, his claim to rule Ireland was now an absurdity.

In his tour of duty Roger did suffer some setbacks. The first of these stemmed from the king's desire to try to control Ireland through Roger, rather than leaving him to govern the country independently. On 7 July Roger appointed his clerk, Nicholas de Balscot, to the chancellorship of Dublin Cathedral. In England, however, the king decided to appoint James d'Ardingel of Florence to the post. Finding that he had clashed with Roger, the king annulled Roger's appointment in favour of his own. This clash may have been connected to the second problem Roger faced at the end of 1317: the influence of his rival Hugh Despenser over Edward. While Roger had found preferment in Ireland, Despenser had found equal success at court. As husband of the eldest of the three heiresses of the Earl of Gloucester, Despenser was allowed to claim the largest third of the inheritance, the county of Glamorgan, in November. This was bad enough news for Roger, but what happened next was truly awful. Despenser celebrated his triumph by removing Llywelyn Bren from the Tower of London without any authority. He had him taken to Cardiff, and there, at the castle, had him executed in the most barbaric manner. The lord of Senghennydd, whom Roger and the Earl of Hereford had both sworn to protect, was drawn behind two horses to a gallows beside the Black Tower where he was hanged. As he was dying, the executioner cut out his heart and intestines with a knife and threw them into a nearby fire. His limbs were hacked off and distributed throughout Glamorgan. The man to whom the king had promised mercy was no more.[33]

Whatever Roger's immediate reaction to the news of Llywelyn's murder, there was nothing he could do about it in Ireland. The disadvantage of his Irish authority was that he was trapped across the sea; returning to the mainland without the king's permission would have jeopardised his standing at court. He could do nothing but wait, and concentrate on governing.

Roger's position as King's Lieutenant allows us to reconstruct a putative itinerary for him far more detailed than anything to date. Although the contents of the Irish Public Record Office were largely destroyed in 1922, calendars of the rolls of letters granted under the king's seal by Roger and the Justiciar, Edmund Butler, were published in 1828. In addition the accounts for his administration survive and have recently been published.[34] Thus we know that shortly after his victory at Okinselagh Roger returned to Trim and then to Dublin, where he remained throughout October. In November he took the government to Cork, where he remained for the rest of the year, spending the sum of £316 14s on curbing the rebellion in Cork and Desmond. In January he moved to Clonmel, and the accounts mention him fighting in 'Waterford, Leinster and elsewhere in Ireland'. In effect what Roger was doing was to use the Justiciar as his deputy while he himself went off to fight battles. Royal grants were made at Thomastown on 28 January and 2 February, presumably under the Justiciar's authority, but Roger himself was already back in Dublin by this time, dusting himself down from battle to grant a manor to Hugh de Turpington.[35] He was acting in a way which was remarkably free from the responsibilities of government, more like a conquering king than the head of a bureaucracy.

In true conqueror style, on 19 February Roger held a great feast at Dublin Castle at which he exercised his right as the king's representative to create new knights. One of those he dubbed was John de Bermingham, a ferociously loyal Anglo-Irish soldier and a commander of considerable ability, as later events would show. Another was Roger's faithful retainer Hugh de Turpington. A third is described in the St Mary's chronicle as 'Lord John Mortimer'.[36] This seems to have been his fourth son, who must have been a very young esquire in his father's service, perhaps between seven and ten years old. In conferring the honour on his son Roger was able to demonstrate his family's high status as well as his own authority.

In early March Roger undertook a last campaign to Drogheda, where he remained for four weeks. He held discussions with the king's council over the partition of estates and the awards of lands to the Irish, and plans were made for the final push towards Ulster. All resistance in Ireland had been crushed; Roger was master of all southern Ireland, but still Edward Bruce held out in the north. If he were to complete the reconquest and kill Bruce, a very great victory would be his, and most probably the dignity of an earldom too.

It was not to be. At the end of April Roger learnt that he was being summoned back to England. He returned to Dublin and set about winding up his activities. He appointed William FitzJohn, Archbishop of Cashel, to govern in his place, and then set about exacting a final shard of revenge upon the de Lacys. It seems that John de Lacy, the son of either Walter or Hugh, had been caught and imprisoned in Dublin. He was now taken to Trim for an audience with Roger. Unlike others, such as Miles de Verdon, who had begged forgiveness for their treachery, the de Lacys had thrown all hope of reconciliation back at Roger by killing Sir Hugh de Croft. Roger sentenced John de Lacy to be starved to death in Trim Castle, which his family had so desperately coveted.[37]

On 5 May Roger relinquished his command and prepared to sail for Wales. He must have left with a heavy heart, for he was passing up his opportunity of completing a glorious reconquest of Ireland from the Scots. When Sir John de Bermingham led the royal army north five months later to fight Edward Bruce, he was in effect Roger's surrogate. In his army were some of Roger's closest retainers: men like Sir Hugh de Turpington, Richard Tuit and John de Cusack. And his enemies amongst the Scots included men like Walter and Hugh de Lacy. It was Roger's campaign, a war which in many ways was of his creation, but he was not there to fight it.

SIX

The King's Kinsman

The Roger Mortimer who left Ireland in May 1318 was a different man from the Roger Mortimer who had left in December 1315. In 1315 he had been defeated, another losing commander in the sorry tale of Ireland under Edward Bruce. But in 1318 he had proved himself one of the most efficient leaders in the king's service. He was a more confident man too. In 1318 he left £1,000 of unpaid bills arising from his household's living expenses, which he expected the Irish Exchequer to pay. The reason for his confidence in this particular instance was that the Deputy Treasurer in charge of the Exchequer was his own man, Nicholas de Balscot.

Roger was not the only one to have changed. Relations between the king and the Earl of Lancaster were at a particularly low point. The rise of Hugh Despenser and three new favourites, namely William de Montagu, Roger Damory and Hugh Audley, had created a great antagonism between the king and Lancaster.[1] Damory was the king's latest infatuation, and had received the hand in marriage of one of the three heiresses of the earldom of Gloucester. Audley, a second favourite, had received the hand in marriage of the last unmarried Gloucester heiress, the third heiress being married already to Hugh Despenser. These men were described by some chroniclers as being 'worse than Gaveston' in their effect on the king. But they were given the largest portion of the Gloucester inheritance, and constituted a real threat to Lancaster's influence and power. Accordingly Lancaster had tried to make a political point of their presence at court, accusing Edward of disobeying the Ordinances and demanding that they all be banished. Edward had refused, and relations between the king and his overmighty cousin had broken down completely, to the point where Edward started mustering an army at York in case hostilities should break out during the parliament to be held there in October.

In this madness, Pembroke and Badlesmere had begun to act together, as the two most experienced and sensible elder statesmen. They urged both parties to come to an agreement but, far from being reasonable, Lancaster would not even attend a conference. He feared he would be murdered at court, and anyway he preferred the distinction of being a leader of the king's enemies to the role of a faithful subject. It was a position which suited his cantankerous nature. But such a stance was likely to lead to a national disaster, as anyone with a clear mind could see. It was impossible to defend the northern border against the Scots without Lancaster's help, Parliament could not function properly, Lancaster acted at every opportunity to impede the government, and there was a constant risk of civil war.

Two papal envoys had finally secured Lancaster's tentative agreement to come to court in September 1317; but then Edward had stupidly let his favourites talk him into attacking Lancaster's castle at Pontefract in retaliation for the occupation by Lancaster's agents of two royal castles in the constableship of Roger Damory. Only Pembroke's intervention had prevented bloodshed and probable war. Once again Lancaster withdrew his agreement to negotiate. Back at the point where they had started, Pembroke and Badlesmere decided on a new approach: they sought to control the king's favourite and thus to direct the king in the way he preferred to be directed: by his closest companions. Accordingly in late November 1317 they sealed a contract with Roger Damory so that Damory would advise the king only in conjunction with Pembroke and Badlesmere. And by the spring of 1318 the two elder statesmen had achieved what they set out to do: a position of real influence over the king and his courtiers, so that civil war could be averted.

While Pembroke and Badlesmere had been working together to restore sanity at court, the English bishops and the Archbishop of Dublin had been working on the Earl of Lancaster. At their suggestion Lancaster met with them at Leicester in April, where negotiations began on a patched-up truce between the earl and the king. Enough progress was made for Pembroke and Badlesmere to join the earl and the prelates. On 12 April an outline agreement was reached on statements of intent, and enough concessions were offered for there now to be hope of a settlement. It was at this point that Roger Mortimer was summoned back from Ireland, to help negotiate on behalf of the king.

Roger did not rush. It seems that he was delayed from sailing until the end of the month, possibly due to adverse weather conditions.[2] He did not reach the English court until July, by which time preliminary meetings between the king and the Earl of Lancaster had taken place. He was not part of the embassy which was sent from Northampton to Lancaster on 4 July. This team, which included the Archbishop of Dublin, the Bishops of Ely and Norwich, the Earl of Pembroke and two barons (Hugh Despenser and Bartholomew de Badlesmere) secured agreement on a number of points: that gifts made contrary to the Ordinances should be revoked and that Damory, Montagu and Audley should be banished from the court, except to answer military and parliamentary summons.[3] They conceded that a permanent royal council, consisting of eight bishops, four earls and four barons, would monitor the king's government over the course of each year, two bishops, one earl and one baron being with him at all times. For his part Lancaster promised he would attend the king and fight against the Scots when ordered to do so. However, having returned to court, Hugh Despenser tried to persuade the king not to confirm the terms agreed on his behalf. With Audley, Damory and Montagu also stamping their feet at the thought of being expelled from court, the king's will gave way, and only the determination of the Earl of Pembroke saved the agreement. A second deputation, with more reliable members, was organised. Hugh Despenser was dropped, and Roger, who was back at court by 18 July,[4] was invited to join, probably at the joint instigation of Badlesmere and Pembroke. On 20 July the new delegation set out from Northampton for Lancaster. They returned on 29 July, having made good progress. A third delegation set out on 1 August, consisting of Roger and the same delegates as the second delegation with the additions of the Bishop of Norwich, Sir John de Somery, Sir Ralph Bassett and Sir John Botetourt. Six days later, between Loughborough and Leicester, Roger witnessed the kiss of peace exchanged between the king and his rebellious cousin. At Leake, on 9 August, the final treaty was drawn up and witnessed.

The treaty secured peace for the time being, and was a significant diplomatic achievement. For Roger it marked a personal milestone in several ways. He was chosen to be one of the four barons on the permanent royal council, and thereby acquired a position of importance in the government. Equally significantly, he had proved himself as a negotiator, a military general and a provincial governor. He was also appointed to the committee to reform the royal household. Roger may well have reflected how far he had come since he had been a mere ward in the household, fourteen years before.

Political authority carried with it financial rewards. Roger's fee for delivering Ireland from the Scots was 6,000 marks (£4,000). Some idea of how large a sum this was, and how much it reflected the king's high regard for him, is revealed by the fact that usually the Justiciar of Ireland received a salary of £500. In addition there were grants towards Roger's expenses, and although payment was not as prompt as it should have been,[5] Roger had every reason to be satisfied with the financial rewards for his period in Ireland. Together with the not inconsiderable sum of £2,000 which he had received from de Badlesmere, he was now a rich man indeed.

As for Ireland itself, Roger could be satisfied that his estates there were now safe from incursions by native Irish and Scots invaders. On 14 October 1318 Sir John de Bermingham, whom Roger had knighted the previous year, met Edward Bruce in battle at Faughart, just north of Dundalk. The English charged through the Scottish ranks and destroyed them, killing many. Philip de Mowbray was so badly wounded that he later died. Several Irish chiefs who had sided with Edward Bruce were also killed, including the King of the Hebrides and the King of Argyle. Hugh and Walter de Lacy escaped but Edward Bruce did not: after the battle John de Maupas's corpse was discovered still lying on top of him; with his last breath he had ended the reign of the first and only Scottish King of Ireland. Sir John de Bermingham came to court with Edward Bruce's head. It was the only successful overseas campaign of Edward II's reign.

*

In December 1318 Roger journeyed back to the Welsh Marches. He was probably at Wigmore Castle for Christmas. Three days later he and his uncle, Lord Mortimer of Chirk, went to Wigmore Abbey to witness the resignation of the abbot, Philip le Galeys, in the abbot's chamber.[6] This was usual practice: frequently when the abbot of an important monastic house became too old to act, he was pensioned off and another monk elected or presented in his place. Thus Philip (who had been one of the executors of Roger's father's will) received a pension, servants and a room near the infirmary. In his place John de Clayhanger was appointed, a man presented to the monks and the lords by the new Bishop of Hereford, Adam of Orleton.

Contemporaries and later generations considered Adam of Orleton a cunning, calculating man, a ruthless cleric with more thought for his own authority than for his flock. Orleton was highly intelligent, cynical perhaps, but with an intolerance of foolish government and a loyalty to the Pope bordering on fanaticism. Therein lies the key to understanding his political career. Orleton had spent a considerable time at the papal court, having been despatched at a very early point in Edward's reign to Pope Clement V. Later he was closely associated with Pope John XXII, whom he counted a personal friend. Edward's poor government exasperated and embarrassed him on an international front. He preferred the dynamic new government espoused by his noble friends, the Mortimers, to whom he felt he owed a loyalty second only to the Pope.

The nature of Orleton's relationship with the Mortimer family is not entirely clear. His name came from one of Roger's manors, and he himself may have done likewise, although it seems more probable that he was born in Hereford.[7] There is no doubt that he was acquainted with Roger from an early point in their respective careers. His appointment by Edward II as an envoy to Pope Clement in 1307 may have had something to do with Roger's influence. Whatever his origins, he proved to be a very political bishop. Now, at the start of 1319, he and Roger had ample opportunity to discuss matters of state, as Orleton spent six days at Wigmore.[8] It was the start of a working relationship which would have the most profound consequences for both men.

It was probably also at this time, or shortly afterwards, that the wedding took place between Roger's daughter, Maud, and John, the heir of John de Charlton, lord of Powys.[9] This brings a curious political alignment to the fore, for John de Charlton's younger brother Thomas had been the king's unsuccessful candidate for the see of Hereford, which had been given to Orleton. Both Orleton and Thomas de Charlton had been clerks close to the royal household, and the two men went together to Avignon to petition the Pope on behalf of the king to appoint Henry de Burghersh to the see of Lincoln. Henry de Burghersh, who was not yet twenty-five, was another of Roger's relatives, being the nephew of Bartholomew de Badlesmere. In fact Badlesmere paid the Pope no less than £15,000 of the king's money for the appointment, which, overriding the previous election by the canons of Lincoln, some considered illegal.[10] Thus it is possible to see Roger, with the help of his son's father-in-law, Lord Badlesmere, promoting the interests of several of the most intelligent and highly educated men known at court: men who, although they were in holy orders, could wield very great power through the wealth and influence associated with an English mitre. In this respect it must be remembered that Roger's father was himself an Oxford-educated man, who had stayed at university even after it became likely that he would succeed to the family titles and estates. In these friendships with ecclesiastics – Orleton, Charlton, Burghersh, as well as Alexander Bicknor (Archbishop of Dublin) and John de Hothum already mentioned – Roger was building an educated and diplomatic power base as well as a military one. He was in effect collecting a series of political forces, and in many respects grooming himself to take over the position of the ageing Earl of Pembroke: the king's most astute, militarily able and independent adviser, and a foil to the antagonistic Earl of Lancaster.

Edward was mindful of Roger's ambition and ability. While Damory or Audley had won the king's unlimited affection for a month or six, Roger had increasingly gained the king's respect. But, as the king's interference in Roger's Irish administration showed, he did not completely trust him. Roger, like Pembroke, was not a pawn. A good example is Roger's move on the young Earl of Warwick. In early 1315, one of Roger's vassals, Walter Hakelut, had died. The Earl of Warwick had claimed some of Walter's lands in Wales, which Roger believed were his.[11] The dispute outlived the earl, who died in 1316, passing to his under-age son. Roger saw an opportunity and purchased from the king the right to marry one of his daughters to the heir. This aligned Roger with members of a family estranged from Edward, following the death of Gaveston. It was justified by Roger on the grounds that it solved the quarrel between him and the late earl, as the disputed lands could pass in dower to the heir and Roger's daughter and their children.[12] In this way Roger was able to strengthen his family alliances, preserve his independence from the king and solve a dispute without recourse to royal favouritism. But although such moves won the king's respect Roger could not command the king's wholehearted trust. It was not through favouritism but through his loyal work as a governor of Ireland, a negotiator, and as a military leader, that he deserved reward, and after the success at Faughart it was obvious where his talents could most usefully be employed. In mid-March Roger was once more made governor of Ireland.

Roger did not set off straightaway. First he had to attend to the burial of his younger brother John, who had been a yeoman in the king's service. Afterwards, in May, Roger also probably attended the marriage of his eldest daughter Margaret with Thomas, the son and heir of Lord Berkeley, which secured an earlier alliance with an important lord of the Welsh Marches.[13] Interestingly Berkeley and his adherents John Maltravers and Thomas Gurney had fallen out with the Earl of Pembroke at this time, and Berkeley's move towards Roger was a long-term political shift, not a mere interweaving of alliances but a vote of confidence in him as a leader.

From Roger's point of view, the king's behaviour towards him only suffered in one significant respect: his preferment of Hugh Despenser. With the king losing Damory, Audley and Montagu from court, his affections fell most heavily on Roger's rival and the sworn enemy of the Mortimer family. And Despenser was no fool: he was working himself into a position at court as strong as Roger's. In 1318 Despenser had been appointed to negotiate with the Scots: he too was being entrusted with more serious diplomatic business. He and Roger were not just hereditary enemies, they were rivals. Now, as Roger made his way towards Ireland, it seemed Despenser's ambitions were on the verge of being fulfilled, as he had already partly persuaded the king to command Hugh Audley to give the castle and town of Newport to him in return for other, less choice, manors in England. He was also making plans for acquiring the lands of Roger Damory which had belonged to the Earl of Gloucester. Despenser was gradually acquiring the whole of the earldom of Gloucester, and there was nothing Roger could do to stop him.

*

Roger's second period of administration in Ireland was far less eventful than his first. Very few Scots had survived the Battle of Faughart, and those who had had fled back to Scotland. All across the country English and Irish joined in one euphoric expression of relief. The satisfaction from the English point of view is easily understandable; the native Irish were just as glad to see the demise of the Scots. Describing the death of Edward Bruce, one Irish writer from Ulster stated that 'there was not done from the beginning of the world a deed that was better for the men of Ireland than that deed. For there came dearth and loss of people during his time in all Ireland in general for the space of three years and a half, and people undoubtedly used to eat each other throughout Ireland.'[14] As a conse-quence of this restored stability, the title under which Roger governed Ireland from his landing on 12 June 1319 was that of 'Justiciar'. It was a less significant position than 'King's Lieutenant', and had no huge fee attached, but it had the ring of permanency about it. In addition the king gave Roger the keeping of the royal castles of Roscommon, Rawdon and Athlone, and ordered the Exchequer not to demand any debts from him.[15]

Roger's main objective as Justiciar was to keep order. In view of the recent war, this included having to make inquiries into who had aided and abetted the Scots, and who had fought well enough against them to deserve reward. Under his direction Thomas FitzJohn, Earl of Kildare, and Sir John de Bermingham (now Earl of Louth), Arnold le Poer and John Wogan were all ordered to root out the adherents of Edward Bruce, and Roger was to hold an inquisition of their findings.[16] At the same time he was commanded to reward men who had fought well against Bruce. Not surpris-ingly he combined his rewarding of the faithful with his punishment of traitors, granting the lands of Hugh and Walter de Lacy and other rebels to his chosen faithful supporters. Among those who benefited were Sir Hugh de Turpington, John de Cusack, Miles de Verdon, Edmund de Bermingham and Adam le Breton. The rewarding of de Verdon, a pardoned rebel, in particular suggests that Roger had the essential diplomatic ability to forgive men as well as to pardon them.

Peace, and one successful harvest, were not sufficient in themselves to ensure a swift return to normality. The Dubliners, who had sacrificed their suburbs for the sake of defending their walls, needed to be pardoned for burning down a royal manor in the process, and begged to have half of the fee of their city remitted, since they could not afford to rebuild and pay their usual dues. Cork was in a similar position, having spent a large sum on a new defensive wall around the city in 1316. Limerick too was in an impoverished state. Then there were the estates of dead men. Many English subjects having been cut down in the wars, their heirs were left under age, and Roger had to grant these wardships to others or take them in hand himself. Just after Roger's departure from Ireland in May 1318, Richard de Clare, one of the greatest lords, was killed in a skirmish with the native Irish, and this too required an inquiry and a distribution of the wardship of his heir. Of course, Roger was in a strong position to affect such inquiries and allocations, and it is noticeable that the Irish estates of the dead Earl of Gloucester, which should have been allocated either to Despenser, Audley or Damory, remained in his hands. Since Roger assisted Audley's steward and Damory's rent collector in 1319,[17] the logical explanation for the Gloucester inheritance not being allocated was that it was all at risk of being given to Hugh Despenser.

In addition to the rebuilding of the country, he had to deal with roaming bands of thieves and foragers who were taking advantage of the weakened law enforcement. Thus, although there was no full-scale military campaign, Roger's responsibility was to stop the looters, and to bring them to justice. A glance at his itinerary shows that he quickly covered most of English-administered Ireland. Arriving in June, he stayed in Dublin for a month before setting out for Cashel. A few days later he was at Callan, just south-west of Kilkenny, before returning by way of Cashel to Dublin. Another long stay there ended in October when he moved to Athboy in Meath, a few miles north-west of Trim, then in another rapid shift he moved south to Wexford in November, settling at Cork for December. He stayed in the south, being at Waterford in February, until in March he moved back up to Drogheda and then back to Dublin, just in time to attend the parliament he had summoned to meet on the 30th. Thus in his tours he was accessible to many of the Anglo-Irish lords, and saw for himself what needed rebuilding and repairing, where force was necessary to protect a lordship, or where a grant of a local customs duty was necessary to finance the building or rebuilding of town gates and walls.

Along with the rebuilding of the wrecked institutions and edifices of the country, the period of Roger's justiciarship allowed significant social progress to take place. Throughout Ireland bridges had been destroyed as the Scots and Irish had fought against each other and the English and the Anglo-Irish. Now a number of bridges at important crossing places were rebuilt in stone. A university was established in Dublin, in fulfilment of a plan first mooted by the then Archbishop of Dublin in 1311, when Roger had previously been in Ireland. It is possible that this was not a coincidence, for while such foundations were the preserve of the highly educated clerical elite, it has been noted that Roger had close links with the higher clergy, and was a man of judgement and intellect. As mentioned, his father had been Oxford-educated, and he seems himself to have had a link with

Oxford University as he mentions the Chancellor of the University and the Bishop of Hereford in a letter to the king which probably dates from about this time.[18] Finally, there is a very good reason why Roger would have been in favour of establishing a university in Dublin: he wanted it to produce educated men of the calibre needed to run the country efficiently.

Parliament sat at Dublin throughout April under Roger's justiciarship, concerning itself principally with establishing law and order on a stronger footing. Statutes were enacted to restrict the activities of bands of outlaws and other criminals, and an Act was passed to prevent 'protection' money being extorted from individuals. It was ordained that henceforth no one should extract rents from his tenants for protection, and that no one could grant protection except the king (in the person of the Justiciar) and the lords of liberties (like Roger). It was also ordained that a well-established lawyer and two knights should hold assizes and set up a gaol in each county. There was also provision for checking the work of sheriffs in administering justice. The Acts passed show a single-minded determination on the part of the representatives under Roger's guidance to return Ireland to the rule of law.

Roger's administration was strong, and it was popular. Its popularity was due to three factors: the famine was seemingly at an end, the destructive Scottish army had been removed, and the thoroughness and speed with which Roger set about re-imposing justice on the country impressed the inhabitants. Judging from the distances he covered, and how readily he applied himself to the task in hand, exercising royal justice was something in which he took pride and pleasure. In May 1320 he was in Dublin; in June Athlone; in August Kilkenny. But his time in Ireland was coming to an end. In early September he returned to Dublin, and by the end of the month he and his knights had gone, leaving the Earl of Kildare as his deputy.[19] A few days later, on 7 October, the mayor and community of Dublin wrote to the king praising Roger's period of office, stating he had 'thought much of saving and keeping the peace of your land'. If their intention was the return of Roger as Justiciar, their compliments fell on deaf ears. Roger's challenges now lay wholly on the British mainland.[20]

After five visits, totalling nearly six of the last twelve years, Roger had left Ireland for ever. The irony is that, when he had first crossed the Irish Sea as governor in 1317, he had been coming to a war zone. Now, having pacified the country, he was going back to one.

SEVEN

Rebel

Sir Hugh Despenser the younger, lord of Glamorgan: there is no other way to begin this chapter but with his name, for by the end of 1320 he had become the pivot upon which the balance of Edward's reign turned. Like Gaveston before him, he had won Edward's confidence completely, and now he won the king's devotion too. But whereas Gaveston had been Roger's friend and jousting companion, Despenser was Roger's sworn enemy, a man who had vowed to destroy him and his uncle and to take their lands. Slowly Despenser's influence had grown. He had killed Llywelyn Bren. He had tried to seize the land of Gwennllwg from Hugh Audley in 1317. He had been made King's Chamberlain in 1318, control-ling access to the king. Now he was trying to make himself Earl of Gloucester in place of the dead Gilbert de Clare. If he and Roger had ever shared any feelings of goodwill towards one another – and there is no evidence that they ever did – then those feelings were nothing more than memories, if indeed either man cared to recall them.

Despenser's desire to become Earl of Gloucester threatened other men besides Roger. When the last earl had died at Bannockburn he had left three sisters as co-heiresses. In 1317 the earldom was divided into three parts between the husbands of these three sisters: Despenser acquired the lordship of Glamorgan, the richest part, and Hugh Audley and Roger Damory acquired the other two thirds. The division only triggered envy and anxiety, especially on the parts of Damory and Audley. The land of Gwennllwg, which had once belonged to Glamorgan, was now legally separated from it, but a technicality like that did not stop Despenser from trying to wrest it from its rightful lord. On his first attempt he failed, but, undeterred, he set about trying to acquire other lands from Audley and Damory by force, intimidation and trickery. In this last aspect he was as wily as Roger himself, convincing the men of Gwennllwg that under his lordship they might enjoy similar privileges to the men of Senghennydd and Misguin and other favoured lordships. The men of Gwennllwg were duped. Despenser also obtained grants in Carmarthen, including the new town of Llandilo, whose constable was one of Roger's most favoured vassals, Edmund Hakelut. This brought him into confrontation not only with Roger but also the neighbouring lord, John Giffard of Brimpsfield. Slowly an alliance was forming against Despenser: John Giffard, Damory, Audley and, most importantly, Roger and the Earl of Hereford, both of whom had not forgiven Despenser for Llywelyn's murder.

Such was the cauldron of hatreds and rivalries into which Roger plunged himself at the end of September 1320. The situation quickly worsened. Even before he had returned from Ireland Gwennllwg was granted to Despenser, against all law and right. Despenser had so completely won the king's heart that the king was more interested in furthering his new favourite's interests than protecting those of his past infatuations. Once again Edward was ruling England as if it were his personal fief. While this was true in theory, it remained so *only* in theory; and Edward had no moral or legal justification for taking one lord's land at whim and giving it to another. Nor did he have any right to overlook the laws of the land in favour of certain men, which is what he did next.

The trouble started in Gower.¹ Having riled his fellow Marcher lords, Despenser now compounded his hatreds with an act of such supreme arrogance that he united most of England against himself and the king. The impecunious lord of the Gower peninsula, William de Braose, had supposedly put his lordship up for sale, soliciting offers from both Lords Mortimer, from Despenser, and even receiving a down payment from the Earl of Hereford. The dissolute de Braose, not particularly caring whom he aggravated, then sold his land to his son-in-law John de Mowbray, who had married one of his co-heiresses, and who was entitled to inherit the lordship anyway. Fearing Despenser's likely response, as Despenser had wanted the lordship in order to round off his lands in South Wales, Mowbray took possession immediately.

Despenser was furious. He spoke to the king. Since Gower had been taken by John de Mowbray without royal licence, he argued, the acquisition was not legal. Had the lands been in England, this would have technically been correct, but even there lords who had a right to a lordship had often received it without royal assent. In the Marches Despenser was entirely wrong. Marcher lords had always enjoyed the right of entering their lands with no need of royal licence. Moreover, if Despenser could persuade the king to overlook this Marcher privilege, what other ones might follow? For Despenser to neglect Marcher law, and moreover to demand possession of Gower himself, was a red rag not just to one bull but the whole herd.

Roger was probably still making his way to Westminster in October 1320, and knew little or nothing of the developments taking place there. On 9 November he had only reached Stratfield Mortimer in Berkshire, and therefore would only have reached Westminster two days later, at the earliest. Thus he missed the whole of the parliament, including the most crucial act. On 26 October the king confiscated Gower from John de Mowbray.

In taking Gower into royal hands Edward was declaring that he would defend Despenser to the last, against all law, all reason and all arms. He did this no doubt out of a supreme wish to please Despenser, but in doing so he showed enormous lack of respect for the other Marcher lords. Immediately he was made aware of the outrage he had caused, and he was forced to placate some of his former friends. To Damory he allowed forgiveness of all his debts, and shortly afterwards he was forgiven a fine of 2,300 marks.[2] To favour Roger, he accepted his advice to assist the heir of the dead Richard de Clare in Ireland.[3] He further confirmed the estates of all three husbands of the co-heiresses of Gloucester – espenser, Damory and Audley – but this was little consolation to the Marcher lords, especially those who saw how intimate he now was with Despenser. To use a phrase employed by tactful contemporaries, 'Despenser was the king's right-hand man'. No one could see the king without his permission. Although this was a flagrant abuse of his position as Chamberlain, there was nothing any of the lords could do. In effect Despenser was shielding the king from the political responsibilities which he found tedious, and was taking the administration upon his own shoulders. England was once more plunging headlong towards civil war, on account of the king placing a personal friendship over and above the interests of the kingdom.

It is difficult to account for Edward's policy without suspecting an emotional reliance upon Despenser as great as that he had felt for Gaveston. True, Edward had had favourites since Gaveston, but his affection for them had not reached the pitch of his love for his brother-in-arms. In fact, at points of crisis, he had let certain favourites, like Damory, be put away from him. Perhaps he did not understand the depth of the crisis in 1320 and imagined it would be smoothed over at a parliament some time in the future. However, by the end of November it was clear that the situation was very serious indeed. When the king's officer tried to take Gower into his own hands, he was met with armed resistance.

Roger remained at Westminster, his accustomed position at times of crisis. He was still apparently at court on 16 November, two days after the king's men managed to obtain control of Gower from the infuriated Mowbray. It was clear that each lord had to make a decision between the king in his support of Despenser's nefarious schemes, or the principle of the Crown's responsibility to the community of the realm.

A telling gauge of the seriousness of the situation was that the Earl of

Pembroke, the arch-moderator of the reign, decided to leave the country. Most of the Marcher lords withdrew from court soon afterwards, before Christmas, and began to arm their castles. Roger stayed for a few weeks longer, until January, trying desperately to reach a compromise, but the king was in no mood to listen to an enemy of Despenser. He had decided to support Despenser no matter what, and the more his enemies criticised him, the more he liked his new favourite.

Herein lies the tragedy of Roger and other men like him. He was forced to choose between supporting corruption and instigating a rebellion. To add to his problems, the man responsible for corrupting the government was his personal enemy, who had declared he would 'despoil him and revenge the death of his grandfather upon him'.[4] Nor was he alone in finding himself forced to oppose the king. Roger de Clifford had seen his mother's lands taken by Despenser with no attempt at compensation. In May 1320 Despenser had finally managed to obtain Hugh Audley's rich portion of the Gloucester inheritance, the lordship of Newport, in return for a few English manors of much less value. For men like Roger, Audley and Clifford, there was no solution in law. There was only war.

In January and February 1321 the battle lines of the opposition were drawn up. Roger, with his customary adherence to the king, and his self-grooming as a moderator, was not at first among them. On 30 January the Earls of Hereford, Surrey and Arundel, and a number of northern barons, were among twenty-eight lords ordered not to attend an assembly called to discuss the estates of the Crown. This is the first sign that the Earl of Lancaster and the Earl of Hereford were renewing their league against the king and his favourite, similar to their alliance against Gaveston, but now implying a new and more dangerous common cause between the Marcher lords and the confederacy of northern barons under the Earl of Lancaster. Probably only a day or two before this Roger had finally given up trying to reason with the king, being the last in a long line of refugee lords to leave court. At the end of January he was at Stratfield Mortimer, on his return journey to Wigmore. Edward acknowledged his opposition by removing him from his office of Justiciar of Ireland. In his place, on 1 February, he appointed one of Despenser's henchmen, Ralph de Gorges.

Roger's royal pedestal had crumbled. In October 1320 he had been the governor of Ireland, and unswervingly loyal to the king. Now, just a few months later, he had been removed from office, he was aligned with the king's opposition, and all because he had opposed a man liable to bring disaster and ruin upon the king. Shocked at this treatment, Roger reluctantly began gathering an army. He and Joan settled all their Irish estates on their second son, Roger, aware of the dangers of the conflict ahead.[5]

In Brecon, the Earl of Hereford was also raising men-at-arms. In the north too, men, armour and castles were being prepared. On 27 February Lancaster held a meeting at which the Marcher lords' representatives were present, and at which it was decided to attack the Despensers in South Wales.[6]

The Earl of Pembroke stayed abroad. The king lamented his absence, since he wanted the earl to treat with the Scots, but Pembroke himself secretly sympathised with the Marcher lords, and would not return to serve the king while Despenser was at court. Thus, with no check on his actions, with all his senior advisers in opposition to him, or abroad, the king trusted his own judgement and that of Despenser. Despenser's advice was selfish and deliberately antagonistic. With clear intelligence that an attack was being planned on his Welsh holdings, he advised the king to take a royal army to defend his lands there.

This mobilisation of royal forces made Despenser's enemies appear rebels against the king. It was an extremely unfortunate move; the Marcher lords were always reluctant to fight a royal army, not for fear of defeat but precisely because they were fundamentally royalists. It was Despenser against whom they were arraying their forces, not the king himself. The king's personal identification with Despenser, however, alienated those who would otherwise have remained in his service. There was no better example than Roger's uncle, Lord Mortimer of Chirk, who was still Justiciar of Wales. He was ordered to inspect all the castles in his authority, and to make sure they were defensible for the king. Thus he was forced to decide between his nephew and his monarch, to choose between his brother's son and nearly fifty years of unstinting loyalty to the Crown. The elder Mortimer, now sixty-six, could not be expected to betray his nephew, especially when he too was threatened by the favourite. In this way the king managed to alienate both Mortimers, the Justiciars of Ireland and Wales, and found himself even more dependent on Despenser's support and advice.

On 27 March, the king issued an order to the Earl of Hereford, Roger Mortimer of Wigmore, Roger Damory, John de Hastings, and John de Charlton,

> to maintain the king's peace . . . and not to permit any assemblies to be made . . . as complaint has reached the king that many of their men . . . make assemblies and musters in a warlike manner, whereat the king is astonished, as it is unknown why such assemblies are made.[7]

The king's pretended astonishment could only grow as the list of rebels grew longer. On the following day, the king ordered those lords whom he still expected to obey him, namely Roger and his uncle, the Earl of Hereford, Lord Hastings, John Giffard and Lord Berkeley, to be at Gloucester on 5 April.[8]

Roger did not go to Gloucester. Instead he and the Earl of Hereford took it upon themselves to answer for all their fellow Marcher lords. They refused to come into the king's presence, they said, while Hugh Despenser the younger remained in the king's company. They put forward a compromise whereby Despenser should be removed safely by the Earl of Hereford to the custody of the Earl of Lancaster, and a parliament summoned at which the earl and Roger could put forward their grievances, and that if this were allowed, they would come to the king at Gloucester as requested.

The king at this point hesitated, and did not reply for some time. It is not difficult to see why. If one takes the list of Marcher lords who were liable to provide fighting men in 1317 for the war against the Scots, there were fifteen major lords in the region besides Roger and the Earl of Hereford; namely Maurice de Berkeley, William de la Zouche, John Giffard, William de Braose, Henry of Lancaster, John de Charlton, John de Hastings, John de Grey, the Earl of Surrey, the Earl of Arundel, Lord Mortimer of Chirk, Lady Mortimer (Roger's mother), Roger Damory, Hugh Audley and John de Cromwell. Most of these were now openly in opposition to Despenser, and, by making Despenser's enemies his own, the king had made enemies of nearly all the lords of the March. Lord Mortimer of Chirk was not openly hostile yet, nor were Lady Mortimer, John de Cromwell, the Earl of Arundel or the Earl of Surrey, but both Lord Mortimer of Chirk and Roger's mother were definitely on the side of the Marchers. Moreover, Despenser's enemies were joined by several southwestern knights, men such as John Maltravers; and of course they were in league with the northern forces under the Earl of Lancaster. The king had miscalculated badly, and so had Despenser.

Despite the increasing strength of the opposition, Despenser and the king remained firm. On 8 April Audley's lands were confiscated. On 13 April orders were sent to Roger, Hereford, Hastings, Damory, Charlton, Giffard and both Berkeleys to maintain the peace in their lands, and 'not to permit assemblies and demonstrations in warlike manner to be made . . . complaint having reached the king that many men of [their lordships] make such assemblies and demonstrations'.[9] A show of equality was maintained by also naming Despenser as one of those preparing for war, but things had gone too far, and there was now no stopping the momentum of the resistance to the favourite.

On 21 April the king finally made up his mind to act, and wrote to more than seventy lords and all seventeen bishops urging them not to attend any musters or to believe 'false news' about a rebellion. Two days later he wrote to Roger and the Earl of Hereford regarding their refusal to come to Gloucester. His letter was effectively a declaration of war. He claimed that their reasons for nonappearance were insufficient because Despenser had been appointed to the office of Chamberlain in Parliament, and in their presence, and that no complaint had hitherto been received against him, and that, in any case, a royal summons was a protection for all who should obey it, so fear of Despenser was no excuse for non-attendance. In addition, conveying Despenser to the Earl of Lancaster would be contrary to the terms of Magna Carta, against the law, and in contradiction to the Ordinances. The letter concluded with the new summons for them to be at Oxford by 10 May.

Edward found it difficult to believe that Roger and Lord Hereford would actually take arms against him. But on 1 May he wrote to the two lords again prohibiting them from taking up arms and stating that he wished to change the place to which they should report from Oxford to Westminster. He was unaware that on that very day the two Lords Mortimer, the Earl of Hereford and all the other Marcher lords were taking up military positions, ready to ravage the lands of Hugh Despenser. This was the king's next great miscalculation: the men he had alienated were the most experienced battle fighters in England. Despenser, by contrast, had very few military knights at his disposal.[10] Lord Hereford and Lord Mortimer of Chirk had fought with the old king in Scotland, Wales and Gascony. Roger had learnt how to command an army in Ireland. More importantly, many of Roger's men were battle-hardened, including Englishmen who had fought with him in Ireland, such as the steadfast Sir Hugh de Turpington and Irish knights who had crossed to help him. Having been dragged to the point of war, they were not going to back down now.

Roger was the prime mover in the attack on the Despensers. He marched south with his uncle from Wigmore on or just before 1 May.[11] His army stayed the night at Bromyard, where his men seized property belonging to local inhabitants.[12] As he marched further south, through Ledbury, his army seized further property. The Bishop of Hereford, Adam of Orleton, sent his own men to help Roger. Approaching Glamorgan he was joined by the contingents of Damory, Audley, Hastings, Mowbray, Sir Roger de Clifford, John Giffard, Henry le Tyeys, Lord Berkeley, Sir John Maltravers and many others. In total they rode with eight hundred men-at-arms, five hundred other horsemen and ten thousand footsoldiers.[13] They rode beneath banners bearing the royal arms, first to Newport, which fell to them after a four-day-long attack on 7 May, and then to Cardiff, which suffered a similar fate five days later. They rode throughout Glamorgan and South Wales, destroying the property of Hugh Despenser in the manner of fourteenth-century war. In the words of Despenser's clerk, their army

> besieged his towns and castles, and took them by force, and slew some of his men, namely Sir John Iweyn, Matthew de Gorges, and others to the number of fifteen Welshmen, and wounded and maimed some of his men, such as Sir Philip Joce, and imprisoned some of them, such as Sir Ralph de Gorges . . . and took and carried away the chattels of Hugh Despenser found in the said towns and castles, including forty destriers and armour for two hundred men . . . siege engines, springalds, cross-bows, lances, quarrels . . . and victuals, such as corn, wine, honey, rye, meat, fish, and divers other necessary victuals amounting to the value of £2,000, and took and burnt all the said charters remembrances and muniments of the said Hugh there found, to the value of £2,000, and burnt part of the gates and houses in the said castles, and took out and carried away the windows, ironwork and lead, and committed many other damages, to the value of £2,000. And with the same power and force they stayed there five days in order to destroy the lands completely, within which time they made by force all the greater part of all the country swear to be of their accord, and they imprisoned and held to ransom those who refused, and burnt their houses and goods. And during the same time they wasted all his manors there, and robbed him of all his movables therein . . . [including 10,000 sheep, 400 oxen, 500 cows, 160 plough-cattle and other animals from a total of twenty-three manors].[14]

This account, being rendered by Hugh Despenser's clerk to the king, is no doubt an exaggeration of their destructiveness, but many elements of it are confirmed by chronicle evidence. The author of *Vita Edwardi Secundi*, for example, supports the figure of eight hundred men-at-arms, and supports the statement about the looting. He also states that

> thirty thousand of the inhabitants of that territory came to the barons saying 'Remit your displeasure towards us, for we have never liked the lordship of Hugh Despenser, and are all prepared to obey your orders.' They were accepted on these terms: that they would wholly renounce their homage to Hugh Despenser, that they would never acknowledge

him as lord, but remain faithful to the lord king in all things, and would maintain their due services for the true heir at the proper time and place . . .[15]

A huge number of people wreaked this damage on Hugh Despenser's lands and castles. As is plain, the hatred which this destruction represented went beyond any single cause. Protest at certain of his actions had grown into a widespread demonstration, in which personal and collective reasons for attacking Despenser were combined. This was the case for Roger also, for the key prisoner who fell into his hands was his appointed replacement as Justiciar of Ireland, Sir Ralph de Gorges. Roger immediately took him back to Wigmore, where he locked him up, before taking his army on to the Earl of Arundel's castle of Clun, which they attacked.

If Hugh Despenser's clerk was more or less accurate in reporting the actions of the Marcher lords, his father's clerk wildly exaggerated their actions elsewhere in England. Roger and his associates are supposed to have done damage to his property to a value which was roughly comparable with two-thirds of a year's royal income. But it is not the amount of damage which leads one to suspect exaggeration, rather the locations. Roger is supposed to have entered Vastern Manor in Wootton Bassett on 11 June and subsequently sacked it and sixteen other manors in Wiltshire, six manors in Gloucestershire, four in Dorset, five in Hampshire, two in Berkshire, six in Oxfordshire, three in Buckinghamshire, four in Surrey, one in Cambridgeshire, two in Huntingdonshire, five in Leicestershire, one in Yorkshire, one in Lincolnshire, five in Cheshire, and five in Warwickshire all before arriving in Parliament on 29 July. Allowing five days for the journey to London, the army had just forty-three days to destroy sixty-seven manors and cover the many hundreds of miles between them. Clearly at this stage the destruction was not being done by a single coordinated army but by a series of forces, many of which are likely to have been local peasants and outlaws eager to take advantage of the war against the Despensers to enrich themselves. The author of *Vita* suggests as much in giving the reasons for the country's hatred of the elder Despenser:

For the brutal and greedy father had in the past wronged many, and promoted the excommunication of many. As a justice of the forest he had accused many of poaching from royal hunting grounds, many of these he vilely disinherited, some he forced into exile, from many he extorted unjust sums of money, and collected a thousand librates of land by means of threats . . . By a general judgement he justly lost what he had accumulated from the losses of others.

Hence his own parks and hunting grounds became a free-for-all for every would-be venison-eater in the country. The claim against the Marchers should be seen in this light: as an attempt by the elder Despenser to pass off the anger against him as their work. It also indicates that, as the lands of the elder Despenser were attacked by the Marcher lords and others,[16] neither the Despensers' men nor the royal forces could do anything to stop them.

While Roger, Hereford and the other Marcher lords were ploughing through the elder Despenser's lands, Lord Lancaster in the north had convened a meeting at Sherburn in Elmet.[17] Roger has usually been thought by historians to have attended this meeting, but in view of the heavy destruction systematically being applied to the elder Despenser's lands in the south, it is likely that the Marchers sent only a representative. This may have been Bartholomew de Badlesmere, who now openly joined Roger's side. The northern lords declared that they understood and sympathised with the Marcher lords' reasons for action. Despite the damage the Marcher lords' forces were wreaking across England, Roger and his co-leader Hereford maintained the full support of the majority of the realm, and the crucial support of the northern barons.

On 29 July 1321 Roger led his army from Waltham to London. Each of the Marcher lords stationed himself at a separate point around the city, practically laying siege to the king and the court. As a mark of solidarity, the Marcher lords and their men all wore an identical livery: green tunics, with the right top quarter and right arm yellow, and with the royal arms on their chests. Roger and his forces encamped in the grounds of the priory of St John at Clerkenwell, just to the north of the capital. And there they waited, while the king refused to negotiate.

The waiting game which the king and the rebel lords now embarked on was a microcosm of the entire reign of Edward II. There was only one basic dispute: the king's right to do whatever he wished. The king and those he happened to favour believed he should have complete liberty. Most other lords, especially those who had lost out to his favourites, believed he had a responsibility to govern the country justly, in accordance with his coronation oath. In the resulting conflicts and resolutions, the whole country suffered, and the only benefit was a careful rethinking of the machinery of government.[18] Only a great statesman like the Earl of Pembroke could break such a deadlock. Ambitious men like Roger and Despenser could never be disassociated from their ambitions; warriors like Hereford could not resolve their differences without the context of violence; and overmighty magnates such as Lancaster could only interpret political settlements in terms of what they personally had gained and lost. Thus it was fortunate for all concerned that at this juncture the Earl of Pembroke returned to England. Although he was still at Dover, the king wrote to him on 1 August asking him to come the next day to Westminster. Pembroke did not delay, and, amazingly, managed to cover the seventy miles to be at Westminster the following day.

It was 1312 and Gaveston all over again, except that the third magnate facing the king with Lancaster and Hereford was Roger, in place of the late Earl of Warwick. And their armies were not encamped a few miles outside the city but right next to the walls. And the royal favourite was not dead, as Gaveston had been when England had last teetered on the brink of civil war, but very much alive. Everything came down to Pembroke, as it had in 1312. The question was: could he persuade the king to accept the Despensers' exile? Or would full-scale civil war break out?

Having discussed matters with the Marcher lords, Pembroke returned to the king. Still he refused to accept the Marchers' terms. It took all the earl's powers of persuasion to make him see that he had no choice.

> 'Consider, lord king, the power of the barons,' he implored. 'Take heed of the danger that threatens; neither brother nor sister should be dearer to thee than thyself. Do not therefore for any living soul lose thy kingdom . . . Let not the king say, to his own injury, that this business was begun by the barons; but since it is for the common good that the country be freed from wicked men, to which end, lord king, you swore an oath at your coronation, if you listen to the barons you shall reign in power and glory; but if on the other hand you close your ears to their petitions, you may perchance lose the kingdom and all of us. For we are sworn confederates, and we cannot oppose our peers.'[19]

Faced with this statement from Pembroke, and the rebel lords' declaration that they would renounce their homage to him and appoint another king in his place if he would not accept, Edward was forced to give in. The Archbishop of Canterbury was sent to summon the rebel lords to Westminster, and on 14 August, in the company of the Earls of Pembroke and Richmond, the king entered Westminster Hall and coldly agreed to the banishment of the Lords Despenser, and that they would be gone by the end of the month. The Marcher lords, it seemed, had won.

Immediately work began on drawing up a formal process against the king's favourites. The accusations against the Despensers were that, although a royal council had been named, of which two bishops, one earl and one baron would be with the king at all times, Hugh Despenser and his father (neither of whom was on the royal council) had become close to the king and taken that role upon themselves unlawfully. This much was true. The Marchers then ascribed to the Despensers the authorship of the 1308 pronouncement that homage was due more to the Crown than the king: a line they themselves had adopted. This was not reasonable, and somewhat undermines the virtue of their position. But the remainder of their accusations against Despenser were substantially correct. The Despensers had limited lords' freedom to see the king; they had removed good ministers (such as Roger) and replaced them with their own men; and they had counselled the king to go in arms to Gloucester against the terms of Magna Carta, thereby provoking war. Hugh Despenser in particular had murdered Llywelyn Bren, had stolen the inheritance of Hugh Audley, had attempted to take that of Roger Damory in order to acquire the whole of the earldom of Gloucester, and had illegally taken the revenues of the estates of the late Earl of Warwick which had rightly been granted to the executors for the benefit of the heir (who was betrothed to Roger's daughter). In addition the Despensers had forced the king to deny hereditary rights in Parliament, so they might acquire them themselves, as in the case of Mowbray. These were the key complaints. There were many more.

For a complete victory, all the Marcher lords now needed was to be acquitted of their own crimes in the conflict. Pardons were granted to the Earls of Hereford and Surrey, Roger, Lord Mortimer of Chirk, Roger Damory, Bartholomew de Badlesmere, John de Mowbray, John Giffard of Brimpsfield, Hugh Audley and his son, Richard de Grey of Codnor, Henry le Tyeys, John Maltravers, Lord Berkeley, Thomas de Berkeley, and a total of 423 of their followers. Their pardon simply stated that they were acquitted of 'anything done' against the Despensers between 1 March and 19 August 1321.[20]

The victory was technically complete.

*

In the fourteenth century the philosophy of the Wheel of Fortune was one with which all people were familiar. It was the cycle of luck which carried men and women to dizzying heights of success and reward, and then tipped over and plunged them into the depths of loss, hardship and humiliation. The Wheel of Fortune now made one of its quickest turns of the fourteenth century, throwing down the Marcher lords who had seemed to sweep all before them, and raising the Despensers from miserable exile to previously undreamed-of heights.

The root of the problem for the Marcher lords lay in the fact that they and their northern allies had been united by their principal enemy, Hugh

Despenser, and he was now banished. Furthermore, unlike Gaveston, who had repeatedly attempted to return from exile, Despenser and his father removed themselves completely. Hugh Despenser became a pirate, robbing any vessels that he could catch, earning a new reputation as 'a sea-monster, lying in wait for merchants as they crossed his path'.[21] His father went to Bordeaux, blaming his losses on his son's greed. Soon the coalition of northern barons, Marcher lords and the Earl of Pembroke, which had brought such pressure to bear on the king over Hugh Despenser, was no longer united.

There was another major factor underlying the Marchers' change of fortunes: the mood of the king. Edward did not care that Hugh Despenser, as a pirate, was jeopardising international relations and damaging English trade, but he cared very greatly about the humiliation he had suffered in being forced to exile his favourite. His determination to exact revenge on the Marcher lords in particular was extraordinary. He believed whole-heartedly that he had been humbled purely for their advantage. Accordingly he put the resources of the realm towards reversing this personal slight and, in so doing, managed to galvanise the many lords who had remained neutral in the recent hostilities into a strong body of royal support. Many of these new royalists were very eager to help the king, for they hoped to win back some of the favour they had lost during Despenser's period in power. As a result, the king was in a much stronger position after Despenser's exile than he was before it. He now had the motive and the means to exact revenge.

Bartholomew de Badlesmere, isolated in Kent, was the first object of his attention.

Less than a month after the departure of the Despensers, Edward went on pilgrimage with Queen Isabella to Canterbury. The king then went on to meet the younger Hugh Despenser alone on the Isle of Thanet, and ordered Queen Isabella to return to London by way of Leeds Castle, which she was to enter if she could by asking for a night's accommodation. Under medieval rules of hospitality, a housekeeper had an obligation to entertain anyone who should ask for shelter, and Lady Badlesmere, who had been left in charge of the castle during her husband's absence, normally would have allowed entry to Isabella and entertained her as a royal guest without a second thought. However, Lord Badlesmere, aware of his delicate position and the heightened state of tension throughout the country, had told his wife not to allow anyone at all into the castle, under any circumstances. On 13 October Isabella asked for accommodation. She was refused. Furious, she ordered her men to try to force the gate. Isabella's company was not equipped to attack a well-defended castle, and nine of her men were killed. Shamed and infuriated, she returned to her husband, and unwittingly provided him with the perfect excuse to raise a royal army to attack Leeds. On 16 October the king announced his intention to make an example of Lord Badlesmere, and the following day he sent the Earls of Pembroke, Richmond and Norfolk to begin the siege.

The garrison of Leeds was under the command of Sir Walter Culpeper. He now saw that overwhelming forces would shortly come against them. Lady Badlesmere nevertheless ordered him to prepare to defend the castle. She sent messages to her husband, who was with Roger and the other Marcher lords at Oxford, to come quickly. Lord Badlesmere asked Roger and the Earl of Hereford to try to relieve the castle. Given his links to Badlesmere, and the marriage bond between their families, Roger could hardly refuse. His uncle and the Earl of Hereford supported him, thinking that everyone who had aided them against Despenser would stand by them now. It was a mistake. By choosing to defend Badlesmere, the Marcher lords were drawn into a new conflict which was not about Hugh Despenser, but about them and their obedience to the king.

Roger and his fellow rebels marched south until they came to Kingston upon Thames. There they halted. Aware of the new trouble, the Earl of Pembroke, the Archbishop of Canterbury and the Bishop of London hurried to meet them. Pembroke urged them not to proceed into Kent. He proposed that if Roger and Lord Hereford retreated, he would mediate with the king on their behalf. They replied that if the siege were raised, and the business discussed in Parliament, they would allow the castle to be surrendered. Pembroke took this message to the embittered king, knowing it would be refused.

At this moment the Earl of Lancaster sent one of the most short-sighted messages of his life. He declared that he did not approve of Roger and Hereford going to Leeds.[22] This instruction, which almost certainly arose out of Lancaster's petty dislike of Badlesmere, put the rebel lords in an awkward position. If the king were to march against them with a significant army, they would need Lancaster's support. They remained at Kingston. With no relieving army on its way, the garrison at Leeds must have suspected that their lives were about to end. The king arrived to conduct the siege personally, and sent for his hunting dogs so that he could hunt Badlesmere's game while he waited for the garrison to capitulate. On 31 October they opened the gates and pleaded for mercy.

Edward had made his point, and he should have left it at that. If he had punished Badlesmere for the insult to Isabella by confiscating the castle, or a few manors, a longer-lasting peace might have been established. But he wanted to make an example of the Leeds garrison. As soon as the king's men-at-arms entered the castle they seized twelve men and hanged them. Sir Walter Culpeper was one of the twelve. His brother Thomas Culpeper was sent to Winchelsea, and publicly killed there. Lady Badlesmere and her children, including her daughter Elizabeth (the eight-year-old wife of Roger's son), were sent to the Tower of London. Badlesmere's sister and her son, Bartholomew de Burghersh, were also sent to the Tower. With the imprisonment of women and children, and the needless execution of men on artificial charges, the tyranny of Edward II had begun.

Roger and Hereford could now see the weakness of their coalition. In order to bolster it they headed north to meet Lancaster. In the words of a contemporary, Roger and the Earl of Hereford 'saw full well that the king was a man without mercy, and thought indeed that he would destroy them as he had done the others, and thus they made their way north-wards as far as Pontefract . . .'[23] There, at the end of November, Lancaster reassured them that they had his full support. Edward, however, had heard of their journey, and forbade them to meet Lancaster. In meeting the northern lords and strengthening the coalition against Edward, Roger and Hereford openly declared their opposition to him.

While they were travelling, the news of the shocking executions of the Leeds Castle garrison reached other rebel lords. Some, like the Earl of Surrey, were cowed by the king's threats. The Earl of Pembroke, who had been so important in securing victory for the Marchers earlier in the year, also sided with the king. But Roger and Hereford remained steadfast in their opposition. They had the Earl of Lancaster's support, Warwick Castle had fallen to their side, and there were stirrings in London in their favour. On 2 December Lancaster wrote to the Londoners stating that he had recently met Roger and the other lords, enclosing for their information the 'Doncaster petition' which Roger and others had sealed. This demanded that the king should stop supporting Despenser in his acts of piracy, and stop pursuing the peers of the realm on Despenser's behalf. The king dismissed it as a further attempt by Lancaster to limit royal authority. The time had come for the Marcher lords' confidence to be put to the test.

The royal army was ordered to muster at Cirencester on 13 December. In the few days beforehand the king increased his pressure on Roger. He ordered him to release Ralph de Gorges, who was still imprisoned at Wigmore. In Ireland, Sir John de Bermingham was given authority to remove all the men appointed by Roger and to appoint new officials, and to review all the acts which Roger had undertaken there in his capacity as Justiciar. It was a vindictive, personal act. Edward was prepared to throw Ireland into disarray just to spite Roger.

Now the tension in the Marcher camp increased to a very high level. They started to withdraw towards Wales, lest they be cut off from their castles by the large royal army mustering at Cirencester. Their allies turned against them – with Despenser banished, they had no reason to refuse a royal summons – and blindly obeyed their king against the royal enemies. The Welsh too took up arms against the Marcher lords, their hated neighbours. In fear, Lord Hastings deserted the rebels, throwing himself on the king's mercy. Then the army left Cirencester and began to advance. At Gloucester the sheriff of the county was accused of supporting Roger. The evidence of his treachery seems to have been his possession of a Marcher tunic of green and yellow. The king's men-at-arms dressed him in it and hanged him.

With the king's large army moving towards them, Roger and Lord Hereford withdrew behind the River Severn. They secured the bridge at Worcester, to which the king came on 31 December. The next crossing place the royal army could use was at Bridgnorth. A royal vanguard raced ahead and secured the bridge there, but on the night of 5 January Roger and his uncle unfurled their banners and charged in upon the king's soldiers. The king's men were defeated with heavy losses, and Roger burnt the bridge and much of the town in the battle.[24] The Mortimers were desperate now. Their forces were being strung out along the river, and their own men were beginning to desert. Remorselessly, the royal army pushed on to the next crossing, at Shrewsbury. Their only hope was that the Earl of Lancaster and the northern barons would come to their aid, as he had promised. But they did not come.

At this point Lord Mortimer of Chirk heard that his own lands in North Wales were being devastated by a Welsh knight, Sir Gruffydd Llwyd, who had remained loyal to the king. Chirk Castle itself had fallen, and the destruction across his lands was great. Clun Castle, held by Roger since the attack on the Despensers, had fallen. John de Charlton's castle of Welshpool had also fallen, and so had Holt. The Marcher lords were being squeezed between a Welsh force and the royal army. Worst of all, it was becoming clear that the Earl of Lancaster was refusing to do anything to help them.

The situation came to a head at Shrewsbury. Roger and his uncle could have held the bridge there, but now saw little point in continued resistance without the Earl of Lancaster's support. Hereford had taken his men north to join Lancaster, and Roger and his uncle were isolated. They could not oppose the king much longer. Perhaps with the noble example of Llywelyn Bren in their minds, they agreed that there was no merit in allowing their men to be killed in a fruitless struggle. They wrote to

Lancaster asking why he had not come as promised. His reply was that it was because they were protecting Bartholomew de Badlesmere, his enemy. Their cause was doomed, all because of Lancaster's petty squabble. Betrayed and alone, Roger and his uncle resolved to abandon Lancaster to his fate, and to petition the king for mercy.

On Wednesday 13 January the king agreed to provide safe conduct until Sunday night for Roger and up to twenty of his companions to come to Betton Strange, near Shrewsbury, 'to treat with the Earls of Richmond, Pembroke, Arundel and Warenne'. The pressure on the king to allow Roger to negotiate is clear from the fact that, in addition to these four earls, Norfolk and Kent also requested that Roger's safe conduct be granted. But the negotiations were not successful, and Sunday night came around with no agreement. Letters of safe conduct were renewed, to last until Wednesday 20 January. The Mortimers were discussing a situation which could end in their deaths, and resisted being rushed into an agreement which did not guarantee their lives and liberty. Ominously, the king was not prepared to guarantee them anything. On 20 January time was running out. That day Roger received a further extension to submit to the king the following day. But still he did not submit.

The earls were anxious now, being detained against their better judgement while Roger negotiated, demanding his life be guaranteed. Elsewhere, especially in the north, other rebel lords were waiting to see how the Mortimers would be treated. Laying aside the king's bitterness, the Mortimers had done nothing for which they deserved punishment, except their attack on Bridgnorth. Both men were far too valuable and experienced as royal servants to be imprisoned or executed, surely? But Edward was, by this stage, almost deranged with his lust for revenge, and demanded their total and complete surrender, without terms. Again the Mortimers refused.

The stalemate was only broken when Lord Pembroke lied to the Mortimers. With no authority from the king, he took matters into his own hands, and promised Roger and his uncle that their lives would be spared, and that they would be pardoned. Having acquired this apparent guarantee, there was nothing else to be gained by further negotiation. On Friday 22 January 1322 Roger and his elderly uncle were conducted into the hall of Shrewsbury Castle, to submit to the king. After a short unfriendly audience, they were ordered to be taken away. They were not pardoned, they were clapped in chains. They were to be sent to the most secure prison in the country: the Tower of London.

EIGHT

The King's Prisoner

The day after Roger surrendered to the king at Shrewsbury, a contingent of men-at-arms approached Wigmore.[1] They rode through the main street of the small town and turned to the west, taking the gently rising road to the castle and under the brow of the low hill on which stood the ancient parish church. Further on they came to the outer courtyard, and presented their letters of appointment to the gatekeeper. Here, on the ridge leading to the castle itself, they passed barns and granaries, cow byres, pigsties, hay lofts and cart houses, and heard the lowing cattle and saw the strutting peacocks about the yard. Beyond them stood the high-standing walls and towers of the castle itself. Crossing over the drawbridge, their leader, Alan de Charlton, addressed Roger's castellan, showed his letters of appointment, and reiterated what King Edward had declared: the castle was forfeit by reason of Roger's rebellion against the king.

It was a pattern repeated all across England. Everything Roger owned was forfeited. Every castle and every manor house, every manorial right and every feudal loyalty. The cattle on his farms were confiscated. So too were the buildings and carts his manorial tenants used to farm his land. Everything was taken into the king's custody. This extended even to his personal possessions: his armour, carpets, wall-hangings, silverware and all his clothes and linen were forfeited; even his wife's books. In surrendering himself to the king he was also surrendering everything he held by right of his lordship or owned as a matter of inheritance. He was left with nothing but the clothes he wore on the day of his surrender.

Adam de Charlton's men inspected the entire castle, from the small chambers in the towers to the keep high up on its mound overlooking the buildings in the bailey. His subsequent inventory of what he found is still extant.[2] For a study of Roger it is invaluable, since it gives us a rare glimpse of the things which he and his wife owned, and an insight into their personal tastes.

There was a large amount of war machinery in the castle. There were six siege engines, called springalds: huge flat crossbow-like wooden machines for flinging rocks and massive bolts. Several similar machines had bombarded Bristol under the co-direction of Roger in 1316. There were twenty-one windlass-operated crossbows, and eighteen foot-operated ones. Although we do not know how large these were, their prominence in the inventory suggests that they were not merely small arms but instruments of strategic warfare. Two hundred and ninety iron crossbow bolts were found, some flighted with brass and some with wood, indicative of a sophisticated, multipurpose nature.

As one might expect, there was a large quantity of armour. Some of this was specialist jousting equipment, including nine helmets and one 'jousting coronet'. Other items were specifically for war, such as the unambiguous 'war helmet'. Among the remainder were two 'suits of plate armour', two helmets 'with visors' as well as a large quantity of older weaponry and items which might have been used in practice combat, such as leather breastplates, suits of body armour, iron and leather helmets. There were collections of lances and shields, lance-shafts and lance-heads, pavilions and tents, indicating that Roger had stored much of his old tournament armour at Wigmore, and that, while he and his men carried their newest war armour with them to Kent and finally to Shrewsbury, the armoury at Wigmore was full of memorabilia: a Saracen arbalest (steel crossbow) and arrows, and an Irish sparth (axe), being two of the more unusual items.

Mixed in among the weaponry were a few hunting tools, such as drums for scaring game and snares and nets for catching animals. Luxury items included a chessboard painted with gold, and another 'gaming board' made of aromatic nutmeg. But there were few luxuries laid aside at Wigmore. Most of the rest of the inventory records everyday practical items: shackles, hooks for pulling down burning wooden buildings and thatch, chests and coffers, table boards, benches, cauldrons and barrels. Eleven wooden vats or tubs were found in the kitchens. The whole picture was one of a castle furnished with the essential rudiments of life. This was where Roger kept his old armour and a few necessary chattels. It was not where he kept his gold or jewels.

To Alan de Charlton it was clear that these items were just the vestiges of the lord's possessions. Where were his spare clothes? Where was his finest armour? Where indeed were his wall-hangings? It was not surprising that they were absent. Medieval lords travelled with a great many of their personal possessions as they journeyed with the court. As it happened, since Roger had never anticipated being imprisoned, de Charlton only had to look as far as Wigmore Abbey. Here he found another huge array of personal arms and armour of very high quality. His men carried it out piece by piece and loaded it on to the wagons to be taken away to be sold. Roger's personal armour alone included eight chain-mail shirts, an iron corset, a pair of gussets (chainmail between pieces of plate armour), a lined gorger (throat-plate), seven pairs of armoured leggings, five chain-mail head coverings, two iron helmets with visors, one war helmet with a 'wicket' (criss-crossed metal face piece), one round iron helmet, one padded tunic covered with brown taffeta, a shirt 'of Chartres' (probably a padded shirt for jousting), five pairs of horses' head-armour, five pairs of iron flank protectors for horses, two pairs of iron covers for horses, two pairs of trappers, a pair of greaves, a pair of shoes of plate armour, a shield, four lances for war, three lances for jousting, a pair of boots topped with iron, and two swords with silver fittings, as well as a small pile of other pieces of plate armour for head, arm, foot, hand, throat and leg protection.

At Wigmore Abbey, Charlton also found Roger's wardrobe: his personal possessions other than his armour and weapons. The clothes found there, which, of course, were those Roger had left behind in 1321–2, show that he was a man of fashion. They included:

Two short jackets of green velvet

A tunic, two supertunics [topmost garments] and a tabard [sleeve-less tunic] of scarlet, without fur or hood

A tunic, two supertunics, tabard and hood of mixed brown cloth, without fur

A tunic of indigo velvet

A supertunic and tabard of scarlet red for summer, without hood

A tunic, two supertunics, tabard and hood of mulberry brown cloth

A supertunic of green with a quarter yellow or grey, and hood lined with red muslin

One black hat furred with high grade lambskin.

The warlord was a man of taste. In addition to fine clothes, and the nutmeg gaming table and gold painted chess set from the castle, his wardrobe keeper also looked after:

One green bedcover embroidered with owls, with four matching hanging carpets

One bedcover with a blue background with several coats of arms embroidered, with three matching hangings

One bedcover of knotted work, with four matching hangings

One great hanging tapestry for a [great] hall embroidered with popinjays and griffons

Two yellow hangings, old and made into curtains, embroidered
   with red roses, with one benchcover of the same work
One hanging of good and subtle work with four matching hangings
One long benchcover striped with yellow and red.

In addition there was an abundance of cloth, including long lengths of 'good striped cloth', 'striped cloth of lower price', 'yellow striped cloth of small value', 'yellow unstriped cloth', 'green unstriped cloth', and 'striped dark blue cloth', some of which may well have gone to furnish Mortimer family retainers with surcoats bearing the family arms, or possibly the yellow and green tunics of the Marcher rebels in 1321. Two final items of interest on the list were 'a brass horn that, together with a certain falchion [a broad, curved sword] . . . is the charter of the lands of Wigmore'. The horn (but apparently not the falchion) were also carried off to become just a horn hung around someone's nect rather than a relic of the family's ancient lordship.

Just as interesting as the list of items belonging to Roger is the separate list which was made for Joan's possessions at the abbey. Not only are such inventories of ladies' possessions rare at this period (as indeed are those for men), this one may be regarded as perhaps more complete than most as Joan was present at the abbey, and so any valuable effects with which she travelled were included. The list in full is as follows:

One wall-hanging, four carpets, one benchcover of a fashion, with
   the Mortimer arms
Four carpets of another type
Four carpets of good and subtle work
Three chequered bedcovers
One red bedcover
One mattress covered with fine linen
Two mattresses covered with canvas
Eight blankets
One red cover furred with miniver
One fustian for the bed
One counterpain for the bed
Fifteen pairs of linen sheets
Three pairs of muslin curtains
One pair of striped muslin curtains
One pair of curtains of striped linen
One pair of red linen curtains
One curtain of white pannelled linen

Two tunics of 'cloth of Thars', of which one is green and the
  other brown
Two supertunics of indigo silk without fur
Three supertunics of brown silk without fur
One tunic and two supertunics of red 'cloth of Thars'
One uncut violet wool cloth
One tunic, two supertunics, one mantel and one hat without fur,
  of mixed brown cloth
One new fur of miniver for a supertunic, and another for a hood
Two red Irish *fallaings*
One old white Irish *fallaing*
One piece of cloth for three altar cloths
One table cloth for a dinner table
Two 'double' towels
Three small towels
Twenty-two ells of linen cloth
One long towel
Three sanap cloths [table under-cloths]
One small piece of linen cloth of double thickness
Two wool cushions of stitched work
One psalter
Four books of 'romances' [stories of chivalry]
Two chests, of which one contains two striped red velvet cloths,
  one comb, one ivory mirror, one small ivory image of the
  Virgin Mary, one ivory scourge [whip?], one belt decorated with
  enamel and precious stones belonging to one of her daughters.
  The second chest contains one enamelled mirror, and one set of
  ivory chessmen, one empty strong box, two wash basins.
Lastly, two silver basins, six silver dishes, four silver salt cellars, and
  two silver cups found with Lady Mortimer.

This list says much about women in a noble household in 1322; for instance, about the provision of washing facilities, and the use of changes of cloth as marks of both wealth and cleanliness. The household Joan controlled was luxurious but not excessively so. She and her husband lived in a style befitting their chivalric and military position. But the list reveals above all that Lady Mortimer was not spared her husband's fate. Her possessions too were loaded on to carts and sent off to be sold or (in the case of the silverware found with her) presented to the king. Lady Mortimer herself was arrested at the abbey and taken under guard to be imprisoned in Hampshire. With her were sent the six men of her household: a knight, Richard de Burgh;

two men-at-arms, William de Ockley and John de Bullesdon; her strikingly named chaplain, Richard Judas, and her two clerks, John de Eldecote and Walter de Evesham.[3]

For modern writers as well as contemporaries this is one of the most shocking aspects of government under Edward and Despenser: women were punished along with their husbands for their husbands' perceived 'crimes'. A precedent had been set with the imprisonment of Llywelyn Bren's wife in 1317, and of Lady Badlesmere in the Tower the previous year. Now Joan, heiress of the de Geneville family in her own right, and a kinswoman of the Earl of Pembroke, was stripped of her belongings and incarcerated. Not since Edward I had exposed the female relations of Robert Bruce in wooden cages had women been treated so harshly. One by one the rebels' wives suffered a similar fate to Joan. With their mothers as well as their fathers in prison, the children of the lords who had dared to oppose Edward II were also incarcerated. Roger's two eldest sons, Edmund and Roger, were imprisoned with the children of the Earl of Hereford at Windsor. His youngest son John was kept under guard in Hampshire. Geoffrey, Roger's third son, would also have been imprisoned had he not been in France at the time of the arrest, probably serving in the household of the de Fiennes family. Three of Roger's eldest four daughters were imprisoned, Maud alone being allowed to remain free owing to her marriage to John de Charlton of Powys, who was pardoned by Edward. In the general enthusiasm to persecute entire families, even aged relatives were not spared. Roger's mother, Margaret de Fiennes, almost lost Radnor Castle and all her household possessions there. Only some outraged complaints, which reveal her to have been a woman of some spirit, prevented her dower lands being confiscated too. Embarrassed by the mistake, the king returned her rightful inheritance to her.[4]

Wigmore was left empty of its lord's possessions, a mere shell. It became a royal castle, but the king had little need of a fortress on the Marches, now that the Marcher lords were divided. In effect it became a royal farmhouse, a place of accounting for the produce of the manor, the revenue from which was supplied to the Exchequer. When, at a late stage in Alan de Charlton's examination of the castle, a chest of documents was found relating to the Mortimer inheritance, this too was packed up and despatched to the royal treasury at the Tower, where its contents were listed and sorted into chests by the king's clerks. All trace of the Mortimer family's lordship of Wigmore was wiped away, with the exception of the painted effigies of the dead warriors lying in their graves in the abbey church, and the family arms in the stained glass shining down on them.

*

Roger and his uncle arrived at the Tower of London 'after dinner on the eve of St Valentine's day', 13 February 1322.[5] They were led through to the inner courtyard, and into the medieval palace. There they were separated. Roger was taken up to a high, narrow cell, 'less civilised than the rooms he was used to', as one chronicler put it, and left to consider his fate.

He knew little of what was going on in the rest of the country, and this must have been infuriating for a man usually at the centre of events. Scraps of news had reached him on his journey to London, passed to him by Herefordshire merchants still loyal and bold enough to bring messages. But such men were few; and they were treated very harshly if caught.[6] Once the doors of his cell had swung shut on him, there was very little news to be had of the outside world. His sole source of information was the castle garrison, as they came and went from his cell.

Roger would have been shocked to hear what was happening elsewhere. He would have been infuriated at the imprisonment of his wife, and he would have been roused to similar anger by Despenser's renewed onslaught on the family of Llywelyn Bren. The Welshman's widow and family were all taken into custody by Despenser on royal authority, and so too were their allies in Wales, including Rhys and Philip ap Howell, friends of the Mortimer family. Edward even took action against clergymen. Bishop Orleton was accused openly of helping the Mortimers to defy the king on their retreat in November 1321. In addition to removing the bishop's income, the king wrote to the Pope asking that Orleton and the Bishops of Lincoln (Henry de Burghersh) and Bath and Wells (John Droxford) should be removed from their offices and exiled for supporting Roger. The Pope refused, angry that Edward should ask such a thing without presenting evidence. This was an important move by the Pope. At a stroke he had demonstrated that the king would never be able to eliminate all opposition as he would not be able to remove the bishops from their sees.

The Mortimers' fate following their surrender was closely observed by their fellow rebels. The Earl of Hereford, who had also been prepared to submit to the king, now realised that he too faced imprisonment, and possibly death, and joined forces with the Earl of Lancaster and the northern barons. Hugh Audley the elder had decided to come with the two Mortimers to Shrewsbury to give himself up, as a loyal king's man. A few days later Lord Berkeley followed suit. But no other Marchers followed them. It was clear that a great battle would be fought in the north, and the fates of Roger and his uncle depended on the success of the man who had hitherto always let them down: the Earl of Lancaster.

For more than a month Roger languished in his cell, knowing nothing of his fate, or the king's actions. His captors had a mere 3d per day for his custody, indicating he was kept in very poor conditions, although not actually starved.[7] It must have seemed that he would receive the worst punishment the king felt inclined to administer. Then, at the end of March, news of events in the north filtered through to London.

Lancaster was dead.

As Edward had marched north, he had summoned men from all over England, even from the clergy and his lands in France. The French king too had been asked to send men. At Lichfield his forces had been strengthened by the return of Hugh Despenser and his father. Fearful of the size of Edward's army, and his unmistakeable purpose, men had begun to desert the Earl of Lancaster. Even Lancaster's own steward, Robert de Holand, had left him. In desperation Lancaster had summoned men to him on the pretence that he needed an army to defend the north against the Scots. Hardly anyone obeyed. Contemporaries were amazed at the transformation: the power of this once mighty prince had simply melted away. His failure to support the Mortimers had made his opposition seem unprincipled, weak and self-interested. Few were prepared to defend him.

Many of Lancaster's allies now pleaded with him to let them throw themselves on the king's mercy, but Lancaster refused. He had ruled the north like a king for years, and would not bow before Edward. Nor would he permit his vassals to do so. But his authority was almost gone. When the king besieged Tutbury Castle, Lancaster's remaining supporters were panic-stricken. They called him to councel at Pontefract, and begged him to retreat north to his great castle of Dunstanburgh. But Lancaster would have none of it, and pointed out that men would say that he was a traitor seeking sanctuary with the Scots. He was convinced that his royal status gave him an immunity from the king's wrath, and that he had nothing to fear from continued opposition. His vassals and allies were more vulnerable. Only a naked blade drawn in his face by Lord Clifford persuaded Lancaster that retreat was the only reasonable course of action. Hereford and the others persuaded him to make for Boroughbridge, a crossing over the River Ure in Yorkshire, about twenty miles north-east of York.

It was a fatal mistake. Both armies were riddled with spies, and a man in Lancaster's ranks informed Sir Andrew de Harclay, Sheriff of Carlisle, about the plan to retreat by way of Boroughbridge. De Harclay roused the men of the counties of Cumberland and Westmorland, and, by forcing them to march through the night, reached the bridge first. As Hereford and Lancaster approached on 16 March 1322, they realised that they would have to fight their way across. With the king's army to the south, they were trapped.

The earls surveyed the battlefield. Besides the bridge there was also a ford, where de Harclay had stationed a number of pikemen. They decided that the Earl of Hereford and Lord Clifford would attack the bridge, while Lancaster would attack the ford with his cavalry. It must have seemed a relatively straightforward task, but they underestimated the redoubtable de Harclay. From long experience fighting the Scots, he knew well how to defend a strategic point, and the rebels were acting in haste, and consequently did not prepare their attack on the bridge with sufficient care. De Harclay's men were drawn up in Scottish *schiltrom* formations, preventing the knights from charging. Hereford led the fight on the bridge, but he and his men were caught in the arrow fire. Then one of de Harclay's pikemen, concealed beneath the bridge, thrust upwards between the planks and skewered the Earl of Hereford through the anus, twisting the head of the iron pike into his intestines. His dying screams turned the advance into panic. Lancaster, amazed, and finding no easy way to cross the river with the arrows coming at him thick and fast, called off the attack, and withdrew from the river, promising to return the next morning, either to do battle or surrender.

That night, the men of the dead Earl of Hereford deserted, many of them leaving their armour in their tents and creeping away in borrowed or stolen old clothes, pretending to be peasants or beggars.

At first light de Harclay, whose scouts had kept an eye on the desertions throughout the night, seized the initiative. He crossed the bridge and moved towards Lord Lancaster. In a short while the Battle of Boroughbridge was all over. Most of the leading lords who had opposed the king, including the Earl of Lancaster, were led to gaol in York.

This was the news that came to London: all opposition to King Edward and Hugh Despenser had been defeated in battle at Boroughbridge. The Earl of Hereford and Lord Damory, two of Roger's closest political allies, were dead. But what was truly shocking, and what astounded the whole country, was what happened to the lords who surrendered to de Harclay or who were captured by him. Six northern barons were drawn and hanged at Pontefract immediately. The Earl of Lancaster was judged by a tribunal of lords, including the two Despensers and the king. He was not allowed to speak in his defence, nor to have anyone speak for him. He was sentenced to be drawn to the gallows, hanged and beheaded. As a mark of respect for his royal blood, the king spared him the indignity of being drawn and hanged. Instead he was dressed in an old surcoat and taken on an ass a mile from his castle of Pontefract, and there beheaded in the king's presence.

This was clearly a tremendous blow to Roger. He had not had the strength to defeat Edward himself, but with the forces of the Earl of Lancaster he and Hereford might have done so. The failure of the Earl of Lancaster to support him had forced him to surrender; but equally it had meant the end of Lancaster too, for on the surrender of Roger and his uncle, the whole opposition movement had faltered. Indeed, when one looks back over the whole anti-Despenser campaign, it emerges as a rebellion heavily dependent on Roger Mortimer and Hereford. It was these two who had led the Marcher attacks on the Despensers, and it was entirely Marcher demands which were presented at Westminster. It was a Mortimer ally, Bartholomew de Badlesmere, who was attacked at Leeds Castle, and it was the Mortimers after whom Edward had taken the royal army at the end of 1321. Roger and Hereford may thus be seen as the focus of the king's attention and the prime movers of the rebellion. Lancaster had merely tried to influence royal favouritism from his lands in the north, an old game which he had played often, but which was in reality a continual bluff. When the Mortimers were removed from the opposition, Lancaster could do nothing to stop the king, even with the worthy Earl of Hereford on his side.

What Roger could not have foreseen, and what indeed the rest of the country could not believe, was the extent of Edward's vengeance. Not only did he hang the northern barons and behead Lancaster, he brought back the Marchers and southern lords to have them killed too.[8] Bartholomew de Badlesmere was taken to Canterbury. There he was dragged to the gallows and hanged beside his nephew, Sir Bartholomew Ashburnham. His head was cut off and exhibited as that of a traitor. Sir Henry le Tyeys, a supporter of Roger who had gone north to fight with Lancaster, was drawn and hanged at London. Sir Francis Aldenham was drawn and hanged at Windsor. Sir John de Mowbray and Sir Roger de Clifford were drawn and hanged at York and their corpses left to decompose on the gallows. Sir Henry de Montfort and Sir Henry de Willington were drawn and hanged at Bristol. More than a dozen peers were killed or executed, and many more knights were killed or died in prison. Hundreds were served crippling fines which acted as security against any future dissent.[9] All opposition to the king had been ruthlessly and very visibly crushed.

Now it seemed it was Roger's turn to suffer the king's retribution. But first Edward headed north, to wage an utterly unsuccessful campaign against the Scots. It was not for another three months that he began to think about his Tower prisoners. Roger's henchman, Hugh de Turpington, who had now served Roger loyally for more than twelve years, was accused of complicity in Roger's 'rebellion' and lost his lands. In June Roger and his uncle were tried for their damage to the king's lands at Newport. On 13 July a complete review of Roger's government of Ireland was ordered, notwithstanding the letter from the community of Dublin commending

Roger's service. Finally, the day after the Irish order, the king at York appointed a jury to sit in London to try Roger and his uncle for treason.

A few days later, the constable of the Tower removed the Mortimers from their cells, and took them to Westminster Hall. There they confronted their judges: Walter de Norwich, Chief Baron of the Exchequer; Sir John de Friskeney, another Baron of the Exchequer; Sir William de Harley and John de Stonor, two judges, and Hamo de Chigwell, the mayor of London. With the exception of the last-named man, this was as impartial a jury as the Mortimers could have wished. But all five men knew they were not expected to produce an impartial verdict. On 21 July they concluded their deliberations. Roger and his uncle were told that each:

> having contrary to his allegiance levied war against his sovereign lord along with Humphery de Bohun, Earl of Hereford (now dead), Roger Damory (now dead), Bartholomew Badlesmere (now dead), John Giffard of Brimpsfield (now dead) and Henry Tyeys (now dead), and having traitorously taken the town and castle of Gloucester and feloniously plundered the king's goods there, and having afterwards as a traitor and enemy, with his banner displayed as in war, ridden to Bridgnorth, assaulted and plundered the king's people there, killing some and wounding others, and burnt the town, and with banner displayed as in war, both before and after, rode in arms destroying and robbing the king's people. All these crimes are notorious, and the king records them against him. This court therefore awards that for these treasons he be drawn, and for arsons, robberies and homicides he be hanged.[10]

The king was satisfied. But in his moment of victory he began to have doubts about the Mortimers' fates, and the renewed opposition that killing his own kin and longstanding servants would have in the wake of the Boroughbridge executions. With Lancaster gone, it seemed he had little to fear from Roger and his sixty-six-year-old uncle. Upon hearing the news of the sentence, he commuted it to perpetual imprisonment. The Mortimers' lands and possessions remained forfeit, and they and their families remained incarcerated in their respective castles and priories, but their lives were spared.

*

All England now lay in the hands of Edward II and Hugh Despenser. Every notable opponent was dead or in prison. Every lord who had so far remained obedient was too terrified to voice dissent. At the York parliament of 1322 Edward enacted a Statute revoking all previous Ordinances which restricted his authority and prohibiting any further attempts to control his power. There would be no royal council, nor would the king be accountable in any way to Parliament. The lords, prelates and commons of the realm were henceforth expected to consent to his will. If they did not, they were expected to suffer his will in silence. Any questioning of the king's authority would be regarded as treason. Parliament became merely an advisory council.

With no check on the king's power, Despenser assumed two roles: that of first minister and that of arch-bully. In the former guise he exhorted the king to gather a large treasury, taking money from whomsoever he could, and paying out nothing unless he absolutely had to, even where he was in debt. In his bullying role, any 'rebels' he wished to constrain were threatened with such crippling fines that they could not possibly step out of line. He took any lands he fancied. Some manors of Roger Mortimer of Chirk and dower lands of the widow of the Earl of Lancaster were made over to Despenser by the king. But these were not the only victims. Even the king's own brother, Thomas of Brotherton, Earl of Norfolk, was forced to rent out lands to Despenser for a nominal amount. Later he was forced to sell them for a ridiculously small sum. Worst of all, Elizabeth, the widow of Roger Damory and the king's own niece, was forced to surrender the lordship of Usk (worth £770 per year) in return for that of Gower (worth £300 per year). Despenser forced her to do this in the king's name, through his control of royal agents, despite the fact that she was his own sister-in-law. He then sought Gower's confiscation on behalf of William de Braose. Thus Lady Damory, the sorry sister and co-heiress of the late Earl of Gloucester, was left with almost nothing of her rightful inheritance.

It would be tedious and depressing to list all of Despenser's misdealings. Through extraordinary connivance, intrigue, extortion, oppression and royal nepotism he acquired whatever he wanted. Lands, money, influence, and prestige all flooded his way. It was only a matter of time before he sought the final victory over Roger. About a year after Roger was condemned, Despenser decided that he would obtain an order from the king for him to be put to death. And what Despenser requested, the king invariably granted.

Despenser had a problem, however, in the person of Queen Isabella.

Isabella hated Despenser's ruthlessness and his manipulation of her husband. She abhorred the tyranny that he had brought on the country, especially the incarceration of so many noblewomen. She loathed the vindictiveness with which he sought revenge on his enemies, and the degree to which he and the king punished whole communities, including the

Londoners. When she had come to London as a young, terrified princess, it had been the citizens above all others who had welcomed her with flags and gaiety, and she had always remained fond of the citizens. Now they were suffering increased taxation from the king on Despenser's advice. As for the imprisoned children, Isabella lamented to see them separated from their families. Despenser was constantly undermining her respect and authority. In late 1322 she decided she had no choice but to act against him, as she believed was right.

For Isabella the breaking point was the English campaign to Scotland in the summer after Boroughbridge. Like all Edward's other Scottish campaigns, this was completely disastrous. Unlike all his earlier disasters, however, Isabella was there in person, close to the border, at Tynemouth Abbey. When the Scots surprised Edward and Despenser at Blackhow moor, the king and his favourite fled, leaving Isabella to the mercy of Robert Bruce.[11] Knowing that Bruce's own mistress and sister had received precious little mercy from Edward I, being exposed in wooden cages on the walls of Berwick and Roxburgh castles for three years, this was an outstandingly callous act. It was only due to Isabella's quick thinking and determination that she managed to escape. Although the coastal routes were controlled by the Scots' Flemish allies, she managed to find a boat prepared to take her to England. Two of her ladies-in-waiting died in the desperate flight from Tynemouth.

As Isabella once again found herself safe on English soil she knew her future course of action: to work towards the release of Roger Mortimer and the overthrow of the Despensers. She was well aware of the dangers, and she knew that any move had to be made in the greatest secrecy. Even to pass a message to Roger was fraught with difficulty. Direct action was even more dangerous. In late 1322 Robert le Ewer was executed by being crushed to death in a linen shirt under a load of iron, over the course of several days, for his part in an attack on the elder Despenser (now titled the Earl of Winchester), in which the Mortimers were believed to have been involved.[12] But Isabella heard that Edward was travelling to the Tower of London, and knew she would soon have an opportunity to act.

Her chance came within a couple of months. In January 1323, as the royal party neared London, Lord Berkeley almost escaped from Wallingford Castle. Certain members of his household arranged to visit him for a feast, and the imprisoned lord invited his gaolers to join them. With a stunning lack of care for security, the guards fell straight into the trap. The men of the Berkeley household drew concealed weapons and threatened to kill them. A further twenty men were allowed into the castle. Their plan was thwarted when a boy living in the outer gatehouse guessed what was happening, and told the mayor of the town, who besieged the castle, and warned the Earls of Kent and Winchester, who were in the vicinity. Lord Berkeley was apprehended in the castle chapel.

Edward and Despenser hastened towards Wallingford to interrogate Berkeley in person, leaving Isabella at the Tower. She was there on 3 February, when she dined with her son, and again on the 17th.[13] While scholars in the past have argued there is no evidence that Isabella was in touch with Roger at this stage, this is not necessarily correct, as on the latter occasion she wrote to the Treasurer on behalf of Lady Mortimer, Roger's wife, who was being badly treated. At that time Joan was in the custody of the Sheriff of Hampshire. Thus Isabella had access to inside information which directly connected her to Roger's wife while she was in the same building as Roger. Although it is clear from other evidence that normally Roger was kept very securely under lock and key, it is also clear that he was able to smuggle letters out of the castle. While we cannot be sure that Isabella received the message about Lady Mortimer from Roger himself, the most probable explanation as to how she learnt that Joan was being mistreated was that Roger informed her. It is thus more likely than not that Isabella was colluding with Roger in February 1323.

This begs the question of the nature of Roger's relationship with Isabella. A meeting on or just before 17 February 1323 does not demonstrate anything more than that they were in contact. However, if Roger passed a message to Isabella, on which she acted, it does suggest they had an understanding. That they were drawn to each other, and were impressed with each other, is not in doubt, given later events. They were both well-born, intelligent, sophisticated people. But the only evidence of the two of them acting together lies in the queen taking up Roger's championing of a disgraced chamberlain of North Wales ten years earlier.[14] While this absence of evidence should not be taken as an indication that they were not in contact, one should not assume at this point that their liaison was anything more than a political one. As to the question of what Isabella could do to help Roger, this is perhaps answered by her returning to court soon afterwards.[15] The likelihood is that Roger asked Isabella to spy on her husband, and to report any discovery by the king of any plots to free him.

Isabella was not the only person to be working towards Roger's freedom. Under interrogation, Lord Berkeley confessed that his attempted escape was just the first part of an elaborate plan to release Roger from the Tower. Thomas de Newbiggin was arrested in South Wales for plotting to free him. Roger himself was working on an escape plan.[16] He had persuaded the sub-lieutenant of the Tower, Gerard d'Alspaye, to help him. D'Alspaye was probably the man smuggling Roger's letters out of the Tower, and passing them on to Roger's contacts among the monastic clergy and London merchants, most notably John de Gisors and Richard de Bethune. In this way Roger was able to communicate with his network of powerful ecclesiastical supporters, such as the Bishops of Hereford (Adam of Orleton), Bath and Wells (John Droxford), Lincoln (Henry de Burghersh), and Ely (John de Hothum), and the Archbishop of Dublin (Alexander Bicknor), all of whom were beyond Edward II's power. Unfortunately his letters to the Priors of Leominster and Wormsley and the Abbot of Wigmore were intercepted.[17] As a result of these plots and Roger's intercepted letters, Edward and Hugh Despenser realised that they would not be safe until Roger was dead. Roger would not have survived much longer if there had not been a spy in the royal household, almost certainly Isabella, who now sent word to London that Roger's murder was planned for early August.[18]

The first of August was the feast of St Peter ad Vincula – St Peter in Chains – the patron saint of the Tower, whose chapel occupied a corner of the inner ward. At the time of the evening meal, most of the garrison made their way to the hall of the royal palace and, seated at the long tables there, began their festive eating and drinking. From the kitchen the cook sent out the meats and various dishes; from the buttery the butler produced the wine to be drunk on the special occasion of the feast. The castle gates were shut, and the prisoners locked in their cells. Almost all the men were present, carousing, with the exceptions only of the gate keepers and perhaps the occasional tower watchman. Stephen de Segrave, the lieutenant in charge of the castle, and Gerard d'Alspaye, the sub-lieutenant, sat among them. But d'Alspaye did not drink. More wine was offered, and slowly the hall filled with drunk, drugged, stumbling men. Stephen de Segrave himself lay unconscious. In the silence which followed, d'Alspaye hurried, with a crowbar and a rope ladder, to the cell in which Roger was locked up with another man, Richard de Monmouth.

The light was dim, but d'Alspaye had to work fast, with only a candle to see by. The door to the cell was heavily barred and padlocked so d'Alspaye had to lever out the stones one by one with the crowbar. The mortar being old, it gave way easily, and soon the first stones fell from the wall. Inside Roger had been praying to St Peter for help. He had sworn a vow that, if successful, he would build a chapel to the saint at Ludlow.[19] Within a short while there was a ragged hole, and a few moments later Roger pushed his way through, followed by de Monmouth.[20] Quickly the three men descended the stairs and made their way into the building next door, which was the kitchen of the king's palace. There the cook, who had been informed about the escape, turned a blind eye as the three men climbed up through the huge chimney on to the roof. In the moonless night Roger and his accomplices felt their way across to the wall, and scrambled over the edge, using a rope ladder brought by d'Alspaye, and climbed down the high walls into the outer ward. From there they slung another rope ladder over the outer curtain wall and climbed up, and by the same rope ladder swiftly let themselves down the outer face to the river bank and into the marshy waters of the Thames. In the darkness they found two men waiting with a small boat. The three fugitives were rowed across the river to Greenwich, where four of Roger's men-at-arms were in readiness, with spare horses. Without pausing for a moment, they mounted and rode off into the night.

Within hours there were men-at-arms in pursuit, riding along the highways up to the Marches, and to the king and Despenser to let them know the news. But they did not find Roger. They presumed he would be heading either to Wales or the south coast, probably Dover. Roger and his men knew that that was what they would expect, and went an indirect way. As the king's men searched for him on the Dover road he was hurrying to Portchester, keeping out of sight of the guards on the highways. Near Portchester he was led to a place to which one Alice de Boarhunt had arranged for a boatswain from the Isle of Wight to bring a small vessel at the request of a London merchant, Ralph de Bocton.[21] Roger and his six companions embarked. He ordered the boatswain to take him to the Isle of Wight, where one of de Bocton's sea-going vessels was waiting to take him to Normandy. Within thirty-six hours of his escape he was out of the country.

Roger was not just at liberty. In attaining his own freedom he had become the most powerful symbol of freedom for all other Englishmen labouring under the tyranny of Edward II and Hugh Despenser. The chroniclers wrote of Roger as following God's will, and being guided by an angel from his cell like St Peter himself. Later he would say that he knew truly that his escape was ordained by God through His mercy, and that he had been freed from the king's hands for a purpose.

NINE

The King's Enemy

The king was thrown into a fury on hearing of Roger's escape. For the last eighteen months he had governed England with little or no check on his power. Suddenly he was thrown back to the days of the opposition of Thomas of Lancaster, except that Lancaster had been neither a clever man nor a difficult man to track down. Roger, on the other hand, was a sophisticated strategist and, more worryingly for Edward, he was nowhere to be found.

Edward was at Kirkham when he was told the news. From there he sent messengers to all the sheriffs and all the keepers of the peace in England to proclaim that 'all and singular who are in the king's peace shall pursue with hue and cry Roger Mortimer of Wigmore, the king's rebel . . . , and that they shall arrest him alive or dead . . .'. The king also declared that any who were contrary or slow in their pursuit should be punished as abettors. He ordered spies to watch all the ports and to inquire whether Roger had yet crossed the sea, and, if so, who had taken him, and whither he had gone. Letters were sent to the constables of eighty castles, instructing them to ensure that all their prisoners were kept securely and that their garrisons were on the highest alert. The king also sent orders to the Justiciar of Wales to prepare all the Welsh castles for war, and he wrote to Sir John de Bermingham in Ireland for the castles there to be secured against Roger. All tournaments throughout the country were banned. Finally, Edward ordered the Bishop of Exeter, Walter de Stapeldon, to go to the Tower of London and take over from Stephen de Segrave. Edward was so unsure of his authority in the city that he ordered the bishop to go in his capacity as Treasurer, and only after entering was he to show his commission to take control of the castle.[1]

Throughout August the desperate commands continued, each one naming Roger as 'the king's rebel' or 'the king's enemy', but none betraying any knowledge of his whereabouts. By the 26th the king seems to have become convinced that Roger had left the country and was sailing to Ireland, as on that day he ordered the Earl of Kent to seize three Irish ships off the coast of Dover. He was still convinced that Roger was in Ireland two days later, when he sent letters to all the principal Irish lords, including several of Roger's own vassals, ordering them to pursue him. Mayors of ports were ordered to search every item coming into and going out of the country for letters to or from Roger. The court was in complete panic. Edward fully expected Roger immediately to gather an army from his lands in Ireland, Wales and the Marches, and to come to do battle. But Roger was not so foolish as to attempt a confrontation without due preparation.

By the end of September the king's spy network had established that Roger was in Picardy, in France, staying with his uncle and cousin, John and Robert de Fiennes. The king wrote to the elder de Fiennes that he was 'astonished' at his harbouring Roger, since John held lands in England and was Edward's vassal, and because Edward had favoured him in the past. Both John and Robert were ordered to arrest Roger. Needless to say, they ignored the command.

One can understand the king's fear of imminent attack. Everything was going Roger's way. He had not only escaped the Tower, he had succeeded in getting out of the country and finding safe refuge beyond the king's reach. He had eluded Edward so effectively that for a long time the king did not know where he was, or where he was heading. Even now the king had only the slightest grasp of Roger's location, and no intelligence regarding his plans. Because of this, and because of the hatred of the Despensers, support for Roger was gathering at home, and various demonstrations in his favour took place, normally in the form of attacks on the manors of the Despensers. But Roger's luck did not end there. His third son, Geoffrey, was also in France, and Geoffrey was the sole heir to the estates of his grandmother, Joan's mother, which included a portion of the de Lusignan inheritance. Just before Roger escaped from the Tower, old age conveniently carried her off.[2] By the end of 1323 Geoffrey had inherited her estates, had sworn fealty to the French king, and was thus able to help support his father.

Even this was not the limit of his luck. War now seemed likely between England and France. Tension had been high between the two countries for the past few years, owing to problems arising from Edward's lordship of Gascony. For this Edward was required to do homage to the King of France in person, a humbling act he had hitherto avoided. Now King Charles had every legal right to confiscate the lordship. Furthermore, the duchy had seen several conflicts which Edward had failed to subdue, and in such circumstances it was incumbent upon the King of France to resolve matters, using a French army to suppress the rebellious Gascon lords, if necessary. This was a highly contentious issue, and one which threatened to flare up into war in the autumn of 1323. Arriving at precisely the right time, Roger was welcomed as an ally and treated with great honour by Charles IV. Edward was naturally infuriated by this, but there was little he could do, for in a final piece of amazing good fortune for Roger, in mid-October 1323 a French attempt to build a fortified town at Saint Sardos was met with resistance from a Gascon lord, Raymond Bernard. Bernard was felt to be acting with the connivance of the Seneschal of Gascony, Sir Ralph Basset, and Basset did not help matters by taking no action against Bernard, despite the murder of a French royal official. When Edward also refused to act to bring the offenders to justice, and refused again to do homage for Gascony (on the advice of Hugh Despenser), the French king confiscated the duchy and sent a royal army to take possession. Thus it is not surprising that Roger was welcomed by Charles: they had a common enemy in King Edward.

With Roger in France, all Edward could do to control him was to keep his spies on the lookout. On 6 December the seneschal wrote to Edward to report that Roger and his companions were travelling towards Germany.[3] A week later Edward's envoys to Paris sent news that 'the Mortimer' (as Edward now referred to him) and the other rebels with him were being entertained by the Count of Boulogne, who was then on his way to Toulouse.[4] It seems that Roger and his French friends were leading the English spies a merry dance. The panic felt at the English court did not diminish. News of the arrival of German ships in the Channel, or a Hainault invasion fleet, or Genoese armed ships, swept the country regularly. Fears of a foreign invasion led by Roger abounded and were widely believed.

The only action left open to Edward was the persecution of anyone in England who supported Roger, such as John de Gisors and Ralph de Bocton, who were accused of helping Roger to escape. De Bocton lost his lands and possessions. So too did John le Mercer of London. So too did William de Boarhunt and his wife Alice, who lost their lands on the Isle of Wight. The English lands of the de Fiennes family were confiscated. Edward even accused King Charles of France of complicity in Roger's plot.[5] The Bishop of Hereford was again questioned, and found guilty of providing arms and horses to help Roger escape, in an irregular – and probably illegal – court, with a jury specially selected by the king for the purpose.[6] The Bishop of Lincoln was also accused.[7] Finally, and most importantly, the king and Despenser took steps against Queen Isabella. Whether she was suspected of complicity in Roger's escape is not known, and with no evidence on which to work the king did not dare accuse her directly, but when she declared herself to be in favour of the accused bishops she incurred the full wrath of the king.

In April 1324 Edward ordered Isabella to write to Charles to try to end the dispute over Saint Sardos. She was the obvious person to make peace: the wife of one king and the sister of the other. But Edward's motive was not just to buy time. He ordered the queen to state in her letter that peace between England and France was the very reason for her marriage to Edward, as the marriage had originally been arranged by Edward I in order to settle a dispute between the two countries. It followed that if war broke out the marriage had failed. In the summer the Pope also suggested that she mediate, but in person, not by letter. Edward would not let her leave the country. He suspected she would meet Roger and form an alliance with him. His preference was to keep her under strict control. He ordered that his debts to her should not be repaid. At the same time, Isabella was aware that she was being spied upon by Hugh Despenser's wife, who was even reading her letters. In September 1324, when Despenser heard rumours that Roger might invade from Hainault,[8] Edward confiscated all her lands and property. It was said that Despenser had sent men to the Pope to request a divorce between Isabella and Edward. The following month the queen's personal living expenses were reduced to a fraction of their former level, to be paid not by her but directly by the Exchequer. All Frenchmen in England were arrested. Twenty-seven of Isabella's household retainers, including her clerks and her doctor, were imprisoned, and she was expressly forbidden to help them. Her income, including the money owed to her by the king, was appropriated for the king's use. Lastly her children were removed from her and placed in the keeping of Hugh Despenser's wife.[9] The woman who had come to England as an innocent and beautiful twelve-year-old bride, who had put up with her husband's affection for Gaveston, who had endured the petty squabbles with the Earl of Lancaster, who had dutifully given birth to four children, who had been abandoned to the Scots at Tynemouth, and who had steadfastly supported her husband despite everything, had now lost her husband's love, her position, her status, her income, her friends, her companions in faith, and her children.

Isabella was just one of the many who were suffering. Bishop Orleton was sent for trial. Assize courts were held in many counties, so that anyone who had helped Roger escape, or who was suspected of having dealings with him in the recent past, or who had sided with the Mortimers and the rest of the Marchers in the rebellion against Despenser in 1321 was to be tried. No matter how great or small, all were judged, and many were imprisoned or hanged. Even Henry of Lancaster was accused. Roger's relatives fared particularly badly. His sons in England were imprisoned. In April 1324 his wife was removed from her lodging in Hampshire, where she was under house arrest, and imprisoned in the royal castle of Skipton-in-Craven in Yorkshire. The men of her household were removed, although she was still allowed a damsel, an esquire, a laundress, a groom and a page; but she was permitted only one mark per day to keep and feed herself and them. Her daughters fared worse. Margaret, married to Thomas de Berkeley, was shut up in Shouldham Priory, with 15d weekly for her expenses – a smaller allowance than the criminals in the Tower were allowed. Her younger sisters fared even worse. Joan, who was twelve or thirteen, was sent to Sempringham Priory by herself, and received only 12d a week to feed her and one mark a year for her clothes. Her young sister, Isabella, suffered a similar fate, being incarcerated at Chicksands Priory.

*

There is little evidence as to where Roger was and what he was doing while on the Continent. Traditionally this has been seen as a period in which he was wholly opportunistic: that he was waiting, with no distinct plan in mind, until Isabella traded her son's marriage for an army. This ignores the fact that Isabella, while known for her intelligence, was not a military leader; her attempts to use force in the past had ended in failure, and it is unlikely she sought military help without first establishing military leadership. It also presumes that, because Isabella maintained the higher profile throughout the later campaign, Roger was dependent on her for direction. It is far more likely that when Roger arrived in France, and was welcomed with 'great honour' by Charles, the seeds of a future attack on England were then sown. This is not to say that Charles and Roger planned the following two years' events at the end of 1323; but it is unrealistic to suggest two men at war with the King of England idled away their time together in jousting and falconry. They almost certainly discussed the possibilities open to them, and probably established a framework for future action. This limited the need for direct communication, and what need there was could be satisfied by Charles's personal messengers. The fact that such a framework was possible was due to one factor which Edward did not understand: Gascony.

Charles and Roger knew that, sooner or later, Edward would have to do homage for Gascony. Edward would have to leave England, and, when he did so, he would have to leave Hugh Despenser behind. As Charles implied in a firm statement about exiles in a letter of 29 December 1323, Despenser was no more welcome in France than Roger was in England.[10] Edward would of course have ignored Charles's request that Despenser be ousted from England in return for Roger being asked to leave France, but there was little doubt that, if Edward came to France, he would be cut off from Despenser in the same way that he had been cut off from Gaveston in 1312. On that earlier occasion Thomas of Lancaster had astutely moved between the two parties and taken Gaveston prisoner. Roger hoped that, with Edward held in France under the watchful eye of the French king, an English lord, perhaps Henry of Lancaster, could move against Despenser. Henry was no friend of the Despensers and very wary of Edward. He had received none of his brother's vast estates, which had all been confiscated by the king on the execution of Earl Thomas. Moreover, when he had supported the Bishop of Hereford, Edward had prosecuted him, and only his extremely able defence in court had saved his life. He was also of royal blood, so he was the obvious candidate for leading the disaffected English lords against the favourite. As it happened, this course of events did not occur, but the clear potential for Despenser to be isolated by a known and predictable event allowed Roger and Charles to discuss possible strategies.

*

It was particularly foolish of Edward to allow Despenser to counsel him to antagonise the French over Gascony. All his experiences in Scotland had proved that he was an incompetent military leader and a poor judge of military commanders. For Gascony he chose to send his young and inexperienced brother, the Earl of Kent. This was equally foolish; not long after arriving Kent greatly angered the people of Agen by trying to extract large sums of money from them and abducting a young girl from the town.[11] Nor were his military engagements any more successful. When Charles de Valois, uncle of King Charles, moved against him in August 1324 his defences crumpled. After losing several key towns, he fell back to the castle of La Réole and was forced to sue for peace. King Charles readily agreed to a six-month truce, but he kept possession of the lands his uncle had conquered.

The truce gave Edward a chance to relieve the army in Gascony, and also a good excuse not to leave England, thus threatening Roger's hopes of separating the king from Despenser. But fortunately for Roger, Edward adopted Despenser's inappropriate bullying tactics. A contemporary account of his attempt to lift the siege of La Réole is to be found in the pages of the *Vita Edwardi Secundi*:

> Then the king ordered all the infantry to board their ships and stand out at sea, until the time should come for crossing to Gascony; and he put in command the Earl Warenne, John de St John, and other great

men of the land, who likewise went on board not daring to resist. The king also sent letters to every county commanding and ordering that all who had returned from the army to their homes without leave should be arrested and hanged forthwith without trials. The harshness of the king has today increased so much that no one however great and wise dares to cross his will. Thus parliaments, colloquies, and councils decide nothing these days. For the nobles of the realm, terrified by threats and the penalties inflicted on others, let the king's will have free play.[12]

With this sort of motivation and poor organisation there was no chance of La Réole being relieved. Hugh Despenser's policy of gathering as much money as he could in his treasury and spending as little as possible meant that the fleet did not carry enough cash to pay the footsoldiers. There was insufficient food even to feed the men who did go. The army rioted. Part of the fleet did not set out at all, as Hugh Despenser was panicked into commandeering the eastern fleet to defend the coast against Roger. At the beginning of October 1324 Despenser wrote to John de Sturmy, the admiral of the eastern ships, that a great fleet was being amassed in Holland which was expected to arrive shortly in East Anglia with a great number of armed men under the command of Roger Mortimer and other banished men.[13] It seemed Roger only had to remain outside England in order to strike terror into the hearts of Edward and Despenser.

Charles now gave Edward four options. All except one involved the loss of Agen and other lands in Gascony. The one exception was that Edward would receive all his lands back as long as Isabella and her son, the prince and heir to the throne, were both sent to France to negotiate. This, clearly, was a trap.[14] The twelve-year-old prince was a suitable alternative figure-head to Edward II, and, in his mother's company, was an eligible candidate for a diplomatic marriage. To remove him from Despenser's control was equally desirable, as Isabella would not be able wholly to take action against her husband while her son was a potential hostage. No doubt Charles also wanted to see Isabella rescued from her English ordeal, if only out of fraternal compassion. But what was so clever about this trap was that, despite the obvious dangers, this option was the most attractive to Edward. At a stroke he could end the war and regain all he had lost at little or no cost. Cautious of the dangers, he reworked Charles's offer, suggesting he would send the queen first, with the promise that his son would follow, as further concessions were made. He also proposed that Isabella should be returned to England if she did not gain a peace settlement satisfactory to Edward by a certain date. An interesting stipulation was that 'the Mortimer' and the other English rebels with him had to leave France in advance of the queen's visit, 'on account of the perils and dishonours' which might befall her.[15] The Pope too was in favour of Isabella acting as a negotiator, and his envoys told Edward that Isabella's presence in France would guarantee the return of Gascony in its entirety. This 'guarantee' convinced Edward: he decided to send Isabella to France in the spring.

Edward was not sufficiently imaginative to see the more subtle and dangerous aspects of the trap. Reassured that Isabella would not disobey his orders in France and relying heavily on Despenser's control of the barons at home, he saw only the diplomatic aspects of the issues confronting him, not their strategic implications. In not sending his son to France he had avoided the most dangerous move he could have made, but he could not see how international diplomacy was so different from domestic political control. At home it was possible for him, or rather Despenser, to terrorise the lords and people into submission, and to keep them there through threats and fines, through the hierarchy of the law. No such control was possible on an international scale; the resources and independence of France, Spain and the Low Countries ensured that a measure of compromise was necessary for an English king trying to keep his foreign possessions. Thus his policy in Gascony should have been one of collaboration with France, not the bellicose stance forced on him by Hugh Despenser.

Unfortunately the one man who would have been able to guide Edward through the process of international compromise, the Earl of Pembroke, had died six months earlier. At the end of June 1324, on his way to Paris, he collapsed after dinner at one of his houses near Boulogne. He died almost instantly, probably suffering from an apoplectic fit, but possibly poisoned. His passing was much lamented by all factions in England. He had personally taken a part in defusing every major crisis of Edward's reign. From now on there were no more arbiters of peace to settle Edward's disputes with his barons.

In March 1325 Isabella set out for her homeland with a company of retainers selected for her by her husband and Despenser. Everyone who went with her was, in effect, a spy or a chaperone. Her ladies were women whose husbands were loyal to Edward, and her male retainers, none of whom was French, were all ardent royalists. Nevertheless she was delighted to leave England. 'The queen departed very joyfully', wrote the author of *Vita Edwardi Secundi* at the time of her leaving, adding that she was 'happy with a two-fold joy; pleased to visit her native land and her relatives, and delighted to leave the company of some whom she did not like'.[16] Had he known of the intrigue which was to unfold, the chronicler could have called it a three-fold pleasure, adding the prospect of plotting revenge.

*

For Isabella, returning to France was an immense relief. She toured the country in no particular hurry, happy just to be away from England. While Edward was worried that she would form a political intrigue with Roger – and indeed a number of French and English chroniclers who wrote about the events in retrospect presumed that her sole purpose in leaving England was to see Roger – this was not overtly the case. Roger was in Hainault, supposedly 'banished' by the French king, in accordance with Edward's instructions. The queen also behaved in total compliance with her husband's directions. After landing she proceeded to Paris via Boulogne and Beauvois with her entourage, dining with the Queen of France at Pontoise before meeting her brother at Poissy. She did not meet Roger, nor did they directly contact one another. For the moment, whatever their secret desires, their relationship was merely a political understanding channelled through Charles IV.

Isabella was under no illusions about what would happen if she thoughtlessly squandered the freedom she had gained from Edward. In the spring of 1314, at the age of eighteen, she had visited Paris and met her father, Philip the Fair. She had unburdened herself of the terrible knowledge that all three of her brothers' wives were having adulterous affairs with two knights in the Tour de Nesles. Philip had the two men watched, and apprehended them. They died cruel deaths: broken on the wheel at Montfaucon. More importantly for Isabella, the women too were severely punished: divorced from their husbands and imprisoned for life.[17]

Gascony also served to keep Isabella on the straight and narrow. The negotiations with her brother were not easy. Although she had had some experience of diplomacy in 1313, when she had been sent to France as an English ambassadress, the principal French negotiator had been her doting father, to whom she had simply presented a petition and waited as he granted almost all her wishes.[18] Now she was negotiating with her clever and careful brother, Charles IV. His principal aim was to extract as much as he could from the situation in Gascony without actually provoking a larger war. He argued forcefully, and, in view of the events leading to the war, he held the upper hand throughout the negotiations. After the initial stages had gone badly for Isabella, she wrote to Edward saying that she had considered returning to England. This was probably a rhetorical device, to encourage his confidence in her, for she also offered to remain in France to see the negotiations through, if he agreed. Edward clearly accepted her letter at face value, as he sent her some money shortly afterwards.[19]

Isabella returned to Paris. By evening she dined with her family and advisers, and entertained distinguished visitors. By day she spent her time visiting churches. She was a devout Catholic, and a keen observer of holy relics, but she now spent more time than usual in contemplation. Her mind was preoccupied, possibly with thoughts of Roger.[20] She must also have been concerned that, as soon as the treaty was signed, Edward would order her to return. He would come to France to perform homage, and Despenser might be arrested; but how would Edward treat her after that? She realised she would have to betray her husband, whom she had sworn holy oaths to obey, and to whom she had sworn to remain faithful. And what if the plot eventually failed? What if Despenser escaped arrest until the king returned? There was no doubt that, in her husband's kingdom, royal status was no guarantee of immunity from prosecution for treason, especially in the case of an undesired woman.

Roger was still in Hainault, at the court of Count William of Hainault, living off the money his son had acquired by mortgaging his recently inherited lordships in France to Charles IV.[21] From there he was able easily to send messages both to France and to magnates in England, who were now collectively turning against Despenser. Hainault also kept him at a safe enough distance from Isabella for Edward not to suspect them of collusion. But even more importantly, Hainault offered an enormous diplomatic opportunity. Some years earlier a proposal had been made to marry one of the five daughters of William of Hainault to Edward's son, Prince Edward. Nothing had come of it; but Roger knew that, if the count was still willing, and if the boy could be procured and married to one of the daughters, the financial and military weight of Hainault would be at Isabella's disposal. Such a plan depended on King Edward sending his son to France. That was not impossible, especially while the question of homage for Gascony remained unsettled. If Edward did not come in person to do homage, then the only alternative Charles would accept was the homage of the prince.

On 31 May 1325 Isabella ratified the terms of the peace treaty between England and France. The terms were heavily in France's favour. Far from the whole of Gascony being granted to Edward, it was first to be surrendered wholly to Charles and then partially regranted. A French official was to ratify Edward's appointments there, and he was not able to raise an army from the land. He kept control of the castles and the military infrastructure, but the area around Agen was to be submitted to a judicial review; if it was judged that Edward had a claim to the title, he was to be liable for the costs incurred by the French army which had invaded it. It was a treaty humiliating and economically depressing, arising not out of Isabella's poor handling but out of an impossible situation.

Edward ratified the treaty on 13 June. He had no choice: he was not in a position to hold out for a better settlement. But there remained the question of who was going to perform homage. Edward insisted that he should go in person, to prevent his son falling into Isabella's hands. Hugh Despenser desperately sought members of the council to prevent the king from leaving England, but failed. The deciding voice was that of Henry of Lancaster. He strongly urged the king to go. Despenser, knowing his own life would be in danger, tried equally hard to dissuade him. It seemed the anti-Despenser faction was about to get its first opportunity to overthrow the favourite. Only later, when Despenser was able to speak to the king privately, was he able to impress upon Edward how vulnerable he would be in the king's absence. Remembering Gaveston's fate, Edward changed his mind and, feigning illness, at the last moment refused to leave England. Henry of Lancaster and the Earl of Norfolk, two men who might have been waiting to act against Despenser, had to bide their time.[22] Instead of going to France himself the king sent the Bishop of Winchester to negotiate an alternative arrangement.

As Charles, Isabella and Roger all knew, there was only one acceptable alternative to the king's attendance, and that was the visit of Prince Edward. Isabella dined with the Bishop of Winchester on 2 September, and suggested then that her son be sent to perform homage for Gascony. The bishop agreed to present this proposal formally to Edward. But just when Isabella might have thought that Edward was playing into her hands, the bishop sprung a surprise upon her. He carried Edward's order for her to return to England forthwith.[23] And to ensure that she complied, her funding was cut off with immediate effect.

This presented Isabella with a dire problem. If she had to return to England, she could not possibly hope to get control of her son. She managed to delay while the bishop returned to Edward with Charles's formal permission that Prince Edward could be invested with Gascony and perform homage. Now it was Edward who was under pressure. He decided that he would invest Prince Edward with the title of Duke of Aquitaine, and send him with a strong party to demand Isabella's immediate return. Prince Edward accordingly set out for Paris in the company of Henry de Beaumont and the Bishops of Winchester and Exeter, arriving there on 22 September. Isabella and her son were reunited, and overjoyed to see one another. Isabella was less pleased to see the Bishop of Exeter, Walter de Stapeldon. It had been on his advice that she had had her estates confiscated the previous year.[24] She refused to dine with him, and attempted to ignore him. But de Stapeldon was not easily ignored. At some point shortly after the prince had performed homage to Charles, the bishop laid before her Edward's demand that she return home immediately, and he did so in public, in front of the king and the court. Edward would not tolerate any excuse, he declared in the hearing of all assembled. He went on to say that he had money to pay her expenses in France, but he would not do so unless she returned to England with him, as she was legally and morally obliged to do. This was the final word, he declared; she had no choice in the matter.[25]

The bishop was wrong. Isabella did have a choice. Now that the matter of homage for Gascony had been resolved, and Prince Edward was with her, there was no longer any point in continuing the charade. Moreover, she felt humiliated by this public demand made on her by the bishop. 'I feel that marriage is a joining together of man and woman, maintaining the undivided habit of life,' she replied in a loud voice, 'and that someone has come between my husband and myself trying to break this bond. I protest that I will not return until this intruder is removed, but, discarding my marriage garment, shall assume the robes of widowhood and mourning until I am avenged of this pharisee.'

Isabella's words amazed and delighted the French court. The bishop had spoken in Charles's presence in the belief that Isabella would not be able to defy him. Now she had made herself plain. De Stapeldon fully expected Charles to rebuke his rebellious sister for her treason. But Charles had played a very clever tactical game for the last two years, and he was not going to let an English bishop jeopardise his plans. 'The queen came of her own free will, and may freely return if she so wishes. But if she prefers to remain in these parts, she is my sister, and I refuse to expel her.'

With the utterance of these words, Roger's and Isabella's lives changed for ever. Isabella had openly defied her husband, and the King of France had supported her. She had declared herself against Hugh Despenser and against her husband the king. She had effectively joined Roger's rebellion.

Now it was the bishop's turn to be alarmed. Isabella was not the only one to detest him. In his time as Treasurer he had made himself rich through extortion. He was universally loathed, and was one of four Englishmen (along with the two Despensers and Robert Baldock, the Chancellor), of whom it was said that, if they were ever found in France, they would be tortured.[26] Within days, fearing for his life, he fled from Paris. Some said he fled disguised as a pilgrim. The men of his household hurried after him and returned with him to England, and went straight to the king to report the news. De Stapeldon told Edward that the men who had threatened his life were 'certain of the king's banished enemies'. From earlier intelligence reports sent back to England, the English exiles seem to have moved about the Continent with Roger as a body. This indicates that now, with the prince safely in the queen's custody, Roger had returned to France.

Over the subsequent days, Isabella's companions realised the implications of her stance. Most of them had been picked because of their
loyalty to Edward and Despenser, and most of them refused to accept
that they would not be returning home with the queen. The queen did
indeed dress as a widow, and played the part of a woman in mourning.[27]
For those who remained loyal to Edward, the knowledge that the queen
was in communication with Roger, and that he was in France despite his
exile, was too much. Isabella gave them an ultimatum: if their loyalty
lay with the king then they should return to England. If, however, they
were loyal to her, they should stay. Rather than defy the king and
Despenser, most returned.

This turning point did not come as a shock to Isabella. She had been
preparing for it since the beginning of September, when the Bishop of
Winchester had demanded that she return. Her reply on that occasion
had been that she would not return 'for danger and doubt of Hugh
Despenser'. Edward referred to this earlier refusal when he wrote back to
her again at the start of December. He stated that he did not believe that
she disliked Despenser, and that:

> The king knows for truth and she knows that Hugh has always procured
> her all the honour with the king that he could; and no evil or villainy
> was done to her after her marriage by any abatement and procurement,
> unless peradventure sometimes the king addressed to her in secret words
> of reproof, by her own fault, if she will remember, as was befitting . . .[28]

Isabella must have been infuriated by this reply. Why should she have
to be grateful that Despenser was supposed to have helped advance her?
She was the queen, and he a mere baron's son! She should not need his
approval. But the king's complete lack of respect for his wife is discernible
not in his pretence that Despenser had helped her, nor in his implication
that Despenser was her superior, but in his refusal even to listen to her.
Her will was something he sought to tame and control. Having sent this
letter he made another crass attempt to control her through the bishops.
Knowing she would accept the order to return more readily if it came
from a clergyman, he ordered all the bishops in England to write to her,
telling her that it was her duty to come home. As if that were not enough,
he dictated to all of them exactly the text they should send, as if they
were all her 'fathers' beseeching their 'dear daughter' to return.

Isabella did not care that members of her household were leaving her.
As far as she was concerned, the more disloyal men and women who left
her service the better. She had no use for spies. Especially not when, in

December, Roger came openly to court. There is no evidence that she had seen him since she left him in the Tower, nearly four years earlier,[29] and we cannot be certain what her feelings had been for him over those years. But now she made no secret of her love, and neither did he. Roger was with her: not the defeated, humiliated and half-starved lord he had been in the Tower but the champion of free England, and the man she loved more passionately than any other in her life.

The relationship between Roger and Isabella is one of the great romances of the Middle Ages. To see them as they were in December 1325, openly defying Edward, is to see two people bound to each other against all the law and authority in the secular and spiritual world. Yet their affection for each other is rarely commented on by historians. In essence it was a relationship formed in adversity. Adultery, especially on the part of a woman, was a terrible sin in the fourteenth century, and doubly so for a queen, for whom it also carried the stain of treason. Isabella's religious fervour made her feel this intensely: breaking solemn vows of fidelity was not something lightly done. Nor was it easy for Roger. Joan, his wife of twenty-five years' standing, was suffering. He was betraying her in her darkest hour, while she was in her cell in Skipton Castle. But their attraction to each other was irresistible, and their affection for each other unshakeable.

For Isabella's part, the rush into Roger's arms seems to have been a reaction against years of self-control and self-denial. All her suffering had resulted in nothing but a husband and who was trying to manipulate her and shame her. She was threatened. She needed someone she could trust, someone, moreover, who would share the risks she was taking. She needed a steadfast and mature adviser on whom she could rely. At thirty-eight, Roger fitted the bill perfectly.

Roger's new companion was one of the most beautiful and intelligent women of the age. She was, furthermore, ten years younger than his wife, whom he had not seen for five years. Her status as the wife of the man who had sentenced him to death, and the chance publicly to cuckold him, added a certain piquancy. If their relationship ended with their executions at the command of the King of England, then so be it. They would go down fighting together.

For a few weeks they tried to keep their closeness a secret. Edward was probably not fully aware of the depth of their relationship until 23 December, when the members of Isabella's household loyal to Edward returned to England. From that day on there was no further pretence. It was a sober Christmas at the English court. For Isabella and Roger, however, it was a Christmas like no other. Not only were they together, and free, they were able to plan the invasion of England. While they had to be careful, aware that Despenser had agents everywhere, and aware too of the dangers of the murderer in the night, or the poisoner in the kitchen, they were relatively safe in the palace of King Charles.

The events of 1323–6 must have been profoundly shocking to the misogynist King Edward. Never before had such an important prisoner escaped from the Tower, and never before had that prisoner been so favoured by heads of state and nobles on the Continent. But worse, far worse for Edward, was this new eclipse of his authority. He, the King of England, had been cuckolded by his enemy. The humiliation was extreme. It was made even worse by the threatened invasion, which Edward was now convinced would come from France. He could do nothing but wait, set up watch beacons, hide his treasure, order the ports watched, and threaten any potential rebels within the kingdom. Such was the personal slight to Edward that he decided he would seek revenge on members of Roger's family. He sent soldiers to old Lady Mortimer, Roger's mother, to accuse her of hosting seditious meetings. They were to take her, immediately, to Elstow Priory, where she was to remain at her own cost, for the rest of her life.[30] When she could not be found, Edward sent more men to seek her out at Radnor and Worcester. A further order to the same effect in April 1326 indicates that she had, like her son, outwitted her would-be captors.

On 8 February 1326 Edward publicly admitted that the queen had turned against him. He sent letters to all the sheriffs in the country ordering them to proclaim that all men should be ready to take arms and protect England against the queen, because, he claimed, 'the queen will not come to the king nor permit his son to return, and he understands that the queen is adopting the counsel of the Mortimer, the king's notorious enemy and rebel'. Four days later an array for the purpose of defending the southeast was ordered. Letters similar to those to the sheriffs were sent to the admirals patrolling the coasts. Edward renewed his orders for searches for messages to be conducted at the ports. Despenser hid his treasure in Caerphilly Castle. All exports of gold were stopped out of fear that aggrieved English lords would help fund the invasion, and all letters leaving the realm were to be inspected for treasonable contents.

Edward had finally realised his blunder. While he might have dismissed his wife as a French irritation, he knew his son to be every bit as royal as himself. Edward took his own royalty very seriously indeed, and recognised that many Englishmen would willingly fight for their future king. When his son refused to obey his order to leave the queen, claiming that out of duty he should stay with her in her great unease of mind and unhappiness, he wrote back to him in the strongest terms, saying of the queen:

> . . . if she had conducted herself towards the king as she ought to have done towards her lord, the king would be much harassed to learn of her grief or unhappiness, but as she feigns a reason to withdraw from the king by reason of his dear and faithful nephew Hugh Despenser, who has always served the king well and faithfully, Edward can see and everybody can see that she openly, notoriously, and knowingly contrary to her duty and the estate of the king's crown, which she is bound to love and maintain, draws to her and retains in her company of her council the Mortimer, the king's traitor and mortal enemy, approved, attainted and adjudged in full Parliament, and keeps his company within and without house, in despite of the king and of his crown and of the rights of his realm, which Mortimer the King of France had banished from his power as the king's enemy at the king's request at another time, and now she does worse, if possible, when she has delivered Edward to the company of the king's said enemy, and makes him Edward's councillor, and causes Edward to adhere to him openly and notoriously in the sight of everybody, to the great dishonour and villainy of the king and of Edward . . .[31]

At the same time he summoned back from France John de Cromwell and the Earl of Richmond, both of whom had stayed with the queen and Roger. The Earl of Kent, the king's own half-brother, had also decided to stay, having married Roger's cousin, Margaret Wake.[32] Despairing that he was losing his authority, Edward further ordered his son not to enter any marriage contracts with anyone in his absence from England. As the king must have known, however, these matters were not in the prince's hands. They were now entirely in the hands of Roger and Isabella.

*

We have only one fact illustrating the nature of Roger and Isabella's relationship at this time, and it can hardly be described as representative. At some point before June 1326 there was an emotional outburst between them in which Isabella, probably confused and frightened, suggested that she might return to her husband. Although the young prince and others were present, Roger angrily replied that, rather than let her go back to Edward, he would himself 'kill her with his knife or some other way'.[33] The prince was profoundly shocked by Roger's threat, as were all those present, including Despenser' spy. But it offers a tantalising glimpse into the relationship. On the strength of it one might say that, after the initial rush of passion, it seems Isabella had doubts about their joint course of action, and considered going back to Edward seriously enough to say so. Roger, on the other hand, did not have this option, and refused to countenance her idea. But that he did this in a way which was sufficiently public for the discussion to become more widely known suggests that his emotions got the better of him, and that his feelings for Isabella were stronger than his self-control. This is the only evidence we have of him being anything other than circumspect in his personal affairs. One last point we can make about this outburst: Isabella's doubts proved only temporary. With Roger's support thereafter she was resolute.

Isabella's wavering might possibly explain why Roger's attack from Hainault, planned initially for February 1326, was delayed. Intervention by the Pope, however, is a more likely explanation.[34] In view of the international situation, Roger and Isabella – particularly Isabella – had to be seen to have exhausted all other options for resolving the dispute with Edward before invading. In February the Pope wrote to Hugh Despenser ordering him to prevent civil war by leaving court, as Isabella had requested. Despenser, lacking the vision to manipulate this intervention to his advantage, told the Pope's legates that the queen had no right to demand his withdrawal. The real reason why she had not returned to England, he claimed, was that Roger was threatening to kill her if she did. Edward himself wrote to the Pope at this time admitting that his wife was sharing her living accommodation with Roger, with the obvious implication that she was also sharing her bed. Only then did the Pope realise that the hatred the English felt for Hugh Despenser, and the hatred Despenser and Edward felt for Roger and the queen, would not be dissipated except by force of arms.

Despenser was trying to find another, simpler solution to his difficulties. In May he despatched barrels of silver to France in an attempt to bribe Charles's courtiers to murder the queen. The plot was discovered when a Hainault ship captured the vessel carrying Despenser's treasure.[35] Time now was clearly running out for Roger and Isabella. The longer their invasion was delayed, the more dangerous the situation. They attended the coronation of the Queen of France together in May, Roger bearing Edward's robes on the occasion in a marked reference to his role at the coronation of Edward II eighteen years earlier. They were probably still in France in June, when the king wrote a final letter to his son, ordering him to ignore Roger's influence and to shun his company.

In July the queen went to her county of Ponthieu to raise money and men for the invasion, and Roger went to Hainault to begin organising the assembly of the fleet. At last he was exercising the function of a commander again, just as he had done in 1317. This invasion fleet, however, was larger than his Irish flotilla. Count William of Hainault ordered one hundred and forty vessels to be assembled between Rotterdam and Dordrecht by 1 September, and ordered his harbour masters to assist Roger in every way. Eventually ninety-five ships were gathered: four warships, fifteen hulks, or transporters, twenty-nine other ships and forty-five fishing vessels.[36] If one assumes that a warship and a hulk could each transport at least thirty men and the requisite horses and armour, besides the crew, and the average ship or fishing vessel large enough to be of use could take an average of six men, it would seem that Roger's army was at least 1,100 men strong, despite some contemporaries' claims that it was smaller.[37] If more foot-soldiers were transported, it is quite possible that the higher estimates of 1,500 or 2,500 men were more accurate. Given the probability that only a fifth of the army, at the most, was mounted it would be reasonable to assume that Roger had an army of approximately 1,500 men at his disposal.

In September, the fleet was ready, and the invasion of England imminent. On the 7th Isabella arrived in Hainault, and from there went to Rotterdam, where Roger had been organising the fleet in conjunction with Sir John of Hainault, Count William's younger brother, who was to command the Hainaulters on the expedition. Roger, Isabella, Sir John and the Hainault court then moved to the port of Brill, ready for the embarkation.[38] On 20 September they feasted together for the last time and prepared themselves for departure.

In his career Roger had led a force which had successfully invaded Ireland; he had been part of an army which had successfully re-established Edward I's control of Scotland, and he had put down a popular revolt in Wales. Now he was about to invade England. He and Isabella stood together on the threshold of either greatness or death. But if his nerve was wavering at this point it must have been made firm by the news which reached him just before sailing. His old uncle, Lord Mortimer of Chirk, was dead. He had died in his cell in the Tower on 3 of August. According to the coroner, the corpse showed no wound, lesion or bruise. But Roger may well have had his doubts.

TEN

Invader

Roger and Isabella and their small army of mercenaries landed in Suffolk, on the north bank of the River Orwell, on 24 September 1326.[1] Although the chronicler Jean le Bel claimed that a storm had blown them off course during their voyage, and that this was to their advantage since the king knew of their plans, it is likely that they intended to land here. It was within striking distance of London, yet defended by rivers from the king's forces in the south. It was also within the lands controlled by the Earl of Norfolk, who loathed the Despensers. Le Bel was probably right in one respect, that the king knew of their plans: three weeks earlier Edward had ordered the admiral John de Sturmy to take a defending force of two thousand men to Orwell. Fortunately for Roger and Isabella, de Sturmy's fleet did not show up, and they were able to disembark quickly and efficiently within a few hours of landing.[2]

Edward was at the Tower of London when he heard the news. Initially he did not believe it: he had been expecting a large invasion force of many thousands of men. A few boatloads from Hainault represented a comparatively minor threat. A day or so later, when further reports confirmed that Roger and Isabella had indeed landed in East Anglia, he saw his opportunity. His enemies were within his grasp, and protected by a comparatively small number of mercenaries. If he could neutralise any local lords who might be tempted to support them, they would be at his mercy. On 27 September he ordered Robert de Waterville to levy and assemble 'all the men-at-arms and footmen of the counties of Norfolk, Suffolk, Essex, Hertford, Cambridge and Huntingdon, and to pursue the rebels and do what harm they can to them'.[3] Other men were ordered to do the same in Kent, Oxfordshire, Berkshire, Buckinghamshire and Wales. Orders were sent to all the sheriffs to forbid anyone from assisting the invaders and to muster the feudal levy. The immense total of 47,640 men-at-arms, hobelers, footsoldiers and archers was summoned, a larger army than had ever before been raised in England. More men were ordered to come to the king to defend him the following day. All the murderers and other criminals held in custody were offered their freedom if they would take up arms against Roger: pardons were issued to more than a hundred murderers straightaway. Finally the king placed a reward on Roger's head. All sheriffs were to proclaim it 'in fairs, markets, and other places at least two or three times a week':

> Whereas Roger Mortimer and other traitors of the king and his realm have entered the realm in force, and have brought with them foreign strangers for the purpose of taking the royal power from the king, the king wills you to go in force against his said enemies to arrest and destroy them, except the queen, his son and the Earl of Kent, whom he wills shall be saved. And, although in such case every man of the realm is bound by his allegiance to come with all his force and power in defence of the king, of themselves and of the realm, the king nevertheless wills on this occasion, for the ease of his people, that all those who shall come to him to set out with him against his enemies – men-at-arms, hobelers and armed footmen, crossbowmen, archers and other footmen – shall be paid wages according to their value promptly, to wit: a man-at-arms 12d, a hobeler 6d, a footman armed with double garment 4d, armed with a single garment 3d, and an archer 2d a day each . . . If any person or persons bring and render to him the body of the said Roger or bring his head, the king wills that he or they shall have his charters of peace for any felony, adherence or other matter against his peace, and he grants that he will pay them £1,000 sterling.[4]

At this point Roger's familiarity with the key members of the court in past years worked to his advantage. They understood his purpose in invading. They knew that he was essentially a loyal servant of the Crown who had been forced into an impossible position, and that his enmity had always been directed at Despenser rather than the king. Even men loyal to the government were swayed. Although a loyal king's man, Robert de Waterville was a longtime friend of Roger and had been one of the guests at the wedding of young Edmund Mortimer in 1316. Instead of attacking Roger in East Anglia he joined forces with him. Similarly Thomas Wake, Roger's cousin, deserted the king upon being ordered to take arms against the invaders. The king, suspecting Henry of Lancaster would do the same, did not even send him orders. He was right to be suspicious. Immediately on hearing the news Henry raised an army at Leicester, stole the treasure which the elder Despenser's agent had deposited in the abbey there, and prepared to march south to join the invaders.

Roger and Isabella spent their first night in England at the Earl of Norfolk's manor of Walton, on the Suffolk coast. They had planned well. In particular they had given considerable thought to how they might sway popular opinion in their favour. Firstly, and most importantly, they under-stood the power of the royal banner. The common people could be relied upon to support – or at least not to defy – their future monarch and those bearing the royal arms. Certainly many more people would follow the banner of the future King Edward than that of a famous rebel. It was also important for Roger to distance himself personally from Isabella: if the leaders of the invasion were seen to be living in sin then people might expect God to exert a moral sentence upon them by having them defeated in battle. Although the military impetus came from him, this was osten-sibly the queen's invasion, and it was a moral campaign with the purpose of ridding England of Hugh Despenser the younger. Isabella had to play the part of a lady in distress. She did this so well that her conquests outweighed those of any number of mercenaries. She conquered the hearts of the ordinary people, who might otherwise have mustered against her.

Roger's role was to plan the strategic movements of the army. The fleet which had carried them from Hainault was ordered to return to the Continent as soon as the army had disembarked. Maybe Roger recalled the tactic employed by Duke William of Normandy in 1066. By ordering the ships to leave he ensured there would be no retreat for the Hainault mercenaries. They would have to fight and die alongside him and the other Englishmen. Roger was also required to discipline the army. At Walton the foreign mercenaries started looting. This was immediately brought to a halt. The queen offered compensation to those whose houses had been affected, and at a stroke regained the confidence of the local inhabitants and obtained the respect of many others who feared her approach. Although Isabella may well have had a hand in planning such gestures, discipline of an army was completely outside her experience, and she was reliant on Roger from the moment they landed. He was in effect her 'strong arm', her Field Marshal.

While Roger's role was publicly played down, Isabella's was exagger-ated. She was given prominence as the religious figurehead of the inva-sion as well as the mother of the future king. She played on her reputation for religious devotion, travelling 'as if on pilgrimage' to Bury St Edmunds. There she stayed in the abbey. This mixing of religion and her righteous grievances was very potent; it gave the invaders' act of war a holy sanc-timony, like a crusade. It also had the advantage of reducing the power of the sheriffs to raise the feudal army. Even those captains and sheriffs willing to support Edward were unable to raise sufficiently large numbers of men to crush the invasion in its infancy. By the time Roger and Isabella reached Dunstable, where they were joined by Henry of Lancaster, their army was far too large to be defeated by a single sheriff. The religious aspect also meant that the bishops who supported the invaders (the Archbishop of Dublin and the Bishops of Hereford, Ely, Lincoln, Durham and Norwich) had no qualms about speaking out in their favour. It was largely due to Isabella that the invasion very quickly acquired the mass support necessary for it to appear a credible opposition to the king.

Edward and Despenser were completely surprised by the growth of the invaders' power. Although they had known for two years that Roger was planning an invasion, although they had a full Treasury, and money to spare, and although they knew when and where he would attack, they failed to stop him, or even to engage him in battle. Rarely can such a well-resourced and well-established authoritarian government have been so paralysed by just a few hundred mercenaries. But therein lay the problem: the government had proved itself too authoritarian. There may have been £60,000 in the Treasury but Hugh Despenser was adept only at amassing huge sums; he did not know how to spend the money to his and the king's best advantage. Roger, on the other hand, was adept at spending money strategically. Both men were intelligent manipulators, but Despenser was all calculation and theory while Roger had the ability to put his ideas into practice, and make his physical force quickly and suddenly felt. Despenser's strengths were the law courts and the Exchequer; Roger's were his power of command and his sword. When it came to fighting a battle, Despenser could only order other people to fight for him. As events now showed, this was something they were unwilling to do.

Edward had complete faith in Hugh Despenser, and trusted both his loyalty and his judgement. But as September turned into October, his position began to crumble. London was collapsing into anarchy around him, and although the Tower was an immensely strong castle, it was not enough by itself to hold back the citizens and the advancing army. Edward and Despenser were aware that their enemies were in contact with the leading churchmen and merchants. The huge army summoned by the king had not materialised. In all the counties the sheriffs had failed to gather enough men. The most loyal gave excuses, the others remained silent, or set about their business with a lacklustre purpose. The king and his favourite began to realise that they were isolated, and would soon be cut off inside a lawless city, facing forces of barbarity which they could not combat and with which they could not negotiate. In desperation the king sought promises of loyalty from the Londoners. He received a very half-hearted response. Alarmed, he prepared to leave London. On 1 October he arranged for the transfer of Roger's three sons to the security of the Tower, and on the following day he abandoned his capital.

On Edward's departure, authority in the city collapsed further. Its inhabitants had hated the Despensers for many years; now they began to persecute their agents. Houses began to be looted, citizens known to be faithful to the king were jeered and harassed. But although the city was turning away from Edward it was not necessarily a safe place for Roger and Isabella to stake their claim to authority. It was fickle, and, like most oligarchies, the controlling forces were principally interested in their own continued prosperity. As Edward left London and rode towards Acton, Roger and Isabella began to turn their army after him. Their pursuit was like the 1321–2 campaign in reverse; this time it was Roger chasing the king across the country from Surrey to South Wales. Although his sons were in the city, and although Isabella's younger son, Prince John, was also in the Tower, their highest priority was to seize the king and Despenser. Only when they had them in their custody could they address the questions of London, the security of members of their family, and government.

On 6 October, when Roger and Isabella were at Baldock, the king was at Wallingford. Three days later, as the king rode into Gloucester, they were near Dunstable. That day, in response to the £1,000 reward set on Roger's head, they set a price of £2,000 on the head of Hugh Despenser. The king and the queen, each equally at the mercy of their favourite's advice, eyed each other across southern England with anger. Their favourites eyed each other with unmitigated and powerful urges to destroy one another. But while Despenser and the king waited at Gloucester, hoping in vain that an army would join them there, Roger and Isabella advanced, their army growing stronger all the time. On 10 October the king learnt that Henry of Lancaster had joined the rebels. Although he had long suspected the earl, the news hit him hard, for he knew now that he had lost control of the country. He sent orders to the garrisons he had positioned across Roger's estates to give up their defence of Roger's castles and lands and to join him at Gloucester with all possible speed. He prepared to set out once again for South Wales, to make a defence of his kingdom in the lands of Hugh Despenser.

Roger and Isabella were in the ascendant but they were not guaranteed success. At any time opinion could turn against them, or the king might decide to make a stand with a contingent of Welshmen. He had with him nearly £30,000 to pay an army for the purpose. Roger and Isabella were certainly very cautious as they neared Oxford. This royal town was the first they had approached as an occupying force. It was notoriously prone to violent clashes; it was a place where opinions from all over the realm met and either melded or struck sparks. At any moment there was the danger of an assassin, or the city being barred to them. As a precaution Isabella sent messengers ahead to arrange her lodgings with the Carmelite friars in the town, while Roger and the other leaders of the army arranged lodgings at Osney Abbey outside the walls. Their cautious approach was appreciated by the townsfolk, who, realising that their houses were not going to be looted, sent a presentation silver cup to Isabella as she approached. The invaders had taken their first town, and no blood had been spilt.

At Oxford the Bishop of Hereford joined them and preached a sermon. His text was from Genesis. 'I will put enmity between thee and the woman!' he declared, comparing Despenser to the snake in the Garden of Eden. Despenser, he claimed, was 'the seed of the first tyrant Satan, who would be crushed by the Lady Isabella and her son the prince'.[5] In the congregation were Roger, Isabella and all the rebel leaders who had now converged on Oxford. Men marched through the streets purposefully: an army determined finally to bring Despenser to justice and to stop Edward abusing his royal power. A feeling of triumph was beginning to spread through their ranks. They marched next to Wallingford, Isabella's own castle, which also surrendered to its lady without a fight.

Edward was now at Tintern, in South Wales, waiting the arrival of his most trusted Welsh knights. At the Archbishop of Canterbury's house at Lambeth, just south of London, a meeting of six bishops loyal to the king had been forced to break up without agreement. Rioting in the streets prevented them crossing the river to the city itself. All was in disarray apart from the invaders' army. At this moment, on 15 October, Isabella issued a proclamation that she had come to rescue the country, the Crown and the Church from the evil of Hugh Despenser, Robert Baldock (the Chancellor), Walter de Stapeldon (the Treasurer), and others. The invasion had become a revolution.

De Stapeldon never got to hear of the proclamation. The day it was issued all hell broke loose in London. Hamo de Chigwell, the mayor, one of the judges who had sentenced Roger to death, was dragged into the Guildhall. He was told that John le Marshal, a Londoner, was one of Hugh Despenser's spies and would be executed. He was told that Walter de Stapeldon was also a traitor who deserved death. He was forced to swear to uphold the cause of the invaders. And then the crowd of Londoners put into effect all their terrible sentences. They dragged John le Marshal from his house and brought him to Cheapside, where they beheaded him. Next they went looking for de Stapeldon.[6] They burnt down the doors of his house, which were barred against them, and stole his jewels and silver. His official register and many of his books were also burnt. At this point the bishop himself recklessly rode into the city in armour with his squires. Foolishly, when told at Holborn of what was being done to his house, he decided not to flee but to ride through the city to the Tower. Halfway across, frightened by the clamour of the crowd baying for his blood, he and his squires rode for shelter to St Paul's Cathedral, hoping that there they might find sanctuary. But before they could enter the cathedral the crowd caught them. At the north door they pulled de Stapeldon from his horse, dragged him through the cemetery, down Ludgate Hill and all the way to the cross in Cheapside. There, by the decapitated body of John le Marshal, they stripped the bishop of his armour and sawed through his neck with a bread knife. Two of his attendant squires were killed in a similar fashion.

De Stapeldon's head was presented to the queen at Gloucester. It is not recorded what she thought of it, but it is probable that she and Roger looked on the bishop's sunken lifeless eyes with grave disappointment. The murder of a high-ranking prelate, even such a hated one, was a definite setback. Shocking proceedings like this only served to undermine the legitimate nature of their campaign. Just as worrying, the capital was up in arms, with lynch mobs and robber gangs ruling the streets. The law courts had been abandoned, and Roger's and Isabella's sons were at the mercy of the mob. The Tower had fallen, and little Prince John had been proclaimed guardian of the city, and forced to swear to uphold the rights of the citizens, but there was nothing he or the city fathers could do to restore order. Not without the army.

Roger and Isabella could not turn back now. Having sent a bodyguard to watch over the nine-year-old prince, they continued in the king's tracks. From Gloucester they advanced to the walls of Bristol. On their arrival on 18 October the townsfolk threw open the gates of the town to them. But the gates of the castle within the town were barred. Here the Earl of Winchester had decided to make a stand.

Ten years earlier Roger had taken the town of Bristol after a week-long siege. Now he set about attacking the castle at its heart. Fortunately, Hugh Despenser, as lord of Bristol, had recently permitted some houses to be built near the castle walls, and these weakened the castle's defences. The siege lasted eight days, during which time the elder Despenser desperately tried to bargain for his life. But Roger offered no quarter. The Despensers had not only accused him of despoiling their property in the war of 1321–2, they had turned the king against him and cost him his lordship, his family, his wealth, his status and his reputation, and tried to have him murdered. Nothing but their complete destruction would do. The Lancastrians, who held the Despensers responsible for the death of Earl Thomas, were of a like mind. On the eighth day, 26 October, the army stormed the castle. In a very short time the elder Despenser was in chains.

The king knew that he was in serious danger. His loyal Welsh forces had not come to his rescue, as he had hoped. This was probably partly due to knights like Hugh de Turpington, Roger's old comrade in arms, who had nominally joined the Despensers the year before but who now disobeyed Edward's order to guard the Marches.[7] Also, in Glamorgan, many of Despenser's tenants remembered Llywelyn Bren's fate, and would not fight to save the man who had butchered their hero, despite their loyalty to Edward himself. The fact that Edward and Despenser were relying on such men to defend them, together with their inability to mobilise even their most loyal forces, reveals the full extent of their strategic incompetence.

Facing defeat, Edward and Despenser decided to take ship and leave, probably hoping to reach Ireland. On 21 October, while Roger and Isabella were at Bristol, they set sail from Chepstow with Robert Baldock and a small contingent of men-at-arms. For five days they battled against the wind – a friar was paid to pray that the weather might change – but it held firm against them. Eventually they put into port at Cardiff, where the royal household rejoined the king. Moving to Caerphilly Castle, Edward made a final attempt to raise an army, summoning all the people of the lordships of Neath, Usk and Abergavenny to defend him, and men from the Despenser lordships of Gower, Pembroke, Haverford and Glamorgan. But it was too late. With his handful of men-at-arms, he could only wait for the end. On 31 October his household servants deserted him, leaving him only Despenser, Baldock and a handful of retainers.[8]

All organised resistance to the invaders had capitulated. Everyone able to raise a force of men had left the king's allegiance and joined them, or were keeping quiet. It was now time for Roger and Isabella to take control of the tatters of government. This posed a problem, since the king had taken the great seal and his privy seal with him. Their solution was simple. Since the king had left the country without appointing a surrogate to govern in his absence, they appointed his son. No one could argue with the selection of the prince; indeed, no other person would have been universally acceptable. But by making the prince custodian of the realm, at just fourteen years old and completely under the influence of his mother and her lover, it meant that Roger and Isabella were, in effect, the unofficial joint heads of the government.

*

Historians have traditionally regarded the *coup d'état* of 1326 as Isabella's personal victory, thereby underestimating or even ignoring Roger's role.[9] The reason for this is not hard to find: the invasion was carried out in her name and that of the prince, and the queen was accordingly the figure-head perceived to be in control, both by contemporaries and historians. There is little doubt, however, that it was Roger who planned the invasion and suggested many of the developments which followed, including the transfer of regnal authority to Prince Edward. The most reliable and well-informed chronicler of the end of Edward's reign, Adam Murimuth, clearly states that Isabella took her direction from Roger and obeyed him in all matters.[10] Roger's presence in Hainault in 1324, before the queen had even left England, strongly suggests that he initiated discussions with the Hainaulters and was primarily responsible for the invasion strategy, whereas there is no evidence that the queen did more than assume titular leadership of the campaign. Also, while there is abundant evidence from those who knew them best – particularly the king and Despenser – that Roger was greatly feared as a military leader, they did not consider Isabella capable of treason on her own, as shown by the king permitting her to travel to France in 1325. The king's confidence that his wife would not turn against him by herself was justified, as shown by her considering returning to Edward even after Roger had joined her in Paris. Thus we may be confident that Roger instigated the invasion and put it into effect, not Isabella, although her approbation was essential to the realisation and success of his strategy.

Responsibility for the progress of the campaign directly after the invasion similarly may be seen to lie with Roger. The earliest evidence of this lies, ironically, in a document in which he is not named. Those listed in the declaration of 26 October (in which the prince was chosen to be the guardian of the realm) were the king's two half-brothers (the Earls of Kent and Norfolk), Henry of Lancaster, Thomas Wake, Henry de Beaumont, William de la Zouche, Robert de Mohaut, Robert de Morley, Robert de Waterville, and 'other barons and knights'.[11] Roger, as the only significant leader of the army not mentioned, is conspicuous by his absence. Isabella would not have excluded him from such a line-up except at his specific direction, nor would any of their episcopal allies, such as Adam of Orleton. Thus it seems the declaration was at Roger's command. By excluding himself from such official processes he avoided being held to account. No one could challenge his authority because, officially, he had none, and no one could point to his abuse of a position for the same reason. It was a technique he practised for the next four years, and partly it explains why so few writers have examined him as the key figure of the period. Unlike almost every other ruler in history, he tried to cover the tracks of his authority and thereby consciously contributed to his own official obscurity.[12]

When it came to exerting judgement on others, however, Roger was not afraid to take a more prominent role. The day after the proclamation of the prince's regency Roger assembled a tribunal of six peers to judge Hugh Despenser the elder. The tribunal consisted of himself, Thomas Wake and William Trussel (former retainers of the Earl of Lancaster), Henry of Lancaster (brother of the Earl of Lancaster), and the Earls of Kent and Norfolk. Although Isabella pleaded that the old man's life should be spared, there was not the slightest chance that such a tribunal would agree. They deliberately conducted the trial to echo that of Thomas of Lancaster. Despenser was not allowed to speak. At the end of the deliberations Thomas Wake read the judgement and the sentence. Despenser was found guilty of encouraging his son's illegal government, of enriching himself at other people's expense, of despoiling the Church, and for his part in the illegal execution of Thomas of Lancaster.[13] He was sentenced to be drawn, hanged in a surcoat of his own arms on the common gallows at Bristol, and beheaded. The sentence was carried out straightaway.

Now there remained only one Despenser to pursue. On the day of his father's death Hugh Despenser the younger was with the king at Caerphilly. Henry of Lancaster was deputed to go after them. For Roger, this had the added advantage of removing Henry from the new court while he and Isabella established their administration. Henry of Lancaster, who showed every sign of being as troublesome as his late brother, was not the sort of person they wanted interfering in the appointment of government office-holders. After his departure they appointed the Bishop of Winchester as Treasurer, and despatched him to London to take charge of what remained of the Treasury. The various departments of government were set up anew. Even while Edward was still at liberty Roger was consolidating Isabella's position, ensuring that no one would be able to supplant her in the event of Edward's cause being championed by a rival or envious lord.

The king retreated to Neath in early November, and attempted to bargain with Roger and the queen through an embassy headed by the Abbot of Neath. The abbot and his companions were sent back with a stern refusal. No terms were acceptable, only complete surrender: just as Roger had been told in January 1322. He did not need to negotiate further. On 16 November, having been informed of the king's whereabouts by Rhys ap Howel, the pursuing contingent under Lancaster caught sight of Edward, Baldock and Despenser and their few companions in the open country near Neath. They pursued them for a short distance, and caught them. The king's men-at-arms were released; Baldock and Despenser were taken to the queen at Hereford. Also taken was Despenser's vassal, Simon de Reading, who had been so presumptious as to insult the queen and to take the lands of Roger's follower, John Wyard. Lancaster, gleeful at his triumph, took the king himself to Kenilworth. On hearing of the king's capture, the last royalist castle, Caerphilly, surrendered.

Hugh Despenser knew he could expect no mercy, and, anticipating the sentence Roger would pass upon him, he tried to starve himself to death. Even as Henry de Leybourn and Robert Stangrave took him to Hereford to meet his fate, Roger was exacting revenge for a lifetime of enmity on another of the king's friends. On 17 November the Earl of Arundel and two of his associates, John Daniel and Thomas de Micheldever, were beheaded. In the words of the chronicler Murimuth, Roger hated these men with a 'perfect hatred'. The earl had been a sworn enemy of Gaveston ever since the tournament at Wallingford. He had moreover taken arms against Roger's uncle in 1312. He had opposed Roger and his uncle during the Despenser war, had taken the lands of Roger's uncle and even some of Roger's own estates. He had been part of the embassy which had persuaded Roger to surrender at Shrewsbury by giving the false guarantee that his life would be saved. His defence of Hugh Despenser was just another reason for him to suffer the full penalty of the law. Roger procured the official order for the deaths from the queen, who followed his advice in this 'as she did in everything'.[14]

If revenge was a dish best served cold, the Earl of Arundel was merely the starter. The main course was Hugh Despenser. In order to legalise the process against him the tribunal that had sat in judgement on the elder Despenser was reconvened.[15] Roger, the Earls of Lancaster, Kent and Norfolk, and Thomas Wake and William Trussel between them drew up a list of Despenser's crimes. Their judgement was thorough, extensive and uncompromising. Only the sentence was in doubt. The Lancastrians wanted Despenser to be sentenced and beheaded at one of his own castles, in the same way that the Earl of Lancaster had died at Pontefract in 1322. Roger, on the other hand, wanted to ensure that Despenser suffered a death every bit as horrific as his (Despenser's) killing of Llywelyn Bren in 1317. Isabella wanted him executed in London.[16] The number of aggrieved parties meant that Despenser was certain to be quartered: every lord wanted a piece to show their followers that they had exacted revenge.

On 24 November Hugh Despenser, Robert Baldock and Simon de Reading were brought to Hereford. A huge crowd had gathered with trumpets and drums, ready to pull Despenser apart with their bare hands if need be. As the prisoners neared the city, with crowns of nettles on their heads and their surcoats bearing their coats of arms reversed, the crowd seized Despenser and dragged him from his horse. They stripped him of his clothes and wrote biblical verses denouncing arrogance and evil on his skin. Then they led him into the city, forcing Simon de Reading to march in front bearing his standard with the arms reversed. In the market square he was presented before Roger, Isabella and the Lancastrian lords. Sir William Trussel read out the list of charges of which Despenser was accused. He had been adjudged a traitor and an enemy of the realm, he declared. In particular, he was guilty of returning to the realm during his period of banishment without the permission of Parliament; of robbing two great ships to the value of £60,000[17] 'to the great dishonour of the king and the realm and to the great danger of English merchants in foreign countries'; of taking arms against the peers of the realm 'to destroy them and disinherit them contrary to Magna Carta and the Ordinances'; of aiding Andrew de Harclay[18] and other traitors in the 'murder' of the Earl of Hereford and others; of falsely imprisoning the Earl of Lancaster and arranging his death in his own castle by illegally assuming royal power; of arranging the executions of seventeen named barons and knights; of putting Roger and his uncle 'in a harsh prison to murder them without cause except for his coveting of their lands'; of imprisoning Lord Berkeley (Roger's son-in-law), Hugh Audley the elder (Roger's brother-in-law) and Hugh Audley the younger (Roger's nephew), the children of the Earl of Hereford (nephews of the king), and the noblewomen associated with these lords, and even 'old women such as the lady Baret . . . whom he had made the butt of ribaldry and whose arms and legs he had had broken spitefully, against his vows of chivalry and against law and reason'; of traitorously assuming royal authority in the war with the Scots and abusing such power, thus endangering the realm; of abandoning the queen at Tynemouth Priory when the Scots were approaching, thus endangering her life; of often dishonouring the queen and damaging her noble state; of cruelty towards the queen; of confiscating illegally the possessions of the Bishops of Ely, Hereford, Lincoln and Norwich and of robbing their churches, and of making war on the Christian Church; of unlawfully procuring for his father the title of Earl of Winchester to the disinheritance of the Crown, and for Andrew de Harclay the title of Earl of Carlisle; of 'ousting the queen from her lands'; of coming between the king and the queen and hindering their relationship; of persuading the king not to perform his royal duty in going to France to perform homage for Gascony, thereby resulting in the loss of lands to the French; of sending money to France to bribe people to murder the queen and her son the prince, or otherwise to prevent their return to England; of making grants of land to his followers against the law; of putting lords such as Henry de Beaumont unfairly in gaol; and of maliciously counselling the king to leave the realm, and taking with him the treasure of the kingdom and the great seal, contrary to the law. Trussel concluded by describing what would be done to the wretched man's body:

Hugh, you have been judged a traitor since you have threatened all the good people of the realm, great and small, rich and poor, and by common assent you are also a thief. As a thief you will hang, and as a traitor you will be drawn and quartered, and your quarters will be sent throughout the realm. And because you prevailed upon our lord the king, and by common assent you returned to the court without warrant, you will be beheaded. And because you were always disloyal and procured discord between our lord the king and our very honourable lady the queen, and between other people of the realm, you will be disembowelled, and then your entrails will be burnt. Go to meet your fate, traitor, tyrant, renegade; go to receive your own justice, traitor, evil man, criminal![19]

And with that a huge roar went up and Despenser was roped to four horses – not just the usual two – and dragged through the city to the walls of his own castle, where an enormous gallows had been specially constructed, with a great fire at its foot. Simon de Reading was dragged behind him. Both men had nooses placed around their necks, and were lifted into the air. Simon de Reading was lifted just to the normal height, a few feet off the ground. Despenser was raised a full fifty feet, up above the walls of the castle, high for all to see. Then he was lowered on to a ladder. A man climbed up alongside him and sliced off his penis and testicles, flinging them into the fire at the foot of the gallows.[20] Then he plunged his knife into Despenser's abdomen, and cut out his entrails and heart, throwing them into the fire below, to the huge delight of the revenge-crazed crowd. The corpse was finally lowered to the ground, and the head was cut off, and raised to a chorus of ecstatic cheers. It was later sent to London, and Despenser's arms, torso and legs were likewise sent to be displayed above the gates of Newcastle, York, Dover and Bristol. Justice was very visibly and viscerally done.

Baldock, who, as a clergyman, had to be handed over to his fellow clergymen for trial, met a similarly brutal fate, albeit an unofficial one. He was taken to London, but there the mob broke into the house in which he was held, beat him almost to death, and threw him into Newgate prison, where he was soon finished off by the inmates.

Roger and Isabella had every reason to be overjoyed at their success. The day of Despenser's death was a mere two months after their landing in Suffolk, and there had been no innocent casualties except those caught up in the London riots. A year earlier Edward had peremptorily ordered the queen to return and urged the King of France to send Roger back to

England in chains. Now Edward was in chains and both Despensers and Arundel, Baldock, and de Stapeldon were dead. In two months they had achieved what no one had managed since the Conqueror. But, in the wake of their victory, it was clear that life could not return to the way it was before Despenser rose to power. Roger's uncle was dead. Many other lords, knights and commoners were dead as a result of the Despenser war. Many more innocent people had lost their lands in the subsequent tyranny. On the personal level, Roger and Isabella were no longer lovers in exile; they were in the same country as their spouses, and had at least to appear faithful for the sake of the government. On the political level, they had to decide the fate of the king and how to keep rival and potentially dangerous lords under control. It was clear, as Christmas approached, that victory brought a new set of problems to the fore.

ELEVEN

Revolutionary

We do not know when and where Roger came face to face with Joan again. Nor do we know what they said to each other when they did meet. They had last seen each other in the summer of 1321, more than five years earlier. In all that time they had both suffered for Roger's war against the Despensers, but Roger had found a surrogate wife, had frequented the courts of Europe, and had become the most important man in the country. Joan on the other hand had spent five years in prison. At forty, having borne so many children, she must have been losing her looks and fast approaching (what was in the fourteenth century) old age. Whenever it was that they met, it seems likely that it was a meeting touched with sadness, regret and possibly some bitterness on Joan's part; not only because Roger had become Isabella's lover but also for the years of her life she had lost.[1]

It is possible that the meeting took place in November 1326, either just before or after the execution of Despenser. Roger seems to have visited his manor at Pembridge, near Wigmore, where he and Joan had been married.[2] The records do not mention Joan (except in a legal capacity as heiress of the de Geneville lands) until two years later when Roger endowed a chantry at Leintwardine, where priests were to sing masses for the souls of Roger's family, closest friends and ancestors. It is probable that four books of 'romances' which Roger obtained at Westminster early in 1327 were presents for his wife.[3] Joan had a taste for romances, as shown by the inventory of her possessions in 1322. Those issued to Roger in 1327 were actually handed over to Walter de Lingaigne, canon of Wigmore, and Walter de Evesham, clerk, on 19 February. Since Roger was at Westminster himself at this time it seems likely that they were given to the two men to take back to Joan, especially as Walter de Evesham was one of Joan's own clerks.[4] This suggests that she was not with Roger at Westminster but back at Wigmore, where she had been staying in 1322, or at Ludlow, where she was living in 1330, and thus perhaps estranged from her husband. There is no evidence that Roger was anything other than regretful that his devoted wife of so many years had suffered for his actions.[5] On balance it seems that the couple had decided to live apart by early 1327, a decision forced upon them by Isabella's affection for Roger and her need of his guidance, and, most of all, by Roger's love for Queen Isabella and his craving for power.

Roger spent Christmas 1326 at Isabella's castle at Wallingford. His stay was not all seasonal frivolity. Several key issues faced him: how to make Isabella's seizure of power legitimate; how to control lords such as Henry of Lancaster, who had now started referring to himself by his brother's title of Earl of Lancaster; how long to keep the Hainault army in England; and, by no means least, what to do with the king.

The first and the last of these could be considered a single question. If the king were executed, his son would naturally assume the title after his father's death. But such a move, while apparently simple, was technically very difficult. It required a state trial on a charge of treason, a guilty verdict and a death sentence. Roger invited various lords and prelates to discuss the matter with him and Isabella. There was little agreement. From the point of view of most of the lords, Edward had repeatedly shown himself to be unconcerned with the country's welfare and deserved to die. Several of the prelates, however, held that he had been appointed by God, and thus could not legally be deposed or tried. This spiritual argument against a trial had wide political implications: if he were tried and found guilty, many people might believe that God would punish the country. There was also a legal argument against a trial: if Edward was not found guilty of treason – and most people believed that a king could not technically be charged with treason – he would have to be released, and possibly restored. While it would have been easy to rig the trial, this might have raised widespread sympathy for him. The hardest line was taken by the Lancastrians, whose world had been shattered by Edward's destruction of Thomas of Lancaster. Roger, on the other hand, had been saved from his death sentence in 1322 by the king's intervention, and indeed had for many years before that been a loyal supporter of the king. Even now he was a royalist, and he wanted to encourage Prince Edward's respect, a respect which was very unlikely to be forthcoming if he were held responsible for the death of his father. Nor did Isabella want her husband destroyed, partly out of marital affection and partly on account of the dignity of royalty. Since Roger's wife was still alive, there was no question of her marrying Roger even if Edward were executed. By the end of December those opposed to killing the king had prevailed. Roger and his associates decided not to have the king tried but to imprison him, without trial, for life.

This decision presented Roger with a much more difficult problem with regard to the legal consolidation of Isabella's power and the establishment of her son's reign. Since the prince had been appointed guardian of the country while the king had been abroad, on Edward's return that guardianship should have come to an end, even though the king was in prison. Roger and Isabella found a temporary solution by having Bishop Orleton take the great seal from the king and give it to Isabella, so she could rule in her husband's name, or the prince's, or her own, as appropriate. In addition, in December the Chancery was ordered to date writs issued in the king's name as if they had emanated from him at Kenilworth. But Roger and his constitutional advisers, such as Bishop Orleton of Hereford and Bishop Stratford of Winchester, knew this state of affairs could not continue. It would only be a matter of time before someone challenged the legality of such writs.

On 4 January 1327 Roger and Isabella entered London with the prince and the court. The rioting had calmed somewhat. The election of Richard de Bethune as mayor in November had placed one of Roger's most loyal supporters in power, and he had returned the city to something resembling normality. Parliament had accordingly been scheduled to meet on 7 January, and the lords, prelates, knights of the shire and representatives of the boroughs and Cinque Ports all assembled in Westminster Hall.[6] But the king and the two bishops sent to accompany him from Kenilworth had not arrived.[7] As a result Parliament could not proceed, for the assembly could not be deemed Parliamentary unless the king were present. Nothing happened until 12 January when the bishops arrived alone.[8] Instead of the king himself they brought his defiant refusal to attend, and his declaration that all who did attend were traitors. Bishop Orleton, in announcing this, declared that it was just as well that the king had not come, for he kept a dagger in his clothes for the purpose of killing the queen, should he ever see her.

Already Roger's propaganda machine was working. Orleton, who was almost certainly exaggerating the king's defiance, knew as well as Roger that, for the first time in English history, the representatives of the community of the realm would be called upon to act as an authority over and above that of the king. At this time, commoners were rarely even summoned to Parliament, let alone asked to judge the monarch. But Roger and his advisers intended to manipulate them to their political advantage. It was no democratic principle which made Roger and Orleton draw the representatives of English boroughs into the debate about the deposition of Edward II, but a calculated attempt to unite all the classes of the realm against the monarch. Hence no representatives were summoned from South Wales, which was known to be strongly in favour of the king, and representatives were only summoned from North Wales (which was strongly anti-Mortimer) when it was too late for them to take part in the debates.

Orleton went straight to the crux of the matter: the king had refused to come to Parliament; so did Parliament want the king to rule the country or did it prefer that his son should rule instead? Orleton's confidence and the rigging of the later debates itself suggests that a wave of approval was expected to follow his speech, together with a unanimous declaration of allegiance to the prince. But such a reaction was not forthcoming. It was too sudden. The Archbishop of York, three other bishops, and various other people refused to give an answer. They declared that this was for fear of the Londoners, who were known to be on Roger's side. Some of them wished to see the king himself speak in Parliament, and openly abdicate, rather than for him to be deposed by Roger and Isabella. Frustrated, Orleton accordingly dismissed Parliament until nine o'clock the following morning, and consulted with Roger as to what to do next.[9]

Roger now used his influence over the Londoners. The waverers were reluctant to answer his demands because of fear of recriminations; rather than reduce that fear he decided to exploit it. He instructed Richard de Bethune to write to Parliament asking whether the members would come to the Guildhall to swear an oath to protect Isabella and her son, and to depose the king. He also called all the great lords to attend a secret meeting that evening, and asked for their unanimous support in deposing the king. This was forthcoming. Roger now had all the weapons he needed.

At nine o'clock on the morning of Tuesday 13 January Roger addressed the mass gathered in Westminster Hall. He spoke eloquently, but did not try too hard to persuade them. Instead he showed the assembly the letter from the mayor and citizens of London, asking that they all swear the oath to support the queen and her son and to depose the king. Roger added that in a meeting the night before all the great lords of the realm had discussed the matter and were unanimous in their opinion that the king should be deposed. He was not saying this for himself, he said, and nor could he speak for the commons, but he had to speak out on the issue because the great lords had urged him to do so. On cue, Roger's cousin, Thomas Wake, jumped up and declared in a loud voice that he for one did not think that the king should be allowed to rule any longer. As the tones of assent were heard around the hall, Orleton rose to his feet. 'An unwise king destroyeth his people,' he preached, going on to give a tremendous sermon, rousing those present in the way he knew best, through the power of the word of God. By the time he had come to the end, Parliament was truly animated. 'Away with the king! Away with him!' they shouted. But the show was only just beginning. As soon as Orleton had resumed his seat, Bishop Stratford took up the call. His theme, obviously prepared well in advance, was that the head of the nation was feeble, and that the king should be allowed to lead the country astray no longer. As he spoke, again Thomas Wake rose and demanded, gesturing to the assembly, 'Do you agree? Do the people of the country agree?' By this stage the representatives of the people who agreed were completely swept away, and those who did not had been silenced by the knowledge that they would have to face the Londoners in the Guildhall later that day. As the commotion died down, the last of the three scheduled speakers stepped forward. This was the old Archbishop of Canterbury, Walter Reynolds. He said that the people of England had been oppressed too long, and that, if it were the people's will that the king should be deposed, then it was God's will, and the reign should come to an end. Again, on cue, Thomas Wake rose and demanded: 'Is this the will of the people? Is it the people's will that the king should be deposed and his son made king in his place?' A tumult of approval answered him. 'Let it be done! Let it be done!' The archbishop then concluded: 'Your voice has clearly been heard here, for Edward has been deprived of the government of the kingdom and his son made king as you have unanimously consented.'[10] Then, as the assembly was carried away, Prince Edward was ushered into the hall to the cry 'Behold your king!' At which point most of the assembly started singing 'Glory, Laud and Honour'. The Bishop of Rochester, one of the few who did not sing, was later beaten up for his lack of enthusiasm.

The overt manipulation of Parliament was entirely Roger's doing. Later that day a large crowd of nobles, prelates and knights followed him to the Guildhall to swear the oath of fealty requested by Richard de Bethune. The first to swear the oath was Roger. The oath itself was different from that requested by de Bethune in his letter. Those who took it swore only to protect Isabella, her son, and those who fought against Despenser, and to observe the Ordinances and the liberties of the city of London.[11] There was no mention of the deposition of the king. Persuading de Bethune to include this had just been a ruse by Roger to intimidate those who were not in favour to keep quiet during the sermons and speeches in Parliament.[12] It did not matter that many of the assembly did not swear the Guildhall oath; the oath itself was irrelevant as far as the deposition went. But it had influenced or threatened Parliament clearly to vote in favour of removing the king, and thus Roger was able to say that the decision was with the assent of the people of England in Parliament. The English monarchy had changed for ever.

*

The agreement by Parliament to dethrone Edward II was a landmark achievement. Never before had an English monarch been deposed, and nor had any European king of comparable status been removed from his throne. The only precedent was a minor German prince of small reputation earlier in the fourteenth century. Thus, for Victorian and early twentieth-century scholars, the key feature of the fall of Edward II was this constitutional development, and especially what this indicated about the role of Parliament. In concentrating on the constitution they failed to notice the most important fact about the deposition of Edward II: it did not actually happen. Parliament's will was not imposed on Edward; rather he was asked to accept its decision.

On 20 January Edward, dressed in a black robe, was led into the hall at Kenilworth Castle. There he saw the faces of those who had come to announce the decision of Parliament. Immediately he collapsed in a faint, and had to be lifted back to his feet by Bishop Stratford and Henry of Lancaster. Orleton read the charges. The king had been found guilty of several crimes. Namely: of being incompetent to govern, and of allowing others to govern for him to the detriment of his people and of the Church; of not listening to good advice but rather pursuing occupations unbecoming to a monarch; of having lost Scotland and lands in Gascony and Ireland through his failure effectively to govern; of allowing the Holy Church to be damaged and its representatives to be imprisoned, and other nobles to be killed, imprisoned, exiled and disinherited; of failing to ensure that all received justice, but instead governing for his own profit and allowing others to do the same, against his coronation oaths; and of fleeing in the company of a notorious enemy of the realm, and leaving the realm without government, thereby losing the faith and trust of his people. Since his cruelty and faults in his character were to blame, the people had agreed that there was no alternative but to depose him.[13] Edward, utterly shaken by this judgement, wept as he heard the charges. At the end, he was offered a choice: to abdicate in favour of his son, or to resist and relinquish the throne to one who was not of the royal blood but experienced in government, with the obvious implication that this would be Roger. Through his tears, the king confessed that he lamented that his people so hated his rule. He agreed that if the people would accept his son, he would resign in his son's favour. Sir William Trussel then stepped forward to renounce homage on behalf of all the lords of the realm, and after him Thomas le Blount publicly broke his staff of office, announcing that Edward's royal household was no more. In this way Edward abdicated and was not deposed, a distinction which later would prove significant.

News of all that had happened at Kenilworth was published in London on 24 January:

Sir Edward, late king of England, has of his good will and by common counsel and assent of the prelates, earls, barons, and other nobles, and commonalty of the realm, resigned the government of the realm and granted and wills the government shall come to Edward, his eldest son and that he shall govern, reign and be crowned king for which reason all the magnates have done homage. We proclaim the peace of our said Lord, Sir Edward the son, and command under pain of disinheritance and of loss of life and limb that no one infringe the peace of our said lord the king. If anyone have anything to demand from another let him demand it by way of law without using force or violence.[14]

The day after the announcement of the abdication was proclaimed the first day of the reign of Edward III. It was thus effectively the start of the reign of Roger and Isabella, who firmly advised the fourteen-year-old boy, looked after his privy seal for him, appointed the Chancellor who held the great seal, and, of course, controlled access to the young king himself.

*

Roger, as the orchestrator of events, had never had any doubts about the discussions concerning the king's deposition, nor about the king's subsequent abdication. Even before the debates had taken place he had fixed the date of the coronation for 1 February, and had decided that his three eldest sons would be among those knighted on the day. On 13 January, the day of his speech and the prelates' speeches to Parliament, he was more concerned with what his sons would wear at the coronation of the new king than the process of removing the old one. He ordered that his sons should be given bannerets' clothes for the occasion.[15] Three days later, he changed his mind and decided they should be dressed in clothing befitting earls.[16] This was four days before the king's abdication. His confidence was so high, and his authority so great, that dressing his sons as earls – implying a rank above himself and far above them – seems never to have crossed his mind as a high-handed act. Nor, in the euphoria of the moment, does it seem to have crossed anyone else's.

On the day of the coronation the young king was knighted by John of Hainault.[17] Edward himself then dubbed a number of young knights, as tradition dictated. First and foremost were Roger's sons – Edmund, Roger and Geoffrey – in their earls' attire, followed by Hugh de Courtenay, Thomas Lestrange and other heirs. The Archbishop of Canterbury performed the actual coronation, while the Bishops of Winchester and London held the crown above the boy, it being too heavy to be placed upon his head. The two bishops who had performed such important roles in the proceedings of the Parliamentary deposition – Orleton and Stratford – were present, as were Roger's other episcopal supporters: William Airmyn of Norwich, Henry de Burghersh of Lincoln, and John de Hothum of Ely. Even the Bishop of Rochester was present, still nursing his bruises. This time he joined with Bishop Airmyn in the singing of the Litany.

The coronation was marked by several propaganda statements, like the earlier parliament. Young Edward proclaimed a general pardon to all criminals then in custody, thereby clearing up the problem created by his father's offer of pardons in return for soldiers to fight the invaders. A special medal was struck for the occasion, and scattered among the crowds after the service. This showed, on one side, the young king laying a sceptre on a pile of hearts, with the motto: 'Given to the people according to their will', and on the other, the king holding his hands out as if to catch a falling crown, with the motto: 'I did not take, I received'.[18] The latter message, loaded and unsubtle as it was, was not incorrect. Edward did not take the crown: Roger took it for him.

With the official handover of the crown to the new regime, the protagonists of the revolution were at liberty to grant themselves all the lands, titles and power they desired. Historians have traditionally claimed that Roger and Isabella took advantage of this to make themselves huge grants, and that they were avaricious, insatiable, and even ruthless in their acquisition of land, castles and power. This sounds like a classic case of conquerors gathering their fortunes greedily, but the image is misleading. A closer examination of the records reveals a marked difference between Roger and Isabella in 1327. On the very day of the coronation Isabella had granted to her an annual income of no less than 20,000 marks (£13,333). This was a phenomenal increase from her previous income of £4,500 before the Despenser regime had confiscated her assets. She thus made over to herself one of the largest personal incomes anyone had ever received in English history, larger even than the income of the late Earl of Lancaster, whose wealth had been regarded as fabulous. Roger did not follow her example. In December 1326 he had been given the keepership of Denbigh Castle, and allocated lands to the annual value of £1,000 in fulfilment of a promise made to him before the invasion. He and Thomas Wake shared a debt of £1,152, owing (but yet to be paid) to the late Hugh Despenser. But as far as direct substantial gifts went, that was all. Indeed, it is remarkable how few direct grants Roger received in 1327. In mid-February he was given the right to marry one of his daughters to the heir to the earldom of Pembroke,[19] and four months later he received temporary custody of the lands of Eleanor de Clare, widow of Hugh Despenser, which he returned to her the following year. He also received the wardships of the heirs of the de Beauchamp and Audley families, but he had already been awarded both of these by Edward II before his rebellion, and so these were merely restorations of his property.[20] His pardon on 21 February for escaping from the Tower, and with it the restoration of his estates in England, was hardly a concession. The remaining grants made to him carried administrative responsibilities: for example, his uncle's old role of Justiciar of Wales, which he held for the rest of his life, and a keepership of the peace on the Marches. Otherwise they were grants he requested benefiting his dependants, such as an award to the townsmen of Ludlow of the right of murage (a toll on all those coming and going from the town so they could rebuild the town walls), and a licence for him to make a small gift of land to Aconbury Priory, at which both Joan's sisters were living. These were not the marks of unbridled acquisitiveness or dictatorship: they amounted to a lump sum of several hundred pounds and an income probably about half as much again as he had earned while he was Justiciar of Ireland. Unlike Isabella he was making relatively modest claims and taking time to explore the limits of his authority and power.

The explanation for Roger's reluctance to seize great wealth immediately is simple. The examples of Despenser and Gaveston could be said to have haunted him. He did not seek huge grants as they did. He did not impose himself on the government's largesse as they had done. Most importantly he did not attempt to stamp on his principal rival, Henry of Lancaster. Instead he cleverly allowed Lancaster officially to dominate Parliament and the regency council. He allowed the Lancastrian supporter, John de Ros, to be appointed Steward of the Royal Household. He did not oppose any of the pardons granted to the Lancastrians for their crimes and sentences in 1322 with the sole exception of that of Robert de Holand, in which he followed the Lancastrian demand for the man not to be pardoned. Henry of Lancaster was permitted officially to receive his late brother's title of Earl of Lancaster. Most importantly a council of twelve or fourteen magnates and prelates was appointed, and Henry of Lancaster, not Roger, was given the chairmanship. This council was filled with members of the Lancastrian faction, for Henry Percy and John de Ros were Lancastrians, and Thomas Wake was not just a cousin of Roger's, he was also a son-in-law to the late Earl of Lancaster. Indeed, it is open to question whether Roger even sat on this council.[21] The only significant issue over which Henry of Lancaster did not gain complete success was in the restitution to himself of all his brother's estates. Isabella herself had appropriated most of the vast wealth of Henry of Lincoln, which had descended to Alice, the miserable and estranged wife of the late Thomas of Lancaster, and thus kept part of what Henry of Lancaster considered his rightful inheritance.

Lancaster was particularly angry that he had not received the honour and castle of Pontefract. This confrontation between Isabella and Lancaster, against the background of Roger's purposeful avoidance of confrontation with the earl, suggests the queen's acquisition of lands was not wholly with Roger's blessing, and that her acquisition of personal wealth was the one area in which she refused to follow her lover's advice.

Between the queen and Lancaster one can discern Roger playing a diplomatic role, playing down his own interests, trying perhaps to restrain the queen from acquiring too many lands, and trying to placate Henry of Lancaster. But as early as the end of March he realised placation was not a long-term strategy. Isabella's acquisitiveness was too great, and Lancaster's propensity to sulk even greater. In addition to her massively increased income Isabella had obtained in January a grant of £20,000 supposedly to pay her debts overseas (which had in fact already been paid) and had earlier received a further sum of £11,843, together with the treasures of Hugh Despenser and the Earl of Arundel.[22] Henry of Lancaster bitterly complained. Roger, of course, stood by Isabella, and as a safeguard he did the one thing essential to preserve her and the regime he had set up in her name. He took Edward II out of the clutches of the Earl of Lancaster.

Custody of the king was vitally important to Roger. If Lancaster turned against the queen and promoted a counter-revolution, Edward II would be a natural rallying point for all those angered by Isabella's greed. Alternatively, the earl could allow Edward to be 'rescued' by some of the extremist groups who were attempting to free the king and restore him. Even the Scots, who were now beginning to take arms again, could have been involved. One such attempt, by the Dunheved brothers, seems to have been made at the end of March.[23] It was time to grasp the nettle.

The removal of the ex-king from Kenilworth Castle on 3 April 1327 was undoubtedly a strategy devised and put into effect by Roger. The two new custodians, Sir John Maltravers and Thomas, Lord Berkeley, were among his closest political supporters. Maltravers been knighted on the same day more than twenty years before, and had subsequently been a companion in Ireland,[24] a fellow rebel in 1321, and a companion in exile on the Continent. Maltravers was close to Berkeley too, being married to his sister and having previously been in the retinue of the Earl of Pembroke with him. Berkeley himself had served in Roger's household in 1318, rode with Roger in his 1321 rebellion, and had married Roger's eldest daughter, Margaret. If the evidence of the propagandist chronicler Geoffrey le Baker is to be believed, one of the men-at-arms acompanying the king from Kenilworth was William Bishop, one of Roger's men-at-arms in 1321.[25] But perhaps the most intriguing piece of evidence indicating Roger's responsibility for the transfer of the deposed king is that now, for the first extended period since invading the country, Roger left the court.

It is much easier to be certain of Roger's whereabouts in the period after the deposition than at any time earlier in his career. From 1327 he frequently took it upon himself to be one of the barons who witnessed the granting of charters under the royal seal. In the first year of the reign of Edward III he witnessed at least fifty-seven of the ninety-one grants recorded on the Charter Rolls, thus indicating his presence on at least fifty-seven occasions. In addition he made about twenty requests for grants to be made to other people, at which his presence would almost certainly have been required. From this regularity of court service, combined with the usual means of establishing a medieval itinerary, we can be reasonably confident that the periods for which we have no positive information regarding his whereabouts indicate times when he was not at court.

There are two periods in 1327 during which Roger was absent from court for more than two weeks, the first being from early March to early May, the second being in the autumn. On both occasions he rejoined the court at Nottingham. Since on the second occasion he returned to Nottingham from South Wales, and thus by way of the Welsh Marches, it is quite possible that during the first period of absence he was also in the region of South Wales. This coincides with the king's removal from Kenilworth in early April. The following year Henry of Lancaster accused Roger of taking the king by force from Kenilworth.[26] Roger's rare absence from court at this time and his possible presence in the region does suggest he was on standby to play a military role in seizing the ex-king if necessary, and, if Lancaster's accusation was true, that he took Edward by force. The ex-king was taken from Kenilworth to Llanthony Priory near Gloucester, and from there to Berkeley, where he was kept in lordly comfort at an expense to the Exchequer of £5 a day.

By now Roger and Isabella had solved virtually all of the problems that had faced them six months earlier. They had forced the king to abdicate and had established the prince on the throne, thereby legitimising their authority, and they had safeguarded themselves from the ill will of the Earl of Lancaster, for the time being at least. Now a new problem raised its head, or rather an old problem, one that had beset and beaten both Edward I and Edward II: Scotland.

*

On the day of the coronation the Scots had launched an exploratory raid on Norham Castle. They had been beaten back, but in March the court was informed by its spies of a build-up in Scottish forces preparatory to an invasion. Accordingly, as a precautionary measure, a general muster was ordered at the beginning of April. Although Roger and Isabella had been wholehearted in their determination to find a diplomatic settlement, peace negotiations between the two countries were constantly collapsing. Four sets of negotiators had been appointed, and one by one they had failed. This was strange, for it was in the interests of both sides to secure a lasting peace. How was it then that England and Scotland now found themselves heading for war?

The explanation lies in the Scots' neutrality during Roger and Isabella's invasion. If there had ever been a time for the Scots to attack England, it was in September 1326, when most of the English fleet had been tied up in the south and the army was reluctant to obey a general muster. But the Scots had not attacked. Before the invasion, Sir Thomas Randolph, Bruce's chief negotiator, had gone to Paris to meet Roger and Isabella. Terms had been agreed: in return for a recognition of Scottish sovereignty, the Scots would not attack England during the invasion. Now the invasion was over, but no recognition of Scottish independence had taken place. Roger and Isabella had delayed their side of the bargain because they had not wanted to alienate the northern barons and Henry of Lancaster, to whom the idea of Scottish independence was anathema. Bruce was close to death now, and he wanted a recognition of Scottish independence in his lifetime. As a result he planned a three-pronged attack on England: through an invasion from Scotland, another from Ireland, and a rebellion in South Wales. Although Roger prevented the Irish rebellion by replacing Despenser's justiciar there with his own former deputy, time was running out for a peaceful settlement.[27]

It was a difficult situation. Roger and Isabella did not want to fight. Scotland was, to all intents and purposes, lost, and the last thing they wanted was the expense of a new Scottish campaign. But they faced the enmity of the Earl of Lancaster if they did not. They devised a compromise strategy. They made the appearance of marching to defend the north, but planned to make no significant inroads into the Scottish position. They raised men from the boroughs and from John of Hainault, who was once more requested to bring a mercenary army. The feudal host was summoned, and, by the end of May, the English army was ready at York.

We know what happened in the ensuing weeks in some detail as Sir John of Hainault brought a chronicler in his retinue: Jean le Bel. His account corresponds well with what we know of the story in John Barbour's poetic biography of Robert Bruce.[28] Thus we have the whole story of what became known as the Weardale campaign from both sides, from its riotous beginning in the unlikely location of the dormitory of the Dominican friary at York.

On 7 June, to celebrate the arrival of Sir John, Isabella held a great feast at the friary where the court was staying. As part of the courtly entertainment, Isabella planned to entertain Sir John alone with sixty ladies-in-waiting at tables set up in the dormitory while the king held court with all the men in the hall and cloisters. The ladies were superbly dressed, and dishes were passed around which had been dyed various colours so everyone had to guess what they were eating. But few of the dishes were tasted, as a violent quarrel quickly broke out between some of the Hainaulters' servants and the English archers lodged with them. Seeing their fellows attacked, the English archers appeared with arrows notched in their bows, and shot some of the Hainaulters, forcing the others to seek refuge in nearby houses. Several householders panicked and refused to let the Hainaulters in to get their weapons. Fences and gardens were trampled in the ensuing panic, and those Hainaulters who managed to arm themselves gathered in a square to attack the archers. There followed a general melee between the Hainaulters and the English in which several hundred men on each side were killed. Le Bel claimed that more than three hundred English archers died. Peace was only restored when the king and the leading English magnates rode through the streets calling for the fighting to stop. But the damage had been done: from then on, the Hainaulters slept in their armour and posted guards on their lodgings. They said they feared the English archers were keener to kill them than the Scots.

The army remained at York throughout June. Several rumours reached Roger of plots being formed against him. Accordingly he took personal control of the situation. On 8 June he had himself appointed chief keeper of the peace in Herefordshire, Worcestershire and Staffordshire, and to this he added Glamorgan four days later. Being the deposed king's keeper made for an uneasy existence, and one which could only become uneasier if he went to Scotland. But on 15 June the Scots launched an overnight attack, and it became clear that a military confrontation was inevitable, not so much to defeat the Scots as to placate the northern English lords.

On 1 July, as the army set out from York, dreadful news came from the south. An express messenger gave Roger a secret message: Berkeley Castle had been ransacked and Edward II had been captured by men faithful to the Dunheved brothers, the same men who had been involved in the conspiracy in March to free Edward.[29] It was a significant blow. One can only imagine the fury and the feeling of powerlessness that he now felt. Here he was, about to set out on a sham war against the Scots, on behalf of a sham king, two hundred and fifty miles away from Berkeley Castle, unable easily to communicate with Maltravers and Berkeley. Edward had to be recaptured at all costs, not just because of the risk of Roger's enemies exploiting the ex-king but for the sake of his control of the present king too. He must have recognised that without Isabella he had no real power over Edward III. This young man wanted to fight, to play the chivalric hero, to rule even; and Roger, without Isabella, could not stop him. The only potential hold he had over the king was possession of his father, and his ability to stop anyone else from setting Edward II up as a rival to Edward III.

Roger waited at York for a day after the army set out. He had no option but to keep faith with Berkeley and Maltravers, and hope that they could recapture the ex-king. The two custodians were given a special commission to keep the peace across the whole of the region, through the counties of Dorset, Somerset, Wiltshire, Hampshire, Herefordshire, Oxfordshire and Berkshire, in the hope that this would help them track down the conspirators. Apart from this official appointment, everything was done in the strictest secrecy – no one was allowed to know the ex-king was at liberty. Then Roger set off to catch up with the army.

Edward III was full of confidence and expectation as he set out on his first military campaign. Le Bel notes trumpets sounding and pennants fluttering as they marched north, through Overton, Myton-on-Swale, to Topcliffe, where they waited a week for intelligence reports, and then on through Northallerton and Darlington to Durham, which they reached on 14 July. Here they paused again, considering their strategy. With a small contingent of men at Carlisle guarding the western approaches to England, it was hoped that any Scottish army intent on reaching York would be held at bay by the risk of being cut off by the king's force at Durham.

The Scots were not daunted. Under the command of Sir Thomas Randolph and Sir James Douglas – Black Douglas as he is known to Scottish patriots – Bruce's army had already crossed into England and was harrying the country. Far from cutting off the Scots' advance the two English armies had created a corridor along which the Scots had skilfully manoeuvred their forces. The first the English knew of the incursion was seeing smoke rising above the villages to the south.

How could an experienced military leader like Roger have allowed this to happen? One explanation may simply be that he was not personally in control. The king had appointed the Earls of Norfolk and Kent to take direct charge of the army, and Henry of Lancaster to be overall commander.[30] Roger received no position of command at all. As the most experienced and successful military leader then in England, this might be considered surprising. But it has to be remembered that Roger and Isabella were not anticipating any great conquests or victories, but rather a campaign merely to hold the Scots at bay prior to agreeing a surrender of the English claim of sovereignty. Moreover one must bear in mind Roger's policy of not offering himself official positions of command in order to avoid being seen to be appropriating power. It is probable that he opted out of any share of responsibility for the campaign on the basis that it was bound to end in a peace which many would find humiliating. The alternative explanation – that his failure to receive a position of command was due to the king's or Lancaster's resentment – is unlikely, since the appointments were made in mid-June, at York, while Edward was still under his mother's watchful eye. The blunder was most probably a failure of collective leadership, in which Roger, in a distracted and unenthusiastic mood, was to blame as much as Henry of Lancaster and the two royal earls.

Jean le Bel, as a Hainaulter footsoldier with the army, had his own explanation as to why the Scottish forces managed to outstrip and outsmart the English. They travelled on horseback, taking no provision wagons, no chests of meat, no tuns of wine. They took no pots or pans either, and so could travel long distances in one day, whereas the English were tied to their long lines of packhorses and supply wagons. In war the Scots relied on local cattle, which they butchered and stewed in cauldrons made of hide, and to balance their diet they carried oatmeal under their saddles which they baked into cakes on flat stones. In addition they were following two very experienced and inspiring commanders; the English by comparison were following a fourteen-year-old boy whom Roger and the other leaders were desperately trying to shelter from danger.

When the English saw the smoke rising to the south, they turned in that direction and drew up in three battalions, expecting to do battle. The Scots withdrew. The English followed as far as a wood near Bishop Auckland, where they waited for their baggage carts while the Scots burnt another village. So long did they wait that they camped in the wood, and set out in formation again the following day. But the terrain was too hilly and marshy for battle formations to be maintained. Their systematic rule-book approach thwarted them. Not only that, it was exhausting, and they were still no nearer meeting the Scots in battle. Smoke now rose from more villages in their path. The army was exhausted. When they camped that night the king ordered his commanders to meet at a nearby monastery to discuss tactics. It was agreed that the Scots were probably now in retreat, unwilling to face superior numbers, and that the English might yet win a victory if they moved north to cut off their route over the River Tyne. The one problem was that this strategy required a very rapid troop manoeuvre. The decision was made that the English mounted men should emulate the Scots and leave behind their provisions. Lacking the knowledge of how to make oatcakes, each man was told to take only one loaf of bread with him, strapped to his saddle. It was anticipated that there would be a battle the next day, so further provisions were considered unnecessary.

Next morning the English mounted men all set off on a thirty-five-mile ride towards the Tyne. The strict battle formation in which they had proceeded earlier no longer applied. Now men rode ahead of their banners and behind them, lacking all order. But the weather had not been good, and horses were trapped in bogs and marshes. The journey became miserable and frustrating. Those whose horses stuck in the mud, or went lame, quickly fell behind, and with no support to help them soon lost sight of the army. They were riding in heavy armour, which made progress even harder and slower. The lack of discipline hampered them: when the front ranks of riders cried out or gestured at the sight of wild animals, of which there were many, the rear thought that the enemy was attacking, and forced themselves forward with all haste. Through marshes and mountains le Bel and his comrades followed the king and Roger, reaching the Tyne that evening. There they forded the river near Haydon, despite the inconvenience of the huge rocks, and collapsed, exhausted and hungry, on the far side.

Now the shortsightedness of the manoeuvre became apparent. Having failed to meet the Scots, they would have to sleep in their armour, out in the open, with no tents, nor the means to make any shelters. This effectively meant no sleep. They had no warmth since they had no hatchets and hooks to get material to build fires, and they had no food, except the loaves they carried. By now these were mostly disgustingly salty and damp, soaked by the sweat of their exhausted horses. Their forces were scattered, their companions were far behind, and their supply wagons were a fading memory. Worse, they had nothing for their horses to eat, and on the bare bank of the Tyne there was precious little to which they could tether them, so men sat out the night on the ground, shivering, holding their horses' reins.

When dawn finally came, their sorrows were swollen by a downpour. The rain was so heavy that within a few hours the river before them had risen dramatically, and it was no longer possible to cross to find out where their supplies were, or where their enemy was. Men drew their swords and hacked branches from the trees to tie up their horses, but otherwise they were in the same parlous state as they had been the evening before: except colder, hungrier, and more hopeless.

That night they attempted to sleep in their armour again.

The following day, about noon, they found some 'poor peasants', who told them they were forty-two miles from Newcastle and thirty-three from Carlisle, and that there were no nearer towns. Men were sent off accordingly to fetch provisions on horseback. They proclaimed in the towns that whoever wished to sell their goods should bring them to the army. The announcement was sufficient to bring a few mules and ponies laden with poorly baked rough bread and thin watered down wine to add to the river water the army had been drinking. Although the food was poor, men fought over it. The rains continued and the saddles and harnesses began to rot, and many horses fell sick and died. Sores developed on the horses' backs, and their hooves rotted. They were unable to replace the horses' shoes. There was no wood except stuff so green and wet it would not burn, and men's armour began to chafe and tear the skin off their shoulders. For eight days this went on, according to le Bel, with the army tramping up and down the north bank of the river between two fords. The official records agree with him: after the long ride from Bishop Auckland on 21 July the privy seal (the most accurate indication we have as to the king's whereabouts) was either at Haydon or twenty miles upstream at Haltwhistle until 29 July.

Meanwhile, the Scots, who had not anticipated the sudden dash of the English from Bishop Auckland, had begun to wonder what had happened to the enemy. They themselves sensibly remained in their well-defended position at Stanhope. On 29 July, a Yorkshire squire named Thomas Rokeby found them, and, having been captured by the Scots guards, was released in order to bring the English back to confront them. At Haltwhistle the army returned to the river, now in full flood, where a number of horses were drowned. Once across they rode down to the burnt-out ruins of Blanchland Abbey. Here, knowing at last where the Scots were, and reunited with their footsoldiers and supply wagons, they prepared for battle. With great solemnity Edward heard mass and made his confession. Then the English mounted and advanced with trumpets sounding behind their banners and rode the last nine miles south from Blanchland to Stanhope, where the Scots were arrayed.

The purpose of the Scots in releasing Thomas Rokeby to lead the English to them was immediately apparent. They were lined up on the side of a steep hill about four hundred yards on the other side of the River Wear. To fight them, the English would have to cross the river and climb the hill under arrow fire. Although the young king did what he could to inspire his forces – riding among his army giving them words of encouragement, knighting several esquires, and drawing his footsoldiers up in battalions – nothing could detract from the strength of the Scottish position. They simply did not move. Edward sent heralds to them, asking them whether they would consider crossing the river to fight on the English side, since they professed to be eager for battle. Sir Thomas Randolph was all for this, but Sir James Douglas restrained him, insisting they should be patient. The Scots sent their reply: the King of England could see that they were in his country, and that they had ransacked and plundered it; if he did not like them being there he should cross the river and force them to retreat, otherwise they would stay where they were.

The English marched several battalions forward, and sent their archers to the front to cross the river and to cover the advance of their knights. But Douglas anticipated this move, and sent a party forward under Donald of Mar and Archibald Douglas to ambush the archers. The archers were warned at the last minute by a squire, Robert Ogle, and although many were killed, they managed to retreat. In the fighting a Scots knight, Sir William Erskine, was captured, and, in anticipation of a general attack, the English brought forward some new weapons they had brought with them. 'Crakkis of wer' Barbour calls them, saying they had never been heard before.[31] They were in fact the forerunners of the first cannon to be used in war in Britain: iron buckets filled with stones and gunpowder, ignited from beneath, making noises considerably louder than anything heard in battle before. As the wily Scots may well have observed from their commanding position, these exploding iron buckets were not yet wholly reliable or even controllable, and required considerable further development before they would become effective weapons. Barbour also remarked that that day was the first time the Scots had seen heraldic crests on knights' helmets. It is ironic that one of the classic hallmarks of the knight on horseback should first appear in the same battle as the first guns, which would eventually make such mounted knights redundant.

On seeing the attack on the English archers, Roger insisted that the advance be halted. Young Edward was furious: this was his great chance to lead a victorious army. Moreover, he had gone amongst his men urging them to fight for England and for God; he could not possibly be seen to withdraw now: it would seem cowardly. But Roger insisted. He overruled the Earls of Lancaster and Kent, countermanded Sir John of Hainault, and persuaded the marshal of the army, the Earl of Norfolk, not to lead the vanguard against the Scots.[32] They all obeyed him. Seething with fury, Edward accused Roger of treason, saying that he wanted the Scots to get away.[33] Roger would not be moved. He had no official position, he ruled only through force of character – he did not even have Isabella at his side to coerce young Edward – but on the field of battle no one disagreed with him or dared disobey. His peers were scared of him.

That night the English encamped in a bitter mood. The Scots, seeing their advantage, decided to keep them up all night. They built huge fires and blew their trumpets and screamed and howled to keep them awake. Morale in the English camp sank; nor did it rise much the next day. The English feigned a frontal attack while an ambush of a thousand men was sent around to attack the Scots from the rear, and to force them closer to the river. But the Scots discovered the ruse, and made to ambush the would-be ambushers. The English advance party was called back. A few men were killed or captured: nothing was gained.

The following day was 1 August, St Peter's day, and the fourth anniversary of Roger's escape from the Tower. Perhaps he reflected that his living conditions were hardly any better than they had been in 1323. At least as a prisoner he had been able to sleep. Again, that night, the Scots did all they could to prevent the English from getting any rest.

After three days of this constant harassment by day and night, the English raised their weary heads to behold a bare hill. The Scots had gone. In the middle of the night Douglas and Randolph had led their men several miles along the river to another wooded hill, one even more defensible than the first. The few Scots whom the English had managed to capture in their skirmishes had let on that the Scots were short of bread and wine, although they did have plenty of cattle to eat. It was resolved once more to starve the Scots from their position. The English army shifted camp, to stop the Scots coming and going. Apart from the odd skirmish, nothing happened for eight days.

One night, when the English were being allowed a good night's sleep for a change, Sir James Douglas secretly led five hundred mounted men across the river.[34] He led them a long way around the English camp, to the far side, and ordered half of them to draw their swords to cut the guy ropes of the English tents; the other half were to have their spears ready, to stab down on the bodies sleeping beneath. According to the Scottish patriot Barbour, as Douglas rode to the English camp he heard a soldier saying how he wanted to stay in the north no longer, for he was much afraid of Black Douglas, to which Douglas replied 'You have good cause!' as he killed him. With Douglas blowing his horn, the Scots galloped through the camp, slashing with their swords and stabbing with their spears by the light of the English fires. Sir James was heard yelling, between blasts on his horn, 'Douglas! Douglas! You will all die, you English barons!' Even the king's tent was attacked: two or three of the guy ropes were cut, and the king was shaken badly. Douglas was attacked by a man with a club on his retreat and was wounded and thrown from his horse, but his men piled towards the sound of his horn, and his assailant was killed. As suddenly as they had arrived, the Scots vanished back into the night.

Thereafter the English once again chose to sleep in their armour. They posted heavy guards on all the approaches to their camp, but no further attacks were staged. On 6 August they captured a Scot who told them that that night the army had been ordered to follow Sir James Douglas's banner wherever it went. He knew nothing more than this. The English leaders were sure that this meant they would be attacked, and so drew up in readiness, fully armed, in their battle formations. The Scottish fires burnt late, as usual. But shortly before dawn two Scottish trumpeters came to them and announced that the Scots had left for home some time before midnight. A party of men sent across the river to their camp next morning discovered this to be true: le Bel saw three hundred leather cauldrons full of meat to be cooked. It was a final insult to the English, as if the Scots were even giving them a farewell meal.

Two days later Roger, King Edward and the army arrived back in Durham. They found their carts and wagons there, each stored in a barn with a little flag on it to help identification. After two days in Durham they returned to York, and Roger rejoined Isabella. The army was disbanded. The Hainaulters were promised £4,000 compensation for their horses, along with all their other expenses, and sent home.

It had been an absolute fiasco, and no one tried to pretend otherwise. Whose fault was it? Given the youth of the king, one would normally blame those who had command of the army, in this case the Earls of Lancaster, Norfolk and Kent. But the king himself blamed Roger, who, as we have seen, was effectively in charge throughout. Responsibility for the initial failure to contain the Scots probably lies with him, and he certainly prevented the English army from attacking them at Stanhope. Edward believed that such failure amounted to treason. But in Roger's defence, it was obvious at the time even to footsoldiers like le Bel that the Scots were in too strong a position for the English to mount a serious attack. In addition, it seems probable that Roger actually wanted the Scots to get away. A massacre of Scotsmen would only provoke reprisals, and he and Isabella were not prepared to countenance year after year of war against the Scots for a few barren acres of no-man's-land, as Edward's father and grandfather had done. They were determined to honour an agreement which recognised the independence of Scotland, and this would have been jeopardised by a major battle. Thus Edward was justified in accusing Roger of treason but not of incompetence. Roger's purposes had been to preserve the king's life on a sham campaign which satisfied the northerners and did not significantly damage the Scots, and this he had done.

Whatever his private motives, the Weardale campaign was publicly embarrassing for Roger. His lack of official command would have done little to lessen Lancaster's anger, for example. The escape of the ex-king, although still a secret, threatened to humiliate him further. Back at York he heard from Thomas de Berkeley that Edward had in fact been recaptured and secured, but also that further plans to free him were being made by groups of dissident royalists in South Wales. Over the course of the next few weeks, Roger planned a final resolution to his various problems. He decided that the Exchequer and courts should be transferred to York, where they could be more directly administered while negotiations took place with the Scots. And at the beginning of September, he and Isabella agreed what they would do with Edward II. On the 4th he left the court at Nottingham, ignored his summons to Parliament, and went to South Wales.[35] From there he would order his final solution to the problem of the ex-king.

TWELVE

The King's Murderer?

Popular legend has it that Edward II died in agony in Berkeley Castle with a red-hot spit thrust through a horn inserted into his anus. Various elaborations on this are to be found in a number of chronicles: that he had been kept half-naked in a pool of cold water with corpses floating around him for weeks beforehand; that he was pinioned by cushions (or a door, or a table) while he was skewered, and that his screams as the spit entered his body could be heard over a mile away. The usual explanation for the extraordinary cause of death is that the king's body would be unmarked when examined. These stories are all characteristic of the vivid popular imagination of the period, and it is tempting to conclude that they are unlikely to be true simply for that reason. But they do have a strong basis in many of the chronicles of the early to mid-fourteenth century, and thus a much closer analysis of these and other sources is necessary in order to determine both what happened and what people believed happened. This narrative of Roger's life must therefore pause in order to establish the limits of what we can reasonably say about the death of Edward II, with a view to determining the nature and extent of his responsibility.

To begin with the official records, we know that Edward III received news of his father's death late at night on Wednesday 23 September at Lincoln, the message being carried by Thomas Gurney.[1] The death was announced publicly on Monday 28 September, the last day of Parliament. It was stated officially that Edward had died of natural causes at Berkeley Castle on the feast of St Matthew the Apostle and Evangelist (21 September).[2] The accounts rendered by Thomas de Berkeley and John Maltravers tally with this date: they claimed £5 a day for their expenses in guarding the living king from the date they received him (3 April) to 21 September, and after that they claimed the same rate for custody of the dead king's body until 21 October, when the corpse was handed over to the Abbot of St Peter's, Gloucester.[3] From these accounts we know also that Edward II was embalmed at Berkeley in the month following his death, and that a number of people watched with the corpse in the traditional manner until his burial in December. One of these was William Beaukaire, who most importantly started his period of 'watching' on the very day of the king's death, 21 September, and stayed with the corpse the whole time until the burial.[4] In addition there was a clerk of the royal household, Hugh de Glanville, who was commissioned to take the body from Berkeley to Gloucester, and who remained with the corpse from 22 October until the burial. He was responsible for paying all the others staying with the corpse, namely, John Eaglescliff, Bishop of Llandaff, for watching from 21 October to the day of the burial; and Robert de Hastings and Edmund Wasteneys, knights; Bernard de Burgh and Richard de Potesgrave, the king's chaplains; Bertrand de la More and John de Enfield, the king's sergeants-at-arms; and finally, Andrew, the king's candle-bearer. All of these men were with the king's body from 20 October at Berkeley Castle to the day of the burial at Gloucester.[5] Finally, we know from official sources that the body was eviscerated and embalmed by a local woman, not the king's physician as one might have expected; and we can be sure that her work was carried out at Berkeley, as many of the expenses, including 37s for a silver vase to contain the deposed king's heart, were charged by Thomas de Berkeley to the royal wardrobe.

Even these few bare facts imply the king died in suspicious circumstances. The first point to note is that only one man, William Beaukaire, participated in the formal 'watching' with the corpse before 20 October, and that for the month after the death sole responsibility for the king's body lay with John Maltravers and Thomas de Berkeley. Beaukaire had been pardoned in March 1327 for defending Caerphilly Castle against the invaders the previous year.[6] As a royal sergeant-at-arms, his arrival at Berkeley Castle on the day of the death and his prolonged stay with the body until the burial suggests that the king's death was premeditated by the person who sent him. It also implies that the person who premeditated the death had authority over sergeants-at-arms of the royal household. The next point to note is that the embalming woman had finished with the body before these other watchers saw it. The embalming process of kings, like most nobles in the fourteenth and fifteenth centuries, involved covering the body with a linen cerecloth (a cloth impregnated with wax).[7] Thus any cuts, bruises or other wounds on the body would have been entirely covered before any of the named watchers saw it, with the sole exception of William Beaukaire, who, as we have seen, appears to have been involved in the plot to dispose of Edward II on 21 September.

The question of who sent William Beaukaire to Berkeley is not a difficult one to answer. To begin with, in 1330 Roger was directly accused of arranging the king's murder by Edward III, and was not allowed to answer the charge, being found guilty by 'common knowledge'. While this does not itself prove his guilt, we also know that the king's imprisonment was entirely controlled by Roger. In addition, Roger was probably in the area at the time, just across the Bristol Channel, supposedly attempting to discover the perpetrators of a plot to bring down the government.[8] He returned to court shortly after the death occurred. Roger, of course, also had authority over royal sergeants-at-arms, and could have sent Beaukaire. Even more damning is some evidence given in a 1331 court case in which William de Shalford, Roger's lieutenant in North Wales, was cited as writing from Anglesey to Roger at Abergavenny on 14 September 1327 with news of a plot being formed to release the deposed king by force. According to the court records, Roger is supposed to have shown the letter to William de Ockley – a member of Roger's wife's household at the time of her incarceration, and thus a particularly close family servant – and commanded him to take it to Edward's guardians at Berkeley with the message that the captors should 'acquaint themselves with its contents and find an appropriate remedy to avoid the peril'.[9] These facts, and Roger's involvement in removing Edward from Kenilworth against Henry of Lancaster's will, allow us to be confident that it was William de Ockley who bore Roger's instructions to Berkeley. In all likelihood, William Beaukaire accompanied de Ockley, and remained with the corpse, to ensure no one inspected it closely before it was embalmed and neatly covered in cerecloth.

So much for the responsibility. What actually happened to Edward is a much more complicated question to answer. It was announced at the time that he died of natural causes, and there was no subsequent official statement as to the cause of his death, not even when those supposedly responsible were tried for his murder in 1330. Thus it is necessary to turn to the various chronicles to establish what was known and what was suspected in 1327.

Before commenting on what the various chronicles say, it is worth first making a general point. Several chronicles of the reign of Edward II were composed or copied several years later by monks who rarely left their monasteries. Some resided two or three hundred miles from Berkeley. They were usually dependent on a variety of sources, including travellers' tales, official proclamations, and other chronicles. Sometimes, as with the case of the clerk Geoffrey le Baker, a contact was known to the chronicler who claimed to be able to shed light on a story beyond the level of general knowledge, but this was very rare. All the extant contemporary chronicles were compiled by men who had no first-hand or (apart from le Baker) second-hand knowledge of the actual process of Edward's death, which was obviously a very closely guarded secret, probably known only to six or seven people. With regard to secret plots, most chronicles reflect contemporary rumour and popular opinion more closely than historical facts. To put the issue in perspective, imagine the results if several amateur historians – perhaps working in retirement homes, which monasteries sometimes were – began to write up accounts of a covert political assassination five, ten or twenty years after the event. Imagine them trying to do the same thing in an age before literacy was common, without television, newspapers, radio or railways.

Two of the earliest chronicles to mention the death of Edward II were both written by canons of St Paul's Cathedral in London. Both were written within ten years of the death. The earlier of the two, the *Annales Paulini*, is anonymous, and simply states that 'on the eve of the feast of St Michael the Apostle King Edward died . . . in Berkeley Castle, where he was held prisoner; and he was buried in Gloucester Abbey'.[10] The other, by Adam Murimuth, gives much more information. He was the only contemporary chronicler who was connected with both the court and the south-west region, being at Exeter from June to November 1327, while he administered the diocese after the death of the bishop, James de Berkeley.[11] Thus he must be considered the nearest we have to a presence in the area at the time of, and just after, the death. Although he did not begin to write his chronicle for another ten years, he kept a book of memoranda at the time, and this formed the basis of his later work.[12] He claimed that Berkeley and Maltravers exchanged custodianship month by month and that Berkeley treated the king well but Maltravers did not; and that for secrecy's sake Edward was moved from Berkeley to Corfe and back. He notes that Isabella sent her husband delicacies and noncommittal messages in his captivity, but refused to see him. He gives an apparently inaccurate estimate of 100 marks per month ($£67$) for the expenses of keeping the king, but although this is less than half the actual figure paid, it is what one might expect to be left after his custodians had taken their fees in proportion to their status and their charge.[13] As for the death itself, he places this at Berkeley a day later than the official date, on 22 September, and, although he does not give a cause of death under his entry for 1327, he does so under an entry for 1330. Here he states his belief that the king was 'suffocated' by Thomas Gurney and John Maltravers with Roger's connivance. Since this does not reflect the official charge as enrolled in Parliament, and as the official charges did not mention Maltravers in the context of Edward's death but did mention Ockley, whom Murimuth neglects, the chronicle must reflect his opinion at the time of writing (1337) and was not merely copied from official documentation. Significantly, he indicates that his opinion was widely shared and he specifically states that 'it was commonly said' that Edward 'was killed as a precaution' by Maltravers and Gurney. The other very important fact in Murimuth's chronicle is his unique statement that 'Many abbots, priors, knights, burgesses of Bristol and Gloucester were summoned to see his corpse intact, and this they saw superficially.'[14] Murimuth is the only contemporary to mention this exposure of the corpse, but as he was the only chronicler in the south-west at the time, this is not wholly surprising. As one would expect, a number of historians have wondered what he meant by the corpse being seen 'superficially': none seems to have considered the embalming process as an explanation. The whole body being covered in cerecloth would go a long way to explain his use of this word, for only the superficial contours of his body would have been visible, and no wounds.[15]

A number of chronicles, possibly contemporary with the St Paul's writers, are continuations of an earlier work, called the *Brut*, which was an ongoing history of the kingdom of England from its legendary foundation by Brutus. These continuations fall into two groups, referred to by historians as the 'long version' and the 'short version'. The originals of both were written in French and were separately completed in the early to mid-1330s.[16] The short version, which was probably compiled in London, survives in a number of manuscripts, including those published as the *Anonimalle Chronicle* and the *French Chronicle of London*. Both of these examples give very little information about Edward's death. The first states merely that Edward was moved from Kenilworth to Berkeley Castle and that 'soon afterwards the king became ill there and died on the day of St Matthew the Apostle before Michaelmas . . .'.[17] The *French Chronicle of London*, which is a later derivation from the short version, states that Thomas de Berkeley and John Maltravers were appointed guardians of the king in his imprisonment, and that 'abetted by certain persons and the assent of his false guardians, he was falsely and traitorously murdered . . .'.[18]

By comparison with the short versions, the long version of the *Brut* is positively rich in detail. It was probably completed in the north, although it may have been begun in London. Either way it was written by someone sympathetic to the Earl of Lancaster.[19] It carries a few obvious mistakes in its entry for 1327: it wrongly claims Maurice de Berkeley, not Thomas, was the king's keeper at the time of the death, along with Maltravers and their assistant Gurney (whom it calls Thomas 'Toiourney' in 1327), and that the king died at Corfe Castle.[20] It corrects these mistakes in a later passage relating to events in 1330, which reflects the official proceedings relating to the death: that the king died at Berkeley under the direction of

Thomas Gurney (now correctly spelled with a 'G').[21] These mistakes ironically increase its value, as they indicate that the entry for 1327 was very
probably composed at an earlier date than that of 1330, probably in the
period 1328–30, and thus records popular rumour at a slightly earlier date.[22]
This is important for two reasons: firstly because this entry supports some
of the lines in Murimuth which are not found in other contemporary
chronicles, for instance that the king lamented that his wife and son did
not visit him; that Maltravers was involved in the death; and that the king
visited Corfe. The second reason is that the entry for 1327 contains the
earliest explicit description of Edward's death. It states:

> Roger Mortimer sent orders as to how and in what manner the king
> should be killed. And later, when the aforesaid Thomas and John had
> seen the letter and the order, they were friendly towards King Edward
> of Carnarvon at supper time, so that the king knew nothing of their
> treachery. And when that night the king had gone to bed and was asleep,
> the traitors, against their homage and against their fealty, went quietly
> into his chamber and laid a large table on his stomach and with other
> men's help pressed him down. At this he awoke, and in fear of his life,
> turned himself upside down. The tyrants, false traitors, then took a horn
> and put it into his fundament as deep as they could, and took a spit of
> burning copper, and put it through the horn into his body, and often-
> times rolled therewith his bowels, and so they killed their lord, and
> nothing was perceived [as to the manner of his death].[23]

None of this is in Murimuth, although he and the author of the *Brut* had
similar background information about Corfe and the king's lamentations.
Indeed, Murimuth seems still not to have heard this story seven years later.
Clearly the Lancastrian author of the longer version of the *Brut* was significantly closer to the source of the red-hot spit story than Murimuth.

The explicit details of Edward's death in the *Brut* seem to have been
known to another northern chronicler, an anonymous canon of Bridlington
Priory, who wrote some time between 1327 and 1340. He states that on 21
September 'Edward of Carnarvon died in Berkeley Castle where he was
held in custody . . . Of his death various explanations are commonly
suggested, but I do not care for such things as now are written.'[24] This is
not directly taken from the 1327 entry in the *Brut*, as it mentions Berkeley
as the place of death, not Corfe, and thus it may be further evidence that
the rumour that Edward died in the circumstances described in the *Brut*
was widespread across the north of England at an early date.

The next chronicle to give details of the death was also written in the north. This is the famous *Polychronicon*, the most popular history of the fourteenth century, written by Ranulph Higden, a monk of Chester. It is an enormous mixture of fables and chronicles, mostly borrowed from other writers. Although Higden was comparatively uninterested in English history, being more concerned to present a comprehensive history of the world, he devotes his last book to his homeland. The passage relating to the death of Edward reads: 'On 3 April the old king was taken from Kenilworth to Berkeley Castle, where however since many people conspired to free him, about the feast of St Matthew the Evangelist, he was killed disgracefully by a burning rod piercing his private parts.'[25] This shows that the story was circulating in Chester by 1340 at the latest. The first version of the *Polychronicon* was completed in 1327, but it is not clear whether this covered the death of Edward. Thus Higden's account can be dated to some time between 1327 and 1340, with the likelihood of the latter being the date of actual completion.[26]

Few chronicles of the next decade mention the death. Most do not give details. The *Historia Aurea*, another northern work, finished in about 1346, states tersely that the king 'was killed in September on St Matthews Day by the introduction of a hot iron through the middle of a horn inserted into his bottom'.[27] Another account completed in that year but in the south, at Westminster, states that 'according to rumour, the manner of his death and the method of his execution was that he was pressed down in his bed with a table, a horn was thrust violently into his anus and through the middle of this horn an iron rod was pushed into his guts, from which he died in torment'.[28] The Westminster writer was undoubtedly using a copy of the long version of the *Brut* for his information, as shown by the wording of this and other entries at this point in his chronicle.

By the 1350s no new writers could remember the events and hearsay of 1327, and they tended to follow existing works. One chronicle dramatically stands out as an exception. This was the work of Geoffrey le Baker, previously attributed to his patron Thomas de la More, written about 1356. Le Baker is the only writer of any originality besides the author of the long version of the *Brut* to give a full and detailed account of the killing of Edward, and he is the only writer to have cited an independent witness. He used a copy of Murimuth's chronicle for a chronological framework, and seems to have supplemented this with readings from the *Brut*, but where he felt he could significantly add information he did so with abandon and in abundance. He states that the king was handed over at Kenilworth to Maltravers and Gurney (not Berkeley, as Murimuth states), led first to Corfe Castle, then to Bristol, where various townsmen conspired to take him overseas, and finally to Berkeley. At Bristol he was tortured and humiliated, deprived of sleep, his food poisoned, and he was left without heat in an attempt to induce madness. On the way from Bristol to Berkeley he was supposed to have been mocked by his guards: they crowned him with hay, and ordered him to walk. They prepared to shave him with ditchwater and when he protested that he would have hot water whether they liked it or not, he began to weep profusely. These things were related to le Baker after the plague of 1347 by one William Bishop, who claimed to have led Edward from Bristol.

This William Bishop is interesting, for he was one of Roger Mortimer's men-at-arms in 1321.[29] He is often cited as a witness for all that le Baker has to say about the death of Edward II; but in fact he is only a witness for what has so far been related of le Baker's narrative. While le Baker may well have received other information from him relating to the death, Bishop was not involved in the killing. Firstly he would have been arrested in 1330 if he had been in the castle at the time,[30] and, secondly, no other role is claimed for him in the chronicle beside that of transporting Edward: a fact most historians seem to have overlooked. But even this transportation seems fabricated. We know that Edward was taken from Kenilworth on 3 April 1327, and that he was at Llanthony Priory near Gloucester two days later.[31] To take a captive man fifty-five miles in less than three days is not a particularly easy task and, although it would not have prevented processions of ridicule and mock crownings with hay, they were likely to have been of short duration. It is also difficult to explain how a three-day journey from Kenilworth to Berkeley by way of Gloucester was supposed to lead first to Corfe, another point certainly to Bishop's discredit as a witness, which raises questions about le Baker's judgement. The whole account fits more with the traditional religious literary form of the 'passion', or suffering of a martyr, and le Baker definitely goes to some considerable lengths to convince us that Edward was indeed a martyr.

To continue with le Baker's evidence. Adam of Orleton is supposed at this point to have sent an ambiguous Latin message to the gaolers, which could be read in two ways: either 'Do not fear; to kill the king is a good thing', or 'Do not kill the king; it is good to be afraid'. Unfortunately for le Baker, at this time Orleton was on a mission from Roger and Isabella at Avignon to see the Pope. He was thus at least two weeks away by letter.[32] And finally, the story le Baker tells has been lifted from a story told by Matthew Paris of the murder of a Hungarian queen in 1252.[33]

Up to this point le Baker has offered only a literary elaboration on what is already known from earlier chronicles, elaborated upon mainly by his bias and William Bishop's testimony. Now he states Edward was looked after by Thomas de Berkeley until the receipt of the bishop's letter with its cryptic message. To give le Baker the benefit of the doubt, let us assume the letter was that of William de Shalford to Roger, which Roger forwarded to Berkeley. According to le Baker, Berkeley is supposed henceforth to have been forbidden to see the king, and the persecution of the deposed monarch began in earnest. He was confined for days in a pestilential chamber deep underground among rotting corpses. Then, 'the tyrants, seeing that a very strong man could not be overcome by the stench of death, by night, on 22 September, while asleep in bed, with great cushions piled in a heap and more than fifteen men pressing down on him, a burning plumber's iron was applied through a ductile tube in his empty secret parts to his lungs after his intestines were burnt away, showing no wound in the region of the body where wounds were normally sought . . .'.[34] Here we seem to have a garbled version of the longer version of the *Brut*, for instance that Berkeley was forbidden to intervene to save the king, and the use of the word 'tyrant' to describe the murderers at the same points in the text. Le Baker has pillows rather than a table, but otherwise there is nothing which could not have come from Murimuth and the *Brut*. Certainly there are no references to key facts which we have in official records, such as the sentences on the accused murderers, or the presence of William Beaukaire. Such details would have been much more convincing than a 'passion' story about a man weeping profusely in order to have sufficient hot water to shave, especially when the king at this stage of his life habitually wore a beard.[35]

There is something both farcical and pathetic about le Baker's evidence. He is so keen to impress upon his readers the strength and suffering of the noble Edward that no fewer than fifteen people had to hold the ex-king down beneath cushions. With such an onslaught as this, one wonders why they bothered with the spit. Why not just smother him, as Murimuth believed, or poison him? Or strangle him? Or starve him? If it was important to have no sign of the death impressed on the king's features, why torture him so terribly? If Roger himself had wanted to arrange a well-concealed death, he could have used poison, having used it very effectively in 1323 on the guards at the Tower. So why encourage the screaming that was reputedly heard throughout the castle? One might speculate that the murderers did not know that a king's body was covered up as part of the embalming process, and they panicked, and murdered Edward with tables, cushions, red-hot spits, dead bodies, cold water, fifteen men or whatever; but such speculation can only hit a wall of suspicion. The method of death described by le Baker and others of the red-hot spit tradition seems to be a reflection of the basic idea that the people who had custody of Edward were both cruel and wicked. This is clearly borne out in le Baker's narrative, which is a polemic against Isabella, whom he calls 'Jezebel'. Indeed, his principal motive for writing was justice, born out of his determination that Isabella should have been punished for adultery and the murder of her husband, and not allowed to live in luxury, as she was when le Baker began writing.

Le Baker's anti-Isabella stance is different from earlier polemicists, who were principally anti-government. This is interesting in the context of the geo-political standpoints of each of the chroniclers in relation to the red-hot poker story. The earliest southern writers – the *Annales Paulini*, Murimuth and the various chronicles based on the short version of the *Brut* – do not mention this means of death. Those who do are all northerners: Higden, the Lancastrian author of the long *Brut*, and John of Tynemouth, author of the *Historia Aurea*. The one northern writer who does not – the canon of Bridlington – clearly has heard a terrible story and has refused to believe it. The first southern chronicle to tell the story of the red-hot poker – the Westminster chronicler – merely copied the story verbatim from the longer *Brut*, in about 1346. The idea that Edward died on a red-hot poker was new in London at this time. Ten years after the death it was still widely believed in the south that Edward had been suffocated by Gurney and Maltravers, as shown by Murimuth. While the source of the red-hot poker story cannot be proved, it is clear that the pattern of its dissemination is the reverse of that which one would expect: the writers geographically most distant from Berkeley were closer to the source of the story than the well-connected Murimuth, who was in the south-west at the time. Thus the story may be explained as a piece of propaganda, probably spread by a Lancastrian sympathiser, and probably arising the following year from the conflict between Roger and Henry of Lancaster. Le Baker seems to have swallowed the northern account whole, placed it within the framework of a well-informed and reliable chronology (adapted from Murimuth), reinforced it with the dubious testimony of the aged and unreliable William Bishop, and created an account so vitriolic and vivid that it seemed better informed and more attractive than any other before or since, and ultimately became the main source for the popular legend.

One may go further than this. There is one detail about the Berkeley Castle plot which allows us to say unequivocally that no chronicler knew anything about what happened inside Berkeley Castle in late September 1327. Not even le Baker, with his long description of the barbarity of Edward's political masters, came close. In this we may learn an important methodological lesson: the most detailed chronicles are not necessarily the best-informed. Indeed, any writer who ventured to comment on the subject was skating on very thin historical ice. While some guessed at murder, and some reported the red-hot poker story, not even the sceptical canon of Bridlington imagined what really happened.

Edward II was still alive.[*]

---

[*]The detailed argument underpinning this statement will be found below in Chapter Twelve Revisited.

THIRTEEN

King in All but Name

The Berkeley Castle plot is without doubt one of the most remarkable events in European history, made more so for the fact that it has remained secret for nearly seven centuries. No other event compares with it. Kings were occasionally deposed, or murdered, and new monarchs took their thrones; but at no other time did a subject dethrone a king, feign his death and burial, and secretly keep him alive in order to influence his successor.

The origins of the plot lie in Roger recognising the importance of the custody of Edward II. This occurred many months beforehand, as shown by his seizure of the ex-king in early April. Taking possession of the ex-king was not just a means of reducing the chances of Edward's escape, or lessening the chance that the Earl of Lancaster would use him as a political weapon; it was also a way for Roger to control Edward III. Since Edward II had been forced to abdicate, the ex-king posed a danger to Edward III as well as to Roger and Isabella. If he were to be rescued, he would have claimed that he had been forced to resign the throne illegally. If powerful men had sought his restoration the young king would have had to choose between opposing his father on the battlefield and resigning the throne himself. The latter was not an option, as he would thereby undoubtedly have sentenced his mother to death along with Roger and many other men who had joined them in France.[1] Thus, with Edward II in Roger's custody, the young king was dependent on Roger for the security of his throne and his mother's life.

There was another strong reason for keeping Edward alive in 1327: Isabella did not want her husband killed. As shown by her sending presents to him in prison, and the tempestuous moment in France when she had suggested that she might return to him, she still felt some affection towards him. It was also an unholy act to murder a man, and doubly so for a wife to murder her husband. Such an act would invite divine retribution. Thus on personal and religious grounds Isabella wanted the same as Roger: to keep the king alive. As an intelligent woman she could also forsee that her husband's continued survival would help to bind her son to Roger. But if the opposite were to happen – if the ex-king were to be murdered – a gulf would open up between herself and Roger and the king. She and Roger would have blood on their hands, and the murdered man's son would doubtless wish to be avenged.

This was what Roger had on his mind after leaving court at the beginning of September: if he kept control of Edward II he and Isabella were safe. But it would not be an easy matter to arrange. Four things in particular were necessary for the plot to work. Firstly, all details had to be restricted to as small and as faithful a group of people as possible. Secondly, the mechanisms of state had to be employed to convince Edward II's supporters and the country at large that the man was dead. Thirdly, a royal funeral had to take place with just as much show as if the man really was dead, and this included exhibiting the corpse. And finally, after the announcement of the supposed death, the ex-king himself had to be kept in the strictest security and secrecy.

By about 18 September, when Roger received de Shalford's letter from Anglesey, everything was ready. He gave the letter to William de Ockley to go to Berkeley Castle to affect the 'suitable remedy'. De Ockley was probably accompanied by Thomas Gurney, Berkeley's retainer,[2] William Beaukaire, and Roger's henchman, Simon Bereford.[3] They arrived at Berkeley on 20 or 21 September, by which time Roger was well on his way back to Lincoln. On 21 September Thomas Gurney was sent with letters to inform the king, Isabella and Roger that Edward II had died that day. Roger and Isabella, of course, knew that the letters were false; but for Edward III it was a shock. As far as he knew, his father was dead.[4] Writing to his cousin late at night on 23 September, Edward remarked sadly that his father had been 'commanded to God'.[5]

Now came the critical part of the plot: to persuade the country that the king was indeed dead. It was crucial that no one should inspect the supposed corpse of the king before it was embalmed. Roger instructed Gurney to return to Berkeley with orders that news of the death should be kept secret locally until 1 November.[6] He persuaded the king not to announce the death until the end of the session of Parliament (28 September). On that day the court went into a period of mourning befitting a man who had been a feckless but characterful king, and the process of preparing for the funeral got underway.

There were two distinct parts to the funeral: the public and the private. The private aspects had been in progress from before the announcement of the death. A corpse was acquired, eviscerated, embalmed and covered in cerecloth. The heart was removed and placed in a silver vase for presentation to Isabella, probably in line with her own request, in order to reinforce the notion that Edward II really was dead.[7]

The public part of the funeral was altogether more ostentatious.

Although a plea by the monks of Westminster for Edward II to be buried alongside his royal father and grandfather in the abbey was turned down, a display appropriate for a deposed king was organised. The royal clerk in charge of the funeral, Hugh de Glanville, was ordered to oversee the carrying of the corpse to St Peter's, Gloucester, the nearest suitable large abbey.[8] It was dressed in royal robes, covered in expensive Eastern rugs and placed inside a lead coffin, which in turn was placed inside a wooden one. The abbot's own carriage was draped in black canvas and used to take the body from Berkeley Castle to Gloucester. Lord Berkeley, the mayor, and many of the townsfolk processed in front of the cortege as it approached the town and passed through the gates of the abbey into the church and up to the hearse in front of the altar.

The hearse was the centrepiece of the show. Specially constructed in London, it bore the gilt images of the lions of England on its sides, each lion bearing a painted mantle emblazoned with the royal arms. At its four corners stood figures of the four evangelists, looking over the body. Around the hearse were eight figures of angels covered in gold leaf carrying censers from which incense wafted. At the centre of all this, on the hearse itself, beneath the gold canopy, lay a figure of the king carved in wood, wearing cloth-of-gold and a gilt crown. This made a fine sight; people travelled long distances to view this rare royal spectacle. So many arrived that four large oak barriers had to be erected around it, so that it was not damaged and the figures and the hundreds of candles on and around it were not knocked over.[9]

Roger may well have attended to some of these arrangements himself. He was one of the few lords who could remember the previous king's funeral, twenty years earlier. His last known appearance at court was on 22 October, the same day that Hugh de Glanville was charged with paying all the bills and keeping an account of the funeral arrangements. He does not appear in the records again until 7 December, when he witnessed two royal charters at Leicester, an interval of six weeks.

On 19 December the court arrived at Gloucester to witness the interment. Only a handful of those present – Roger, Isabella and a few trusted men like Berkeley and Maltravers – knew that the whole spectacle was a charade. For the vast majority it was the genuine burial of the ex-king. Roger himself played his part scrupulously, wearing a black tunic made specially for the occasion.[10] After hearing mass, he and Isabella stayed one more night at Gloucester and then left.

It was at Worcester, two days later, that Edward III finally learnt the truth from his mother.[11] One can only guess at his shock. The whole country believed his father was dead as a result of his solemn proclamations. He himself had believed it for the last three months. But now, it turned out, his mother's lover was secretly holding his father prisoner. And there was nothing he could do. If he issued a proclamation stating that his father was still alive, Roger would have denied it and called him a fool. If he issued such a proclamation and people believed him, he would make an enemy of his mother and risk starting a civil war. At fifteen, Edward was not strong enough to stand up to his mother and Roger, so he did the only thing he could: he demanded proof that his father was alive. Isabella summoned the woman who had performed the embalming of the corpse. Although we cannot know for certain what was said, we may imagine that he was fully informed about the implications of his father's continued existence: that his throne and his mother's life – not to mention his father's – were dependent on his not revealing to anyone that Edward II was still alive, and not doing anything to threaten his mother's lover. From now on, both he and Isabella were dependent on Roger for their political lives.

*

The success of the Berkeley Castle plot changed everything for Roger. He could now afford to exercise authority openly. More than a year had passed since he and Isabella had received the royal seals, but only now did he dare to use them against Henry of Lancaster. On 23 December, three days after the funeral at Gloucester, Robert de Holand, the prime enemy of the entire Lancastrian faction, was restored to his lands.[12] The alliance which had toppled the Despensers and Edward II had come to an end.

Roger did not break from the Lancastrians simply out of dislike for Lancaster or revenge for being deserted in 1322. The split was a result of the conciliatory policy which he wished to pursue with regard to Scotland. He wanted a permanent settlement which would guarantee borders and save the expense of further wars. To this end he sent a delegation to Bruce in October offering to recognise Scottish independence. Bruce offered the sum of £20,000 in return for Scottish sovereignty. Most of his terms were acceptable to the English, namely that the borders should be restored, that Bruce's son David should marry Isabella's daughter, Joan, that a mutual defence alliance should bind the two countries, and that the English should drop proceedings against Scotland at the papal court.[13] But he made one stipulation which would never be acceptable to the northern English lords: Bruce demanded that they should renounce their rights over their Scottish estates. He wanted to make a clear distinction between peers of the realm of Scotland and those of England.

This was a real problem. From the English point of view, an English lord could have territories in France, and so be both a French lord as well as an English one. Bruce's opposite point of view was born out of bitter experience. If English lords were also Scottish lords, to whom did they owe their allegiance in time of war? They would side with their more powerful English monarch, naturally. Thus he insisted that Henry of Lancaster, Henry Percy and Thomas Wake, among others, had to give up their claims to lost Scottish estates. The northerners were outraged, but Roger refused to listen to them. Bruce's agreement was vitally important to the question of peace with Scotland, the northerners' less so.

After Christmas at Worcester, Roger and Isabella made their way north to York to attend the king's marriage to Philippa of Hainault. Philippa had been accompanied to England by her father, Count William of Hainault, now struggling with gout, and her uncle, Sir John. On Friday 30 January, the fifteen-year-old king married his sixteen-year-old bride in the minster under the auspices of the Archbishop of York and Bishop Hothum. It was an occasion for celebration by all. Isabella and Roger were happy to cement the tie with Hainault, and the Hainaulters were happy to see their count's daughter married to the king. For a few days there was feasting, music, dancing and jousting, and the full medieval chivalric ideal was lived out to the full. Then it was back to politics.

Parliament met at York on 7 February with Scotland the only important subject on its agenda. There were a few other items besides, such as why Adam of Orleton had presented himself at the papal court as a candidate for the recently vacated see of Worcester, against Roger's wishes, and the continued imprisonment of the widow of Hugh Despenser, Eleanor de Clare, who was ordered to be released from the Tower, along with her children and chattels;[14] but these were minor issues by comparison. The disinherited northern lords bitterly refused to give up their Scottish claims. Their protests divided the council between supporters of Henry of Lancaster on the one hand and of Roger and Isabella on the other. The debate raged for a whole month, but ultimately there was only going to be one conclusion: the king would support Roger's policy, and Scottish independence would become reality with or without the agreement of the Lancastrians.[15] The shallowness of Henry of Lancaster's authority was exposed.

*

Roger's newly won power did not tempt him to award himself huge grants of land and authority straightaway. He was still wary of appearing the sole dictator of royal policy. Unlike Despenser, he had no need directly to control manors, towns and men in order to affect government. His grants to himself were largely made with his family in mind. On 2 September 1327 he requested a small grant to Isabella Mortimer, and on the following day a more significant one, that of the right of marrying the widow of the late Earl of Pembroke to his second son, Roger.[16] In the next six months he himself accepted just one administrative office – that of the chief keepership of the peace in Herefordshire, Shropshire and Worcestershire – one personal gift, of the manor of Church Stretton, at the request of the Earl of Kent, and one wardship: the heir to the earldom of Pembroke.[17] Although this last lucrative grant suggests that Roger had designs on the Pembroke estates in the way that Despenser had coveted the earldom of Gloucester, there was no possibility of his becoming earl himself, and his relationship with the family suggests that he sought a future political association rather than personal territorial gain. Evidence of his authority lies not so much in grants to him as an individual but in his exercise of patronage and his appointments to government offices.

In the six months after the king's death Roger directly requested a number of royal grants be made. There was nothing new in this, and indeed Roger had exercised such a right since 1308. But now the numbers began to increase, modestly at first, and then in greater number and value. In October 1327 he requested that John Wyard, his man-at-arms, be granted a licence to crenellate the manor of Stanton Harcourt, which Roger had given him. In December he requested that the prior and convent of Wormsley be allowed to dispose of certain lands. Having unofficially appointed himself the right to adjudicate who had suffered arrest unfairly under Hugh Despenser, he put forward hundreds of names of less important men whom he requested be pardoned outstanding fines. In the same month he requested that Master Thomas de Chandlos be allowed to receive the manor of Lugwardine. In January he requested that a grant should be made to Richard le Gayte, custodian of the Conway ferryboat, and that Richard de Hawkeslowe should receive the office of Chirographer of the King's Bench, and that the people of Evesham should be allowed to exact a toll for three years to pave their streets, and that his man John Wyard should be granted the right of free warren on his estates. In February 1328 he requested the same right be granted to Thomas Gurney, that a grant of land be made to John Mauvas, that Hugh Morvill be appointed forester of Inglewood Forest, that William de Ayte be appointed forester of Galtres Forest, that Gerard d'Alspaye be allowed to keep the £40 annual income Roger had granted him for helping him escape from the Tower, and that Richard de Cleobury, the old cook of Edward I and Edward II, who had also helped Roger escape from the Tower, should be given a pension. In March he requested that the townsmen of Montford should be granted the right to levy a murage toll for five years, and that a grant be made to Thomas de Vere, his distant kinsman, and that a grant be made to the monks of Buildwas Abbey (where he may well have had family or retired household retainers living). This type of patronage, which was always of small amounts, secured for Roger a large number of supporters, and through it he satisfied the claims of existing supporters, and fostered relationships with newcomers.

This behaviour was exactly what was expected of a great magnate, and although Roger was operating on a grander scale than he had done in Edward II's reign, it was nevertheless calculated not to cause envy or offence. In some acts he jointly requested a gift along with other barons and earls, including the Earl of Surrey, John de Cromwell and Gilbert Talbot, companions of long standing. But these official requests were only a minor aspect of his power. Much more significant were the gifts made to his friends, allies and supporters through his influence over Isabella and, more specifically, his power over the king. It is noticeable that all the grants to Roger's friends and allies, whether ecclesiastical or secular, were made on the authority of the privy seal (the king's private seal).[18] There is insufficient space here to enumerate all the various people who benefited, but a few examples are particularly worthy of mention. John de Hothum, Bishop of Ely, was forgiven all his debts in Ireland in January 1328. John de Fiennes, Roger's French cousin who had sheltered him in 1323, was licensed to sell his manorial holdings in England in February. The same month John Wyard, Roger's man-at-arms, was granted safe passage to go abroad on pilgrimage. And in March the Earl of Kent received a large grant of manors which had belonged to Hugh Despenser. This last grant is interesting in that Roger seems to have appointed himself the sole arbiter of all ex-Despenser lands and rights, and probably established what Kent (his cousin's husband) was to receive. Some of these privy seal grants were significant and important; others were minor and merely administrative. But since they were all made supposedly by the king, in none of them does Roger's name appear as patron. In other words, his patronage went right to the heart of the administration, and he was exercising authority not only in his personal capacity as a magnate but also in an executive capacity comparable to that of a monarch.

Roger's unofficial royal power extended also to the appointments of the great offices of state. In January 1327 John de Hothum was appointed Chancellor, and in the same month Roger's fellow rebel in 1322, Bishop Orleton, was appointed Treasurer. Hothum's successor as Chancellor in July 1328 was another close friend of Roger: Henry de Burghersh, Bishop of Lincoln, whose niece had married Roger's son and heir. When Orleton was replaced as Treasurer after his departure for Avignon in March 1327, the office was filled first by Henry de Burghersh, and, when Burghersh became Chancellor, by Thomas de Charlton, brother of Roger's long-time ally John de Charlton, and uncle to Roger's son-in-law. It is noticeable that all these men were members of the coterie of prelates which Roger had gathered around him in his earlier career, and that he had had personal or official links with all of them since at least 1319, and with de Hothum since at least 1309.

The above appointments are interesting, for they demonstrate that Roger held the upper hand in government appointments even before the Berkeley Castle plot. The only major office which seems not to have been held by Roger's appointee was that of the Keeper of the Privy Seal. The holder of this office from 26 October 1326, Robert Wyvill (later Bishop of Salisbury), was Isabella's own clerk. It seems that initially Isabella had a policy of allowing Roger to appoint government ministers while she maintained control of the king's privy seal. In this way she passed much of the responsibility for government to Roger while maintaining a veto, in her own interests and those of her son. However, this situation did not last. Wyvill was replaced on 1 March 1327 by Richard Ayrmin. The post changed hands again on 24 April 1328, when Adam Lymbergh took the seal. Neither of these two men is known to have had strong personal ties to Isabella.

With regard to the lesser positions of power Roger exercised as much if not more influence over appointments than Isabella. It was probably owing to his early policy of appeasement towards Henry of Lancaster that the appointment of John de Ros as Steward of the Royal Household can be attributed. In March 1328, two months after the successful completion of the Berkeley Castle plot, de Ros was dismissed and John Maltravers was appointed, albeit temporarily. Such a promotion was designed not just to reward Maltravers for his part in the Berkeley Castle plot but to restrict Lancastrian access to Edward III. Another key appointment in the royal household made by Roger was that of Gilbert Talbot, who became King's Chamberlain in August 1327.[19] Additionally Roger controlled keeperships of the peace, the appointment of sheriffs, and custodians of castles. In April 1328 he requested openly that his man be appointed Sheriff of Anglesey. A good example of how he exercised authority anonymously in the appointment of custodians of castles is the appointment in November 1327 of Sir Hugh de Turpington to the keepership of Newcastle Emlyn in Carmarthenshire, a key fortress for the control of South Wales (of which Roger was Justiciar) and the protection of the lands of the earldom of Pembroke (in Roger's guardianship). From the very top of the hierarchy of royal service to very nearly the bottom, the majority of government offices were filled by men appointed by Roger.

The consequence of this series of high-profile appointments and this power structure of personal loyalties was that Roger was able to administer the realm without the widespread series of territorial grants which Despenser and Gaveston had received, and without repeatedly having to use his trump card, the possession of the ex-king. That he granted himself relatively little land and few positions of authority in local government was immaterial. In terms of power his authority was every bit as wide-ranging as that of a monarch. The only difference was that it was largely unofficial.

*

Now, completely unexpectedly, one of those deaths occurred which caused medieval society to lurch suddenly in a new direction. It was that of King Charles of France, and he left no heir. All three of Isabella's brothers had become king in turn, and had died young before their wives had given birth to a son. Unless Isabella herself acted to secure the throne of France for Edward, her father's ruling line was dead, and it would be Philip, the heir of Charles de Valois, who would inherit. Isabella and Roger were now confronted with one of the most far-reaching political questions of the fourteenth century. It would eventually end in the Hundred Years War.

News of the death probably reached the court on 1 March. Two days later Roger and Isabella left the court quietly together. We do not know where they went. They gave instructions for Parliament to be summoned to Northampton for 26 April, and disappeared for more than a month. It is likely that they took with them a large amount of money, for Roger now claimed the outstanding portion of the 6,000 marks which he was owed for his service in Ireland, of which he had received only a fraction.[20] None of the contemporary chronicles records their whereabouts, and so it appears that their departure – the first time that Isabella had left her son since the invasion – was a private affair. They seem to have rejoined the court in mid-April, in time to enter the lion's den of an angry Parliament.

Roger anticipated hostility. He stipulated in advance that no retinues of men-at-arms were to be brought, and no proctors would be allowed to stand in for their lords. All tournaments were banned, so no opposition forces could be gathered in that guise. Roger also planned to choreograph proceedings: a strategy towards France was already in place. He would attempt to unite northerners and southerners against Philip de Valois rather than dividing them against Robert Bruce. In requiring full attendance of all the lords in person, and by offering unavailable French lordships in compensation for unavailable Scottish ones, Roger was trying for one last time to placate the Lancastrians who had objected so vehemently to his policy at the previous Parliament.

All Roger's attempts to coerce the northerners failed. He declared that the treaty with Scotland should be ratified since they could not afford to fight a war with both France and Scotland, and that the king, as rightful heir of the French Crown, now had a responsibility to protect his interests there. The Lancastrians accepted that a deputation should be sent to claim the throne of France, but they did not accept that it was necessary to relinquish all claim on lordships in Scotland. Roger realised that no amount of discussion would persuade them. Accordingly he announced that he would not reveal the wording of the charter for Scottish independence.[21] Outraged, the Lancastrians declared the whole matter treason, decided between Black Douglas, Roger and Isabella. Roger replied that the terms of the peace had already been agreed, and had been announced in London, seven days before Parliament had met. He seems to have been utterly indifferent to his peers' and the king's opinion, but he then went even further: he stated that this was the king's will. This was a lie, and Edward was furious, but he was unable to overrule him. The Earl of Lancaster protested that this 'shameful peace' was none of his will. Only the Bishop of Ely, John de Hothum, seems to have spoken in favour of Roger's strategy. On 8 May Roger forced the young king to ratify the treaty with Scotland, against his own judgement, as he bitterly but belatedly complained.

The confirmation of the treaty with Scotland was only one of many issues discussed at Northampton. In addition a number of judicial points and law-enforcement measures were discussed and passed. These included restrictions on the issuing of pardons and the use of the privy seal, the prevention of men riding while armed, the prohibition of groups of armed men attending fairs and, most significantly, the extension of the powers of the assize judges who travelled from county to county to sit in judgement on the most important cases. Some of these points, especially the restrictions on pardons and the use of the privy seal, were aimed at reducing Roger's authority. But, as with his negotiations in Scotland, Roger was prepared to give a lot of ground in order to achieve what he wanted. Now what he most desired was an extension of central government authority, which he, of course, could control. In increasing the powers of the central administration, he was attempting to reduce the power of the crowd to act as a political force. Nowhere would this have worked so much to his advantage as in London, where riots had accompanied his assumption of power and threatened the stability of the administration. Riots had also broken out at Abingdon and other places in the south. Through the central courts and local law-enforcement measures he sought to control the people as efficiently as he controlled the king and the peers.

*

Following the parliament of Northampton, which ended on 15 May, Roger and Isabella made their way to Hereford, where a double wedding was to take place. Roger had had the rights of marriage of several important young men for a number of years, two of whom were now of an age to marry. He also had a large number of unmarried daughters. Although the details are confused by Adam Murimuth, the only chronicler to mention the event, it seems that on 31 May 1328 his daughter Joan was married to his ward James Audley, the fifteen-year-old lord of Heleigh.[22] Probably at the same time, his daughter Catherine was married to another of his wards, Thomas de Beauchamp, the fourteen-year-old Earl of Warwick. After the event the wedding party made its way north, to Ludlow, for feasting and entertainment in the ancient castle of the de Geneville family, now Roger's most spectacular residence.

Herein lay a problem. Ludlow Castle was Joan's inheritance, and taking the royal party there raised the question of how to bring Isabella and Joan face to face without one or the other losing dignity. Under the laws of hospitality and precedence, when the queen came to Ludlow, Joan would have been expected to give up her position as lady of the castle. Normally there would be no problem in this, but when the queen was her husband's mistress, the situation was potentially fraught. But Roger had anticipated the problem and had constructed a solution.

On entering the inner ward of Ludlow Castle, Isabella and members of the court would have found a newly completed but unfamiliar arrangement of buildings. The centre of a great building was always the great hall, and one could expect normally to find the private, solar accommodation (where the lord and his family mainly lived), at one end of this hall, and the kitchens, buttery and other catering and storage rooms at the other. At Ludlow, Joan's father and mother had rebuilt the great hall and solar about forty years earlier. Recently, Roger had added a new top storey to the de Geneville solar block, and had built an entirely new complex of solar buildings at the other end of the hall. The kitchens were moved across to the other side of the courtyard. In effect the castle had two splendid and luxurious solars: one for Joan, and one for Isabella. Roger's solution to the problem of housing both his wife and mistress under one roof, without his wife having to cede precedence to his mistress in her own castle, was an architectural masterpiece, two semi-detached medieval palaces. Joan presumably remained in the extended de Geneville building while Isabella, Edward and Philippa stayed in the new solar, surrounded by the sculptures of kings and queens which formed part of the decoration. History does not relate which wing Roger himself retired to that night, or whether discretion proved the better part of valour and he slept in the gatehouse.

The rebuilding of the interior of Ludlow was not undertaken simply out of duty; Roger enjoyed spending his money on building work. It was one of his pleasures, along with exotic clothes and fine textiles, jewellery, silverware, armour, wine and jousting. At the same time as working on Ludlow, he was continuing the rebuilding of Wigmore Castle, which was probably why he asked the king to give him all the lead then being stripped from the royal castle at Hanley.[23] He was also having a chantry added to Leintwardine church, probably building an extension to the parish church at Wigmore for the use of the parishioners,[24] and, in the outer ward of Ludlow Castle, he was having a chapel to St Peter built. Building chapels might appear a little out of character for Roger: by comparison with his contemporaries, and especially compared to Isabella, he was not an overtly religious man. He went on no pilgrimages – although he did once promise to go[25] – and he made few grants to monastic institutions. Most of those he did make were on account of members of his family. It was only when extreme situations faced him that his mind turned to God. One such occasion had been in the Tower on the eve of his escape. Then he had promised that if St Peter would deliver him from the Tower he would build a chapel dedicated to the saint, hence the chapel under construction in the outer ward of Ludlow Castle. He also constructed a semi-circular tower adjacent to this chapel, now known as Mortimer's Tower. Two priests, for whom the tower was probably built as a residence, were paid to sing masses in the chapel daily, to celebrate for eternity the miracle of his escape from the most daunting prison in the country.[26]

Roger was now at the height of his power. He could afford to relax and feast with the royal entourage, to go hawking with the young king, and to joust with his sons and members of the court. Perhaps he joined in the dancing, or listened to romances read aloud in the company of his wife and Isabella. He was surrounded by splendid embroideries and tapestries, exotic armour and silver and gold ornaments. Although the bedspreads and cushions and tapestries and luxurious fabrics and textiles mentioned in the inventories of Roger's and Joan's possessions in 1321–2 had all gone, a glimpse of the interior of the castle is possible from an inventory of Roger's goods found at Wigmore and Ludlow in 1330. Roger's personal travelling possessions and Joan's personal items were not recorded, but there were several gilt silver-lidded cups, including one which, inside, was decorated with the figure of a baboon with a bow in his hand, and another which had a shield engraved at the bottom with the arms of England and France. There were several silver water vessels, and a great hall curtain illustrating historical scenes from Welsh history. Most suggestively, there was a set of silk bedclothes with a bedspread embroidered with a castle of love, with accompanying hangings of green silk with ray taffeta, and four matching green rugs covered with white and red roses. In addition there was a set of white linen bedcovers, decorated with butterflies, with an accompanying bedspread and four matching carpets, and a set of red woollen bedclothes with a matching bedspread and two carpets. There was a great arras tapestry for the hall, of eighteen pieces, in white, again decorated with butterflies. There were two tunics emblazoned with the arms of Roger's uncle, Lord Mortimer of Chirk, one of velvet, the other of silk covered with yellow velvet and lined with red sindon (a fine linen), and a yellow padded tunic decorated with lilies and yellow roses.[27] With regard to the possessions which travelled with him, a few silver items were recorded in a London goldsmith's in 1330, and this short list reveals more of the splendour in which Roger now lived on a daily basis. He had a great silver dish weighing nineteen pounds; a large silver wine goblet, the lid and base of which were gilt and enamelled with his arms. There was a cup with a cover and tripod, all of silver, engraved with foliage, gilt and enamelled with the arms of Mortimer and de Geneville, and a silver wine jug enamelled with the various arms of Roger's ancestors, with a matching water jug. There were four wine goblets of which one had a gilt interior and the others had bases enamelled with Roger's arms. There was a great salt cellar with a silver cover weighing more than six pounds, and a cloth-of-silver table cover.[28] There is no doubt that from the silk bedclothes to the silverware, Ludlow Castle in June 1328 was as opulent and luxurious as any palace in the kingdom.

Besides architecture and fine living, Roger's principal entertainment was still the tournament. Although all his old armour had been sold by Edward II after his imprisonment in 1322, he had acquired more. At Ludlow and Wigmore he kept what was spare, including a pair of armour plates covered with gold cloth, and another pair covered with red sindon; a red velvet jousting suit with silver embroidery, an accompanying shield decorated with butterflies whose wings were the Mortimer coat of arms, and a matching banner of sindon; a set of green velvet horse trappings for jousting, two banners of the arms of Mortimer, one of sindon, the other old and battered; various pieces of metal armour for the shoulders, arms, hands and legs; three hardened leather thigh protectors; two pairs of shoes;

ten coats of Welsh cloth quartered with one sleeve red; four tournament bascinets (close-fitting helmets), four jousting helmets (three of which were gilt); six iron corsets; three war helmets and various other odds and ends. The velvet suit for jousting sounds very similar to those given by Edward II to Piers Gaveston in 1307, and the quartered coats with one arm red are reminiscent of the green tunics quartered with one sleeve yellow which Roger's men wore in the 1321 rebellion. This was more than mere nostalgia. This was his attempt to create his own knightly court: to promote himself in men's estimations and to live up to the highest chivalric ideal.

Chivalry was an elusive concept even in 1328. King Edward still seethed with anger at being forced to surrender Scotland. It was, in his eyes, an appalling act, an act of cowardice. It belittled him as a king, and he wanted everyone to know exactly what he thought of it. While Roger had the honour of entertaining the king at Ludlow, the honour was greater than the pleasure. After two days the royal party with all its noise, servants, clerks, general bustle and scowling young monarch moved on, first to the nearby manor of Bromyard, and then to Worcester.

At Worcester, while the royal party waited to discuss the French war with Henry of Lancaster, the king agreed to give Roger the roof lead which he had requested. It seemed that the king's anger was abating. Then Lancaster arrived, and, petulantly, he refused to discuss France. This council, he said, referring to Roger and his coterie of lords and prelates, was too small to discuss such a weighty issue.[29] This was an open accusation: that Roger was appropriating power to himself. Edward agreed with the earl, again expressing his anger at how Scotland had been taken from him. Lancaster insisted Parliament be called in the north. Roger acquiesced, and ordered that such a meeting would take place at York six weeks later. The king protested that he did not want the treaty with Scotland to go ahead. It was too late, Isabella explained: the king's own sister, Joan, was due to be married to David Bruce, the future King of Scotland, in a month. Edward declared defiantly that he would never recognise Scottish independence and that he would not attend the wedding. The end of the argument was its solution: if the king did not wish to attend, they would leave him behind. And they did.

*

Roger and Isabella went north with Henry de Burghersh and Isabella's daughter, Joan, leaving the king in the Welsh Marches with Henry of Lancaster. It appears at first sight that they were taking a risk, placing the king in their enemy's hands; but they had taken precautions. They had the great seal with them, in Burghersh's keeping, and, although they had left the privy seal with the king, Edward knew better than to incur Roger's anger. Ministers and spies kept watch on the king and what he ordered. As for Lancaster, he was powerless for, most importantly, Edward did not trust him.[30] Furious and frustrated, Lancaster declared his enmity towards Roger and Isabella. The author of the *Brut* chronicle dated Roger and Isabella's tyranny from this time onward.

As Isabella rode north to Berwick in early July, her feelings may be imagined. She was giving away her seven-year-old daughter to the Scots, the mortal enemies of England. For little Joan the journey must have held many terrors. At the age of four she had been separated from her mother when Isabella had gone to France. Now it was happening again, but this time it was for ever. The Scots did not help by calling her 'Joan Makepeace', as if that were her sole purpose. At Berwick, on 16 July, she was married to the five-year-old David Bruce and handed over to Thomas Randolph and Black Douglas. The English and Scots appeared to get on well – there was much feasting and celebration – but the emotions must have been burning in the hearts of both bride and bride's mother.

Roger too had reason to reflect. Although he had learnt by now that his eldest son's wife was expecting his first grandchild, he had also heard that his second son, Roger, had died. In the summer of his glory, following the wedding of his daughters in the king's presence, and after the honour of entertaining the king at Ludlow, Roger suffered the most humbling of blows. The aftermath of his triumphant summer was arranging for his son's corpse to be taken to Wigmore Abbey for burial.

We know nothing of Roger's emotional life, nor anything of the private lives of any of his family, thus it is very difficult to say what this loss meant to him. It seems he held his family in high esteem. A cynical explanation might be that he valued his children for their potential to make political alliances through marriage; but this would only be partly true, for inter-family marriages tended to be most meaningful when the individuals were close. Furthermore, rather than forging new alliances, marriages tended to cement existing ones. It is significant that Roger and Joan were not like previous generations of their families, marrying off the eldest son and the eldest daughters and putting the younger ones into the church. Instead all their children were given the opportunity of marriage and independence. The younger sons were all knighted and provided with lordships of their own. Edmund and Geoffrey spent time at court, and Geoffrey especially seems to have been favoured by both his parents.[31] All the daughters who had been placed in nunneries by Edward II and Despenser were redeemed and allowed the greater luxury, and the relatively greater freedom, of an aristocratic married woman's lifestyle. Only one daughter, Isabella, did not marry, but this may indicate merely that she did not live to receive a husband. Just as the number of children Roger and Joan had together indicates a greater than usual propensity to spend time with each other, so too his treatment of their children seems to reflect a loyalty deeper than that normally borne by power-obsessed magnates for their offspring.

As for Roger's relationship with his wife, he obviously continued to see her, on occasion at least, and she may well have visited court in addition to the visits he made to her at Ludlow. His feelings towards her were respectful, as shown by his sending the present of books in 1327, his occasional small gifts to her sisters' nunnery, Aconbury Priory, and his inclusion of her name in the list of those whose souls were to be the object of prayers in December 1328. There were no grants made to her which were not also to him, but this was due to the nature of medieval land tenure. In all legal matters touching Ireland and Ludlow her name is usually mentioned with his, but again this is only as one would expect. It is possible that the extended grants to them in Ireland benefited both of them, and certainly Joan was not left penniless. But it is perhaps in the strange arrangements of the solar wings at Ludlow Castle, and the silverware which bore their arms combined – which Roger still had with him in London two years later – that one can perhaps detect elements of their relationship lasting. Because of these hints of closeness with Joan and his children, one suspects that the death of his son Roger was a real blow, and perhaps one of the reasons why he started building the chantry at Leintwardine church.

*

Whatever Roger's and Isabella's personal feelings must have been on heading south from Berwick, they had to put them to one side and gather their resources for the meeting at the end of July at York. The Earl of Lancaster, disgruntled with Roger's hold on power, had decided not to attend the York meeting which he himself had demanded, to the king's ill-concealed disapproval. Thus Edward was at York on the appointed day to meet his mother and Roger, but Henry of Lancaster was not. Lancaster's supporters, including Thomas Wake, were also absent. Of most concern, however, was the absence of the king's two uncles, the Earls of Kent and Norfolk.

The court remained in York for most of August. Orders to attend a special parliament at Salisbury were despatched at the end of the month. The Controller of the King's Wardrobe, Thomas de Garton, was sent on a special mission to Lancaster, presumably to try to persuade him to come to Salisbury.[32] But Lancaster remained defiant. On 7 September he met Roger, Isabella and the king at Barlings Abbey near Lincoln. He had an army with him, and, shouting at Roger and Isabella in the king's presence, he threatened to use it.

It was a foolish move. The king was genuinely shocked by the earl's behaviour, and, faced with the reality of an aggressive vassal, Roger had no difficulty in persuading Edward of the merits of taking military precautions. The following week all armed followings were once again forbidden. He began to review positions of authority, removing any sheriffs or constables whom he did not trust, strengthening his hold on the country and the government. On hearing that in London, the Bishop of Winchester and Thomas Wake were negotiating with important London merchants on Lancaster's behalf, Roger advised the king that a rebellion was underway, and sent Bishop Burghersh and Oliver Ingham to demand an explanation from the Londoners. They replied in the form of a letter sent by Hamo de Chigwell on 27 September which listed the grievances of the Earl of Lancaster.

The accusations were numerous. Lancaster demanded firstly that Isabella give up her huge estates and return to the level of income more traditionally allowed a queen, and secondly that Roger be banished from court and forced to live upon his own lands, since he had disinherited so many people in order to acquire them. Thirdly he demanded an official inquiry into the fiasco of the campaign against the Scots, to establish who had betrayed the king. Fourthly he demanded that an inquiry be held as to why the rule that the king should be controlled by a council of twelve men ordained at the coronation was being neglected. Fifthly he claimed that the deposed king had been

> taken out of the castle of Kenilworth, where he was in ward, and through the influence of the Queen Isabella and of the Mortimer, without consent of any parliament, they took him and laid him there that none of his kindred could see him or speak to him again, and afterwards they traitorously took him and murdered him, for whose death a foul scandal arose throughout all Christendom when it was done.

Sixthly he claimed that Edward II's treasure had been frittered away without the consent of the young king. Seventhly that through the advice of Roger and Isabella the king had given up the land of Scotland for which many men had died, 'to the disinheritance of himself, his successors and his vassals and great reproof to all Englishmen forever more'. And finally, that Princess Joan had been married to the son of a traitor, on Roger and Isabella's advice.[33]

The seriousness of the accusations underscored the seriousness of the rebellion. Lancaster did not see this as a move to reduce Roger and Isabella's authority but entirely to destroy it. But he was not a great strategist. What did he offer in place of their rule? Only his own. This was a marked contrast to Roger's revolution with Isabella at the fore: they had been seen to offer a preferable alternative to the existing government, untainted by corruption. Lancaster offered an alternative which was partisan and every bit as corruptible as Roger and Isabella's rule. But most of all Lancaster was perceived not to have the subtlety to control public and noble opinion. Evidence of this was to be seen in his armed entourage confronting and challenging the king at Barlings Abbey. Proof of it came a few days later when he heard that the king was by himself in East Anglia, and took his army to capture him. Only a high-speed flight saved Edward. He forced the court to ride or march 120 miles to Salisbury from Cambridge in under four days, and, learning there that Roger and Isabella were at Gloucester, travelled the remaining sixty miles to meet them equally rapidly.

As a result of Lancaster's aggression, Roger obtained permission on 6 October to travel armed with his men. It was a sensible precaution. Shortly afterwards Lancaster's retainer, Sir Thomas Wyther, ambushed Sir Robert de Holand in a wood in Hertfordshire, hacked off his head and sent it to the earl. There had been no pretence at a trial. Far from distancing himself from this murder, Lancaster condoned it, and took Wyther and his accomplices into his protection.[34]

Outright civil war now seemed inevitable. The Salisbury parliament was only five weeks away, and the two sides were bound to come armed. At Gloucester Roger was gathering a large army from Wales and the Marches, ready to put down Lancaster's revolt and restore order. Lancaster was raising troops in London. The citizens had promised a force of six hundred men to support him. They had ousted Roger's supporter, Richard de Bethune, from the mayoralty and replaced him with Hamo de Chigwell, one of those who had sentenced Roger to death. They had kidnapped the Abbot of Bury St Edmunds and looted his monastery. Lancaster moved his army to Winchester, ready to attack Roger on Salisbury Plain. Roger advanced to Salisbury, where he ordered that Parliament should sit, with or without the Earl of Lancaster.

Desperately the Archbishop of Canterbury, who had already given some encouragement to Lancaster, tried to intervene. He requested that, as a sign of his impartiality, Roger should swear upon the archbishop's crozier that he intended no harm to the Earl of Lancaster, nor to his supporters. Roger did as requested. Slightly mollified, the archbishop proposed that the Bishops of London and Winchester should be sent to Lancaster, again asking him to attend Parliament. This was done. But Lancaster refused to come. He sent his list of grievances once more, stating he was prepared to come if his demands were met, and if he received guarantees of safe passage from those whom he thought were 'determined to do him harm'.

Roger replied to his demands on the king's behalf. With regard to the first of these, he said, the king was impoverished not by Isabella's grants of land but by the present likelihood of war, although, he added with wry humour, 'if any man knew how to make the king richer he would be made most welcome at court'. Quite simply the earl had no right to determine the level of the queen mother's dowry. With regard to the fourth complaint, Roger explained that the reason the King's Council did not more frequently advise the king was that Lancaster himself refused to attend, even when summoned. Lancaster could have letters of safe conduct if he should so require them, but if he took advantage of them he would have to abide by the terms of Magna Carta. This document held that he would be answerable in court if any man accused him of any crime, such as complicity in the murder of Sir Robert de Holand, or treason for riding against the king.[35] There was no reference to the other matters raised by the earl and the citizens of London. Accusations such as murder, conspiracy with the Scots and of frittering away Edward II's and Despenser's fortune were best left unanswered, being on the one hand beneath contempt, and, on the other, justified.

Lancaster recognised that he had no option: he could not go to Salisbury. The threat of arrest loomed too large, since he would undoubtedly have been accused of both murder and treason. Moreover there was a real risk of his being assassinated himself. Bishop Stratford, who had now wholly adopted the earl's cause, returned to Salisbury to attempt to win over more of the bishops gathered there for the parliament. He held secret meetings in his own house, but spies were at work in the town, and Roger's men soon drove him out of the city. He took shelter in the nunnery at Wilton, but there he was informed that Roger intended to murder him, and, mindful of de Stapeldon's fate, he fled across the fields by night.[36]

With the Earl of Lancaster and his supporters silenced, there was no need for Parliament to sit. But since it had gathered, Roger used the opportunity to recall the courts and the Exchequer from the north, safeguarding them from falling into Lancaster's hands, and restoring to London some of the favour which he now realised was necessary to maintain his popularity there. The only other significant business of the parliament was transacted on the last day, 31 October, when the king created three earls. The first was his brother, Prince John of Eltham, to whom he gave the title Earl of Cornwall. The third was James Butler, son of Edmund Butler of Ireland, to whom the king gave the title Earl of Ormond. Between these two grants the king strapped the belt and sword on Roger himself. To him the king gave the title Earl of March.[37] Roger's greatest moment had arrived. To cap it all, eleven days later, at Ludlow, his eldest son's wife gave birth to a son and heir.

Contemporaries were amazed by Roger's new title. Normally earldoms were associated with specific counties or county towns. A more usual style would have been for Roger to call himself 'Earl of Shrewsbury' or 'Earl of Radnor', taking his title from the county town of one of the shires in which he held a significant lordship. Instead he chose March, referring to the Welsh March. This was for two reasons. Firstly it harked back to his wife's ancestry, the French counts of La Marche, and drew attention to his connections with several of the ruling houses of Europe. Secondly it set him apart from all the other earls because it related to such a vast area. Despenser might have coveted the earldom of Gloucester, Roger himself might have controlled most of the earldom of Pembroke, but the earldom of March . . . Such a title implied supremacy over the existing earldoms of Pembroke, Hereford and Gloucester, and would naturally be far superior to those of Chester and Shrewsbury, if they were to be recreated. By comparison with such a magnificent title, what was an Earl of Lancaster?

Lancaster was furious when he heard of the title. Immediately he marched into Winchester and cut off the king's approach to London. Roger sent the Sheriff of Hampshire to force Lancaster to withdraw. Thomas Wake came out from the city to meet the sheriff, and negotiations continued for several days before Roger's army drew close. Desperately Wake tried to persuade Lancaster not to fight, suspecting that Roger would have little mercy on them. Only at the last minute did Lancaster relent. His soldiers were still leaving when Roger's army marched into the city. Men from both sides skirmished with each other, jeering and shouting. The two armies scraped each other but they did not clash.

In London frantic negotiations were taking place as the Lancastrian supporters battled with the more moderate aldermen. Bitter recriminations were thrown across the Guildhall, as both factions realised the court was coming to London. In the end the neutral John de Grantham was elected, and he created a fiction that London had remained totally loyal to Roger. As the court entered the city in late November, both Roger and the Londoners had learnt a lesson: neither could afford to neglect the other.

Roger was satisfied for the time being, but he had not gone to London to make peace. He knew now for certain there would be war. There could be no return to the charade of Lancaster as head of a council. Only one of them could wield power. Thus his purpose in taking the court to London was to break the citizens' support for Lancaster. The earl stationed himself at Higham Ferrers in Northamptonshire, and sent his messengers to the king with proposals for a meeting of the royal council. Roger sent them back angrily, stating that Lancaster should show more humility: that he should approach his king as a vassal and make an unconditional surrender. Roger listed the king's grievances, including protests that the king had the right to surround himself with such advisers as he chose, and that Lancaster had stayed away from court when he had been summoned, and had appeared in arms before the king on the few occasions when they had met. While Roger awaited a response, he took measures to control the capital. He prohibited the carrying of arms in the city and reinforced law and order. Finally, confident that London would stand firm, he and the court withdrew from the city to Gloucester, to arm, plan and begin the war with Lancaster. Force of arms could determine which of them was loyal and which the traitor.

At moments of grave crisis, it seems, Roger turned to God. Now he made the endowment for his chapel at Leintwardine. On 15 December at Gloucester he granted lands and rent to the value of 100 marks (£67) per year for a college of nine chaplains to sing masses daily in the church of St Mary for the souls of King Edward and Queen Philippa, Queen Isabella, Bishop Burghersh, and himself, his wife, his children and their ancestors and successors.[38] It had been a long time since he had fought a campaign, and he knew he would be fighting the combined forces of the Earls of Lancaster, Norfolk and Kent. He might not live much longer. His mind had grown a little colder, since the loss of another of his sons. Not long after the death of his second son, Roger, his youngest son, John, had been killed in a tournament at Shrewsbury.[39] Besides the dead there were grand-children being born whom he realised he might never see grow to adult-hood, who would inherit the fruits of his labours and merely wonder at his name. Chantries and sepulchral monuments were one way for noblemen to communicate across the centuries with their descendants. And finally there was the matter of his wife and Isabella, with whom he could neither be together nor apart, being wrenched between them both. It was a strange extended family – a king, two queens, a wife, a mistress, the living and the dead – but these were the people for whom Roger cared most, and he wanted them to be together at peace, if only in the prayers of the chaplains of St Mary's, Leintwardine.

There was one other reason for the timeliness of this foundation: Roger was not just going to war over his policy towards Scotland or Henry of Lancaster's treason, he was fighting for his and Isabella's lives. The Earl of Kent had learnt that Edward II was still alive. And he had told Lancaster.

We do not know how the Earl of Kent learnt about the ex-king's continued existence. Perhaps the most likely explanation is that Edward III confided in him while Roger and Isabella were travelling to Berwick for the marriage between David and Joan in July 1328. This may explain why he and his brother, the Earl of Norfolk, refused to attend the meeting at York which was to take place on their return. In his later confession, Kent claimed that he had heard the news at Kensington from a Dominican friar of London who 'had raised up the devil, which declared unto him for certain that Edward, his brother, sometime King of England, was alive'.[40] This was almost certainly a means to cover up the identity of his true informant. It remains a possibility that friars of the Dominican order had learnt for themselves that Edward was alive, and informed the earl. Whichever was the true source of his information, if Kent informed Lancaster between July and September, then Lancaster's accusation of murder in the autumn was an attempt to call Roger's bluff, to force him to reveal the living ex-king. While this remains uncertain, it is highly likely that Lancaster had been informed by the end of October, as on 5 November he wrote to the Mayor of London stating that he would send some information by messenger he dared not have written down which he had heard from the Earl of Kent.[41]

The consequence of this information was further to alienate Edward II's half-brothers from Roger. In December they issued a joint circular statement accusing their nephew the king of breaking the terms of his coronation oath and abusing Magna Carta.[42] The latter was a tacit reference to Edward II's custody, for which they held Edward III partly responsible, indicating that they were aware that he knew of his father's survival.[43] They called for a general gathering in London to discuss further action. It was sent to all those likely to be sympathetic to the Earl of Lancaster's cause, as well as to the king. The Archbishop of Canterbury, the Bishop of Winchester and the Bishop of London responded, as did Lancaster's northern supporters. On 18 December the archbishop preached a sermon against the king at St Paul's. Three days later a very full reply was received in the city and read aloud at the Guildhall. The archbishop, who by now had given up all pretence to impartiality, wrote back to the king and the court threatening him and them with excommunication. This outrageous letter, which implied the king was guilty as charged, coincided with the completion of Roger's preparations for a military campaign. There was nothing left to do but fight.

On 29 December Roger declared war on Henry of Lancaster in the king's name.[44] A letter was sent to London stating that Edward intended to march to Leicester, via Warwick, and that those who surrendered before

7 January would be pardoned for their transgressions, with the exceptions of Henry de Beaumont, Thomas Roscelyn, Thomas Wyther and William Trussel, whose disloyalty could never be forgiven. The letter was read aloud on 1 January to Lancaster and the other leaders at St Paul's, who even now thought they could mediate. But the royal army was already on the march. They left Warwick that same day and went to Kenilworth, where the king asked for access to the castle. Upon being refused, Roger decided to bring forward the deadline for action. He took the army to Leicester and began to sack the Earl of Lancaster's manors. Then he ordered the town and all the earl's property to be destroyed by sword and fire, including the property of his dependants. Over the years Roger's men had grown experienced in the art of wanton destruction. They took the earl's deer, cut down his woods, emptied his fish ponds, emptied his granaries, took his cattle and sheep, and destroyed his manor houses, barns, fences, sheds and cottages. The entire town and hinterland was devastated in a few days. The army was, however, restrained when it came to killing people: the majority of the fatalities arose from Henry Percy's massacre of a crowd of peasants marching to serve Lancaster.

Hearing of the attack on his lands, Lancaster marched north. At Bedford he held a council with his fellow lords. He declared that they now had no choice: they would have to fight the king. At this the Earls of Norfolk and Kent recoiled. They refused to ride in arms against the royal banner, for the double risk of being presumed traitors by their nephew, who was obviously Roger's pawn, and for fear of Roger himself, who seemed unbeatable with a royal army behind him. They grew angry, and denounced Lancaster, accusing him of sedition, of trying to destroy the king. They abandoned the earl and rode off to seek peace before it was too late.

Roger was at Northampton. When he heard that the Earls of Norfolk and Kent had deserted Lancaster, he ordered his troops to prepare for an immediate night attack. Even Isabella took part, dressed in armour and mounted on a war horse. Through the night he led them, for twenty-four miles, arriving within sight of Lancaster's camp near Bedford at daybreak. Henry made no attempt to defend himself. He came out of his pavilion and walked slowly forward through the cold January morning, and knelt down, alone, in the mud. He waited there until Roger, Isabella and the king rode up. They watched him from their horses as he begged for forgiveness.

FOURTEEN

King of Folly

The moment the Earl of Lancaster knelt at the feet of the young king, Roger was able to claim a personal victory far greater than merely that of defeating Lancaster. All England, Wales and Ireland was under his control. The king was in his power, Isabella was more dependent on him than ever, and all the key office-holders in the country were his appointments. If people sought pardons, they sought them from him. If wardships were distributed, it was to men of whom he approved. He had been granted the most prestigious title in the country, and no one dared face him with an army. His only real threat had been the vanquished, humiliated earl, kneeling in the mud before him. This, he may have reflected in his moment of glory, was what it felt like to be a king.

Like a king, but not actually a king. He did not enjoy this power by right but through duplicity and force. He could never be secure. Knowledge that Edward II was still alive was now circulating among the nobility: if he had previously had any doubts about remaining at court, this resolved them. He could never go back now to live on his own estates, as the Earl of Lancaster had demanded. And why should he? He had won the right to dictate his own fate, as well as Lancaster's. Besides, there was Isabella to consider. She needed him. Henry of Lancaster's rebellion had demonstrated that no one could be trusted. If Isabella's second son John, the newly created Earl of Cornwall, were to die, the Earl of Norfolk would be next in line to the throne. Norfolk had initially sided with the rebels, and had only sought peace at the last moment. What if he were to take arms? And how many others were there like him? It was Roger's duty to stay and show the king how to rule his realm, and how to control his opponents. In this way he justified to himself the necessity of maintaining his grip on power. The result was that he ruled the kingdom for the next two years with less regard for its people than for himself.

Those who had dared oppose him had to pay the penalty, especially the less important men, the Londoners. Only a matter of days after Lancaster's submission the new mayor of London and twenty-four leading citizens were summoned and ordered to hold an inquiry to root out all those who had supported Lancaster. They held a council at the end of the month. Powerful figures within the city hierarchy tried to protect the Lancastrian sympathisers, but spies ensured that this information found its way to Roger. A few days later the city's inquiry was replaced by a group favourable to Roger, namely Oliver Ingham, Sir John Maltravers, John de Stonor, Robert Mablethorpe and John de Grantham, the mayor.[1] Trials continued throughout the first half of February. It tried even the most powerful merchants, including Hamo de Chigwell, the former mayor, who was sent to the Tower.[2]

Londoners could be stamped on hard. Peers were a different matter. Obviously all positions of authority were removed from lords who had joined Lancaster. There was an unstated but implied death sentence on those whom Roger felt had betrayed him most of all: Thomas Roscelyn, Henry de Beaumont and William Trussel. To these he added Thomas Wyther, for the murder of Robert de Holand. All four of these men fled to France and lost their lands. But otherwise Roger was lenient. The Earls of Norfolk and Kent were not punished. Thomas Wake, being Roger's cousin, was bound over for £10,000. Hugh Audley, Roger's nephew, was also not driven into exile but was allowed to keep his estates on penalty of £10,000. The Earl of Lancaster himself was treated similarly, being bound over for £30,000 and fined £11,000. Many more leaders were allowed to remain and keep their estates on recognition of an impending fine. Roger did not need to exact revenge; he merely consolidated his victory by financial punishments and by forcing all rebel lords to swear to protect the king, Isabella, and all the other members of the king's council, including, of course, Roger himself.

There are several reasons why Roger showed such leniency to his opponents. The first is that he did not want to provoke the reaction which would surely follow a cold-blooded massacre of the nobility, like the one after the Battle of Boroughbridge. In addition, he had sworn an oath on the Archbishop of Canterbury's crozier that he meant the Earl of Lancaster no harm. Thomas Wake and Hugh Audley were close relations, and he did not want to alienate them. Similarly he did not want to damage the Earls of Kent and Norfolk; rather he wanted to thank them for turning the tables on Lancaster. Besides, he wanted to draw closer to the royal family, not to distance himself from it. But probably the most important reason was that he was cautious of the weight of the opposition which had dared to face him. Even now, Henry of Lancaster was very popular, especially in the north, for having led the resistance to Roger's peace treaty with Scotland. To punish him severely would be to incite a popular uprising. Lastly, news of the ex-king's survival was now spreading among his opponents beyond his control, and becoming common rumour. In the words of the longer *Brut* chronicle, 'all the commons almost of England were in sorrow and dread' whether the king was alive at Corfe or not.[3]

In addition to the rumours and and the whispers behind closed doors, there was the problem of France. When Philip de Valois ascended the throne, against the claim of Edward III, he dealt a diplomatic as well as a political blow to the English royal family. In the autumn of 1328 the new French king insisted that Edward should come in person to France to do homage for Gascony. Isabella retorted that the son of a king would never do homage to the son of a mere count.[4] Philip de Valois responded by confiscating the revenues of Gascony and, in February 1329, sent an ultimatum. Roger and Isabella, still tidying up the legal loose ends of Lancaster's rebellion, realised they were in no position to go to war with France. Instead they loaded the envoys with gifts for the French king and promised that Edward would perform homage in the near future. In April an apology for the delay was sent. Finally in May the court went into Kent to see the young king off to France. As they said goodbye to one another at Dover, Edward gave Roger a diamond amulet worth £20, a token perhaps of his confidence in him rather than Henry of Lancaster.[5]

The king was away for sixteen days. He performed homage to Philip at Amiens on 6 June. He did so in an unsatisfactory manner, so far as the French king was concerned, for Philip wanted Edward to swear to serve him in war, knowing there was a high risk of Edward (as a rival for the French throne) attacking him. But the English advisers with Edward, notably Roger's close friend, Henry de Burghersh, had been instructed not to let this happen, and Edward himself had no wish to serve his mother's cousin. As soon as the ceremony was over Isabella summoned her son to return to England as quickly as possible, and he obeyed, without even taking formal leave of the King of France.[6] On 11 June he was back at Dover. Three days later he was with Roger and Isabella at Canterbury.

We cannot know for certain the reason why Isabella summoned him back so abruptly. Perhaps she did not want him to fall under Philip's influence; perhaps she did not trust Philip not to detain her son. But there is another possibility, more plausible than her fear of Edward falling under Philip's influence; and although it cannot be proved it needs to be considered seriously.

She was pregnant.

*

The subject of Isabella's pregnancy has to be approached with enormous caution. If she was at any time pregnant with Roger's child, the fact was kept secret for two very good reasons. Firstly, the child was proof of an enormous impropriety on the part of the queen mother, and a public insult to the king. Secondly, a male child would have had a claim to the throne of France, after King Edward and Prince John, and thus his very existence would have constituted an international scandal, very probably affecting Edward's claim to the French throne. To Edward, who clearly found Roger's hold on him irksome, the thought of having to acknowledge Roger's son as his half-brother was unbearable. The irony was that Edward was the one person from whom Roger and Isabella could not hide the truth. Being so close to his mother, and seeing her every day, any protracted period apart would have made him suspicious. But with his help, a pregnancy might be kept secret, especially under the more voluminous dresses to be seen at court now that Philippa was queen.

In these circumstances it is surprising that there is any evidence at all regarding a pregnancy. But there are some details which, taken together, indicate that it may well have happened. Firstly there is the chronicle of Froissart, which states bluntly that Isabella was rumoured to be pregnant in 1330.[7] Froissart is somewhat erratic in his chronology of the early years of the reign of Edward III, and regards dates as less important than deeds of valour, but it is unlikely he would have completely fabricated a story which brought no credit to the mother of his hero. He may have heard a rumour and supposed it related to Roger's arrest in 1330, or he may have picked up on rumours concerning a second pregnancy.

Support for Froissart's statement that Isabella was pregnant is to be found in less explicit but more official sources for the previous year. In September 1329 Isabella made a form of will: a settlement of some of her estates which in the event of her death were to go to Roger. This was unusual for a thirty-three-year-old woman; most people made bequests only in the last months of life, when they knew they were dying. But it was not the first time Isabella had made such a settlement: she had made a similar one when pregnant with her first child in 1312, facing the uncertainty of giving birth.[8] The only credible alternatives to a pregnancy are that Isabella was ill, or feared an attempt on her life. There is no evidence for any illness, and no evidence that anyone was plotting to murder her at that time.

The next piece of evidence that Isabella was pregnant in the summer of 1329 relates directly to Roger. In the grant he had made to Leintwardine church the previous December he had specified nine chaplains to sing masses daily for the souls of King Edward III, Queen Isabella, Queen Philippa, Bishop Burghersh, himself, his countess Joan, and their children, their successors and their ancestors.[9] There are nine constituencies here – six individuals and three groups – corresponding with the nine chaplains endowed. On 10 February 1330 Roger added another chaplain and another individual, acknowledging that there was now a further member of his extended family for whose soul prayers had to be offered daily. Roger named him as the 'Earl of Lincoln'.[10]

This choice of title is interesting because there was no Earl of Lincoln in 1330.[11] The last man to bear this title had been Thomas, Earl of Lancaster, who had borne the title by right of his wife, Alice, the last surviving child of Henry, Earl of Lincoln. The Earl of Suffolk had seized the countess and taken her away from Lancaster, to her great delight, and so Henry of Lancaster was unable to inherit the Lincoln title after the overthrow of the Despensers. She was forty-eight years old, and knew she would not bear an heir herself, although she was married to Sir Ebulo Lestrange, a Shropshire baron. Thus the title was bound to become extinct on her death. Moreover, most of the Lincoln estates had already been granted to Isabella, and those which had not were soon to be granted to Roger and his son Geoffrey.[12] Thus, although the Leintwardine grant evidence is not conclusive, it is clearly significant. It suggests that there was a son, gives him a highly plausible title which he could have expected to be granted on the death of the countess, and explains how Roger and Isabella might have managed to bring him into the front rank of the nobility, despite his illegitimacy.[13]

If there was a child born to Isabella at this period one would expect this to be indicated by a prolonged pause in her itinerary. When Queen Philippa was heavily pregnant with Edward's son in 1330, the court stayed at Woodstock from 29 March until 20 June, a period of about twelve weeks, moving on a few days after the birth took place (on 16 June). Apart from this instance there are only four other periods of five weeks or more when the court stayed in one place in the years 1326–30. All but one of these can be linked to major political developments in 1327, as the government was being more firmly established.[14] There are no such prolonged pauses in Isabella's itinerary in 1328. The only other stay in the whole of Roger's period of authority was at Kenilworth Castle from 29 October 1329 to 3 January 1330. This is without obvious explanation. Indeed it was the quietest period of Roger and Isabella's time together. Thus, if Isabella was pregnant by Roger, the most likely time and place for the child to have been born was December 1329 at Kenilworth. This coincides with the evidence of the revised Leintwardine grant, which implies a date not long before 10 February 1330.

If an illegitimate son was born at Kenilworth in December 1329, it would help explain several other events in the summer of that year. For example, it would explain why Edward returned from France so quickly in June. Isabella and Roger realised the necessity of informing Edward at an early opportunity and summoned him back without an explanation. This caused him to hasten, fearing the worst. It would also explain a gift-giving ceremony which took place at Windsor that summer.[15] Edward gave Roger a number of valuable jewels and other gifts, including seven silver goblets, four of which were gilt, one patterned with shells, one enamelled, and one encrusted with jewels.[16] Such gift-giving between the king and his most important vassal may be accepted as routine, but it is not so easy to explain Edward's gift of a French goblet later that summer. This was a valuable silver-gilt enamelled goblet bearing the royal arms of France and Navarre.[17] These were the arms of Isabella's parents, and thus this cup had been a possession of the French royal family, and a gift to Edward. Giving it to Roger was perhaps a confirmation, prompted by Isabella, that Roger was now linked to the royal family.

Any part of this evidence by itself would permit only tentative suggestions regarding a pregnancy. Taken as a whole, however, it suggests that Isabella gave birth to Roger's son in December 1329. Moreover it seems that Edward was told about it. This is highly significant, as it would explain the worsening of Roger's and Edward's relationship with one another which took place at this time. Up to late 1329 Roger dominated the king and the court, but he remained deferential to Edward. All the marks of disrespect to the king – remaining seated in his presence, walking by his side, and, eventually, commanding that his own word was to be obeyed, and not the king's – date from after the late summer of 1329.[18]

This is the real importance of a pregnancy in 1329: the effect it would have had on Roger and Isabella, and on their relationship with Edward. How did they cope with the pressure of keeping the pregnancy hidden while being seen publicly to be in control of government? What happened to their relationship with each other? Since Isabella was already bound to Roger by her dependency on him to keep Edward II safely concealed, it probably only reinforced the knowledge that they could never leave each other, as this secret could have destroyed both of them. But what did it mean for Roger's relationship with Edward? It meant that Roger was even more closely tied to the royal family. He not only had possession of the ex-king and the love of the queen, he was biologically linked to the king through a half-brother. Edward could no longer hope that one day Roger would withdraw from court. If Isabella was pregnant, Roger was bound into the royal family by blood. To unbind him, blood would need to be shed.

*

The stakes had been raised in the power struggle between the two men, so the spying and the machinations, the devious plots and the subterfuge increased. John Wyard, Roger's retainer for a number of years, was now a king's sergeant-at-arms and a spy. Possibly he informed Roger that the Earl of Kent had visited the Pope at Avignon and had spoken of Edward II's imprisonment. At Paris, in the Duke of Brabant's chamber, Kent had discussed the matter with the exiled Henry de Beaumont and Thomas Roscelyn.[19] Maybe it was Wyard who learnt that Kent and his wife were going on a pilgrimage to Santiago de Compostella in northern Spain. Whatever the case, Roger formed a plan to have the earl murdered. But Edward clearly had spies of his own: he learnt of Roger's plans, and managed to inform Kent in time that his life would be in danger if he went to Santiago. The king and Roger were playing out their private battle like a deadly game of chess across Europe, while politely giving each other formal presents at home.

In late August 1329 Roger decided to hold a Round Table tournament in the style of his famous grandfather.[20] The reason for the celebration was another Mortimer double marriage, like the one of the previous summer, but this time with far more powerful men as the bridegrooms. Since the previous family wedding, Roger had become an earl, and thus his daughters could expect to be married to earls and the sons of earls. One daughter, Agnes, was to be married to the young Earl of Pembroke, Laurence de Hastings, whose right of marriage was in Roger's hands. The other was an even more eminent match, a marriage into the royal family. The Earl of Norfolk, the king's uncle, was persuaded to let his son and heir marry Roger's daughter, Beatrice. Normally one would have expected the fourth in line to the throne to make a better marriage than the sixth daughter of the recently created Earl of March, but these were not normal times.

Just before setting out for Wigmore, the possibly pregnant Isabella made her settlement in case of her death. On 2 September she ordered that Roger was to receive Montgomery Castle and the adjacent lordship of the hundred of Chirbury. He was also to keep Builth Castle at a nominal rent. With this sealed and settled, the royal party moved up the Welsh border, reaching Leominster the following evening. From there, on the following day, they made the short journey to Wigmore.

A large crowd had arrived for the tournament. Everything was paid for by Roger out of the treasure which he had taken from the Despensers and with a grant from the king of £1,000.[21] Earls and barons had encamped in the valley below the castle and around the small town of Wigmore. Pavilions stretched through the hunting grounds. As at the Kenilworth

Round Table held by Roger's grandfather, gifts were given, love tokens exchanged, and knights jousted while spectators watched from platforms above the ring. Roger himself took the part of Arthur, and Isabella, seated next to him, played Guinevere, overseeing the events.[22] On each day of the tournament the king gave Roger formal presents of jewels and gilt-silver goblets, including, on 5 September, the French royal goblet bearing the arms of France and Navarre mentioned above.

The Wigmore tournament lasted for two or three days. Throughout, Roger himself was the talking point, overshadowing even his daughters on their wedding day. People remarked on his familiarity with the royal family. Roger, crowned as King Arthur, and with his queen beside him, was setting himself very publicly above the real king. If Roger had taken the part of Lancelot, it would have been amusing and ironic, and King Edward (as Arthur) would not have been threatened. But Roger was not just play-acting; he was self-importantly reminding everyone that he, not Edward, was of the line of Arthur. Rumours swept around the crowd that Roger now sought to make himself king. People did not need to have the prophecy of Merlin explained to them to understand the symbolism of Roger wearing a crown.

Herein lay Roger's mistake. He was not a member of the royal family and his attempts to appear as such seemed perverse. His elaborate and 'wondrously rich' clothes, which were strange in style and colour,[23] were particularly remarked upon. His jewellery attracted envy. His casual manner with the king offended everyone, for he walked alongside him and sat in his presence. People were shocked at his temerity. It did not help that the size of his personal household was vast – nearly two hundred people – as many armed men as the king himself maintained. And inviting comparisons with King Arthur was more than just faintly ridiculous. His grandfather might have got away with a Round Table tournament fifty years earlier, at the end of his illustrious career, but Roger compared unfavourably with the peerless Arthur of the Round Table myth, a man who had supposedly fought giants, won all his battles, conquered France, saved ravished maidens, and led a glorious band of knights. How could Roger compare with 'the most worthy lord of renown there was in all the world'?[24]

Roger's self-creation of chivalric magnificence and power had become over inflated. He was surrounded by royal people and all the trappings of courtly magnificence, all the ancestry, wealth and power; but he and everyone else knew that he was a mere baron's son from the Welsh Marches. He had not won glory like his hero William Marshal, Earl of Pembroke, he had cheated his way to it. His power had been achieved not through wisdom but through cunning. Only one person was courageous enough to stand up publicly and tell Roger to his face that he was ridiculous. At Wigmore, Sir Geoffrey Mortimer, Roger's favourite son, declared him to be 'the King of Folly'.[25] It was a telling phrase. Roger had foolishly come to confuse his proximity to royalty with being royal himself and, equally foolishly, he had lost his ability to gauge and control public opinion. He had grown too mighty.

*

In the wake of the Wigmore tournament the conflict at the heart of government became more heated. Edward had not reacted well to Roger's display, and now he took his first steps towards regaining his royal power. On 12 September he sent abroad his trusted friend Sir William de Montagu. His mission was ostensibly to visit Gascony but he had secret instructions to go to the Pope in Avignon to let him know what was happening in England.[26] On hearing that Montagu was going abroad Roger became suspicious and insisted that he be accompanied by Sir Bartholomew de Burghersh, brother of the Bishop of Lincoln. But at Avignon, Montagu managed to evade Burghersh and was granted a private audience with the Pope. He brought back a message that the Pope wished to have some sign by which he could distinguish the king's own letters from those Roger issued in his name. Edward wrote back early the following year, signing the letter with the words 'Pater Sancte' in his own hand, the earliest extant autograph of an English king.[27]

The court moved on. At Gloucester on 16 September the king was successful in replacing Roger's appointed Treasurer, Thomas de Charlton, with Robert Wodehouse, formerly Keeper of the King's Wardrobe. A week later Edward forced the appointment of his personal secretary, Richard de Bury, as Keeper of the Privy Seal. The writing was on the wall: Edward was slowly increasing his influence. Roger and Isabella were having to balance a possible secret pregnancy and the secret existence of the ex-king at Corfe against the growing enmity of the nobility and the powerful ambitions of the seventeen-year-old king. In addition there may have been an attempt to free Edward II in August 1329.[28] At the end of September, Roger appointed John Maltravers the official custodian of Corfe Castle, to protect his royal prisoner.[29]

In early October the court was at Dunstable for a tournament.[30] Immediately afterwards it moved north, directed by Roger and Isabella, to Kenilworth. If Isabella was pregnant by Roger, this was where she was going to give birth to their child. Being a castle of the Earl of Lancaster, it might seem an odd place to choose. But there were several good reasons.

One was Roger's sense of history and individual destiny, linking his family stories of Kenilworth and his grandfather's victories with the destiny he imagined for his unborn child. Another was more pragmatic. Roger's estates on the Welsh Marches were not far away. In addition, Henry of Lancaster was in France, acting on the king's behalf in negotiations with King Philip about the imperfect homage Edward had performed in June for Gascony.[31] Thus in that vast castle, surrounded by Roger's bodyguard of nearly two hundred men-at-arms, they were relatively safe.

If Isabella gave birth in December 1329, it was probably at the very beginning of the month. Roger was still at Kenilworth on 3 December, but then left for a short visit to his estates on the Welsh Marches. On the 5th he was at Ludlow, where he made a grant of land to one of his retainers (Walter le Baily of Leinthall), and to the man's wife and first heir.[32] Three days later he was at Clun. The business which we know he conducted there was very minor – about fishing rights, for which he merely ordered an inquiry to be made – and was probably incidental to the real purpose of his visit, which is not recorded.[33] But Clun was close to Montgomery Castle and the hundred of Chirbury, the lands which Isabella had settled on him in case of her death and which thus presumably she intended to be settled on their child. The route also took him through Leintwardine, where he could have explained the intended extension of his grant. By 12 December he was back at Kenilworth, administering royal business.

*

For the last couple of months Roger had been relatively cautious and quiet. Now he went back on the offensive. It was only nine months before Edward turned eighteen, and as the young king grew in age and stature, so he grew in authority. Roger realised that it would only be a matter of time before he and the king clashed openly.

In January the court returned to the capital, to stay at Isabella's palace at Eltham. Roger granted himself all the possessions of Hugh Despenser which had been concealed from the king in Pembrokeshire. At the end of the month he further granted himself custody of lands of the earldom of Kildare, together with the right of the heir's marriage. In February the court moved to the Tower, to prepare for the coronation of Queen Philippa, now heavily pregnant. This required Isabella to relinquish lands and castles destined to be granted to the new queen, for which, of course, she sought even greater grants in compensation.[34] But opposition forces were once more growing. In late January Hamo de Chigwell had been released from custody by the Bishop of London, and the Londoners were beginning to voice openly their support for merchants who had suffered under Roger's judges a year earlier.[35] The Earl of Kent was also back in the country, and he was scheming.

Two days before Hamo de Chigwell's release Roger issued summonses in the king's name for a parliament to be held at Winchester. Kent and his brother, the Earl of Norfolk, played their part at the coronation of Queen Philippa on 18 February, dressed as simple grooms and riding alongside the queen as she made her way to Westminster from the Tower. None of this pageantry was of importance to Roger. His plan was set. He had proof that Kent had hatched a plot to free Edward II, written in the hand of Margaret Wake, his own cousin, the earl's wife.

As the lords gathered for the parliament, Kent was quietly arrested, along with certain of his followers. A few days later, Roger announced the news to the lords. The charge was treason.

Kent had attempted several times to gain access to Corfe Castle: he had written to two men of the castle garrison, Bogo de Bayeux and John Deveril, seeking access, but had been refused. However, these two men, who were either Roger's or Maltravers' agents, agreed to pass a letter to Edward II on the earl's behalf. Trusting them completely, Kent persuaded his wife, Margaret, to write a letter to the ex-king. Deveril and Bayeux received the letter and, after the earl had returned to his estates, dutifully took it to Roger. Roger read the letter. It showed that the earl had attracted considerable support in his plot to free Edward.

This placed Roger under huge pressure. Secrets that would ensure that he went to the gallows were being passed around among his enemies. He could deny the accusation, of course, but his credibility depended entirely on Edward III's support. This was exceedingly dangerous, as the king was anxious to oust him from court. Roger had to trust in the protection afforded him by his secret custody of the ex-king.

It was a tense situation for all concerned. Roger was relying on the king to condemn his own uncle rather than admit his father was still alive. No doubt Isabella repeatedly reminded her son of the danger they would all be in if it were widely known that Edward II lived. For his part, Roger once more choreographed proceedings. He convened a court specially for the purpose of trying the earl, presided over by the coroner of the household, Robert Howel.[36] Roger himself acted as the prosecutor. The author of the longer *Brut* chronicle seems to have been close to someone there that day, and reports that Roger addressed the accused as follows:

Sir Edmund, Earl of Kent, you should understand that it behoves us to say, and principally unto our liege lord, Sir Edward, King of England – whom Almighty God save and keep – that you are his deadly enemy and his traitor and also a common enemy unto the realm; and that you have been about many a day to make privily deliverance of Sir Edward, sometime King of England, your brother, who was put down out of his royalty by common assent of all the lords of England, and in impairing of our lord the king's estate, and also of his realm.

Kent is supposed to have replied: 'In truth, Sir, understand well that I never assented to the impairment of the state of our lord the king, nor of his crown, and that I put myself to be tried by my peers.' But Roger paid no attention to the earl's plea. Instead he produced the letter which Kent had sent to the deposed king by way of Bogo de Bayeux and John Deveril. He held it up, with its seal, for all to see. 'Sir Edmund, know ye not the print of this letter that you took unto Sir John Deveril?' The earl, not knowing which letter it might have been, as he had sent several, agreed on inspecting the seal that it was one of his, but he claimed it was of no consequence. Roger asked him again if the seal was his, and the earl said he would not deny it. And then, in the words of the chronicler, 'with that word the wily and false Mortimer began to undo the letter and started to read it in the hearing of all the court'.

> Worships and reverence, with a brother's liegeance and subjection. Sir knight, worshipful and dear brother, if you please, I pray heartily that you are of good comfort, for I shall ordain for you that soon you shall come out of prison, and be delivered of that disease in which you find yourself. Your lordship should know that I have the assent of almost all the great lords of England, with all their apparel, that is to say, with armour, and with treasure without number, in order to maintain and help your quarrel so you shall be king again as you were before, and that they all – prelates, earls and barons – have sworn to me upon a book.[37]

The implications did not need to be spelled out to those in the court. This was proof that a number of lords were plotting against the government, and thus against the king. More importantly, Kent would be forced to name names, and to implicate these lords, great and small, including some lords present. If the king's own uncle could be charged in this way, no one was safe.

It was Robert Howel who delivered the final judgement:

> Sir Edmund, since you have admitted openly in this court that this is your letter ensealed with your seal, and the tenor of the letter is that

you were on the point of delivering the body of that worshipful knight Sir Edward, sometime King of England, your brother, and to help him become king again, and to govern his people as he was wont to do beforehand, thus impairing the state of our liege lord the present king, whom God keep from all disease . . . the will of this court is that you shall lose both life and limb, and that your heirs shall be disinherited forevermore, save the grace of our lord the king.

The court was horrified. The Earl of Kent was to die for the crime of trying to rescue his own brother. And all his family were to be disinherited. It was incredible. Everyone presumed that this was an anomaly, that the earl would appeal to the king, and that the king would spare the earl's life. Edward II had lost his crown because of such acts of tyranny; surely his son would not uphold the death sentence on his own uncle for a crime fabricated by Roger.

But this extraordinary charade was not yet over. On 16 March a fuller confession was extracted from the earl, and it was read aloud in Parliament. It was declared solemnly that the Earl of Kent had acknowledged that the Pope had charged him to deliver Edward II from prison, and had promised to fund the plot. Many lords and prelates were implicated, including the Archbishop of York, Sir Ingelram de Berengar and Sir William de la Zouche, who had all promised to help rescue Edward II from Corfe. It was confessed that the archbishop had pledged £5,000. Sir Fulk FitzWarin was accused, so too were Sir John Pecche, Sir Henry de Beaumont, Sir Thomas Roscelyn, the Scottish Earl of Mar, Lady Vesci and the Bishop of London. The earl implicated certain Dominican friars, claiming they had informed him his brother was at Corfe. He gave everything away; everything, that is, except the real source of his information. Instead he told the story about the friar who had summoned up the devil. This suited both Roger and the king: if Kent had admitted he had heard of Edward II's existence from the present king his testimony would confirm to everyone that Edward II was alive.

Having confessed so much, and so wholeheartedly, the earl threw himself on Edward's mercy. He admitted that he was guilty, and that he had borne himself badly towards the king, and wholly submitted himself to him. He promised, if it was the king's will, to walk in his shirt through the streets of Winchester or even all the way to London, barefoot, with a rope around his neck, or wherever the king pleased, in atonement for his offence. The picture of the earl is that of a sincerely contrite, terrified human being, begging for forgiveness with all his heart, not fully able to grasp that he was to be executed for trying to free his brother.

He was right to be terrified. Roger was unmoved by his pleading. To the earl's horror and the astonishment of all present, Roger boldly urged that the death sentence be upheld. Edward, seeing that Kent had betrayed him by trying to restore his father, thereby jeopardising his life, had no choice but reluctantly to assent to the earl's death.[38]

It was the most profoundly shocking act of tyranny that anyone could remember. There was no evidence against Kent apart from his confession and his letter. Roger himself had been forgiven far worse in 1322 by Edward II. But Roger knew that his life and Isabella's life were at risk, and he was ruthless. There could be no half-measures. He ordered the arrest of Kent's pregnant wife and their children. Like Hugh Despenser before him, he was locking up whole families and confiscating their estates. That Kent and his wife had both once been in exile in France with Roger simply made matters worse: as with Roscelyn, Beaumont and Wake, he had trusted these people implicitly. To be betrayed by them was an act of personal enmity, and he could not bear such betrayal.

The day before Kent's execution Roger ordered about forty men to be arrested. Every layman mentioned in the earl's confession was proscribed, as well as many others. He used the moment to take action against everyone whom he wanted behind bars.

The Earl of Kent was led out of his cell to be beheaded on the morning of 19 March 1330. There he waited, in the midst of a crowd. The man appointed to wield the axe refused to do so. Men-at-arms were ordered to cut the earl's head off, but none dared. Their captains sympathised. And so the earl stood there, for several hours. The crowd grew restless. Furious with the delay, Roger offered a pardon to anyone in the local prison who would cut off the earl's head. At last a latrine cleaner, facing the death penalty himself, was found and he agreed to kill the earl in return for his life being spared. The axe came down, the blood spurted on to the ground, and the earl's head was lifted to the traditional shout of 'behold the head of a traitor'. But the crowd was silent. The earl had not been a popular man but he was undoubtedly a victim of Roger's tyranny, ensnared in his misguided search for his brother. Roger had taken advantage of his fraternal honour. His judicial execution amounted to murder.

*

There could be no significant parliamentary business after the earl's death. No one had the stomach for it. Roger had called for a parliament with the intention of impressing everyone with a demonstration of his power, which he had very effectively done. But while the lords were frightened, as he intended, they were also appalled. They were more determined than ever to remove him from power. But as long as the king kept silent, as long as he tolerated Roger, they could do nothing.

For the forty men whose names were on the list which Roger issued the day before the execution, the king's position was an irrelevance. They were preoccupied with trying to save their own lives. Most fled the country as quickly as they could, before Roger closed the ports. Those who managed to escape joined Roger's other enemies on the Continent. Many others did not wait for the next list, which was issued at the end of the month, or for the list after that. Thomas Wake, for example, fled long before his arrest warrant was issued. Like most sane men, he realised that Roger was now acting without any limit on his power, and without any regard to the destruction he was causing. Throughout the country commissioners were appointed to arrest political opponents and agitators. Despenser's brutal tyranny had been reborn.

The increased violence and fear following Kent's arrest and death were accompanied by Roger's increased demands for money. At Winchester Roger had asked Parliament to grant a tax to be levied on both the clergy and the ordinary folk of the country, to pay for the defence of Gascony. Not surprisingly, after the execution of Kent, he received assent. Having heard of the unrest in London and the boldness of the Londoners, he berated their representatives and demanded a special tax be levied on the city. At the same time the Pope was prevailed upon to allow an ecclesiastical grant. Huge amounts of cash were needed to prepare to defend England from the risk of invasion by the exiles. There was stiff resistance from the Church, especially when it emerged that the money granted at an earlier date for a Scottish campaign had been spent on other things. But refusal was not an option: Roger and Isabella had already spent the £20,000 that the Scots had paid for the recognition of sovereignty; and the reserve of £60,000 which Edward had left in his treasury at the time of the revolution had also long since gone.

In addition to this urgent drive for public cash, Roger now sought personal grants on an unprecedented scale. On 20 April he ordered that he be pardoned all his own and all his ancestors' debts at the Exchequer.[39] Two days later he arranged that a certain John Galeys, in return for his service to Roger, should be allowed to keep a manor which he held from Queen Philippa, even after her death.[40] The royal purse was now publicly rewarding men for service to Roger. On his forty-third birthday, he celebrated with a whole string of grants. To himself he gave the lordship of the manor of Droitwich and custody of the castle of Athlone in Ireland. To himself and Joan he granted palatinate rights in Meath. To his son Sir

Geoffrey, who had obviously been forgiven for his earlier outburst, he granted the lordship of Donnington Castle, as well as other lands forfeited by the Earl of Kent in Leicestershire, Gloucestershire, Surrey, Lincolnshire, Derbyshire, Nottinghamshire, Rutland and Wiltshire.[41] In May he granted himself an extra 500 marks (£333) annually, in addition to his usual salary, for governing Wales. In June he granted himself an extra 500 marks in return for his continued attendance on the king as well as the lordship of the manor of Westhall and the town of Folebrook. At the same time his son Geoffrey received the manor of Miserden, another of the Earl of Kent's properties. A few days later he extended his control of the Pembroke wardship which he still held. The list goes on and on . . . In August he received Clifford Castle, the manor of Glasbury, the custody of the manor of Gormanstown, and a grant of all the goods and chattels of the Earls of Arundel and Hugh Despenser in the Marches of Wales which had escheated to the king. This last grant especially was an example of Roger interpreting his earldom of March in the widest possible sense, claiming authority over a vast area, and appropriating the huge wealth of the Despensers, which had supposedly been surrendered to the government, rather than to him personally.

No one was safe from Roger's rapacity, not even his relations. His judicial murder of his cousin's husband (the Earl of Kent) and the imprisonment of his thirty-eight-weeks-pregnant cousin (the Countess of Kent) have already been mentioned. Similarly he claimed that John Mortimer, grandson and heir of Lord Mortimer of Chirk, was illegitimate, and therefore could not inherit the Chirk lordship. Roger took it for himself, and thereby disinherited another cousin. Thomas Wake was another cousin whom he disinherited. He let nothing, not even kinship, stand in his way.

There were those who benefited from Roger's tyranny. The lands of the Earl of Kent did not just go to Sir Geoffrey; they were distributed among men such as Hugh de Turpington, John Maltravers, John Wyard, Thomas de Berkeley, Sir Simon Bereford, Edward de Bohun, Sir Bartholomew de Burghersh, the Earl of Surrey and Oliver Ingham. Many of them had to promise to perform military service in return, ostensibly to the king but in reality to Roger. Orders were issued for the protection of Roger's favoured merchants. Others benefited from grants made at his request as before, and more of his supporters were appointed to key positions. Maltravers was made Steward of the Royal Household again, and was followed in that office by Sir Hugh de Turpington. But whereas once Roger would have made such appointments out of patronage, now he was acting in self-defence.

Edward had tolerated Roger for nearly five years now, during which time their relationship had been borne with great frustration on the king's part. The two men had not been enemies the whole time: like Roger, Edward enjoyed jousting and hawking, and was enthusiastic about the whole chivalric world. Nevertheless by 1330 the companionship had worn very thin, and Edward had built up a catalogue of grudges against Roger, such as the Scottish fiasco and the secret custody of his father. With the execution of Kent in March, Edward and Roger became outright enemies. Edward could see that Roger's domination of the government had to be brought to an end, but he could not find a way to act. Roger had too much power over him. Someone else would have to act on his behalf. But Roger had so many spies about the court. Sir William de Montagu was one of the few men whom the king could trust. Accordingly, in the summer of 1330, Montagu began tactfully and cautiously to prepare a band of supporters who would help the king throw off the yoke of Roger and Isabella.

Taking action against Roger was, however, exceedingly dangerous. In early June Richard FitzAlan, the disinherited Earl of Arundel, plotted to end Roger's rule through a rising of men in Shropshire and Staffordshire. He was found out and swiftly arrested.[42] A larger and more elaborate plot was hatched by the band of exiles from the English court on the Continent. They were now of sufficient strength and financial leverage to attempt an invasion, following Roger's own example. A contingent in Wales was prepared to strike at Roger's estates there, and the exiles themselves and their forces planned to attack the English coast, forcing a war on two fronts. But Roger was alert to their plans. In July all the counties and towns were forced to array troops for the defence of the realm, and Roger and his son Edmund themselves inspected many of the men. The Londoners were required to swear loyalty to Edward. With England on the alert, Wales being purged of would-be rebels under Roger's justiciarship, and the court taking up a defensive position at Gloucester, within striking distance of Roger's estates, the invasion plans of the exiles were brought to a halt.[43]

Roger's unpopularity was now widespread. Several contemporary chroniclers refer to his pride, and reflect suspicions that he was about to seize the crown for himself. The *Anonimalle Chronicle* states that Roger 'usurped royal power and great treasure and had thought to overthrow the king'.[44] The *French Chronicle of London* says that the huge host of Welsh and English men-at-arms following Roger wrought great destruction wherever they went, so that there was not a woman, wife or girl who had not been 'played with' in all the country through which they passed.[45] Although both canons of St Paul's writing in the 1320s and 1330s were distant and objective about the Earl of March, they said nothing in his defence. The author of the longer *Brut* particularly disliked Roger, stating that he was 'so proud and high that he held no lord of the realm his equal'. The chronicler also claimed that he was covetous, and let his servants eat at the same table as the king's servants, and he allowed himself to eat from the same plate as the king, and to share carriages with him.[46]

The court moved north from Gloucester in July. Roger knew there were plots against him everywhere, and he sought to root out all conspirators. But the principal coordinators of the movement now forming against him were very careful men. By the time the court reached Northampton at the end of July, Montagu had sounded out and recruited several reliable supporters. He was able to tell Edward that he had a body of men who were prepared to act. It seems, however, that the king was still very cautious about removing Roger, and one chronicle states that Montagu had to persuade Edward to agree to action, saying to him that it was 'better to eat the dog than be eaten by the dog'.[47] Edward assented, acknowledged his friend was right, but urged that they bide their time.

Roger's spies were hard at work. By the time the court arrived at Nottingham Castle, perched on a rock above the town, Roger knew that there was a new plot afoot. Some men were suggesting that he be prosecuted for the murder of the king's father, and that a legal means be found to remove him. John Wyard and his fellow spies reported back to Roger that some of the king's friends were holding secret meetings and discussing action against him. All September Roger worked at establishing who was doing what and which plots were being hatched in the town below. But cocooned by his bodyguard, and cut off on his rock, there was little he could do but wait for his spies to bring him news. Little official business was transacted. When Henry of Lancaster arrived in preparation for the parliament that was to be held in mid-October, and sought accommodation in the castle as befitting his rank, Roger angrily demanded to know who had let so dangerous an enemy of Queen Isabella be housed so close to her? To the fury of the earl, who had lost his sight since his rebellion against Roger, he was moved out of the castle and down into the town. Roger told Isabella to take the keys of the castle into her own keeping, and ordered the guards to obey his orders before those of the king. Like Edward, Roger trusted no one but his own close friends.

By 15 October, when Parliament was due to meet, Roger and the court had been in the town for six weeks, and the tension had not abated. Was the forthcoming assembly going to be a show trial like the last? Was the Earl of Lancaster to be the victim this time? Or were Roger's spies pointing to someone else? Everyone understood that the next few days would be crucial. The king and his close friends had to move fast.

Roger himself precipitated the final confrontation. From his spies he knew that some of the king's friends, including William de Montagu, were accusing him of the murder of the king's father in Berkeley Castle. Roger, 'as a devil for wrath', summoned each of them to him.[48] One by one he interrogated them: Montagu, Edward de Bohun (whom Roger had recently rewarded for his support), Ralph Stafford, Robert Ufford, William Clinton and John Neville.[49] All remained silent, except Montagu, who denied strenuously that there was any plot afoot. Without further evidence, Roger let them go, to have them watched and to lure them into providing him with the proof he needed. But this time the men he was dealing with were the cream of the young generation of knights at court. They were quick-witted and active, and had been bred on Roger's own prescribed diet of loyalty and courage. Most importantly, they were men whom Roger wanted to believe would not betray him, as they were sons of his old comrades in arms. But while Roger might have given them the benefit of the doubt on this occasion, they for their part could not risk being interrogated a second time.

On or just before the third day of the parliament Montagu was approached by a local man, William Eland. He had grown up at the castle, he told Montagu, and he knew all the passages through the rock on which the castle was built. One particular secret tunnel led out of the castle and into the park. Despite Isabella having taken the keys, and despite Roger doubling the guards on the castle gates, and ordering that his commands alone were to be obeyed, it was still possible to get inside the fortress, and even to get into the royal apartments, through these subterranean passages. There was a door, bolted, at the top of the tunnel, but Edward himself could undo the bolt and allow his men in. Montagu was struck by the tremendous opportunity this presented, and sent a message to Edward immediately. No one was to try to enter the castle, he said, without first consulting him.[50]

On the evening of 19 October, after the gates to the castle had been secured, Edward asked to leave the hall, claiming he was unwell. His physician, Pancio de Controne, agreed that he should go to his chamber, and went with him.[51] He and his physician pretended he was ill until Roger and Isabella and their supporters had withdrawn from the hall and retired to Isabella's chamber to discuss what was to be done about the conspirators who now faced them. Sir Hugh de Turpington was with them. So too were Sir Simon Bereford, Oliver Ingham and Bishop Burghersh. Squires and household officers were about in the candlelit corridor leading to the royal chambers. But the guards were outside, in the bailey, on the walls and at the gates. The castle was on high alert, but not in a state of alarm.

Meanwhile, in the park below the castle, in the pitch dark, two dozen men gathered, led by Sir William de Montagu. They had publicly left Nottingham that afternoon, pretending they were fleeing Roger's investigation; but they had come back in the moonless dark. They were waiting for more men to join them. As they waited, tense, in the cold, they decided their fellows had got lost. It would be just the few of them who would attack. Montagu gave the order to William Eland, and they moved in the direction of the castle.

Eland led them to the foot of the crag on which the castle was built, and felt his way through the tunnel within. The men moved with caution, and as silently as they could. Up above in the castle itself, Isabella's old clerk, Robert Wyvill, who had also been recruited by Montagu, came to the king to tell him that Roger and Isabella and their council were in her chamber. Perhaps he also said that the signal at the door to the secret tunnel had been given. Edward stopped feigning illness, got off his bed, and slipped out into the corridor. He pulled back the drawbar on the door to the tunnel and admitted the armed and determined figure of John Neville, mace in hand, followed by William Eland, Montagu and the others.

Suddenly Sir Hugh de Turpington came around the corner and saw them. 'Traitors!' he yelled, drawing his sword, and despite the numbers facing him he charged them, shouting, to warn Roger, 'It is for nought that you enter this castle! All of you shall die an evil death here!' And with that he hurled himself at the foremost of them, household squires following his voice, terrified in the candlelight. In Isabella's chamber, Roger hastily drew his sword and hastened out into the corridor. But, before he could do anything, Sir Hugh de Turpington, his lifelong comrade, was struck on the head by Neville's mace, collapsing under the blow. Richard de Monmouth, the squire who had escaped with Roger from the Tower and who had faithfully served him for the last seven years, was the next to go down defending his lord. There was no hope of holding back the assailants. As Robert de Walkefare struck down an usher, Richard de Crombek, the leading knights pushed past and fell on Roger. Isabella, realising her son had betrayed them, knew that all was lost. 'Fair son,' she screamed out into the dark corridor, 'have pity on the gentle Mortimer! Do not harm him, he is a worthy knight. Our beloved friend, our dear cousin.'[52]

Roger was overpowered, bound and gagged. Behind him, Isabella was forced back into her chamber and placed under guard. Montagu, or one of his men, made a quick search of the chamber and found Bishop Burghersh trying to climb down the latrine chute. He was told that he was in no danger. Bereford and Ingham, however, were placed under arrest, also bound and gagged, and led down through the passage out of the castle with Roger. Meanwhile a few men had gone to the chamber of Sir Geoffrey Mortimer. They entered and told him his father had been arrested, and that he too was under arrest. He followed them quietly.

In the course of a single night, Roger and several of his key advisers had been apprehended and silenced. Isabella had been isolated, and placed under guard in her chamber. After all the failed, carefully prepared large-scale plots, twenty-four knights had managed to surprise Roger and arrest him in a hastily contrived attack. The difference had been the king's support. Edward now saw a clear path towards power. He would claim that his father had indeed been murdered in Berkeley Castle, and that Roger had perpetrated the deed. If his father dared to present himself in public, Edward would face the problem squarely, not as a dependant of Roger Mortimer but as a rightful king, who had assumed the throne in good faith and who had the support of his knights and the trust of the realm.

Edward had at last inherited his royal power.

*

Roger was removed from Nottingham that same night and taken by the king to Leicester. There Edward wanted him to be hanged immediately, but the Earl of Lancaster persuaded him that Roger should be judged in Parliament. Writs were hastily despatched requiring that the lords gather in London. Accordingly Roger was sent to the Tower, where six king's men-at-arms were ordered to watch him.[53]

Parliament heard the charges against Roger at Westminster on Monday 26 November 1330.[54] There was never any doubt about the outcome. This was the show trial of the show trial king, the condemnation of the chief prosecutor of the reign, and the execution of a dictator. The only real question was how he would die: like Despenser on a high gallows, or more mercifully, by an axe, like the Earl of Kent.

Roger was led, bound and gagged, into the same hall in which he had feasted after he had been knighted, which he had known since his youth.[55] Unable to speak, he was accused of fourteen crimes:

1. Ignoring the royal council of regency and taking royal power and full government himself, appointing and sacking ministers in the king's household, and sending John Wyard to spy on the king;
2. Removing Edward II illegally from Kenilworth Castle and having him murdered at Berkeley;

3. Using his royal power to grant himself the title of Earl of March, and to force the king to march against the Earl of Lancaster;

4. Using his royal power to keep the Earl of Lancaster and other advisers away from the king, and banishing others from the realm contrary to Magna Carta;

5. Luring the Earl of Kent into a treasonable plot and procuring his death;

6. Using his royal power to grant himself, his children and his supporters castles, towns, manors, and franchises in England, Ireland and Wales;

7. Raising money for a Gascon war through a Parliamentary grant which he had then spent himself;

8. Using his royal power to take the fines and ransoms paid by individual knights who did not want to serve personally in his fictitious Gascon war;

9. Falsely and maliciously putting discord between Edward II and Isabella, and 'for saying to her that if she had gone to him (Edward) he would have killed her with a knife or murdered her in some other way';

10. Using his royal power to enrich himself and his supporters with money and jewels from the royal treasury;

11. Using his royal power to appropriate to himself the twenty thousand marks paid by the Scots for their sovereignty;

12. Gathering many knights and men-at-arms at court, so the king was surrounded by enemies;

13. Using his royal power to grant two hundred pardons to men of Ireland who had killed great men loyal to the Crown; and

14. Acting to destroy the king's supporters and his closest advisers, and ordering at Nottingham that his word should be obeyed rather than that of the king.[56]

Roger was then told he had been found guilty of these crimes 'and many others which are not listed here' by the earls, barons and peers. These accusations were 'notorious and known for their truth to you and all the realm'. Having been adjudged guilty he was sentenced 'as a traitor and enemy of the king and of the realm, to be drawn and hanged'.

Three days later Roger was taken from his cell in the Tower. He was dressed in the same black tunic he had worn at the funeral of Edward II. He was placed on an ox-hide, tied to two horses, and dragged all the way along the uneven roads between the Tower and Tyburn, a distance of nearly two miles. The cuts and grazes must have been numerous; the bone-breaking bumps, ditches and stones in the road must have made him feel that, by the time he heard the crowds at Tyburn, he was half-dead already. But he was still alive, and was able to make a speech to the crowd in which he confessed that the Earl of Kent had been the victim of a conspiracy. What was left of his tunic was then stripped off him, leaving him naked. Psalm 52 was read to him: 'Why do you boast in mischief, O mighty man? The goodness of God endures for ever. The tongue devises mischiefs, like a sharp razor, working deceitfully. You love evil more than good, and lies more than honesty . . .' Then a rope was placed around his neck, and over the beam of the thieves' gallows, and he was lifted off his feet into the air. Within a few minutes he was dead.

The crowds drifted away. His naked body swung there for the rest of the day, through the night, and through the following day and night. On the second day it was cut down, and handed over to some Franciscan friars for burial.

Epilogue

Roger's body was probably first taken to the church of the Greyfriars in London. It is usually said that he was buried there,[1] but it seems that there was an attempt to return him to the Welsh Marches shortly after the hanging, as Roger's widow, Joan, received permission a year after the death to remove his body from the Greyfriars church in Coventry.[2] If he was dug up, he was probably reburied at either the Greyfriars Church in Shrewsbury or at Wigmore Abbey. Both churches were destroyed in the Dissolution.[3]

Joan was implicated in Roger's treason, although she was at Ludlow at the time of his arrest. In 1336 she was pardoned and her possessions were apologetically restored to her, together with her loss of income. She did not remarry. She died in 1356, at the age of seventy, and was probably buried at Wigmore, possibly with her husband. Two years before she died, her grandson managed to reverse the judgement on Roger and inherited the family estates. Edward III declared the original sentence void owing to Roger not being allowed to speak in his own defence. The grandson thus became the second Earl of March, and Joan once more the dowager countess.

Isabella was never accused of adultery with Roger. Nor was she accused of complicity in the Berkeley Castle plot. She was treated very leniently indeed, and given a very respectable income, and, in time, some measure of freedom. She did not go mad and she was not locked up in Castle Rising, as is often claimed. If she had a son by Roger, he did not inherit the earldom of Lincoln or any other title, and nothing more is known of him. She died in 1358 at Hertford Castle, at the age of sixty-two, and was buried in her wedding dress in the Greyfriars church in London, where Roger's body had briefly lain. Beneath her grave was buried the heart of Edward II. The grave was destroyed in the Great Fire, and although the church was rebuilt by Wren, this too was almost completely destroyed in the Second World War. A busy road now runs across the site.

One question outlived Roger: the fate of King Edward II. It suited Edward III perfectly to be able to accuse Roger of his murder; and he later expressed his gratitude to Sir William de Montagu for thinking up this means of turning the Berkeley Castle plot to his advantage. The death of the ex-king in Berkeley Castle has consequently become an established historical fact. However, as this book has already stated, Edward II's fate is a much more complex issue than a murder. It is a question of corruption and power: of knowledge and how that knowledge was used. Thus one must answer the question as to what happened to the ex-king after Berkeley. Did Roger leave a political legacy in the form of a dethroned Edward II?

Just as a man's life story may begin many years before his birth, so it may end many years after he is dead.

Chapter Twelve Revisited

There are two main reasons why we have commonly come to believe that Edward II died in Berkeley Castle. The first is that this was the official pronouncement both at the time and after Roger's arrest, repeated by contemporary chroniclers, sometimes with attractive embellishments which made the event notorious. The second is that until about one hundred years ago medievalists depended almost exclusively on the direct evidence of these sources (official pronouncements and chronicles). Historical methodology tended to be restricted to a literal interpretation of a document, or a comparison of alternative texts. Possible biases, hidden agendas and secret agreements were largely ignored by scholars. The work of amateurs, which sometimes strayed into fictionalisation, confirmed to most intelligent readers that the scholars were right to be dismissive of anything not supported by authoritative records and contemporary chronicles. When huge numbers of official medieval documents began to be calendared and published in the nineteenth and early twentieth centuries, historians reacted by placing an even greater emphasis on the importance of the written record. This drive towards greater documentary authority was a very positive development, but it had a side effect. It created the illusion that the basic chronology of English political history was fixed, and that the modern historian's role was one of refinement: adding detail and providing perspective. Scholars became reluctant to pursue fundamental revisionist lines of inquiry for the very good reason that, on the whole, they were unnecessary and counterproductive. The result is that, among scholars, revisionism has come to be associated with amateurism. With regard to the death of Edward II, scholars today tend to regard the story that he was murdered in Berkeley Castle as the safest historical narrative because it is the best documented and thus professionally the most acceptable. However, as the chronicle of Geoffrey le Baker shows, the most detailed and widely accepted narrative does not necessarily indicate the most reliable series of events. This chapter will show that, far from being the safest assumption, the death of Edward II in Berkeley Castle and his subsequent burial in December 1327 were undoubtedly fictions, initially devised by Roger and later reinforced by Edward III.

The logical starting point for demonstrating this claim is the issue which has most frequently been the stumbling block for those considering the narrative put forward in this book: that is to say how Roger managed to have the corpse of another man buried in Gloucester Abbey in December 1327, and more particularly how he managed to convince those who viewed it that it was the body of Edward II. Academics and laymen alike have made many wayward statements on this subject, from stating that the ex-king's naked corpse was inspected to claiming that the wooden effigy at the funeral was used in place of the king's body. Amazingly, no previous writer has considered the problem in the light of the burial and embalming practices of fourteenth-century English kings. As mentioned in Chapter 12, by the time Maltravers and Berkeley handed the corpse over to Abbot Thoky, it had been eviscerated, covered entirely in cerecloth, sewn into the ex-king's garments, and placed inside one coffin of lead and another of wood. Even if both coffins had been opened in the abbey, the corpse would not have been recognisable as a result of its being entirely covered with cerecloth and obscured from view.[1] Any doubts as to whether the process of embalming obscured the features may be answered by referring to the archaeological report on the body of Edward I, whose face still bore traces of cerecloth when his tomb was opened in 1774.[2] Confirmation that it was necessary to remove the cerecloth in order to recognise an embalmed corpse may be found in the case of Richard II, for whom this was done specifically so he could be recognised when being brought south from Pontefract in 1400.[3] There is no evidence that this removal of cloth happened with Edward II. Indeed, there is evidence to the contrary in the testimony of the only chronicler in the West Country at the time, Murimuth, who stated that those summoned to view the corpse only saw it 'superficially'.[4] Thus, while it is possible that one or both of the coffins were opened at some point, we can be confident that the features would not have been visible and that a false corpse would not have been suspected after its removal from Berkeley Castle on 20 October.

Prior to this date it would have been easy for Maltravers and Berkeley to have had a false corpse embalmed. The watchers attending the corpse did not begin their period of watching until 20 October, almost a month after the supposed death. The key question is whether the face was viewed by anyone other than the conspirators before it was covered in cerecloth. Normally the embalming process would have started very soon after the death, probably within three days and certainly within a week.[5] Since the public announcement of the death of Edward II was not made until 28 September, at Lincoln, and since it would have taken at least three days for any lord or prelate to cover the 110 miles to Berkeley to view the corpse, we can be confident that no independent person could have seen the body within ten days of the date of the supposed death, by which time the face and body of the corpse would have been covered. The possibility that anyone saw the corpse in an uncovered state is diminished even further if one accepts Smyth's statement that Gurney returned with orders to keep the death secret locally until 1 November.[6] The only exception to this was the dubious figure of the royal sergeant-at-arms, William Beaukaire, who arrived at the castle on the day of the supposed death and who stayed with the corpse until burial. Finally, conclusive evidence that the exhibition of the corpse lacked credibility lies in the actions of the Earl of Kent and his fellow conspirators, who were convinced that Edward II was still alive despite their having been at the funeral.

There is a great deal of difference between demonstrating how something could have happened and proving that it did. Indeed, the burial of a false corpse raises a large number of questions. These are, most notably, why did Edward not mention Roger's custody of the king in his charges against him? Why was such a magnificent tomb erected in such a prominent position within the abbey if the body beneath was not genuine? Why did Isabella have the heart of 'Edward II' buried with her if it was false? Why did John of Trevisa, the rector of Berkeley who translated Higden's *Polychronicon* for Lord Berkeley's grandson in 1381, repeat the story about Edward's murder if it was not true, to the great discredit of his family? And, most of all, why did the men accused of complicity in Edward II's murder flee in 1330 if they had not killed the king?

One may counter these objections in a number of ways. For example: Edward III would not have mentioned the secret custody of his father in the 1330 trials because Edward II was still a potential danger to him. If news that the ex-king was alive had leaked out, Edward III might have come under pressure to restore him; he might even have run the risk of being accused of treason himself, having assumed his father's power despite a poor track record of filial loyalty. One must also remember the danger to the old king; even if Edward III was sure of his throne in November 1330, his father's life would have been jeopardised if it had been widely given out that the man was not dead. No chronicler reported the ex-king's survival because even those that recorded the rumour that he was alive – the authors of the *Annales Paulini* and the longer *Brut* – were convinced that the rumours were false, and they had no evidence to the contrary. Later fourteenth-century writers merely followed their predecessors in declaring that Edward II died in 1327. As for why such a magnificent tomb was erected in such a prominent position if the body beneath was false, there is no reason to doubt that it was erected in good faith, probably by the abbey itself, to whom the glory of being seen to hold a king's corpse guaranteed a stream of visitors, pilgrims, noble benefactors and wealth.[7] Similarly the hearse was an elaborate work of art because it was undoubtedly ordered in good faith by royal officials. Furthermore, the possibility that the tomb did not contain Edward II's body in December 1327 does not mean that it never contained it. Indeed, Edward II's bones – if not his entire body – could have been secretly interred in the grave at a later date.[8] This would explain why so many royal visitors later came to Gloucester on pilgrimage, including Edward III himself in March 1343.[9] A similar explanation may be extended to the burial of the king's heart. Isabella did not die until 1358, when Edward II would have been seventy-four, an age to which no medieval king lived. Thus he almost certainly predeceased her. It is therefore possible that the heart buried beneath Isabella in 1358 was not the organ that she had been given as her husband's by Lord Berkeley in 1327 but one she had received more recently.[10] As for why Trevisa stated, in his English *Polychronicon*, that Edward was killed in Berkeley Castle, one would hardly have expected a scholar of Trevisa's standing to alter a widespread work so fundamentally, especially as it had been universally accepted that Edward II had been murdered there, and Trevisa himself had probably never heard a different story. Thus it can be seen that none of these objections is incontrovertible. On the other hand, none of these counter-arguments is anything more than conjectural.

Only one objection and counter-argument provide a way to take the analysis forward: the flight of the men involved in the alleged murder, namely Bereford, Berkeley, Maltravers, de Ockley and Gurney. Their individual cases must be examined.

Simon Bereford was the only man apart from Roger executed as a result of the palace revolution of October 1330. He was hanged the following month because he had helped Roger 'in all his treasons, felonies and plots', including the Berkeley Castle plot. His precise role is unknown, although it may be noted that a later piece of evidence to be discussed at the end of this chapter offers an explanation.

John Maltravers fled the country on hearing of Roger's arrest, escaping from Mousehole, in Cornwall, in a fishing boat. A writ for his arrest was issued to the sheriffs of the counties on 3 December 1330, more than six weeks after Roger's fall. In his absence he was tried in Parliament and sentenced to be drawn, hanged and beheaded.[11] A reward was offered for him, 1,000 marks alive or £500 for his head. The crime for which he was sentenced, however, was not connected with the death of the ex-king but that of the Earl of Kent. Thus it can be shown on paper that, although he fled, this was not because of complicity in the murder of Edward II.

However, this is a superficial reading of the evidence. Maltravers was an official keeper of the king with Berkeley, charged with protecting the king's safety, and so implicated in the same charges as brought against Berkeley. This was stated explicitly by both Berkeley and the prosecution in the course of Berkeley's trial. After the acceptance of Lord Berkeley's second statement, that he was away from his castle at the time of the murder, Maltravers was even more strongly implicated. But he was not accused. In March 1334 he wrote from Flanders to Edward III saying he had certain information about the 'honour, estate and well-being of the realm'.[12] It was no slight underling but Edward's closest companion, Sir William de Montagu, who was sent to receive the information. By 1339 Maltravers was being employed by Edward III on official business in Flanders, and in 1345 he made a formal submission there to Edward, having served in Ireland the previous year.[13] He received a guarantee of safe passage at that time to return to face trial for the charge of procuring the death of Kent, but he did not immediately take it up. He continued to be employed by Edward, and was restored to all his estates after he returned to England to face the judgement of Parliament in 1352 for Kent's death, at which time he was acquitted.[14] Thus, although he was involved along with Lord Berkeley in the supposed murder of Edward II, he was never charged with involvement in the killing, even when in custody in 1352.

Thomas de Berkeley did not flee. He faced trial in Parliament on the same day as Roger, 26 November. When asked how he wished to acquit himself of responsibility for the death of the king, he answered that he had never consented to it, helped with it, or procured it, and 'nor had he ever heard of his death until this present parliament. And in this way he wished to acquit himself, just as the king's court would consider it.'[15]

Berkeley was claiming that he was not guilty of the murder because, as far as he knew, Edward II was still alive. Unfortunately for Berkeley, he was refused permission to put his case to a jury. Allowing him to plead that Edward II was still alive was the last thing the king or his close advisers wanted, as it was in their interests to maintain that Edward II was dead. Forced to play along with the prosecutor, Berkeley said that at the time of the king's murder he was away from the castle at his manor of Bradley. This was in fact a lie, as he was not at Bradley until a week after the supposed death.[16] He further claimed he could not recall anything from the time as he had been so ill. This again was not true, as he had been well enough to send Thomas Gurney to Nottingham on the day after the supposed murder with letters about the king's death.[17] He was then asked how he excused himself for appointing the men who had killed the king. He could not deny that the appointment of the guards had been his responsibility without shifting the blame on to his father-in-law, Roger, which he was not prepared to do. Thus he was acquitted of the murder himself but charged further with the appointment of William de Ockley and Thomas Gurney to look after Edward II.[18] This charge technically hung over him until 1337, when he was absolved of all responsibility for the supposed death.[19] In fact Edward III never punished him, allowing him to retain the shrievalty of Gloucestershire after Roger's arrest and ordering a large debt owed to him by Edward II to be paid a few months later.[20]

William de Ockley did flee the country, and was in his absence found guilty with Gurney, the other messenger in the plot, of murdering Edward II. Gurney himself did not initially flee but was protected by Lord Berkeley until the trial. After Berkeley's line of defence had been refused, and Gurney had been sentenced to death in his absence, Gurney was given money by Berkeley in order to escape.[21] A reward of £100 was offered for him alive and 100 marks for his head. From England he fled to Spain, where he was captured at Burgos in 1331. Having escaped, he remained at large until William de Tweng caught him in Naples in 1333, but he died at Bayonne in de Tweng's custody on the return journey, despite the efforts of two physicians to save him.[22] De Ockley carried a lower price of 100 marks alive or £40 for his head. After fleeing, he was never heard of again.

This comparison of the later careers of the protagonists shows that there was no band of men who collectively knew and felt their guilt and fled into the night. Of the five men accused in Parliament, two were arrested, one fled, and two remained in England until the trial, the less important man fleeing after his protector's plea on their joint behalf had been disallowed and he (Gurney) had been sentenced to death. Berkeley did not flee, confident he could refute the allegations against him. There were other people involved in the supposed murder – presumably Berkeley's household men-at-arms – who did not flee. In 1332, one of Edward's agents found William de Kingsclere at Rochester and Richard de Well near Northampton, both of whom he stated were connected with the Berkeley Castle plot.[23] Apart from Roger and Bereford, Gurney was the only man to suffer in any way for the murder, and his death was not the result of judgement. Some men who were involved, like William Beaukaire and William de Shalford, were never accused or arrested. De Shalford in fact was rewarded for long loyal service in 1337 at the request of Richard of Arundel and William de Montagu.[24]

Much of the evidence given in the foregoing passages is either circumstantial or tangential to the supposed death of Edward II. Some, however, is not. Careful sifting of the facts reveals three details in particular which together demonstrate that he did not die in Berkeley Castle. Firstly, there is a hitherto unnoticed inconsistency in the official records which undermines the government pronouncement that he was killed. The records of the trials in the *Parliamentary Rolls* show that Maltravers and Berkeley were acknowledged to have been jointly and equally liable for the safe keeping of the ex-king. As has already been mentioned, Maltravers was not charged with murder or with failing in his responsibility to keep the ex-king safely, whereas Berkeley was, on both accounts. As only one of the two men equally liable was charged, either the charges which ought to have been brought against both of them lacked substance or the king was protecting one man, Maltravers. That Edward III was not protecting him is clear in the full traitor's death sentence passed on him for the lesser crime of being an accessory in the plot against Kent.[25] It follows that the charges of murder and of failing to prevent Edward II's death, brought successively against Berkeley, were groundless.

The above argument is important in itself but its greater historical significance is that it independently corroborates Berkeley's initial trial statement that Edward II was still alive, as far as he knew, in November 1330. Furthermore, it supports an implication of that statement which explains the method of deception. Berkeley himself had led the funeral cortege into Gloucester, and so his claim that he had not heard of the death 'until this present parliament' implies a confession that his announcement of Edward II's death to Edward III in September 1327 was a lie. The announcement of the death to Parliament, the arrangements for the funeral, and the subsequent spread of the news throughout the country were all consequences of this flow of misinformation from Berkeley.

To sum up: the chronicles which state that Edward II died in Berkeley Castle were based, either directly or via subsequent rumour, on the official announcement of the death which was made for the first time in Parliament on 28 September. This statement and its successors were based on information supplied by Lord Berkeley during the week following 21 September, first received by the king on the 23rd. This information was, by Berkeley's own admission in 1330, false. That Edward III knew this in 1330 is made clear by his bringing groundless charges against Berkeley, his acceptance of a demonstrably false alibi which preserved the fiction that Edward II was dead, and his inability in 1330 to charge Maltravers with the 'murder' of Edward II, or even to charge him with failing in his legal responsibility to look after the ex-king. The correlation of these perspectives shows that the principal defendant and the prosecution were essentially in agreement in November 1330: Edward II was, as far as was known to both of them, still alive. This undermines all previous government announcements that the ex-king was dead, and demonstrates that all subsequent official statements that he had been killed in Berkeley Castle were unfounded. It does not prove that Edward II was actually alive at this time, merely that he was not believed to be dead, and known not to have died in Berkeley's custody.[26]

*

The above passages do not include all the evidence relating to the survival of Edward II, only the key facts relating to the period between 21 September 1327 and the end of November 1330. As some later evidence explains and enlarges upon the findings laid out above, and as the later life of the ex-king was a direct consequence of Roger's connivance, the rest of this chapter will contain the evidence pertinent to Edward II after Roger's execution.

In the late nineteenth century, Alexandre Germain, a French archivist working on an official register of the medieval Bishopric of Maguelonne in the Archives départementales d'Hérault at Montpellier, found an official copy of a letter from Manuele de Fieschi, a papal notary and later Bishop of Vercelli who died in 1348, addressed to Edward III of England. This is a full translation:

> In the name of the Lord, Amen. Those things that I have heard from the confession of your father I have written with my own hand and afterwards I have taken care to be made known to your highness. First he says that feeling England in subversion against him, afterwards on the admonition of your mother, he withdrew from his family in the castle of the Earl Marshal by the sea, which is called Chepstow. Afterwards, driven by fear, he took a barque with lords Hugh Despenser and the Earl of Arundel and several others and made his way by sea to Glamorgan, and there he was captured, together with the said Lord Hugh and Master Robert Baldock; and they were captured by Lord Henry of Lancaster, and they led him to the castle of Kenilworth, and others were [held] elsewhere at various places; and there he lost the crown at the insistence of many. Afterwards you were subsequently crowned on the feast of Candlemas next following. Finally they sent him to the castle of Berkeley. Afterwards the servant who was keeping him, after some little time, said to your father: Lord, Lord Thomas Gurney and Lord Simon Bereford, knights, have come with the purpose of killing you. If it pleases, I shall give you my clothes, that you may better be able to escape. Then with the said clothes, at twilight, he went out of the prison; and when he had reached the last door without resistance, because he was not recognised,

he found the porter sleeping, whom he quickly killed; and having got the keys of the door, he opened the door and went out, with his keeper who was keeping him. The said knights who had come to kill him, seeing that he had thus fled, fearing the indignation of the queen, even the danger to their persons, thought to put that aforesaid porter, his heart having been extracted, in a box, and maliciously presented to the queen the heart and body of the aforesaid porter as the body of your father, and as the body of the said king the said porter was buried in Gloucester. And after he had gone out of the prisons of the aforesaid castle, he was received in the castle of Corfe with his companion who was keeping him in the prisons by Lord Thomas, castellan of the said castle, the lord being ignorant, Lord John Maltravers, lord of the said Thomas, in which castle he was secretly for a year and a half. Afterwards, having heard that the Earl of Kent, because he said he was alive, had been beheaded, he took a ship with his said keeper and with the consent and counsel of the said Thomas, who had received him, crossed into Ireland, where he was for nine months. Afterwards, fearing lest he be recognised there, having taken the habit of a hermit, he came back to England and proceeded to the port of Sandwich, and in the same habit crossed the sea to Sluys. Afterwards he turned his steps in Normandy and from Normandy, as many do, going across through Languedoc, came to Avignon, where, having given a florin to the servant of the pope, sent by the said servant a document to Pope John, which pope had him called to him, and held him secretly and honourably more than fifteen days. Finally, after various discussions, all things having been considered, permission having been received, he went to Paris, and from Paris to Brabant, from Brabant to Cologne so that out of devotion he might see The Three Kings, and leaving Cologne he crossed over Germany, that is to say, he headed for Milan in Lombardy, and from Milan he entered a certain hermitage of the castle of Melazzo, in which hermitage he stayed for two years and a half; and because war overran the said castle, he changed himself to the castle of Cecima in another hermitage of the diocese of Pavia in Lombardy, and he was in this last hermitage for two years or thereabouts, always the recluse, doing penance and praying God for you and other sinners. In testimony of which I have caused my seal to be affixed for the consideration of Your Highness. Your Manuele de Fieschi, notary of the lord pope, your devoted servant.[27]

Historians have puzzled over this letter ever since it surfaced, privately published by Germain, in Montpellier in 1878. A few years after it appeared, the great constitutional historian, Bishop Stubbs, included it in his edition of the *Chronicles illustrative of the reigns of Edward I and Edward II*. His opinion was that it 'must have been the work of some one sufficiently well-acquainted with the circumstances of the king's imprisonment to draw up the details without giving an opening for ready refutation'. He admitted that the letter tallied with the facts as they were then understood, but could not believe its story to be true, and attempted to dismiss it on grounds of improbability. This was an admission of defeat, as he himself stated. He made a few suggestions as to why it might have been created, then carefully showed how each suggestion was implausible, and gave up, saying 'There the fact remains, at present inexplicable.'

The next great British historian to consider the document also drew a blank. Thomas Frederick Tout's lines on the subject in his article on the captivity of Edward II, published in 1919, are full of scholarly despair: 'It is a remarkable document, so specious and detailed, and bearing none of those marks by which a gross medieval forgery can generally be detected. Yet who can believe it true? Who shall decide how it arose? Was it simply a fairy tale? Was it the real confession of a madman? Was it a cunning effort of some French enemies to discredit the conqueror of Calais?'[28]

Since then advances have been made, but no one has been able to assess the matter objectively with any illuminating results. Scholars have fallen back on the Stubbs/Tout confusion, unable to comprehend how an escape could have taken place against the backdrop of the chroniclers' evidence. A couple of writers have taken a contrary view, and have so blithely accepted the letter at face value that they have committed equally great sins of misinterpretation. Most guilty of the latter is Anna Benedetti, an Italian professor of English, who in 1924 identified the Lombardy castles at which Edward was supposed to have stayed as the castles of Melazzo d'Acqui and Cecima sopra Voghera, and the hermitage in which he died as the Abbazia di Sant'Alberto di Butrio, this being situated near the latter of the two castles.[29] The fundamental weakness in her working was that she identified a carved capital as relating to Roger, Isabella and Edward, although this capital was made more than a hundred years earlier. To bolster her theory she highlighted a legend at Sant'Alberto that an English king had taken refuge there. A modern plaque in the monastery states that there was 'The first tomb of Edward II, king of England' and that 'his bones were taken by Edward III and transported to England and reburied in the tomb at Gloucester'.[30] There is no evidence for this latter statement but it is a plausible suggestion in view of Edward III's later pilgrimages to Gloucester. G.P. Cuttino has pointed out that it is practically impossible now to determine whether the legend existed before the publication of the Fieschi letter.[31] Natalie Fryde, in her book *The*

Tyranny and Fall of Edward II, suggested that it would be wrong to dismiss the Fieschi letter, although she did not go further into details about the evidence and left the matter unresolved. Only two scholars in the last thirty years have commented in academic journals on the Fieschi letter: G.P. Cuttino and R.M. Haines.

Cuttino's article, 'Where Is Edward II?', appeared in 1978. He summarised the debate to date, and brought together a number of sources not previously collated. He drew attention to the fact that Manuele de Fieschi held several benefices in the Church in England, that he was a distant relative of Edward II, that he held an ecclesiastical position which carried responsibility for the region in which Melazzo and Cecima are situated, that there are weaknesses in the evidence of the chronicles which mention the death, and that some aspects of the funeral arrangements of the late king are open to doubt. His conclusions were that, while it was not possible to prove anything, the implications of Berkeley and Maltravers being forgiven at around the time of the letter 'are obvious': presumably that Edward III forgave them on the strength of the letter. Unfortunately there are huge assumptions and gaps in his arguments, and some of his statements are misleading. He states that the William Bishop who gave evidence to Geoffrey le Baker about the death of Edward II 'has never been traced', although there is little argument that Bishop was a member of Roger's retinue in 1321. On the subject of Bishop and the chronicle of Geoffrey le Baker, Cuttino claims that Bishop gave le Baker his evidence about the king's death but the chronicle clearly states that Bishop was a source only for the king's transportation to Berkeley. Like historians before him, Cuttino also failed to note the inconsistencies in the chronology of the Fieschi evidence (the letter states Edward was at Corfe for only a year and a half, whereas he was probably there for two and a half years, September 1327–March 1330). Finally he declared that Edward could not have received the letter, had it actually been sent, before 16 March 1337 owing to the forgiveness of Berkeley on that date, a peculiar assumption.

The 1996 article by R.M. Haines, 'The Afterlife of Edward of Carnarvon' is a much more valuable addition to the literature on Edward's supposed death. He corrects a number of Cuttino's and other writers' more obvious errors, and points out facts which should have been noticed at the outset, most particularly the inconsistency in the chronology of Edward II's stay at Corfe Castle. He refines the dating of the register's compilation to probably the time of Arnaud de Verdale, an earlier Bishop of Maguelonne, and notes that the last dated document in the register is from 1337, although there are other undated documents within it which may be later. He notes the strange style of the Latin, which is particularly Genoese and informal.[32] He relates the contents of the letter to verifiable facts, checks the Berkeley Castle accounts for the relevant years (which reveal the purchase of locks among other possible precautions), and relates these and other details to connected evidence. Despite all this, he discounts the possibility that Edward was not buried in December 1327 on two accounts: firstly that a public viewing of Edward's corpse 'must have taken place at Berkeley prior to embalming' – although he provides no evidence that it did – and secondly that Isabella herself did not doubt the body was Edward's, otherwise she would not have had Edward's heart buried with her in 1358: again, an unwarranted assumption.[33] He suggests the Fieschi letter was a religious forgery, put forward to claim Edward as a martyr, but produces no evidence to support this allegation; nor does he explain how the forgery could have benefited the forger. His discussion on the writing of the document suffers from his assumption that Fieschi would have expected a clerk to have had to translate his Latin for Edward III, whereas the king could read both Latin and French, as shown by his letter to the Pope, and could at least write individual letters.[34] The article also suffers from chronological errors of Haines's own making, most notably that the document could have been written as early as 1333, despite the fact that it clearly describes a four and a half year sojourn in Italy after a journey of more than two thousand miles around Europe, begun no earlier than January 1331.[35]

Perhaps because of the traditional conviction that Edward II died in Berkeley Castle, no historian has examined what the Fieschi letter actually is. It is not a confession but a report from Fieschi supposedly gleaned from information obtained through the 'confession' of the deposed king – that is to say in his own words – not necessarily through a holy confession, although the information may have been gathered in this way. Also none of the historians who have so far discussed the document have attempted to state why it might have been written, with the exception of Bishop Stubbs, who proved all his suggestions implausible. Thus no historian has pointed out that its message is a political one. During the years when this letter might have been written, 1335–43, England was on the verge of starting a European-wide war, and Genoa, the city of the powerful Fieschi family, was attempting to win independence from Milan, which it achieved in 1339 under Simon Boccanegra, the first Doge of Genoa.

A closer examination of the Fieschi letter shows that it can be divided into several parts. Firstly there is information of a kind which Edward III would have already known, details of the capture of Edward II, included in order to demonstrate the authenticity of the letter at the outset. Then there follows a description of events at Berkeley Castle expressed by the supposed Edward II as an attempt to explain what happened: specifically, whose body was in Gloucester, how he 'escaped', how Isabella came by 'his' heart, and the reactions of the guards. This included information presumed by, or imparted to, the supposed Edward II after his escape, and during his later incarceration at Corfe. It is written from the point of view of one explaining not how he escaped incarceration but how he escaped death, being secretly transferred to Corfe. It is noticeable that Fieschi states Edward's keeper was with him all this time: in other words, he did not 'escape' as claimed but was transferred secretly under the pretence of an escape. The letter then moves on to explain what happened to him after his removal from Corfe. It is written in the past tense entirely, but nowhere does it refer to Edward being dead. Although the translation above has been taken verbatim from that given in Cuttino's article, it should be pointed out that the last passage of evidence – 'he was in this last hermitage for two years or thereabouts' – could also be read as 'he has been in this last hermitage for two years or thereabouts'. The implication that Edward was in Lombardy, and that his identity could be verified, gives the letter a potent political force, and indicates it was written not just for Edward II's benefit but primarily to further Genoese interests.

Given the political implications of a letter such as this coming from Genoa in the 1330s or early 1340s, and the motive for forging such a document, a systematic analysis of its reliability is necessary. Here it is significant that the surviving text is in a bishop's register, and thus is a copy. Moreover it is probably a copy of a copy, if the original manuscript was sent to Edward. There are five possibilities:

i.   that there was no original letter, and the copy in the register is a forgery;

ii. that the original was not by Fieschi, and that it was made in bad faith, and his seal applied with or without his knowledge, and thus that the register copy is from a forgery;

iii. that the original was by Fieschi in good faith but upon the evidence of an imposter, and thus that the register copy is not a forgery but contains no information derived from Edward II;

iv. that the original was by Fieschi but was fraudulently compiled for political purposes from received information, and thus that the register copy is not a forgery but contains no information derived from Edward II;

v.   that the original was by Fieschi in good faith based on evidence derived from Edward II directly or indirectly (for example, through a confessor).

The first of these possibilities can be dismissed immediately. According to Haines, the letter is in a singularly different style from any of the other entries in the register, and in an altogether more Italian form.[36] In addition, the register was compiled no earlier than 1337 (the date of the last document) and no later than 1368, probably before 1352.[37] Thus we can be confident that the entry is a contemporary copy of a document that once existed. Access to a bishop's register was very limited indeed, and thus this was a poor place to forge a text. This is why the text was unknown to the rest of the world for so many centuries.

With regard to the second option, that the original was a forgery: forged medieval documents are plentiful, but there are reasons for doubting this is one of them. Fieschi's seal, as a papal notary, would have been very carefully guarded. One could imagine that it might have been temporarily stolen to authenticate the document, but this theory requires an individual or group to have stood to benefit from such a fraudulent document being created. If the document was to be used by a state or political force to effect a policy change, it would have been worthless stealing Fieschi's seal on account of the risk of his denying the document's veracity to his kinsman, Edward III. Thus, if the document was a forgery, it was the work of a small group, or an individual.

The motive of an English lord or knight wishing to clear his name of the murder of Edward II can be dealt with fairly briefly as there were very few candidates. Gurney was dead by the time the letter was written, as on internal evidence it cannot be dated before 1335. De Ockley had successfully disappeared by this stage, but even if alive it is difficult to see how he could have gained access to Fieschi's seal to forge the document. Also it is doubtful whether de Ockley had all the detailed information supplied in the letter. Maltravers, of course, almost certainly had custody of the deposed king at Corfe, but he had relayed his information to Edward in 1334 via Montagu, before this letter could have been written. The only individual who had the status, knowledge, contacts and motive to forge this letter was Lord Berkeley. But since he did not leave England, it is doubtful that he ever met Fieschi, who seems rarely, if ever, to have visited England. It is very unlikely indeed that he knew about Genoese castles and hermitages or the sequence of towns and pilgrim routes on the Continent. Finally one can rule Berkeley out on the grounds that, by his own testimony to Parliament, he knew that Edward II was alive, and thus there was a high risk his information would clash with genuine information given secretly to the king, and incur further displeasure.

To answer the question whether Fieschi could have been fooled by an imposter it is necessary to ascertain the reliability of the evidence in the document. For a start it contains at least two factual errors and one important lacuna. The first factual error, as Haines noted, is that the period of time between Edward II's supposed death and the execution of the Earl of Kent, at which time he supposedly left Corfe, was two and a half years, not one and a half as stated by Fieschi. The second error is that the name of John Deveril does not appear, but instead the name 'Thomas' is given as the name of the castellan. The surprising lacuna is the fact that the abduction of Edward in July 1327 is not noted, a detail which would give the letter real strength, as very few people knew this secret information. The chronological error was probably a simple mistake, as this information would have been relatively easy for even a forger to get right, and it has to be noted that the testimony is not directly that of the supposed Edward II but his confession written at one or two stages removed.[38] With regard to 'Thomas' being the castellan, not John Deveril, one could offer the simple explanation that Deveril did not tell the captive his real name, a fact made more likely by the absence of a surname. The failure to note the abduction in July 1327 is harder to account for, but the most likely explanation is that, if this information was genuinely derived from Edward II, this secret escape might be presumed not to have been known to Edward III, and therefore be valueless or negative evidence of its authenticity. Alternatively the letter might only preserve the bare bones of the king's more complete testimony or confession, a possibility strengthened by the spelling mistakes of the names.

In this context it is remarkable that the letter contains a lot of accurate information. No single extant chronicle written before 1343 (the date that Fieschi became Bishop of Vercelli and thus the last possible date for the letter to have been written) includes all these details. Significantly, no surviving chronicle states that Edward took ship at Chepstow, a fact which has to be verified by recourse to the chamber account now in the possession of the Society of Antiquaries.[39] This also confirms that he landed in Glamorgan, at Cardiff. Every subsequent verifiable fact is correct with the exception of the detail that the castellan at Corfe was not 'Thomas', as mentioned above.[40] There is also the interesting but hitherto unnoticed fact that, if Edward II was moved from Berkeley Castle to Ireland at the time of the arrest of the Earl of Kent, or just before, his period in Ireland (where Roger had very extensive powers and estates) ended just after the November 1330 trials and execution of Roger. It must also be noted that his departure from Ireland at that point is the first time that Fieschi states the deposed king went anywhere without his keeper. The presence of the keeper with the supposed Edward II until December 1330 tallies very well with the probability that he remained in custody, probably under

Maltravers' orders, until Roger's death. Putting these facts together we can safely say that if Fieschi was dealing with an imposter, the imposter would have had to be not only well informed about Lombardy and continental geography but also better informed than any contemporary chronicler about Edward II's movements in South Wales, and in particular familiar with his fateful attempt to sail from Chepstow, at a time when Edward II had only a few dozen men with him. Finally the supposed imposter would have had to make his impersonation in the Genoa region, and also to convince Manuele de Fieschi himself who, as Cuttino noted, was a distant relative of the English royal family. It is far more likely that Fieschi spoke to the real Edward II, who had all this information, rather than to an imposter.

This leaves us with just two options: that the letter was fraudulently compiled by Fieschi on behalf of his countrymen for political purposes from received information, and that it contains no information derived from Edward II himself, or that it is a genuine account of the latter days of the later life of Edward II. On account of the details of Edward's arrest, and in particular the detail about Chepstow, the former can be discounted. Since the continued existence of the king was still such a secret in 1335–43 that no chronicler in England mentioned it, we can discount the theory that Genoa could have used this information against England with any force if it was not predominantly true. If Edward II really was in Italy at the time the letter was written, however, this would make the letter very powerful material for the Genoese.

Working on the theory that the letter is a genuine statement by Fieschi that Edward found his way to Lombardy, we can build a historical model of events. The letter must date from between 1335 and 1343, as noted above. The last dated document in the register is 1337, so it is likely that the document was written at the beginning of this period rather than towards the end. Furthermore, given the systematic accounting for periods of time in the letter (albeit with one mistake noted above), it is probable that only time spent travelling has not been accounted for, and thus the letter was written in the 1335–7 period. Since Fieschi does not express any context for the letter, and in particular does not express any hesitation over the identification of the hermit, it seems the context was to be provided by the bearer of the letter, who thus must have been someone trusted, and of high status.[41] Looking through published calendars of records, the date of 4 July 1336 stands out as the prime candidate for the model. On that day Edward III wrote to the community of Genoa granting it 8,000 marks (£5,333) in compensation for an act of piracy by Hugh Despenser in 1321, although he (Edward) denied any responsibility for the deed.[42] It is quite extraordinary that, after fifteen years, this money was granted, especially as the Genoese had previously sought compensation and been turned down.[43] The possibility that Edward paid up such a large sum in the summer of 1336 partly on the strength of the letter from Manuele de Fieschi is suggested by the fact that the new envoy who made the claim was noted to have brought certain letters with him from Genoa. The new envoy's name was Nicholinus de Fieschi, a kinsman of Manuele.[44]

If we take as the basis of our model the late spring/early summer of 1336 for the receipt of the letter, certain other details fall into place. Lord Berkeley was completely acquitted of all charges against him in the next parliament following the Genoese embassy, on 16 March 1337. Two days later, at the same parliament, William de Shalford was rewarded, despite his part in writing the letter to Roger which was later sent to Berkeley Castle. Maltravers was employed in the king's service in Flanders in 1339, as mentioned above, effectively being exonerated of any crime deserving of outlawry by then. Isabella's income was considerably increased in 1337; from that date she received half as much again as she had previously.[45] One might suggest that the Genoese envoy announced at the English court that his kinsmen had custody of the ex-king in such a way that Edward had no choice but to drop all actions against those he had held responsible for the Berkeley Castle plot. No one else was pardoned for charges against them, with the possible exception of Joan, Roger's widow;[46] but this is what one would have expected as Gurney was dead and de Ockley, if he was still alive, was not sufficiently well-connected to the English court to be let in on the news from Genoa.

A final reason for favouring a date of about 1336 for the receipt of the letter is that Edward III seems to have been aware that his father was under Lombard protection prior to October 1338. Although both Cuttino and Haines noted the source for this, neither scholar realised its significance.[47] In September 1338 Edward went to Germany to be made Vicar of the Holy Roman Empire.[48] At Koblenz, one William le Galeys – William the Welshman – was brought to him from Cologne by an Italian, Francisco Forcet.[49] This William claimed he was Edward II. The records state he had been 'arrested' at Cologne. But the 'arrest' was patently a fiction, as he was brought to the king not by a local arresting officer or an officer of the English court but by an Italian, a Lombard, and he was brought to Koblenz – a distance of fifty-seven miles – at a cost of 25s 6d, and afterwards accompanied the royal party to Antwerp,[50] where he stayed for three weeks in December. This was just after Queen Philippa had given birth to Edward III's second son, Lionel, on 29 November.

This information has been dismissed as evidence for Edward II's itinerary by several historians, but on very flimsy grounds, their scepticism normally rooted in a conviction that Edward II died in Berkeley Castle. Pierre Chaplais, who first discovered the entries, suggested William the Welshman's claim was an early form of 'demonstration during a royal visit'. This is not supportable, due to the preferred treatment of the supposed criminal. Royal imposters were normally punished severely; Edward II had once hanged a half-witted Exeter man who had claimed to be a son of Edward I. Not only was this William the Welshman not locked up locally in Cologne as a petty criminal and an imposter, he was not locked up at all. He was escorted first to the king at Koblenz and then to Antwerp. In the royal accounts which mention him, there are no pejorative references to his royal claim, such as that he 'traitorously' or 'falsely' claimed he was father of the King of England. The bottom line is that if Edward III had believed in 1338 his father had died in Berkeley in 1327, or subsequently, he would not have paid for an imposter to be brought fifty-seven miles to him at Koblenz, and then entertained him, and taken him back to Antwerp. He would have ordered him to be hanged in Cologne.[51]

The point about the Lombard escort, Francisco, or Francekino, Forcet, requires further comment, for it raises the possibility that William the Welshman was escorted to Edward III from Lombardy, the region in which Manuele de Fieschi claimed Edward was living. Indeed, the fact that Edward II was not free but in custody at this period is the key to understanding the Fieschi document. Just as the letter itself was written for political purposes, so Edward II was carefully guarded for political reasons. Once his identity was known in Lombardy, he was protected, but at a cost to his freedom. He did not 'change himself' from Melazzo to Cecima because he was frightened off by the war; far from it, the lord of Melazzo (the Bishop of Acqui) knew Edward's political value, and moved him to the hermitage near Cecima to safeguard Genoan political interests. Thus, for probably the four and a half years prior to Manuele de Fieschi's writing the letter to Edward III, the Lombard higher clergy had had custody of Edward II. Nicholinus de Fieschi himself was a cardinal, and Francisco Forcet was probably one of his or his kinsmen's retainers. When William the Welshman appeared with Francisco Forcet before Edward III at Koblenz in September 1338, Nicholinus de Fieschi was also present. Furthermore Nicholinus de Fieschi returned to Antwerp with the king and William the Welshman (still in the custody of Francisco Forcet) afterwards, staying there until January 1339.[52]

In conclusion: in late 1338 a man who claimed with impunity to be the king's father was brought to the king at Koblenz by a Lombard, and was there in the company of a member of the same political Genoese family which had previously written a letter to Edward III concerning their custody of the ex-king in a Lombardy monastery. Given that we now know Edward II did not die in Berkeley Castle in 1327, and given that the man in question was not summarily dismissed but entertained at Koblenz and at Antwerp, there can be very little doubt that this William the Welshman was Edward II. Although questions must still remain about the accuracy of Manuele de Fieschi's letter, which was written with specific political purposes in mind, and which was at best a copy of the ex-king's verbal testimony recalled several years after his escape, there is no good reason to doubt that Edward II was still alive in 1338, and that the Fieschi letter broadly outlines the facts as Edward II understood them.

*

Finally, after 675 years, we can confront a much more coherent and historically useful narrative of the later life of Edward II. On Roger's orders, Maltravers or Berkeley directed the ex-king's gaoler to effect an artificial 'escape' from Berkeley Castle. The gaoler brought Edward II to Corfe Castle, where he maintained him under the auspices of one 'Thomas', who was probably John Deveril using an assumed name. There, believing he was now on the run, Edward was effectively still a captive. No one tried to free him, as everyone thought him dead. And there Maltravers kept him on Roger's behalf, until Kent learnt of his whereabouts, possibly receiving this information from Edward III. When Roger realised that Kent was on the point of freeing Edward II, he was able to convince the king to order Kent's execution. Edward III did it in order to save his throne, his mother's life, and possibly even his own life.

After the discovery of the Earl of Kent's plot it was too dangerous to keep the deposed king in England, and so Maltravers ordered the ex-king's gaoler to take him to Ireland, where Roger had influence and the young king had few close friends. Edward II himself still believed he was on the run. But Roger could not afford to lose control of his secret prisoner. Edward III was constantly growing in age and authority. Edward II stayed in custody in Ireland for nine months. Then Roger was arrested, Maltravers fled from England, and Edward's gaoler probably decided it was wise to disappear too. Edward II now found himself truly free, but only as long as no one recognised him. If his son knew he was alive, he would be locked up again. Hence he went to the Continent, dressed as a pilgrim, to see the one person who could advise him: the Pope. John XXII convinced him to give up all thoughts of becoming king again, and may have helped him find his spiritual path.

It is just possible that Edward III heard a reliable report about his father, for in the spring of 1331 he and fifteen of his knights dressed as merchants and went 'as if on pilgrimage' in France at the same time as Edward II was probably crossing that country dressed as a pilgrim. The usual explanation for this mission is that Edward III wanted to keep his performance of homage to King Philip quiet; and indeed Edward did perform homage at this time. But it is not beyond possibility that he hoped to find his father as well. If so, he failed. The next he would have known about his father's fate was possibly the information of Gurney; it was for his information, not his head, that Edward wanted him brought back to England alive. After that the next news about his father's fate was the testimony of John Maltravers, in March 1334. Then came the letter from Manuele de Fieschi, probably brought by Nicholinus de Fieschi in 1336. Edward III paid Nicholinus 8,000 marks, and, later, asked him to bring Edward II to meet him in Cologne. Edward III then summoned his father to Koblenz to see him crowned Vicar of the Holy Roman Empire, and took him to Antwerp, albeit in disguise and under guard, to see his grandson there. After this Edward II disappears from the sources. He may have died in 1341, when Nicholinus de Fieschi was paid the sum of one mark per day, being sent by Edward 'to divers parts beyond the sea on certain affairs'.[53] Edward visited his father's tomb on his pilgrimage to Gloucester Abbey two years later.[54]

In subsequent years no one did more to perpetuate the myth of Edward II's death in Berkeley Castle than Ranulph Higden, the monk of Chester who wrote the *Polychronicon*, in which he explicitly repeated the story of the red-hot spit. This chapter cannot end without noting that, in 1352, when Edward III finally forgave John Maltravers for his part in the death of the Earl of Kent, he summoned Higden to an audience at Westminster 'to have certain things explained to him'.[55] The monk was to bring all his histories and parchments with him. We do not know what was said during that audience, but it is not beyond the bounds of possibility that Edward told Higden that the murder was an untruth, and that the encyclopaedic *Polychronicon* was wrong. All we know is that, there and then, Higden's life work came to an abrupt end. He never wrote another word.

As for the tomb in Gloucester, this was opened for a brief moment on 2 October 1855. The wooden coffin was found and a part of it removed. The lead coffin inside was seen but not opened.[56] From the evidence of Nicholinus de Fieschi's continued secret work and Edward III's pilgrimages to Gloucester in 1343 one can be relatively confident that Edward II's remains do indeed lie inside, but that they were placed there not in December 1327 but some time after January 1339, probably in 1341. It is one of the wonders of British history that beneath that spectacular tomb lies the body of a man who was both a king and a penniless hermit, who lost his wife, his kingdom and everything he possessed to his childhood companion, Sir Roger Mortimer.

Everything except his life.

Author's Note: Since completing the text of this book (in January 2002) I have spent a great deal of time considering the Berkeley Castle plot and have uncovered much more information on the ex-king's supposed death and the plot of the Earl of Kent. I have also reconsidered the arguments put forward in this chapter in considerably greater depth, and have conclusively proved that the announcement of Edward II's death was made without any check on the veracity of the information, i.e., before it was possible to know whether it was true or not. I have discussed these matters with a number of academic specialists, including one who alerted me to a hitherto unknown letter from the Archbishop of York attesting to Edward II's survival. The result of all this is an extended essay which was published in the foremost peer-reviewed journal, The English Historical Review, *in November 2005. This strongly reinforces the conclusions of this book: that Edward II was still alive in 1330 and that the Earl of Kent's plot was a genuine one to rescue him. Research into Edward II's whereabouts and the political consequences of his survival after 1330 continues, with a preliminary conclusion that he probably died abroad in late 1341 and was buried in his tomb in Gloucester not long after August 1342.*

Afterword

And seeing there was no place to mount up higher,
Why should I grieve at my declining fall?
Farewell, fair Queen, weep not for Mortimer
That scorns the world, and as a traveller,
Goes to discover countries as yet unknown
Christopher Marlowe, *Edward II* (1594)

At the beginning of this book, the question was asked: did Roger Mortimer deserve to go down in history as a crooked, selfish, adulterous traitor? The answer to this has to be that this description is inappropriate for it is lacking in depth. As has been shown, the scope of his activities towards the end of his life, and, in particular, his actions against the English royal family, amounted to treason on a scale never known in Britain before or since. No man in English history could be so deserving of the title of this book. He did not just depose King Edward II; he judicially murdered the king's brother, executed the king's friends, went to war with the king's cousin, seduced the king's wife (and possibly had a child by her), and forced the king's nephew into a marriage with his daughter. In addition he took the king himself illegally into custody, feigned his death, and kept him alive secretly like a piece of political veal for three years. He controlled the king's heir, reduced his patrimony and ruled in the heir's name. He undermined the monarchy, and insulted the occupants of the throne and their families. In short, he stole the royal power, just as Edward III claimed at his trial.

This extremely negative historical judgement begs the question: are there any mitigating circumstances which might excuse his behaviour? This is an interesting question, for it demands that we make a more considered moral judgement on the man, independent of the judgement of his contemporaries. For example, if he committed acts of treason for the greater good of the country, are we right to uphold the accusations levelled by contemporaries who were personally threatened by him, such as Henry of Lancaster and Edward III? From this moral point of view, a very different picture of Roger emerges, in which we may sympathise with most of the pivotal decisions he made in his career. In his early years he was a loyal friend to the king and a capable public servant with an almost unblemished record. His rebellion in 1321 was morally justified, as Hugh Despenser was a menace to the nation, and Roger was not alone in wishing the man stopped. Edward II himself forced Roger to take arms by so closely supporting the Despensers. While Roger badly miscalculated in 1321 by supporting Badlesmere, he was at least doing so against the unwarranted oppression of Edward II. After his imprisonment and a second death sentence, Roger can hardly be blamed for saving his life by escaping from the Tower. His plot against Edward II in France, and the close association with Isabella, although certainly treasonable, were merely extensions of the conflict which Edward II had provoked by attacking Badlesmere in 1321. Although he orchestrated the king's deposition and enforced abdication, it is clear that the move had many supporters and was to the benefit of the country. One can find a mitigating factor for his restraint during the Weardale campaign, for, although he was very probably to blame for the fiasco, his wider policy presented an opportunity of a permanent peace with the Scots. Even his decision to feign the ex-king's death and keep him secretly in custody at Corfe may be excused, for this was at least more merciful than murdering the man. It goes without saying that there was a personal element to his actions – and it is clear that he kept Edward alive not for humanitarian reasons but to secure his own position – but ambition is not a crime in itself. While he may be justly accused of dictatorship from 1328, his administration was more acceptable than the last years of the reign of Edward II, and thus his appropriation of power may, in part at least, be excused. It corrected some of the wrongs of the old regime, it did not lead to huge self-aggrandisement on Roger's part (although it did allow Isabella to acquire and spend a fortune), and it did not result in the unmitigated destruction of his personal enemies. It would be fair to say that he governed England as best he could, but was increasingly compromised by his most controversial policies, especially Scottish independence, his failure to restrain Isabella's acquisitiveness, and keeping the ex-king secretly alive.

In this light one has to say that Roger's greatest crime was that he was not a member of the royal family. If it had been possible for him to inherit the throne, he would undoubtedly have made a much better king than Edward II. He was courageous, successful, clever, far-sighted and (on the whole) fair. He was able to forgive most men who turned against him, and sensible to his own limitations and those of his people, as shown by his reluctance to carry on the war in Scotland or to begin a war in France. But his lack of royal blood meant that, as a leader, he was exceptionally vulnerable and constantly under pressure. His unpopular policies, however far-sighted they may have been, led to repeated calls for his removal from court, a fact which makes him more akin to a modern government minister than a medieval king. His familiarity with members of the royal family made him act as if he were himself royal, and this encouraged the envy of others, which added to the pressure. Finally, his policies allowed his enemies to undermine his position to such a great extent that he was isolated, able only to wield power destructively as he struggled to maintain his and Isabella's position at the heart of government.

The one aspect of Roger's later life which has appealed to modern readers is his relationship with Isabella. While there is little doubt that this was morally wrong at the time, such all-consuming passions among historical characters today have a more sympathetic audience. There is no reason to doubt that Roger did love Isabella deeply, as shown by his blurted out threat to kill her if she returned to her husband in 1325. Similarly, the likelihood that she had a child by him and remained at his side for the rest of his life suggests she was, after her initial hesitancy, equally devoted to him. That she chose to be buried in her wedding dress does not necessarily indicate she turned from Roger's memory, for he may well have been in Edward's company at the royal wedding in Boulogne, and thus would first have seen her in this dress.[1] If one were to ask whether Isabella, not Joan, was the love of his life, one would have to say that she probably was. However, the true extent of their devotion to one another continues to be something of an enigma, as does the fate of any offspring.

Finally, we may turn to the question of Roger's integrity. As indicated above, there is a constant sense of natural justice which runs throughout his career. He was prepared to act against the interests of his fellow peers – and even against his king – on moral principles, and was not prepared to let those principles be hijacked by self-interested semi-royal grandees like Thomas of Lancaster and his brother, Henry of Lancaster. One could argue that this sense of natural justice continued with him right up until 1329, when he dealt very fairly with those who had been prepared to take up arms under Henry of Lancaster. But after this, in the summer of 1329, when repeated criticisms made him frightened of losing power and when Edward III started to stand up to him more openly, that sense of justice was obscured. In 1330 he was a frightening example of a man corrupted by both power and fear, and therein lies the tragedy of his last years, for he was not by nature tyrannical. He was a believer in chivalric virtue, the ideals of knighthood and duty to the Crown. He believed in Arthurian romance and the noble deeds of his ancestors. But so desperate was he at the end of his life that he betrayed all these things: king, country, chivalry, vows of knighthood and justice. That he understood this in the last moments of his life is evidenced by the single vestige of his gallows confession which has come down to us: that the Earl of Kent was the victim of his conspiracy. One can say little more damning about a historical character than that he knowingly acted in his own self-interest against what he believed was virtuous, just and right.

NOTES

Introduction

1. Dramatic works which have dealt with Roger Mortimer include: Christopher Marlowe, *Edward II* (1594) and J. Bancroft, *The Fall of Mortimer* (1691), late editions being attributed to William Mountfort. The verse satire is Francis Richardson, *An Ode to the Pretender . . . to which is added Earl Mortimer's fall* (1713). Mortimer's usefulness as an object of satire in the eighteenth century is evident in two works, *The Lives of Roger Mortimer, Earl of March, and of Robert, Earl of Oxford &c . . .* (1711) and *The Norfolk Sting, or the history and fall of Evil Ministers* (1732). Alma Harris, *In Days of Yore: Queen Isabella and Sir Roger Mortimer: A Royal Romance* (Nottingham, 1995) is the only recent non-academic part-biography of Roger Mortimer. An earlier part-biography was J. Adamson, *The reigns of King Edward II, and so far of King Edward III, as relates to the lives and actions of Piers Gaveston, Hugh de Spencer, and Roger, Lord Mortimer* (1732). A fictional account of Roger Mortimer (apart from those primarily concerning Isabella) is Emily Sarah Holt, *The Lord of the Marches: or the story of Roger Mortimer: a tale of the fourteenth century* (1884).

2. The sole doctoral thesis concerning Roger Mortimer has only recently been completed by Paul Dryburgh at the University of Bristol. The text of this book was completed while Dr Dryburgh's thesis was still unsubmitted, and the author has not had access to any part of Dr Dryburgh's written work.

1: Inheritance

1. 25 April 1287 is the most probable date of Roger's birth. The ages given for him in the various *Inquisitions Post Mortem* relating to his father's death (1304) suggest two dates. The first of these is derived from the statement that he was seventeen on the feast of St Mark last, i.e. born on 25 April 1287. The other is that he was seventeen on the last Feast of the Invention of the Holy Cross, i.e. 3 May 1287. The date of the Feast of the Invention of the Holy Cross was the date of the demise of the estates of Edmund Mortimer (Roger's father) to Geoffrey de Geneville in 1300, and this has probably been confused with his birth. A family chronicle, written almost a century later, states he was sixteen and a quarter at the time of his father's death, which would imply a birthdate about April 1288, and the *Complete Peerage* indeed notes that the Chronicle of Hailes (British Library, Cottonian MSS, Cleopatra D3) states he was born on 17 April 1288. Also the Wigmore Annals in the John Rylands Library (transcribed in B.P. Evans's Ph.D. study of the family, for details of which see Bibliography) mentions Roger was born 'circa festum apostolorum Philippi et Jacobi' in the year 1288 (1 May). This chronicle is a year out on a number of details, however; with regard to the birth of Edmund FitzAlan it

269

is two years adrift, a reflection on its being written a long time after the event. Also with regard to the fifteenth-century family chronicle, which has clearly been compiled from earlier sources (including, quite possibly, the Wigmore Annals in the John Rylands Library), although this correctly dates Edmund's death in one paragraph, in the paragraph in which it states Roger was sixteen and a quarter at the time it places the death a year early, in the thirty-first year of the reign of Edward I: i.e. November 1302–3. The *Inquisitions Post Mortem* are the nearest to a contemporary source we have, all being written in the summer of 1304; none of these mentions 1288 as the date of his birth, and most favour the St Mark date. The date of 25 April 1287 was probably supplied centrally by a clerk of the family within a few weeks of the death of Edmund Mortimer, and this, being legally binding, and the only date of birth definitely associated with him in his lifetime, must therefore be considered the most trustworthy evidence we have. Confirmation of the day, 25 April, is perhaps to be found in the number of grants that Roger awarded himself and his son Geoffrey on that day in 1330 (see *Cal. Charter Rolls*, pp. 172, 175).

2. Each head of the family had named his first-born son after his father since the mid-twelfth century. See *Complete Peerage*, ix, pp. 266–85. This custom seems to have held true for the Mortimers from the mid-twelfth century to the fifteenth. It was also true for the inter-related family of Berkeley, for almost exactly the same period (until the death of the fifth lord in 1404).

3. See 'Chronicles of the Mayors and Sheriffs', in *English Historical Documents 1189–1327* (1975), p. 183, for details of de Montfort's testicles.

4. Roger Mortimer's epitaph, 1282, appears in Dugdale, *Baronage*, I, p. 143.

5. Dugdale, *Monasticon*, vi, part i, p. 351.

6. The date of Edmund Mortimer's marriage is given as the 'feast of the birth of the Blessed Virgin Mary' in the Wigmore Annals transcribed in B.P. Evans, 'The Family of Mortimer'. See the caveat mentioned in the note concerning Roger's birth regarding the accuracy of the dates of this chronicle.

7. According to the *Complete Peerage*, Joan de Geneville was born on 2 February 1286. She was thus fifteen and a half at the time of her marriage to Roger. Her younger sisters, Beatrice and Maud, were born in 1287 and 1291 respectively.

8. *Calendar of Inquisitions Post Mortem Edward I*, iv, p. 161. The date of the demise of the estates was 3 May 1300.

9. See the Wigmore Annals transcribed in Evans's unpublished Ph.D. thesis, 'The Family of Mortimer' (original: John Rylands Library, Latin MS 215) for the details of the marriage. See also Holmes, *Estates of the Higher Nobility*, p. 11, n. 5.

10. See Appendix 2.

11. The prince's five other guards were John de St John, Robert de Tony, Henry le Tyeys, William Latimer and William de Leyburn. See Johnstone, *Edward of Carnarvon*, p. 51.

12. Larking, 'Inventory of the Effects of Roger Mortimer' discussed in Chapter 9, and Swynnerton, 'Certain Chattels of Roger Mortimer of Wigmore'. For Roger's borrowing books, probably on behalf of his wife (see Chapter 10), see Vale, *Edward III and Chivalry*, p. 169. For the king's similar books in French, see Johnstone, *Edward of Carnarvon*, p. 18.

13. Johnstone, *Edward of Carnarvon*, pp. 7–8.
14. *Complete Peerage*, ix, p. 283. B.P. Evans has 16 July, derived from the Wigmore annalist.

2: *Youth*

1. The evidence for Roger being able to read is touched on later in the book. The fact he was the son of an educated man is an indication that his reading may have started in youth. In 1322 his wife was in possession of books of romances at Wigmore, and Roger was issued with four similar books in early 1327 which he may have used himself or may have sent to his wife. There are several direct references to him reading, one in a court case of 1331 which appears transcribed in Tout, 'Captivity and Death', pp. 109–10, in which Roger is supposed to have 'shown' a private letter to his man William de Ockley; the other, more explicit one, is in Brie (ed.), *The Brut*, ii, p. 265, where Roger reads a letter aloud. It is unlikely that Roger or Edward ever themselves wrote, however, and it should be noted that, although Edward's son certainly could write, we only have two words in his hand, 'Pater Sancte' on a letter to the Pope. This in itself shows that the fact that a man could write did not mean that he actually did so. For Edward III's writing see Crump, 'Arrest of Roger Mortimer', p. 332. Having said this, it is possible that Roger himself wrote the secret letters to the monastic clergy smuggled out of the Tower by him in 1323 (see Chapter 8).
2. PRO E101/370/9, E101/371/8/97.
3. *CPR 1301–1307*, p. 244.
4. Roger's cousins were members of the de Fiennes family who were also at court. See Tout, *Chapters*, ii, p. 172.
5. A full discussion of the relationship between Gaveston and Edward is given in Chaplais, *Piers Gaveston*, pp. 6–22.
6. PRO E101/371/8/97.
7. See the Wigmore Abbey chronicle of the Mortimer family, quoted in *Complete Peerage*, viii, p. 433.
8. *CPR 1301–1307*, p. 308.
9. BL Harley 1240 f62v.
10. Roger's son, Edmund, was probably born before 1303, as he was using his own seal at the time of his marriage in 1316. See PRO DL 27/93, or, alternatively, the *Appendix to the 35th Report of the Deputy Keeper of the Public Records*, 31–32. In this context it is worth noting that, according to the *Complete Peerage*, Joan's ancestors, the Counts of the March in Gascony, customarily came of age at fourteen.
11. See Appendix 2.
12. The old *DNB* notes Roger and Joan both travelling to Ireland to take seisen of Geoffrey de Geneville's property on 28 October 1308; Joan also accompanied Roger on his 1310 trip to Ireland, and was present at the coronation with him and his mother. See *CPR 1307–1313*, p. 282, and *CCR 1307–1313*, p. 52. It is also highly likely that she accompanied him on his trip to Gascony in 1313, where her family held lands.
13. Roger's love of the tournament is shown several times later in his life, but most

strongly in his deserting the royal army in October 1306 to take part in a tournament along with Piers Gaveston, Sir Giles d'Argentein and several other notable tournament fighters. He also in later life encouraged tournaments, holding many of his own.

14. *CCR 1303–1307*, p. 377.

15. *Calendar of Inquisitions Post Mortem*, 1304, no. 235.

16. Shaw, *Knights of England*. Gaveston was not actually knighted on the same day but four days later, on 26 May. Chaplais, *Piers Gaveston*, p. 21.

17. For Edward's speech see Wright (ed.), *Langtoft*, p. 368; Hutchinson, *Edward II*, p. 46; and Johnstone, *Edward of Carnarvon*, p. 108.

18. See, among other commentators, Johnstone, *Edward of Carnarvon*, p. 116; Hamilton, *Piers Gaveston*, p. 33. Tout's assertion in the old *DNB* that it was Lord Mortimer of Chirk who deserted is wrong.

19. Chaplais, *Piers Gaveston*, pp. 20–2.

20. Johnstone, *Edward of Carnarvon*, p. 121; Rothwell (ed.), *Chronicle of Walter of Guisborough*, p. 382.

3: The King's Friend

1. Hamilton, *Piers Gaveston*. pp. 44–5.

2. Fifteen weeks was not an abnormally long period. The body of Isabella, Edward II's consort, waited the same period before burial, and that of Philippa, consort of Edward III, waited even longer. See Blackley, 'Isabella of France, Queen of England (1308–1358), and the Late Medieval Cult of the Dead', p. 27.

3. Thomas of Lancaster also acquired the earldom of Lincoln after the death of Henry de Lacy in 1311. From this date his income from all five earldoms amounted to about £11,000. Thomas of Lancaster's disposable income was approximately fifteen times that of Roger Mortimer's.

4. *CCR 1307–1313*, p. 46.

5. *CPR 1307–1313*, p. 28. It is not clear which Roger Mortimer is intended here but it was probably Roger, as his uncle, being made Justiciar of Wales just after this, would have had responsibilities in that country which prevented him from leaving for France, even for a week.

6. The evidence for Roger's appointment as seneschal comes from Renouard (ed.), *Gascon Rolls*, no. 9. This reference to 'Roger Mortimer' is a single isolated entry, and therefore probably reflects an intention which was never carried out. That it refers to Roger of Wigmore and not his uncle is evident in the fact that the uncle had no estates in Gascony whereas by 1308 it was clear that Guy de Lusignan, Count of La Marche, would die with no children, making Joan's mother an important landholder in the region. These lands eventually formed the lordship around Couhé which was settled on Geoffrey, Roger's and Joan's son, in 1323. Roger was also associated with Gascony in 1313.

7. Lord Mortimer of Chirk was almost certainly with the king at Dover on 19 January 1308 as he witnessed a grant there of that date. PRO, C53/94.

8. See Chaplais, *Piers Gaveston*, pp. 41–2, for a good example of how Gaveston avoided controversy.

9. See the passage in Hamilton, *Piers Gaveston*, pp. 45–6 where he suggests that this regency was only superficially the zenith of Gaveston's authority.

10. See Phillips, *Aymer de Valence*, pp. 25–7 for a discussion of the Boulogne agreement.

11. Menache, 'Isabelle of France, Queen of England – a Reconsideration', p. 118.

12. Blackley, 'Isabella of France, Queen of England (1308–1358), and the Late Medieval Cult of the Dead', p. 26.

13. *CCR 1307–1313*, pp. 52–3. With Joan and Margaret was Joan Wake, Margaret's sister, another French noblewoman.

14. Chaplais, *Piers Gaveston*, pp. 42–3.

15. Most writers state the giving away of the wedding presents occurred back in England; but Doherty states in his thesis that the presents were sent from France to Gaveston. See Doherty, 'Isabella', p. 26, where he quotes BL Cottonian MS Nero D X, f108.

16. On 16 March, in the midst of Edward's preparations, he obtained a pardon for murder for one of his associates, William d'Esturmy. See *CCR 1307–1313*, p. 52.

17. Bishop Walter Reynolds is the only other person known to have acted with Gaveston, in the previous year. See *CPR 1307–1313*, p. 56; Hamilton, *Piers Gaveston*, p. 155, n. 53.

18. See Maddicott, *Thomas of Lancaster*, p. 87, for the five others who are known to have remained at court.

19. Chaplais, *Piers Gaveston*, p. 48.

20. With regard to Duleek, see *Justiciary Rolls of Ireland 1305–1307*, pp. 188, 241, 277, 307.

21. O'Donovan, *Annals of the Kingdom of Ireland by the Four Masters*.

22. Gilbert (ed.), *Chartularies of St Mary's Abbey, Dublin: With the Register of its House at Dunbrody and Annals of Ireland*.

23. Charlton was King's Chamberlain from 1310 to 1318, and replaced only by the king's second great favourite, Hugh Despenser. See Tout, *Place of Edward II*, p. 315. Regarding his being a yeoman of Gaveston's, see Hamilton, *Piers Gaveston*, p. 88.

24. On the question of Gaveston's influence resulting in de Thornbury's appointment, see Hamilton, *Piers Gaveston*, p. 63. De Thornbury had been a close friend of Roger's father, and was the executor of his father's will. See *CPR 1301–1307*, p. 260.

25. De Hothum remained a supporter of Gaveston's until his death, being associated with the favourite in the Ordinances of 1311. See Hamilton, *Piers Gaveston*, pp. 76, 88, 92, and Phillips, 'John de Hothum', in Lydon (ed.), *England and Ireland in the Later Middle Ages* (Dublin, 1981), pp. 64, 77. That de Hothum was a lifelong supporter of Roger Mortimer is evident throughout his career; but it is worth noting how close a companion he became through contact with Roger in Ireland, for Roger made him an executor of his own will in 1316. For more contemporary evidence of their association it is also worth noting that de Hothum loaned Roger money in October 1309 after Roger had returned to England. See *CCR 1307–1313*, p. 197.

26. John de Sapy was also one of those who, along with John de Hothum and John de Charlton, were specifically noted in 1311 for a past close association with Gaveston. See Hamilton, *Piers Gaveston*, p. 88.

27. Curtis (ed.), *Calendar of Ormond Deeds*, p. 172. The precise date is 12 April.

28. Maddicott states that Roger was at the Dunstable tournament on the strength of

the heraldic roll. This tournament he dates to the end of March or the beginning of April 1308. However, there is only one Roger Mortimer noted on this roll; and although the arms stated are those of Roger, this must be a mistake. The fact that Roger was with Gaveston in Ireland on 12 April, and had been in Ireland before this date, rules out his attending this tournament unless it was held later in the summer. See Maddicott, *Thomas of Lancaster*, p. 100.

29. *Parliamentary Writs*, iv, p. 1203.
30. *CPR 1307–1313*, p. 231.
31. BL Harley 1240, f42v, f54v.
32. The date of Roger's landing is given in Gilbert (ed.), *Chartularies of St Mary's, Dublin*, p. 339.
33. *CPR 1307–1313*, pp. 282–3.
34. In December 1309 he had obtained a pardon for all his men in Ireland who had committed murder and burnt houses 'in repelling and pursuing John FitzThomas and other malefactors and breakers of the peace of the king's land of Carbury, who invaded Trim lands, committing manslaughter, destroying by fire and other damages'. See *CCR 1307–1313*, p. 188.
35. The entry in the Annals of Clonmacnoise is quoted in O'Donovan, *Annals of the Kingdom of Ireland*, iii, p. 405. In 1317 Roger marched against Geoffrey O'Farell again.
36. Lydon, 'The Impact of the Bruce Invasion 1315–1317', in Cosgrove (ed.), *Medieval Ireland*, p. 276.
37. Denholm-Young (ed.), *Vita*, p. 12.
38. See Maddicott, *Thomas of Lancaster*, pp. 140–1, for a full discussion of the events concerning Welshpool.
39. Roger Mortimer of Wigmore is commonly said to have been involved with this. As may be seen from his itinerary, and from the patent and closed letters sent to the Justiciar of Wales, there is no doubt that Roger was not directly involved in this attack as he was in Ireland, fighting the de Verdon brothers. It was rather his uncle, Lord Mortimer of Chirk, who was the agent responsible. The writers who have him taking part in the conflict have taken their information from the fifteenth-century chronicle of the family printed in Dugdale's *Monasticon* (1817–30), vi, part i, p. 351, which seems to have confused its earlier sources.
40. Conway Davies, *Baronial Opposition*, p. 213.
41. Otway-Ruthven, *Medieval Ireland*, p. 223; Lydon, in Cosgrove (ed.), *New History of Ireland*, p. 280; *Chartularies of St Mary's, Dublin*, pp. 340–1; *Calendar of Close Rolls 1307–1313*, pp. 525–6.
42. Wood *et al* (eds), *Calendar of the Justiciary Rolls, Ireland*, pp. 237–9. A year later he showed clemency and obtained a pardon for them, on condition they went to fight in Scotland.

4: Bannockburn and Kells

1. Hamilton, *Piers Gaveston*, p. 98.
2. Hamilton, *Piers Gaveston*, p. 103.
3. Denholm-Young (ed.), *Vita*, p. 30.

4. *CCR 1307–1313*, p. 522.

5. Phillips, *Aymer de Valence*, p. 53.

6. Tout, *Place of Edward II*, p. 349.

7. Barrow, *Robert Bruce*, pp. 204, 207.

8. Barrow, *Robert Bruce*, p. 209. The author of *Vita Edwardi Secundi* says twenty leagues. Denholm-Young (ed.), *Vita*, p. 50.

9. Denholm-Young (ed.), *Vita*, p. 51.

10. Barbour, *The Bruce*, p. 301.

11. There is no definite proof that Roger was at Bannockburn, but that is not very surprising as the names of men most frequently reported by chroniclers to have fought in a battle were those killed. Thus some discussion is required of the evidence. Firstly, Roger was summoned to perform service in person, and he only seems to have ignored summonses when he was in Ireland or already had permission to visit Ireland, as in 1310. Secondly, he was at York with the king very shortly after the king arrived there on his retreat from Scotland, thus suggesting that he travelled back with the king. Thirdly, there is the evidence of the Trivet continuator discussed later in Note 15. Against this there is the fact that a confirmation of a grant made by Roger's father was supposedly made by Roger at Wigmore on 17 June 1314 (see BL Harley 1240 f58v). Normally one would suppose this indicated his presence at Wigmore, far too far behind the army to be able to meet the battle six days later. However, it is noticeable that the grant is a confirmation of a charter whose text would only have been found at Wigmore, and that it is a grant to the men of Maelienydd. A hundred of Roger's men from Maelienydd were summoned to Scotland, and it is possible that this confirmation is a response by Roger to their grievances en route to the battle. If so, this would actually confirm his presence in the army marching against the Scots, as he would have had personally to authorise the charter at Wigmore to be sought, copied and regranted, and to send his seal so that the confirmation could take place. As for the Mortimers' position in the battle, the knights most closely associated with the king's person in this battle, such as Pain Tibetot, Sir Giles d'Argentein and Robert Clifford, were part of a hardly changing royal bodyguard, with whom Lord Mortimer of Chirk had certainly been associated in 1300 at the Battle of Caerlaverock. Although older now, it is possible that this group was still performing a similar role in 1314. Even if Lord Mortimer of Chirk was considered too old for the duty of protecting the king, it is still probable that he maintained his position of dignity close to the royal personage, if only to offer advice or to take orders for the men of Wales. In addition, five of the six bodyguard of 1300 (with the exception of Lord Mortimer of Chirk) were with Roger in leaving Edward I's army in 1306 to attend a tournament. Thus it may be supposed that this group, including Roger, represented the diehard military elite, and that most of these men, if not all, were with the king's person at Bannockburn.

12. In view of Roger's status and experience he was most probably with the king during the battle, as mentioned above. His capture is thus most easily explained by participation in a defence of the king's retreat. It is unlikely that he was among the knights who were captured with the Earl of Hereford for two reasons: (a) the chroniclers do not mention him with Hereford, although they mention several men

of lesser rank; and (b) Roger was soon back with the king at York, and was probably sent with the seal and the body of Gilbert de Clare. See Note 15.

13. Phillips, *Aymer de Valence*, p. 75.

14. Gilbert de Clare (d. 1314), Earl of Gloucester, was a second cousin of Bruce, Bruce's grandmother on his father's side being Isabel de Clare, sister of Richard de Clare, Gilbert's grandfather. Richard and Isabel's mother was Isabel Marshal, Roger's great-great-aunt. See Table 2.

15. All we know on this matter comes from the continuation of the chronicle of Nicholas Trivet. This piece of work was written by a Dominican friar with a penchant for details concerning seals. Roger de Northburgh, the keeper of the king's privy seal, was killed in the battle, and the seal, like the king's shield, was found afterwards. The friar records only that Bruce sent the seal with 'Roger Mortimer' to the king at Berwick. As is so often the case with the Mortimers, one has to ask: which Roger Mortimer is intended? Although at first one might suppose that it would be more likely that the older knight, Lord Mortimer of Chirk, would be released without ransom, there is good reason to believe it was Roger, because of the situation of some of his lands close to the author's friary. The writer was probably a friar of Ilchester, as he mentions two churches damaged by storms within four miles of the town in his chronicle. Also within four miles of the town was the manor of Odcombe, a demesne lordship of Roger's, and thus Roger would have been well known by name to the writer. Also Roger, rather than his uncle, had connections with the Earl of Ulster in Ireland, father of Bruce's wife. Finally, if the Roger Mortimer referred to by the Trivet continuator was the lord of Wigmore, it would explain how Roger rejoined the court shortly after the battle, and much sooner than most of the other knights who were captured. See Antonia Gransden, *Historical Writing in England*, ii, p. 9. I am grateful to Paul Dryburgh for pointing out to me the reference in the continuation of the chronicle of Nicholas Trivet.

16. Denholm-Young (ed.), *Vita*, p. 57.

17. Both the new Chancellor, John Sandall, Bishop of Winchester, and the new Treasurer, Sir Walter de Norwich, were later (in 1318) selected by the king to form a panel with Roger and others to administer the reform of the royal household, and Sir Walter was trusted by Roger so much that, although Walter was forced to sit on the committee which in 1322 would sentence Roger and his uncle to death, Roger later forgave him and allowed him to remain in office.

18. Philips, *Aymer de Valence*, p. 83.

19. *CPR 1313–1317*, pp. 276, 279, 285.

20. Connolly (ed.), *Irish Exchequer Payments*, pp. 242–59.

21. Barrow, *Robert Bruce*, p. 314.

22. Otway-Ruthven, *Medieval Ireland*, p. 226.

23. Hennessy (ed.), *Annals of Loch Cé*, p. 567.

24. Phillips, *Documents on the Early Stages of the Bruce Invasion of Ireland, 1315–1316*.

25. Gilbert (ed.), *Chartularies of St Mary, Dublin*, pp. 407–16.

26. If this suggestion is correct it may mean the whole 'Coigneris' campaign described in Barbour's *The Bruce* (pp. 347–61), which refers to the Battle of Connor at great length, has mixed up elements of later battles in one long description of Connor. Orpen, in *Ireland Under the Normans*, iv, pp. 167–8, suggests as much, and Frame in

'The Bruces in Ireland' does not discount the possibility. However, the chronology in *The Bruce* is not strong enough to warrant a reconstruction of what may have happened at Kells, and we constantly fall back on the annals in the *Chartularies of St Mary's, Dublin*, and the 1317 court case (printed as an appendix in the second volume) for guidance, and these give only the slightest details.

27. Gilbert (ed.), *Chartularies of St Mary's, Dublin*, ii, p. 348.
28. Gilbert (ed.), *Chartularies of St Mary's, Dublin*, ii, pp. 407–16.
29. Orpen, *Ireland Under the Normans*, iv, p. 173.

5: The King's Lieutenant

1. Palgrave (ed.), *Parliamentary Writs*, iv, p. 1203.
2. Denhom-Young (ed.), *Vita*, p. 66.
3. Denholm-Young (ed.), *Vita*, p. 67.
4. See Griffiths, *Conquerors and Conquered in Medieval Wales*, pp. 84–91, for a good overview of this campaign.
5. Wilkinson, 'Attack on the Despensers, 1321', p. 25.
6. *CCR 1313–1318*, p. 376.
7. Denholm-Young (ed.), *Vita*, pp. 69–70.
8. An overview of the background to this dispute is given in the first part of the article by Fuller, 'The Tallage of Edward II and the Bristol Rebellion', pp. 171–278.
9. On 21 May 1316 Badlesmere acknowledged a debt of 2,000 marks to Roger, to be levied on his lands in Kent in default of the payment (See *CCR 1313–1317*, p. 339). On the day of the wedding itself Badlesmere bound himself to pay £20,000 to Roger, in case of default on the marriage. See BL Harley 1240 fol. 114.
10. Elizabeth de Badlesmere was reportedly twenty-five in 1338. See *Complete Peerage*, ix, p. 285.
11. PRO DL 27/93. In addition the Abbot of Wigmore's seal is appended to the charter.
12. Some rolls and accounts from the Mortimer family archive, dating from the later fourteenth and early fifteenth centuries, survive in the British Library in the two Egerton series (Egerton Charters 7350–54; Egerton Rolls 8723–60). Egerton Roll 8723 is a list of charters and other muniments confiscated from Roger's treasury at Wigmore in 1322. Also in the British Library is the Black Book of Wigmore, the principal family cartulary, in the Harleian collection (BL Harley 1240). A contemporary abstract of this is BL Add. MS 6041. These cartularies were drawn up c. 1380 but contain transcripts of deeds extant at that time from much earlier periods. A reference system in the Black Book shows that the originals of the grants mentioned were stored in the treasury at Wigmore. A single receiver's account for 1384 is in the National Library of Wales (see *Bulletin of the Institute of Historical Research*, 10 (1932–3)). At least one late fourteenth-century Wigmore court roll is in the custody of the Harley family of Brampton Bryan, one-time vassals of the Mortimers, who owned the castle when it was dismantled in the seventeenth century (HMC: NRA 686 (Harley family papers)). Certain other odd muniments have found their way into the British Library (e.g. BL Add. Roll 58896, Harley 704 f1,

etc; these references may be supplemented with others noted on the British Library MSS catalogue) and other repositories (e.g. PRO DL 27/93). The family chronicles in the John Rylands Library (12th century to 1307; Latin MS 215), Trinity College Dublin (1355–77; MS E. 2. 25) and Chicago University Library (eleventh to fifteen centuries MS CS 439 fM82 W6) were almost certainly compiled within Wigmore Abbey and formed part of the abbey's library, so did not form part of the family's muniments. At the Dissolution it is quite likely that such chronicles were removed from the abbey separately to the charters and records; in 1574 the abbey's administrative records were lying in a disused chapel of the castle, as shown by a letter from Dr Dee to Lord Burghley published in T.H. Bound, *History of Wigmore* (1876), and the likelihood is that the family's archive was then in the same place. Nothing more is known of it after this date.

13. Denholm-Young (ed.), *Vita*, p. 73. This is also the source for the previous quotation.

14. The account of the siege of Bristol is taken from *Vita*, pp. 73–4.

15. Phillips, *Aymer de Valance*, p. 103.

16. The chronology of Edward Bruce's advance through Leinster is derived from Otway-Ruthven, *Medieval Ireland*, p. 228.

17. Phillips, *Documents on the Early Stages of the Bruce Invasion of Ireland, 1315–1316*.

18. Roger had decided to lead an army by 20 November. The date can be fixed since Hugh de Croft was granted pardon (for a fine waived contrary to the ordinances) on 20 November 'on the king's service with Roger Mortimer'. See *CCR 1313–1319*, p. 563.

19. *CPR 1313–1317*, p. 563.

20. *CPR 1313–1317*, pp. 563–4.

21. *Calendar of Chancery Warrants 1244–1326*, p. 455. The Earl of Lancaster, of course, ignored this summons.

22. The description of Roger as 'the king's cousin', or 'the king's kinsman', appears on several writs at this time and in this context. See *CPR 1313–1317*, p. 632, for 'kinsman', and *Calendar of Chancery Warrants, 1244–1326*, pp. 455, 461 for 'cousin'.

23. Otway-Ruthven, *Medieval Ireland*, p. 232.

24. *Calendar of Chancery Warrants 1244–1326*, p. 461.

25. The date of 16 February and those following are from Otway-Ruthven, *Medieval Ireland*, p. 230. Orpen (iv, p. 184) has 13 February for the Scots at Slane.

26. The assumption that the Earl of Ulster was a Scottish sympathiser was logical, given his daughter's marriage to Robert Bruce and his failure to make an impression on the Scots at every stage of their advance. However, the evidence points to the earl being loyal, as his principal objective in this ambush was to kill Robert Bruce, as shown by his allowing Edward Bruce to pass with the vanguard ahead. It was no sham attack either, for the Scots considered this the hardest fought battle of the war. Roger later released him.

27. These royal letters are calendered in *CCR 1313–1318*, p. 404. The full Latin texts are in Gilbert (ed.), *Hist. & Mun. Docs*, pp. 397–403.

28. Roger's tendency to pardon killers in order to obtain their services was well known, and was one of the causes for complaint against him in later years; it was also a method followed to extremes by the king himself in 1326.

29. Gilbert (ed.), *Chartularies of St Mary's, Dublin*, ii, p. 411.

30. Gilbert (ed.), *Chartularies of St Mary's, Dublin*, ii, p. 356.
31. The arrest of the Bishop of Ferns was ordered by Edward on 6 August. See *CCR 1313–1318*, p. 561.
32. 'Okinselagh' appears as 'Glynsely' in the original. See Gilbert (ed.), *Chartularies of St Mary's, Dublin*, ii, p. 356, and Orpen, *Ireland Under the Normans*, iv, p. 195.
33. For details of the execution of Llywelyn Bren see Griffiths, 'Conquerors and Conquered', p. 90.
34. Connolly (ed.), *Irish Exchequer Payments*, Irish Manuscripts Commission (Dublin, 1998).
35. *Calendar of Irish Patent and Close Rolls*, p. 21.
36. Gilbert (ed.), *Chartularies of St Mary's, Dublin*, ii, p. 357. The possibility that it was his brother John may be discounted as when that man died in early 1319 he was described not as a knight but as a 'king's yeoman'. See *CFR 1307–1319*, p. 396. Also when his three other sons were knighted in 1327, John was not, so it is likely that he was previously knighted, this being the only known possible occasion. The knighting of children in the period is not unknown.
37. The starving to death of John de Lacy was not necessarily a personally chosen punishment but an Irish custom. Instances of a court sentencing someone to starvation are rare in the British Isles, but other examples have cropped up with regard to Ireland. Certain Irish Templar knights were executed in this way in the early fourteenth century. Also Roger's ancestor, Matilda de Braose, and her son were probably starved to death by King John after the rebellion of her Anglo-Irish husband, William de Braose. John had pursued William to Ireland in 1210 and may well have sentenced the family to such a fate in that country.

6: *The King's Kinsman*

1. Phillips, 'The "Middle Party" and the Treaty of Leake, August 1318', *passim*.
2. See Gilbert (ed.), *Chartularies of St Mary's, Dublin*, ii, p. 358, which states Roger returned to England on the 'Sunday before the Ascension of the Lord', i.e. Rogation Sunday, which in 1318 was 28 May.
3. Phillips, *Aymer de Valence*, pp. 166–70, and Wilkinson, 'The "Middle Party" and the Treaty of Leake, August 1318', *passim*.
4. Walter de Wogan received a discharge of his debts in respect of his good service in Ireland with Roger on 18 July. See *CCR 1318–1323*, p. 2.
5. The Chamberlain of Carnarvon still owed Roger 1,600 marks in 1320. See *CCR 1318–1323*, pp. 179, 182.
6. Brakspear, 'Wigmore Abbey', p. 42; Haines, *Adam of Orleton*, p. 218.
7. Haines, *Adam of Orleton*, pp. 1–3.
8. Haines, *Adam of Orleton*, pp. 218–19.
9. According to the *Complete Peerage*, this marriage took place before 13 April 1319. It almost certainly took place on a manor belonging to one of the families. Since Roger was at court until early December in York, at Wigmore after Christmas, and back at court in York by March, the marriage probably took place between late December and early February 1318/1319.

10. Thompson (ed.), *Murimuth*, p. 31. Badlesmere was able to spend this money since he was the royal envoy to the papal court. The author of *Vita Edwardi Secundi* certainly thought the appointment illegal. See Denholm-Young (ed.), *Vita*, p. 105.

11. *CCR 1313–1318*, p. 229.

12. See grant of the marriage, *CFR 1307–1319*, p. 369, and dispensation, *Calendar of Entries in the Papal Registers Relating to Great Britain and Ireland 1305–1342*, p. 186. Eventually Catherine Mortimer married the earl, although probably not until early 1327.

13. Phillips, *Aymer de Valence*, pp. 264–6. It should also be noted that Lord Berkeley had served in Roger's household in 1318.

14. *Annals of Ulster*, ii, p. 437.

15. *CFR 1307–1319*, p. 393.

16. *CPR 1317–1321*, p. 371.

17. Frame, *English Lordship in Ireland*, p. 159.

18. The letter, BL Cottonian Charter 26/27, is in a bundle of letters to Edward along with one from Pembroke dating to early 1319. In the context of the first foundation of Dublin University one might also remark that Pembroke College, Oxford, was later founded by the widow of the Earl of Pembroke, to whom Roger betrothed his son, Roger, on whom he settled his Irish estates, suggesting a connection between Roger and a major educational benefactor.

19. Connolly (ed.), *Irish Exchequer Payments*, states Roger left on 27 September; Richardson and Sayles have 30 September.

20. Gilbert (ed.), *Hist. & Mun. Docs*, p. 392.

7: Rebel

1. For the origins of the Despenser wars, see Davies, 'The Despenser War in Glamorgan', pp. 21–64.

2. Phillips, *Aymer de Valence*, p. 199.

3. *CPR 1317–1321*, p. 523.

4. Denholm-Young (ed.), *Vita*, p. 109.

5. *CCR 1318–1323*, p. 359. Butler was to pay Roger and Joan £1,000 over three and a half years for the marriage. The payment was to be made at Bristol, not in Ireland, thereby signifying Roger's break from Irish affairs for the forseeable future. The Pope granted his permission for the marriage on 21 August 1320. See Blom (ed.), *Papal Registers*, ii, p. 208.

6. Phillips, *Aymer de Valence*, p. 201.

7. *CCR 1318–1323*, p. 363.

8. *CCR 1318–1323*, p. 364.

9. *CCR 1318–1323*, p. 366.

10. Waugh, 'For King, Country and Patron', p. 26, n. 10.

11. Phillips states that the Earl of Hereford attacked Newport and Cardiff, while Roger separately attacked Clun (Phillips, *Aymer de Valence*, p. 205). However, the Wigmore chronicle he quotes clearly notes that Roger personally led the attack on Newport and Cardiff 'with his associates, Humfrey de Bohun, Earl of Hereford, and Roger Mortimer, lord of Chirk' and that after Cardiff he took de Gorges to Wigmore and then occupied Clun. See Dugdale, *Monasticon*, vi, part i, p. 352.

12. Hereford Cathedral Muniments, calendared in NRA 1955, pp. 825–6.
13. *CCR 1318–1323*, pp. 541–3.
14. *CCR 1318–1323*, pp. 541–3.
15. Denholm-Young (ed.), *Vita*, p. 111.
16. The reference to the Marchers attacking the lands of the elder Despenser on the way to London is supported by a line in Stubbs (ed.), *Chronicles illustrative of the reigns of Edward I and II*, i, p. 293, which records their attacks on the way.
17. See Wilkinson, 'The Sherburn Indenture and the Attack on the Despensers, 1321', appendices. For the references to Roger's supposed presence there, see *Complete Peerage*, ix, p. 436 and Phillips, *Aymer de Valence*, p. 206. The meeting supposedly took place on 28 June.
18. For example, the *Modus Tenendi Parliamentorum* – 'the way of holding Parliaments' – was written at this time. See Fryde, *Tyranny and Fall*, pp. 46–7.
19. Denholm-Young (ed.), *Vita*, p. 113.
20. *CPR 1321–1324*, p. 15; BL Harley 1240, f45r. This was dated 20 August.
21. Denholm-Young (ed.), *Vita*, p. 115.
22. Childs and Taylor (eds), *Anonimalle Chronicle*, p. 103.
23. Phillips, *Aymer de Valence*, pp. 217–18. The quote is from Childs and Taylor (eds), *Anonimalle Chronicle*, p. 105.
24. Denholm-Young (ed.), *Vita*, p. 115.

8: The King's Prisoner

1. Roger's goods and chattels were confiscated on 23 January 1322. See *CCR 1318–1323*, p. 415.
2. Adam de Charlton's account was published in 1858. See Lambert B. Larking, 'Inventory of the Effects of Roger de Mortimer at Wigmore Castle and Abbey, Herefordshire, dated 15 Edward II, AD 1322'. The original is in the Public Record Office.
3. *CPR 1321–1324*, p. 77.
4. *CCR 1318–1323*, p. 419.
5. Childs and Taylor (eds), *Anonimalle Chronicle*, p. 107.
6. Arnold le Glover of Hereford was fined 20 marks for speaking to Lord Mortimer of Chirk, and Thomas atte Barre of Hereford received the crippling fine of 100 marks (£66) for speaking to Roger. See *CPR 1321–24*, pp. 64–5.
7. Fryde, *Tyranny and Fall*, p. 62.
8. These details have been taken from Childs and Taylor, *Anonimalle Chronicle*, p. 111. A fuller list is given in Appendix C to the second volume of *Complete Peerage* (2nd edn).
9. Fryde, *Tyranny and Fall*, p. 75.
10. *CPR 1327–1330*, pp. 141–2.
11. Doherty, 'Isabella', pp. 92–4.
12. Fryde, *Tyranny and Fall* p. 155; Denholm-Young (ed.), *Vita*, p. 128.
13. Doherty, 'Isabella', p. 96.
14. Doherty, 'Isabella', p. 98–9.
15. See Doherty, 'Isabella', pp. 94–6, for details of the queen's movements, and the

year-long pilgrimage she was expected to go on, which would have kept her away from Edward until September 1323.

16. Isabella has been accused of plotting to free Roger, as have various other people, including de Gisors, de Bethune, and Adam of Orleton. In all probability the escape was planned by Roger himself, as suggested by the most detailed chronicle (Riley (ed.) *Johannis de Trokelowe*, pp. 145–6). There is supporting circumstantial evidence for this. The escape plan involved a route which required an 'ingenious rope-ladder', or rather a ladder made of ropes slung together, which must have been brought into the castle by Gerard d'Alspaye. This suggests the route out of the castle was planned by someone who knew the castle well: almost certainly someone who was on the inside who knew where Roger was imprisoned. Then there is the form of the rope ladder itself. One cannot help but recall the excellent use of the rope ladders employed by the Scots in capturing the English castles north of the border. The unsuccessful attempt on Berwick Castle demonstrated that these rope ladders allowed not only very quick entries to castles, they allowed very quick exits too. It is likely that whoever dreamed up its application for an escape from the Tower had some knowledge of the Scottish rope ladders, and knew someone in the city who could make one. Then there is the aspect of the *pestiferum potum* used to drug the guards. Whoever organised the plot was able to order the poison to be brought to the castle at short notice, and administered to the guards at a certain time and in a certain place. Finally there is the hole in the wall of the cell, which would have required a crowbar to be used to lever out the stones quickly. Thus whoever planned the escape was in the castle, knew it intimately and had knowledge of people who could work to order on the outside of the city. This could have been d'Alspaye, but it is unlikely that, without Roger's initiative, d'Alspaye could have persuaded his men to be ready for him, or to persuade several high-status merchants to get involved. The most probable explanation is that Roger himself planned his escape, making use of d'Alspaye to smuggle his requests and commands to the many contacts he had made in London over the years. These external collaborators organised the provision of the necessary tools and the means by which Roger could flee.

17. Fryde, *Tyranny and Fall*, p. 143.

18. This is conjecture, based on two facts. These facts are that it is an enormous coincidence that Roger escaped just three or four days before his intended murder or execution, having spent more than eighteen months in the Tower; and that Isabella had been let go to spend a year away from Edward on pilgrimages, able to go where she wanted, and yet she returned to Edward and Despenser, where she was most unwelcome. That Isabella had probably met Roger in the Tower and received a message from him there makes it very plausible that these two facts are connected, and that Isabella was acting as Roger's spy.

19. This is an assumption based on the fact that the chapel he later built at Ludlow was dedicated to St Peter ad Vincula, and it was common at this period for men in extreme situations, such as mariners at sea in a storm, to promise to build chapels in return for their safe delivery. Also the very nature of the saint – St Peter in Chains – may be linked to chroniclers describing St Peter leading Roger out of the Tower.

20. When he received an official pardon for the escape Richard de Monmouth was pardoned in the same words and at the same time. This probably indicates that Roger was not alone at the time of the escape. There is no chronicle evidence that he was accompanied by anyone other than Gerard d'Alspaye, but this is probably due to de Monmouth's relative unimportance. See *CPR 1327–1330*, p. 14.
21. Evans, 'The Family of Mortimer', p. 228.

9: The King's Enemy

1. *CCR 1323–1327*, p. 13.
2. Watson, 'Geoffrey de Mortimer and His Descendants', pp. 1–16.
3. Chaplais (ed.), *St-Sardos*, p. 2.
4. Chaplais (ed), *St-Sardos*, p. 5.
5. Fryde, *Tyranny and Fall*, p. 134.
6. Haines, *Church and Politics*, pp. 144–5.
7. Maunde Thompson (ed.), *Galfridi le Baker*, pp. 16–17.
8. Chaplais (ed.), *St-Sardos*, p. 72.
9. Doherty, 'Isabella', pp. 103–4; Blackley, 'Isabella and the Bishop of Exeter', pp. 225–6.
10. Despenser had been exiled from France in 1321. In 1323 Charles wrote to Edward saying he would banish from France the English exiles and hoped that Edward would banish from England the French exiles living there, i.e. Despenser, reminding him of the opprobrium in which Despenser was held in France. See Chaplais (ed.), *St-Sardos*, pp. 180–1.
11. Fryde, *Tyranny and Fall*, p. 143.
12. Denholm-Young (ed.), *Vita*, p. 136.
13. Chaplais (ed.), *St-Sardos*, p. 72.
14. The authorship of the four options presented to Edward has been considered in detail by Doherty, who concludes that it was Charles's initiative. Given that there was a strong possibility that the prince would be married off to Hainault, and given that Roger was already in Hainault, it seems very probable that the fourth of these options represents a stage in a joint plan to the mutual advantage of Roger and Charles. The lack of any letters or evidence to corroborate this theory has meant that historians investigating this stage of affairs have been unable to conclude that Roger was involved in any planning at all in conjunction with Charles and, more particularly, Isabella, until the end of 1325. In the case of highly secret proceedings, however, probably conducted by the King of France's personal messengers, one would not expect to find any written evidence. Whether one accepts that Charles and Roger were acting in accordance over this issue is entirely a matter of whether one believes later events – particularly the marriage of Edward to Philippa – can be taken as evidence of planning by Roger and Charles at the end of 1323. I believe later events in this case are a strong indication, especially as such a marriage had already been discussed before Roger's rebellion, and thus Roger was aware of its acceptability to the Count of Hainault.

15. Chaplais (ed.), *St-Sardos*, p. 196. One might regard this as evidence that Edward suspected Isabella had colluded with Roger before his escape.
16. Denholm-Young (ed.), *Vita*, p. 135.
17. Brown, 'Diplomacy, Adultery, and Domestic Politics'.
18. Brown, 'Diplomacy, Adultery, and Domestic Politics', pp. 66–72.
19. Doherty, 'Isabella', p. 119.
20. The most perplexing subject in the story of Roger and Isabella's affair is when their personal relationship started. Some scholars insist on the validity of a document-based approach. Doherty states that there is no evidence for Roger and Isabella being in a relationship of any sort before December 1325 (p. 126) and then states that the liaison between Roger and Isabella 'was formed after the queen's refusal to return home, and that Mortimer was not the cause of this refusal' (p. 168). This is too empirical: both Roger and Isabella were quite capable of leading Edward and Despenser astray. There is no proof that Roger and Isabella had *not* formed an attachment before September 1325. One would hardly expect to find written evidence of it before the prince was in France, nor while Isabella sought to obtain favours and money from England under the cover of continued loyalty.
21. Chaplais (ed.), *St-Sardos*, p. 103.
22. The reasons for supposing these two men might have been waiting to act against Despenser are firstly their immediate support for Roger and Isabella when they landed in September 1326; secondly, Henry's actions in trying to persuade the king to leave England in August 1325. It was to Thomas, Earl of Norfolk's lands that the invaders went in 1326. That Despenser had intelligence as early as September 1324 that Roger was expected to land in Thomas's lands in Norfolk and Suffolk (Chaplais (ed.), *St-Sardos*, p. 72), suggests that some contact on the subject of rebellion had been made between Roger and Thomas two years before the invasion actually occurred.
23. Although there is no record of Isabella directly being asked to return to England before October, the cessation of funds and her moving to the King of France's palace in mid-July suggests that with his reply ratifying the treaty, Edward sought his wife's return. On her failure, he cut off her money, the last payment being made four days after the ratification of the treaty by Edward. On 18 October, when he wrote to the Pope on the matter, he stated that he had asked her to return before his son was sent to France. Hence it seems that the initial demand for her return was made in late June, and had been repeated from July onwards. See Doherty, 'Isabella', pp. 122–3.
24. Denholm-Young (ed.), *Vita*, p. 142.
25. See Denholm-Young (ed.), *Vita*, p. 143, written within the year, for the source that the declaration was delivered in the presence of Charles and Isabella together.
26. Denholm-Young (ed.), *Vita*, p. 142.
27. Aungier (ed.), *French Chronicle of London*, p. 49.
28. *CCR 1323–1327*, p. 580.
29. It is possible that on the occasion they communicated in the Tower they had not actually met, in which case they had not seen one another since August 1321. They would have parted on very poor terms on that occasion, as it was before the attack

on Leeds Castle. However, it is much more likely that they met and confided in one another in the Tower in February 1323, as stated in the previous chapter.

30. *CCR 1323–1327*, p. 533.

31. *CCR 1323–1327*, p. 578.

32. The marriage of the Earl of Kent and Margaret Wake was given papal permission on 6 October and probably took place in December, thus possibly being the reason for Roger's coming to the French court at that time. The marriage would have been negotiated some time earlier, suggesting that the earl was in consultation with Roger's camp for some time beforehand. Margaret was the daughter of Roger's mother's sister, Joan de Fiennes. See *Complete Peerage*, vii, p. 146, and xiv, p. 623.

33. There are two sources for this detail. The briefer one is Despenser, who mentioned the fact to a papal legate, according to the *Historia Roffensis* quoted in Doherty, 'Isabella', p. 135. The other, which mentions the knife, is Prince Edward himself, at Roger's trial. See *Rotuli parliamentorum*, ii, p. 53.

34. Doherty, 'Isabella', p. 135.

35. Doherty, 'Isabella', p. 140.

36. Doherty, 'Isabella', p. 150.

37. Froissart claims three hundred men only.

38. Doherty, 'Isabella', p. 150.

10: Invader

1. The date and exact location are confused in the various chronicles. The clearest and most explicit is the 'Annales Paulini' in Stubbs (ed.), *Chronicles*, pp. 313–14. Saul states at the beginning of his 'The Despensers and the Downfall of Edward II' that the army landed on 26 September at Walton-on-the-Naze. With regard to the date he is following Murimuth, among others, who places the invasion at Orwell (with the exception of one copyist, noted as 'C' in the Rolls series publication, who has corrected the entry to 'Wednesday before Michaelmas' (24 September)). The matter is dealt with in more detail by Round, 'The Landing of Queen Isabella', pp. 104–5. The exact location agreed on by most modern scholars is the Colvasse peninsula.

2. One possible explanation for this is that de Sturmy was a supporter of Roger's. The name de Sturmy was not a common one, and sixteen years earlier one William de Sturmy had been pardoned for murder – and thus his life had been saved – at Roger's request. Even if this pardon did not affect John de Sturmy's allegiance, it is noticeable that he supported the invaders very soon after their landing. This might explain how Roger managed to pass messages to English lords despite the king's orders for all ports to search all cargoes coming into the country. For the pardon of William de Sturmy in 1308 see *CPR 1307–1313*, p. 52. For grants to John de Sturmy see the numerous references in *CPR 1327–1330*.

3. *CPR 1323–1327*, p. 327.

4. *CCR 1323–1327*, pp. 650–1.

5. Doherty, 'Isabella', p. 159.

6. Buck, *Politics, Finance*, p. 220.

7. Saul, 'The Despensers and the Downfall of Edward II', pp. 14–15.

8. Doherty, 'Isabella', p. 164; Fryde, *Tyranny and Fall*, p. 191.

9. Doherty's thesis is a prime example. But he admits that it is very strange that Edward II was destroyed by his queen, whom he describes as being of relatively minor political importance before her invasion. Only a biographer of Isabella would resist the obvious conclusion: that it was not Isabella but Roger who was the mastermind in the toppling of the regime, although Isabella was the crucial figurehead. Doherty merely states it is ironic that the invasion showed the previously hidden aspect of Isabella's personality, which was a genius for organising and plotting completely contrary to her character in earlier years. May McKisack more accurately points to Roger as the real influence on the government of the realm at this time in her classic work, *The Fourteenth Century*, p. 97.

10. Thompson (ed.), *Murimuth*, p. 50.

11. *CPR 1323–1327*, p. 655.

12. In establishing the relative roles of Isabella and Roger one should also consider later evidence, particularly Roger's role in the deposition of the king in January 1327 and the Berkeley Castle plot the following September. Since he was in charge of both of these latter two processes, there is every likelihood he was the principal protagonist in the declaration of 26 October.

13. Harding, 'Isabella and Mortimer', p. 17; Stubbs (ed.), *Chronicles*, pp. 317–18.

14. The phrase is slightly paraphrased. The original states that the Earl of Arundel, John Daniel and Thomas de Micheldever were beheaded 'per procurationem domini R[ogeri] de Mortuo Mari, qui perfecto odio oderat illos et cujus consilium regina per omnia sequebatur'. Thompson (ed.), *Murimuth*, p. 50.

15. Holmes, 'Judgement on the Younger Despenser, 1326', pp. 261–7; Taylor, 'The Judgement on Hugh Despenser the Younger', pp. 70–7; Doherty, 'Isabella', p. 166.

16. Brie (ed.), *The Brut*, ii, p. 239. He was not taken to London since he may have been able successfully to starve himself to death before then.

17. It is interesting that this figure exactly matches the amount of damage supposed to have been done by Roger and the Earl of Hereford in their war against the Despensers in 1321.

18. After Boroughbridge de Harclay had been made Earl of Carlisle, but had been executed as a traitor a year later for negotiating a peace settlement with the Scots and discussing recognising the independence of Scotland without the king's permission.

19. Holmes, 'Judgement on the Younger Despenser, 1326', pp. 261–7.

20. The cutting off of his penis and testicles is on the authority of Froissart, who states his private parts were removed. In view of the unofficial but known practice of severing the genitals of traitors – for example de Montfort's testicles (see p. 8) – it is likely that Froissart reflects the actual punishment more closely than the official sentence.

11: Revolutionary

1. Joan never remarried after Roger's death, nor did she enter a nunnery. One can only interpret this as a sign she was content to be Lady Mortimer for ever, and remained faithful to her husband's memory.

2. Eyton, *Shropshire*, xi, p. 329. If Roger and Joan did not meet up at Pembridge in November 1326, then, unless she came to court in the meantime, the next most likely date is March or April 1327, when Roger was probably in the Marches and away from Isabella.

3. Vale, *Edward III and Chivalry*, p. 169.

4. *CPR 1321–1324*, p. 77.

5. Roger, as mentioned, included her in the Leintwardine chantry list of prayers, and never sought a separation from the Pope. Joan was close enough to Roger in 1330 that Edward III accused her of complicity in some of Roger's dealings. Roger occasionally made trips to the Welsh Marches, sometimes with and sometimes without the royal family; and those undertaken by himself may well have been to see Joan.

6. The chroniclers are very confused on the order and details of events concerning the deposition of Edward II. Several writers have attempted reconstructions, most notably Clarke, 'Committees of Estates'; Fryde, *Tyranny and Fall*, pp. 195–200; Harding, 'Isabella and Mortimer', pp. 35–53; and most significantly Valente, 'Deposition and Abdication'. Valente's is the most recent, convincing and useful of these. The parliament had originally been summoned for 14 December; it had probably been delayed owing to the continued rioting.

7. I suspect that they never intended to bring the king to the parliament. Had the king's presence been truly desired, a more important delegation would have been sent to him, headed at least by an earl, and a stronger retinue would have been sent than that likely to have been commanded by two bishops.

8. Fryde, in her *Tyranny and Fall*, p. 197, states that the bishops went to Kenilworth on 7 January and that the assembly adjourned during their absence, until their return on 12 January. As Harding points out, this is not realistic, as Kenilworth is ninety miles from London and the round trip in January would take at least seven days. See Harding, 'Isabella and Mortimer', p. 38. Valente agrees, although she seems not to have consulted Harding. See Valente, 'Deposition and Abdication', p. 855.

9. Valente's otherwise convincing account is very slightly marred here by her error in timing the events of 13 January. She places the Guildhall meeting before the session in Parliament at Westminster on the grounds that Orleton ordered Parliament to turn up in the afternoon. The text of the *Historia Roffensis* which she uses here, which reads that Parliament should return 'at the third hour after eating and drinking', does not indicate an afternoon session but a morning one. The medieval day was counted from about 6 a.m., and thus the third hour was about 9 a.m. The reference to eating and drinking is due to the fact that in the fourteenth century most people ate two meals a day, one at about 10 a.m. and another in the late afternoon. Thus they were being asked to assemble earlier than usual, and to eat earlier than usual in preparation for a long session.

10. Fryde, *Tyranny and Fall*, p. 200. This speech, which is longer in the unreferenced passage quoted by Fryde, may have been part of a speech delivered at a later occasion. So confused are the chronicles on the actual details of these proceedings that it is difficult to say for certain which prelates' speeches were delivered when, except Orleton's, which was definitely given on 13 January.

11. *Notes and Queries*, 6th series, viii, pp. 404–5.

12. Doherty states that the only explanation of why the eventual oath was different

to the oath de Bethune mentioned in his letter was that de Bethune overstepped the mark. It is equally possible and far more likely, given the order of events of the day, that the deposition oath was held as a threat over those not in favour during the Parliamentary discussions, enforcing the silence of the opposition. Once the deposition had been agreed in Parliament, there was no need to include this element of the oath. The prince is still referred to as Isabella's son (rather than as the king) because the deputation to Kenilworth had not yet seen the king to force the king to abdicate, which was always the prime intention of the deposers, and to do the official acts of renouncing homage and disbanding the royal household, etc. See Doherty, 'Isabella', p. 187, and Valente, 'Deposition and Abdication', *passim*.

13. Valente, 'Deposition and Abdication', pp. 880–1.
14. *CCR 1327–1330*, p. 1.
15. Harding, 'Isabella and Mortimer', p. 41, quoting PRO E101/382/8.
16. Harding, 'Isabella and Mortimer', p. 54, quoting PRO E101/382/8.
17. Some sources state Henry of Lancaster, not John of Hainault, knighted him. The matter remains in doubt.
18. The description of the medal comes from Barnes, *Edward III*, p. 4.
19. *CPR 1327–1330*, p. 22. Note at this time only the marriage was granted; wardship of the lands was not granted until October.
20. The wardship of Warwick was granted in 1318; that of Audley in 1316. These should not be regarded as new grants as some writers suggest.
21. The only known membership of the council appears in *The Brut*. This lists the Archbishops of Canterbury and York, Bishop Stratford and Bishop Orleton, the Earls of Lancaster, Norfolk, Kent and Surrey, and four barons: Thomas Wake, Henry Percy, Oliver Ingham and John de Ros. See Brie (ed.), *The Brut*, pp. 254–5. However, as Doherty has pointed out, the Rolls of Parliament mention fourteen members of the council, there being six barons. See Doherty, 'Isabella', p. 199.
22. Doherty accounts for the queen's expenses, and points out that she only needed from this vast wealth to pay her mercenaries' expenses for one month. See Doherty, 'Isabella', pp. 203–4.
23. Doherty, 'Isabella', pp. 208–9.
24. Clarke *et al.* (eds), *Foedera*, iii, p. 309.
25. Thompson (ed.), *Galfridi le Baker*, p. 31. For his service with Roger, see *CPR 1321–1324*, p. 17.
26. Doherty doubts that Edward was removed by force from Kenilworth, claiming that there is evidence of a peaceful transfer of custody because there was a contract drawn up between Berkeley and Lancaster, and also because Roger would have had to use an army to take the king. One suspects that some trickery was afoot. It is possible that Isabella prevailed upon Lancaster, who was still at court, to draw up the indenture with Berkeley, while Roger at or near Kenilworth prevailed upon the constable to hand over the deposed king. It seems very strange that Lancaster should have accused Roger the following year of taking the king from Kenilworth by force if it was a false accusation, as he was trying to keep the moral high ground. One suspects that, even if the indenture was made in good faith, Roger was nearby with a force of men-at-arms. See Doherty, 'Isabella', p. 208.
27. See Doherty, 'Isabella', pp. 214–34, and Harding, 'Isabella and Mortimer',

pp. 203–28, for the basic narrative. To Doherty is due the credit for discovering the dealings between Roger and Isabella in exile and the Scots.

28. Barbour, *The Bruce*, ii (1968 reprint of vols ii and iii in one vol.), pp. 473–94. Certain allowances have to be made for Barbour's glorification of his hero, his being a literary work in praise of Bruce. Numbers of opponents and Englishmen killed are exaggerated. However, so complete was the Scottish success in outwitting the English on this campaign that Barbour did not have to exaggerate very often to make the Scots appear glorious in their retreat.

29. Our knowledge of Edward's escape from Berkeley Castle is based on a letter from Thomas de Berkeley dated 27 July. This was addressed to the Chancellor, John de Hothum, and so Roger had probably already been informed several days earlier by express messengers. Thus the release of the deposed king could have been achieved at any time before this. The dating of the receipt of the news to 1 July (Harding revised the calendered date of 11 July) is because on that day Maltravers and Berkeley were granted the position of keepers of the peace for almost all of the region in accordance with the Statute of Winchester. See *CPR 1327–1330*, p. 154; Harding, 'Isabella and Mortimer', p. 136; Doherty, 'Isabella', p. 229; Haines, 'Afterlife', pp. 69–70.

30. *Complete Peerage*, vii, p. 399.

31. Barbour, *The Bruce*, ii, p. 479.

32. Brie (ed.), *The Brut*, pp. 250–1.

33. This is touched upon, although not explicitly with reference to Scotland, in the final accusations against him at the end of his life, for which see *Rotuli parliamentorum*, ii, p. 52; Roger is more specifically referred to in the longer *Brut* as a traitor for his actions. See Brie (ed.), *The Brut*, pp. 250–1.

34. Barbour says this was after eight nights; le Bel, quoted by Froissart, says the first night. Barbour seems more reliable, although not an eyewitness like le Bel, since he states that for eight days nothing happened while the Scots tried to find a way to attack the English from their well-defended position.

35. *CCR 1327–1330*, pp. 217–18. This order has possibly been very slightly misunderstood by certain writers. Roger had lieutenants in both North and South Wales, therefore he did not need to go in person to root out the 'malefactors and disturbers of the peace', and so the order cannot be seen as the reason for his departure. Significantly it was issued under the privy seal, i.e. probably at Roger's order, and so was in reality an order to himself. Thus it was probably a cover for Roger's departure from court at this time, not the reason for it.

12: The King's Murderer?

1. Harding, 'Isabella and Mortimer', p. 145. Thomas Gurney carried the message from Berkeley, as shown by the sole entry in the Berkeley expenses. See Haines, 'Afterlife', p. 85, n. 98. Smyth, *Lives of the Berkeleys*, i, p. 296.

2. Doherty, 'Isabella', p. 228.

3. Moore, 'Documents Relating to the Death and Burial of King Edward II', p. 217. With regard to the date, although Doherty states that the corpse was moved

sometime after 10 November, the account states definitely that Maltravers and Berkeley on 21 October 'liberaverunt corpus dicti defuncti Abbati Sancti Petri Cloucestrie apud Gloucestriam per breve Regis . . .' See Doherty, 'Isabella', p. 231; Moore, 'Documents', p. 223.

4. Moore, 'Documents', p. 226. The text of the account specifies his watching from the day of the death, 'videlicet xxj Septembris quo die Rex obijt usque xx diem Decembris proximum sequentem'.

5. Moore, 'Documents', pp. 223–6.

6. *CPR 1327–1330*, p. 37.

7. Hope, 'On the Funeral Effigies of the Kings and Queens of England', pp. 517–70, especially with reference to the bodies of Edward I, pp. 528–9, and Richard II, p. 533. See also report of the opening of Edward I's tomb in the first volume of *Archaeologia*. The embalming process would have been expected to occur immediately after death, as happened with Edward III.

8. According to PRO C53/114 (no. 20), Roger was at Doncaster with the court on 26 August. He was ordered on 4 September to inquire into conspiracies in South Wales against the government (*CCR 1327–1330*, pp. 217–18), and probably left the court at Nottingham at about that time. We have no certain information as to his whereabouts apart from the later court case involving William de Shalford in 1331, mentioned in the text, until he was once more back at Nottingham on 4 October (PRO C53/114 (no. 15)). The possibility that he met Berkeley and discussed the fate of Edward II with him is not out of the question. The acknowledgement in March the following year that he owed Thomas de Berkeley £850 might or might not reflect a deal between the two men. See *CCR 1327–1330*, p. 369.

9. Tout, 'Captivity and Death of Edward of Carnarvon', pp. 109–10. Confirmation that William de Shalford was indeed Roger's deputy in North Wales at this time is to be found in *CPR 1327–1330*, p. 194.

10. Stubbs (ed.) *Chronicles illustrative of the reigns of Edward I and Edward II*, i, pp. 337–8.

11. According to the *DNB*, he travelled to Exeter in June, after the death of the Bishop of Exeter, James Berkeley. He remained in Exeter until the autumn, as John de Grandison was appointed in October.

12. Gransden, *Historical Writing*, ii, p. 30. She refers to it as a diary but, as the 'diary' genre as we know it did not evolve until the late sixteenth/early seventeenth century, this description is perhaps a little misleading.

13. Lords travelling on the Continent, of the status of minor earls or bishops, might expect about £2 for themselves. Maltravers and Berkeley, while lesser men, were doing a very dangerous and unusual job. A combined fee of £3 would not be unreasonable.

14. Thompson (ed.), *Murimuth*, pp. 52–3, 63–4.

15. The word 'superficialiter' has allowed historians all sorts of looseness in interpreting the death. One in particular goes so far as to translate the word as meaning the observers' view was 'a very distant one' and she goes on to use this evidence in conjunction with oak barriers mentioned later in the text to suggest that Edward was kept out of sight. See Fryde, *Tyranny and Fall*, p. 202. The matter is dealt with more fully in Chapter 12 Revisited.

16. Brie (ed.), *The Brut*, pp. 252–3. See also Taylor, 'The French *Brut*', pp. 423–37.
17. Quoted from the translation of the French in Childs and Taylor (eds), *Anonimalle Chronicle*, p. 135. This version was finalised after 1337. See Taylor, *English Historical Literature in the Fourteenth Century*, p. 139.
18. Aungier (ed.) *French Chronicle of London*, p. 58. The most concentrated writing on the background of the *Brut*, by Taylor, has suggested that the original shorter *Brut* was begun in London by a clerk connected with the courts or a government office, and that he moved to York with the shift of the administration in 1332–6. Taylor favours a date for the *French Chronicle* about ten years after the compilation of the shorter *Brut*. See Taylor, *English Historical Literature*, p. 123.
19. Gransden, *Historical Writing*, ii, pp. 74–5. On the Lancastrian nature of the longer *Brut*, Taylor comments that 'no other chronicle of the period carries Lancastrian partisanship quite so far'. See Taylor, *English Historical Writing*, p. 124.
20. The mid-fourteenth-century English translation in the Early English Text Society series has been used. Bried (ed.), *The Brut*, pp. 252–3.
21. Brie (ed.), *The Brut*, p. 264.
22. See Taylor, 'French *Brut*', p. 435, in which further evidence of this journal-like method of compiling the chronicle is mentioned. The reason for picking 1329 as the most likely date for writing the earlier entry is a suspicion that the war between Roger and Lancaster at the end of 1328 triggered the red-hot poker rumours of the king's death. It could be as early as 1327 or as late as 1332.
23. This has been modernised from the mid-fourteenth-century English translation in Brie, *The Brut*, p. 253.
24. Stubbs (ed.), *Chronicles illustrative of the reigns of Edward I and Edward II*, ii, p. 97.
25. Lumby (ed.), *Polychronicon*, viii, p. 324.
26. Taylor, *Universal Chronicle, passim*; Gransden, *Historical Writing*, ii, pp. 44–5.
27. This is also known as the continuation of the chronicle of Walter of Hemingburgh. See Hamilton, *Hemingburgh*, p. 297.
28. Tait (ed.), *Chronica Johannis de Reading and Anonymi Cantuarensis*, p. 78.
29. *CPR 1321–1324*, p. 17.
30. See Hunter, 'Measures Taken for the Apprehension of Thomas Gurney', p. 283, which shows that as late as 1332 very minor characters were being arrested for complicity in the plot.
31. Tout, 'Captivity and Death', p. 83, quoting Stubbs (ed.), 'Annales Paulini' in *Chronicles illustrative of the reigns of Edward I and Edward II*, i, p. 333.
32. Haines, *Church and Politics*, pp. 26–9, 228. In the course of this mission news was received by the Pope that the Bishop of Worcester had just died, and Orleton sought and obtained the see for himself, trusting Roger and Isabella would support him. When he returned to England, he found them less than happy with his new title. However, in September 1327 he was not yet out of favour, as some historians have suggested, just a very long way from Berkeley.
33. Doherty, 'Isabella', p. 224. Gransden points out it is an often used device. See Gransden, *Historical Writing*, ii, p. 41.
34. Thompson (ed.), *Galfridi le Baker*, p. 33.
35. See the tomb of Edward in Gloucester for the clearest evidence of Edward's beard. While it can be argued that this is not in fact a portrait but rather a stylised emblem

of a monarch, all the images of Edward in his later years are bearded, and one must presume therefore that, even if all of these were emblematic rather than portraits, the king himself would definitely have tried to look like the emblem. Shaving the beard off therefore might have been an insult to the king. If this was the case, though, the temperature of the water was not the issue.

13: *King in all but Name*

1. Edward II had sought a divorce from Isabella even before the invasion; after the death of the Despensers he would have sought a separation from the Pope and shown her no mercy.
2. As well as being Berkeley's retainer, Gurney had served alongside John Maltravers in the household of the Earl of Pembroke and had been a fellow prisoner with Roger in the Tower of London in 1322–3. Phillips, *Aymer de Valence*, pp. 256, 262. Fryde, *Tyranny and Fall*, p. 160.
3. The first and last of these names are tentatively included from the Fieschi letter. See Chapter 12 Revisited.
4. Harding, 'Isabella and Mortimer', p. 145. Haines, 'Afterlife', p. 85, n. 98. The accounts of Lord Berkeley mention Gurney being despatched with letters for the king, Mortimer and the queen mother. See Smyth, *Lives of the Berkeleys*, i, pp. 296–7.
5. Harding, 'Isabella and Mortimer', p. 145, quoting PRO DL 10/253.
6. Smyth, *Lives of the Berkeleys* i, p. 297. The most likely reason for this was that the king was being transported in disguise across the south-west.
7. Isabella was eventually buried with the heart of the real Edward II beneath her tomb, many years later. The correlation of the presentation of a false heart and the burial of the real one suggests that this was her specific request. It is, of course, possible that the removal of the heart was merely customary. Heart burial was not at all uncommon in this period: the heart of a royal kinsman of Roger's, Henry of Almaine, lay in a silver vase on the altar of Westminster Abbey.
8. There is no doubt that Gloucester was specifically chosen; Abbot Thoky's claim that he was merciful in giving the king's corpse a resting place when others did not dare do so is pure fiction. See Doherty, 'Isabella', p. 230.
9. Doherty, 'Isabella', pp. 231–2; Harding, 'Isabella and Mortimer', pp. 147–9; Moore, 'Documents', *passim*; Haines, 'Afterlife', p. 75; Tout, 'Captivity and Death', pp. 92–3.
10. Roger was drawn to his execution in the same tunic three years later. See Thompson (ed.), *Murimuth*, p. 62, n. 11.
11. The question of whether Isabella was involved equally in the Berkeley Castle plot is a complicated one. The only directly relevant piece of evidence we have is Hugh de Glanville's account, which states that, having spent four days at Gloucester after the burial of the king, he spent two days travelling to Worcester 'bringing a certain woman who embalmed the king to the queen by the king's order, staying there one day, and from there for four days returning to York'. It is interesting that de Glanville states that he took her to Isabella. On the face of it this suggests that it was Isabella who had doubts about the corpse, not the king. However, there are reasons to doubt that Roger deceived her over her

husband's death. If Isabella was of the opinion in September 1327 that, regretfully, her husband had to die, then the plot to keep him secretly alive would not have met with her approval, and the rewards heaped upon Berkeley and Maltravers for their part in the Berkeley Castle plot would not have come from her hands. It is unlikely that Maltravers in particular would have become Steward of the Royal Household if he had jeopardised her position in this way without her approval. Thus we can be relatively confident that Isabella knew and sanctioned the plot to keep her husband secretly alive, even though it placed her in increased danger. From this we may infer that there would have been no advantage to Roger pretending to her that Edward was dead between September and December 1327, and indeed, such a pretence of the man's death and tricking of Isabella would have been a heavy strain on their relationship. Thus it is highly likely that Isabella knew in September 1327 that her husband was not dead. When the woman who had embalmed the corpse was taken to Worcester, she was probably led to the queen so that Isabella could question her in front of her son privately in order to demonstrate to him that his father was, indeed, alive. See Moore, 'Documents', p. 226, for Hugh de Glanville's account and the detail of the woman being summoned. It is interesting that there was an attempt to suppress this piece of information, suggesting that the visit was sensitive and needed to be eradicated from the official account. The text of the account submitted to the Exchequer does not mention the woman. She only appears in Glanville's own particulars, which read: '*Et eidem moranti apud Gloucestriam ad computandum cum ministris Regis per iiij^{or} dies post sepulturam corporis dicti Regis et redeundo de ibidem usque Wygorn' ducendo quandam mulierem que exviceravit Regem ad Reginam precepto Regis per duos dies morando ibidem per unum diem et abinde redeundo usque Eboracum per iiij^{or} dies capienti ut supra xxxv.s ix.d.*' In the submitted account de Glanville simply spent seven days returning to York.

12. *CPR 1327–1330*, p. 192. Holand's lands had been granted back to him on 2 December after his petition to Parliament in September. The Sheriff of Lancashire refused to hand them over. See Doherty, 'Isabella', p. 238. Holand's wife had been restored her lands the previous March, and Holand himself had been given a pardon for escaping from gaol during Despenser's regime in February, so there may have been a deliberate courting of Holand by Roger and Isabella in anticipation of the Earl of Lancaster's opposition.

13. Doherty, 'Isabella', p. 229.

14. *CCR 1327–1330*, p. 261.

15. Doherty, 'Isabella', p. 234.

16. *CPR 1327–1330*, pp. 163, 166.

17. *CPR 1327–1330*, p. 326.

18. See also Doherty, 'Isabella', p. 244, for a second opinion on the use of the privy seal. He uses evidence from the parliament at Northampton which sought to curb the use of the privy seal.

19. Tout, *Chapters in English Administrative History*, vi, p. 46. Obviously this appointment was to the king's satisfaction, as Gilbert kept the post until 1334.

20. *CCR 1327–1330*, p. 262. Roger had been promised 2,000 marks at the English Exchequer, and the same at the exchequers of Dublin and Carnarvon. He had

bought the right of marrying Thomas de Beauchamp for his daughter with 500 marks of the English debt, and had received only 225 marks from Wales and 348 from Dublin.

21. Thompson (ed.), *Murimuth*, p. 57.

22. Murimuth (p. 57) states that at this time there was a double wedding at Hereford in which two of Roger's daughters married two heirs, namely Laurence de Hastings and Edward of Norfolk. This is almost certainly a mistake. It is unlikely that Roger's daughters, Agnes and Beatrice, could have been so advantageously matched before Roger was himself an earl, which did not occur until October 1328. Also it is unlikely that the Earl of Norfolk would have allowed his son and heir to marry Roger's daughter when he was considering rebellion against him, as he was in the summer of 1328. The jousting mentioned by Murimuth in the context of the double wedding is probably the same as the jousting mentioned by Knighton and the longer version of the *Brut* as a Round Table tournament. The earliest of these sources, the *Brut*, places this in 1329; Knighton (p. 449) seems to have copied Murimuth in having one Hereford event, a Round Table tournament, in 1328 (his copyists in turn have mistaken 'Hereford' for 'Bedford' in one manuscript and 'Hertford' in another). It is likely therefore that there were in fact two Mortimer double weddings, one at Hereford at the end of May 1328, and one in autumn 1329, possibly also at Hereford. If this is correct, the pair of daughters married on the first occasion were Catherine and Joan, not Agnes and Beatrice, whose husbands were granted their lands in February and June 1329 respectively. Since Murimuth was working from his memoranda book, it seems likely that he copied his entry relating to the wedding in 1328 at Hereford correctly, since the court was indeed at Hereford at the time he mentions, but then in 1337 he added from memory the names of two of the most eminent heirs to have married Mortimer daughters, who were married at the later event. The text only includes the names of the heirs as an afterthought, the original seems merely to have read that Roger's daughters married 'quosdam nobiles'. See Appendix 2.

23. *CCR 1327–1330*, p. 293. The association of this lead with Wigmore is an assumption based on the fact that Ludlow was probably completed by June 1328, as indicated by Roger's invitation to the king to visit, but Wigmore was not fit for royal inspection for another year. It is also possible that Roger rebuilt one of his manor houses which has not survived, and that the lead went there instead.

24. While there is every possibility that the good burghers of Wigmore themselves paid for this, the architectural style of the early fourteenth-century south aisle, its features in common with Ludlow and Wigmore, its demonstrative and aristocratic use of light, and the dramatic rise in Roger's fortunes at this time suggest he was involved in this project.

25. Blom (ed.), *Calendar of Papal Registers*, ii, p. 349.

26. Dugdale, *Monasticon*, vi, part iii, p. 352. The priests were not financed until later in the year, but it is probable that in Roger's presence a mass was sung on the occasion of its consecration.

27. This inventory is from an account made by William de Shalford in the PRO, dated 25 November 1331, and transcribed as appendix iii of Harding, 'Isabella and Mortimer', pp. 389–91. The original is PRO E372/179, m22.

28. *Notes and Queries*, 11th series, x, p. 126.

29. Doherty, 'Isabella', p. 249.

30. Edward did not trust Lancaster enough to tell him of the survival of Edward II, as shown by later evidence from 1328 showing Lancaster almost certainly learnt this from the Earl of Kent. Lancaster also approached Edward in a hostile fashion later in the year.

31. Geoffrey appears several times on the Charter Rolls as a witness. He was also made heir to Joan's inheritance of the lordship of Trim in Ireland in 1336, although her grandson Roger was the rightful heir.

32. Harding, 'Isabella and Mortimer', p. 162; Doherty, 'Isabella', p. 251.

33. The accusations are from Brie (ed.), *The Brut*, i, p. 259.

34. The usually accepted date is 7 October, but 15 October has been proposed as more likely. See Harding, 'Isabella and Mortimer', pp. 166–7 for a discussion of the actual date.

35. Thomas (ed.), *Plea & Memoranda Rolls*, p. 82; Doherty, 'Isabella', p. 260.

36. Doherty, 'Isabella', p. 260; Harding, 'Isabella and Mortimer', p. 170; Thomas (ed.), *Plea & Memoranda Rolls*, p. 82.

37. PRO C53/115 (no. 26, dated 30 October). This shows Roger was not referred to as an earl on the second to last day of the parliament, so either he was created that night or the following day. He is referred to as Earl of March in PRO C53/115 (no. 11, dated 3 November).

38. *CPR 1327–1330*, p. 343.

39. There is no hard evidence as to the dates of either of these deaths. Roger died some time before 27 August 1328, as shown by the shift of the grant of all the Irish estates to John at this time. See *CPR 1327–1330*, p. 317. John's death is recorded by the Wigmore chronicler as occuring some time in 1328, and was clearly after 27 August. See Dugdale, *Monasticon*, vi, part iii, p. 352.

40. Thompson (ed.), *Murimuth*, p. 255.

41. Doherty, 'Isabella', p. 294, quoting Thomas, *Plea & Memoranda Rolls*, p. 77.

42. Doherty, 'Isabella', p. 265.

43. The clause in Magna Carta to which they were probably referring was no. 39: 'No free man shall be seized or imprisoned, or stripped of his rights or possessions, or outlawed or exiled, or deprived of his standing in any other way . . . except by the lawful judgement of his equals or by the law of the land'. See Davis, *Magna Carta*, p. 28.

44. See Doherty, 'Isabella', pp. 253–68 for a good outline of the move towards war in 1328–9.

14: King of Folly

1. Harding, 'Isabella and Mortimer', pp. 180–1; Doherty, 'Isabella', p. 274.

2. Later his supporters managed to organise his removal to the custody of the Bishop of London, on his estates in Essex.

3. Brie (ed.) *The Brut*, ii, p. 262.

4. Doherty, 'Isabella', p. 279.

5. PRO E101/384/1 f17v. My thanks to Paul Dryburgh for this reference.

6. Brie (ed.), *The Brut*, ii, p. 261.

7. Joliffe (ed.), *Froissart's Chronicles*, p. 52.

8. Doherty, 'Isabella', p. 287. Although she had not made a similar settlement before the births of her other three children, as Doherty says, there was no need as the initial grant would have held good for all four.

9. This is taken from the account in the published version; *CPR 1327–1330*, p. 343.

10. Eyton, *Shropshire*, xi, p. 324. This relates to BL Harley MS 1240, the later fourteenth-century Mortimer family cartulary.

11. This is according to *Complete Peerage*. It is to be noted that the *Anonimalle Chronicle* mentions an Earl of Lincoln arrested in March 1330 along with the Earl of Kent. This is difficult to explain. Ebulo Lestrange, who is the most likely person mistakenly to have been called Earl of Lincoln, seems not to have been arrested at this time. He was no friend of Roger's, however, as shown by the fact that his lands were assumed late in 1330 by Roger. Also he, together with Thomas Wake, and the sons of the Earl of Hereford, were ordered to bring Isabella to Edward after Roger's death. See *CPR 1327–1330*, p. 36.

12. See *Rotuli parliamentorum*, ii, p. 57, for a list of what was claimed. Clifford, Donnington and Dinbaud castles were among those Roger had acquired or would acquire for himself and his family, along with the manor of Glasebury.

13. A few further words might be added to this theory. Firstly it is highly likely that any child of Roger's and Isabella's would be created an earl, as all English royal sons for the past century had been created earls. This was despite the illegitimacy: a son would have been the half-brother of the King of England, half-brother of the Earl of Cornwall, a half-brother of the future Earl of March, a first cousin once removed of the King of France, and a brother-in-law of the King of Scotland and the Earls of Warwick, Pembroke and Norfolk. The Countess of Lincoln could have been induced to adopt the boy as her own, perhaps by pretending he was her own offspring, and thus to perpetuate the title while removing from Roger and Isabella the possible embarrassment of having very publicly to create a new earldom. This was not possible with any other English earldom at this time. As for making a baby an earl, Edward III himself had been made Earl of Chester at the age of eleven days, so such a move was not strange to Isabella. Finally if this theory is correct, it may possibly explain the unidentified Mortimer effigy in Montgomery church. This figure, which is normally said to be that of Sir Edmund Mortimer, d. 1409 (Roger's great-great-grandson), dates from about 1400. It is of a member of the main line of the Earls of March, but the arms are differenced by a bend. Montgomery Castle was granted to the Mortimers after Isabella's death in line with her settlement, and it would be expected that, if allowed to live, the illegitimate son of Roger and Isabella joined the retinue of his elder brother's son, Roger Mortimer, second Earl of March, of whom he would have been a contemporary. See 'Two Effigies in Montgomery Church', pp. 76–9.

14. The otherwise explicable periods of stasis are: the stay at London during and following the deposition and abdication proceedings, the Scots campaign that same year (during which Isabella remained at York), and the prolonged stay at

Nottingham just after the death of Edward II. Although one might suggest that a confinement could have taken place during these periods, there is no other evidence for a pregnancy in 1327 or 1328.

15. The date usually assigned to this gift-giving, recorded in the original MS (PRO E101/384/1, f18v) is 20 June. The court was still at Canterbury at this time, and so if this date is accurate, the gift-giving took place in private and a long way from the court, and very shortly after Edward's return from France. A possible later date for the gift-giving is 20 July, when the court was indeed at Windsor. Junii/Julii errors are quite common in manuscripts.

16. PRO E101/384/1, f18v. My thanks to Paul Dryburgh for this reference. Also see Harding, 'Isabella and Mortimer', p. 295.

17. PRO E101/384/1 f16v, f18r. My thanks to Paul Dryburgh for his transcription of this.

18. See Rotuli parliamentorum, ii, p. 53 for Roger ordering that his word was to be obeyed before the king. This was at the very end of his administration, at Nottingham, in October 1330.

19. Thompson (ed.), Murimuth, p. 256.

20. Knighton records a Round Table tournament held by Roger at Bedford in 1328, probably drawing his information from Murimuth. The royal party did not visit Bedford in 1328 except late in the old-style year, on 19–21 January 1328–9, when Roger was just finishing his war with Henry of Lancaster. A Round Table tournament was certainly not held then. Although some writers like the old DNB have taken Knighton at his word, it seems far more likely that the Round Table tournament took place in 1329. Robert of Avesbury states it happened at Wigmore, which would place it in early September 1329. See Thompson (ed.), Murimuth, p. 284. It is significant that another Knighton manuscript records 'Hertiford' as the place, and a few pages further on, 'Bedford' appears mistakenly written in place of 'Bereford'. It seems possible therefore that Knighton's Round Table is the same as the jousts Murimuth records at Hereford, mistakenly at the end of May 1328, and which Avesbury mentions at Wigmore. The issue is probably confused by the various Mortimer weddings of 1328–9. See Appendix 2.

21. Edward acknowledged a debt to the Bardi of £1,000 for the marriage of Beatrice with Edward, daughter of the Earl of Norfolk, 21 March 1330. See CPR 1327–1330, p. 502.

22. Murimuth records that Isabella oversaw the proceedings, and if this was a Round Table as suggested above, her role would naturally be that of Guinevere.

23. Brie (ed.), The Brut, ii, p. 261.

24. Brie (ed.), The Brut, ii, p. 262.

25. The recent translation of the Anonimalle Chronicle's original French reads that 'Sir Geoffrey through madness even called himself king'. This is not convincing, not least because it does not make historical sense. The mid-fourteenth-century English translation of the longer Brut, which would reflect the commonly understood meaning of the original French much more closely than a modern literal translation, is much more creditable, reading 'Sire Geffray the Mortymer the yonge, that was the Mortymer's sone, lete him calle Kynge of Folye; and so it bifelle aftirward indede, ffor he was so ful of pride and of wrecchednesse, that he helde a rounde

table in Walys . . . and countrefetede the maner & doyng of Kyng Arthures table.'
The fourteenth-century sense of the longer *Brut* was undoubtedly that Roger drew
attention to himself as a king, and that Geoffrey called Roger 'King of Folly', or
that Geoffrey, in folly or madness, addressed Roger as king. See Brie (ed.), *The
Brut*, ii, p. 262; Childs and Taylor (eds), *Anonimalle Chronicle*, p. 145.

26. Crump, 'Arrest of Roger Mortimer', pp. 331–2.
27. Crump, 'Arrest of Roger Mortimer', pp. 331–2.
28. Small defensive repairs were made to the walls of the castle in August, to be
    completed to the satisfaction of John Maltravers. *CCR 1327–1330*, p. 487. Maltravers
    was not appointed custodian of Corfe until the following month, and so this may
    well relate to Maltravers' responsibility for guarding the king.
29. *CFR 1327–1337*, p. 149.
30. Doherty, 'Isabella', p. 287.
31. *Complete Peerage*, vii, p. 399.
32. BL Harley 1240 f41v.
33. Eyton, *Shropshire*, x, p. 116.
34. Doherty, 'Isabella', p. 289.
35. Doherty, 'Isabella', pp. 289–90.
36. The *Brut* refers to Howel as Hammond, and Harding follows this; Howel is the
    name in the original confession printed in Thompson (ed.), *Murimuth*, pp. 255–6,
    and Doherty follows this. Both original sources have the office as coroner of the
    king's household. Tout in his *Chapters* uses the title clerk of the marshalsea of the
    household for Robert Howel, but the coroner title has been preferred in this
    instance, owing to the tally of the two primary sources.
37. This is from the mid-fourteenth-century English translation of the French longer
    Brut chronicle. The original letter would have been in French, but it is not known
    on what authority the author of the chronicle quoted it.
38. For the King wanting to forgive Edmund see Brie (ed.), *The Brut*, ii, p. 267. For the
    king being given the chance to revoke the death sentence, see *ibid*. For the fact that
    the death sentence was forced upon him by Roger, see *Rotuli parliamentorum*, ii, p. 52.
39. *CPR 1327–1330*, p. 511.
40. *CPR 1327–1330*, p. 514. John Galeys was probably a servant also of the royal house-
    hold: on Isabella's death a man of this name was paid for the time the body of
    the queen mother lay in his house. See Blackley, 'Isabella and the Cult of the
    Dead', p. 31.
41. *Calendar Charter Rolls 1327–1341*, p. 172.
42. Harding, 'Isabella and Mortimer', p. 302. The proximity of the Arundel estates
    to Roger's was a probable factor in the failure of the plot.
43. Doherty, 'Isabella', pp. 304–5.
44. Childs and Taylor (eds), *Anonimalle Chronicle*, p. 145.
45. Aungier (ed.), *French Chronicle of London*, p. 63.
46. Brie (ed.), *The Brut*, ii, p. 268.
47. Maxwell (ed.), *Scalacronica*, p. 157.
48. Brie (ed.), *The Brut*, ii, p. 268.
49. Shenton, 'Edward III and the Coup of 1330', p. 4.
50. This is partly conjecture. It is unthinkable that one of the strongest military forti-

fications in the country could have an undefended passage into its heart which was not kept locked from the inside, especially given the castle's high state of alert. It is equally unthinkable that the constable and others within the castle did not know of the existence of the tunnels. An internal lock would explain their confidence, and why 'enemies of the queen' were not permitted within the castle, and also why the author of the *Scalacronica* calls the passage a 'postern gate'. An internal lock would require someone to open it, however; Edward's presence at the scene being assumed by the queen in both the *Brut* and Geoffrey le Baker's account suggests she was assuming he had undone the fateful lock and allowed in the assailants.

51. The king's feigned illness is an attempt to explain how Edward joined the conspirators, having been in the castle after the gate was shut, and why his physician was rewarded for probably playing a part in the plot. Caroline Shenton's suggestion that he was rewarded for his role on account of his tending to the wounded and dying is unconvincing, as such a role was associated with no risk, and therefore would have been very unlikely to merit a very valuable reward. See Shenton, 'Edward III and the Coup of 1330', pp. 24–6.

52. 'Fair son, have pity on the gentle Mortimer' are the words attributed to Isabella by Geoffrey le Baker. I have concatenated them with the similar but more wooden phrases in the *Brut*. In fact probably neither chronicler was informed as to what the queen's words were, but one cannot write a book about Roger Mortimer and ignore the most famous phrase associated with him. See Thompson (ed.), *Galfridi le Baker*, p. 46; Brie (ed.), *The Brut*, ii, p. 271.

53. Harding, 'Isabella and Mortimer', p. 317. Isabella was sent to Berkhamsted Castle.

54. *Rotuli parliamentorum*, ii, p. 53.

55. Doherty, 'Isabella', p. 317.

56. *Rotuli parliamentorum*, ii, pp. 52–3.

Epilogue

1. Maunde Thompson (ed.), *Murimuth*, p. 62.

2. *CCR 1330–1333*, p. 403. Roger's body may have been appropriated by the Coventry friars eager to obtain such an eminent corpse.

3. Some doubts remain as to whether Roger's body was relocated to Wigmore. A petition from Joan dated 1332, now in the Public Record Office (PRO SC8/61/3027), suggests he might have remained buried in Coventry, despite Edward's order of the previous year. Since Coventry was a city within Isabella's sphere of influence, it is possible that she persuaded her son to leave Roger buried in the friary there. I am grateful to Paul Dryburgh for alerting me to this argument and to Barbara Wright for sharing her knowledge of the original petition. All I can add is that the Wigmore Chronicler states that Roger was buried in the Greyfriars Church in Shrewsbury a year and a day after his execution (Dugdale, *Monasticon*, 6, iii, p. 352). If he *was* removed from Coventry in 1331 it is by no means certain that he was reburied in Wigmore Abbey.

12: Chapter Twelve Revisited

1. Hope, 'On the Funeral Effigies of the Kings and Queens of England'. Elizabeth Hallam, writing more recently but less specifically, states that in fourteenth-century England, in contrast with thirteenth-century practice, 'a funeral effigy occupied the place of the royal corpse on the bier', adding that the first time this happened was 'probably at Edward II's funeral'. See Hallam, 'Royal Burial and Cult of Kingship in France and England 1060–1330', pp. 366–7.

2. Hope, 'Funeral Effigies', p. 529.

3. Hope, 'Funeral Effigies', p. 533.

4. Thompson (ed.), *Murimuth*, pp. 52–3, 63–4. The text reads: '*Et licet multi abbates, priores, milites, burgenses de Bristollia et Gloucestria ad videndum corpus suum integrum fuissent vocati, et tale superficialiter conspexissent . . .*' There is no context to support Fryde's interpretation of the word *superficialiter* as 'from a distance'. See Fryde, *Tyranny and Fall*, p. 203.

5. Edward III was embalmed 'immediately' after his death. See Hope, 'Funeral Effigies', p. 532.

6. Smyth, *Lives*, i, 297. The body was publicly taken from Berkeley before this date.

7. Cuttino quotes H.M. Colvin to this effect. See Cuttino and Lyman, 'Where is Edward II?', p. 525.

8. The monument is generally considered to be some years later than the supposed burial. See Cuttino and Lyman, 'Where is Edward II?', p. 525.

9. Thompson (ed.), *Murimuth*, p. 135.

10. To clarify this point: because the funeral service in 1327 had to be seen to be correct in every respect, the heart was given to the man's widow as part of the aristocratic burial procedure. After the ceremony, she might have disposed of the false organ discreetly, probably placing it in a church where it could still be noticed as Edward's and thus perform a propaganda function. Her husband's heart may have been procured for her on the actual death of her husband, and later buried with her. There were plenty of precedents for burying hearts separately after death; for example, Henry of Almaine's, for one, was brought back in a silver vase from Italy.

11. *Rotuli parliamentorum*, ii, 53.

12. Harding, 'Isabella and Mortimer', p. 332.

13. *CPR 1338–1340*, p. 378; *CPR 1343–1345*, p. 535; Rymer (ed.), *Foedera*, iii, p. 56. For his service in Ireland see *CPR 1343–1345*, pp. 244, 245, 334.

14. *Rotuli parliamentorum*, ii, p. 243.

15. *Rotuli parliamentorum*, ii, p. 57. To the line '*Qualiter se velit de morte ipsius Regis acquietare?*' Berkeley's reply was unambiguous: '*Dicit, quod ipse nunquam fuit consentiens, auxilians, seu procurans, ad mortem suam, nec unquam scivit de morte sua usque in presenti Parliamento isto.*'

16. Tout, 'Captivity and Death', pp. 91–2; Smyth, *Lives*, i, p. 296.

17. Haines, 'Afterlife', p. 85, n. 98; Smyth, *Lives*, i, pp. 296–7.

18. *Rotuli parliamentorum*, ii, p. 57.

19. Rymer (ed.), *Foedera*, ii, p. 960.

20. *CCR 1330–1333*, p. 270.

21. Smyth, *Lives*, i, p. 297.

22. Hunter, 'Measures Taken for the Apprehension of Sir Thomas de Gurney, One of the Murderers of Edward II', pp. 274–97.
23. Hunter, 'Measures Taken', pp. 282–3.
24. *CPR 1334–1338*, p. 399. This was two days after Berkeley was finally acquitted of any part in the death of Edward II.
25. The possibility that there was an error in the recording of the charges is ruled out by the fact that no charges relating to the ex-king's death were mentioned on the two occasions when Maltravers received permission to return to England to face trial in 1345 and 1347, or when he was in custody in 1352.
26. However, it is worth noting that he was almost certainly alive in March 1330. Even if Edward III was uncertain about his father's existence, Roger was certainly better informed. His ability to convince the king that Kent's plot to reinstate Edward II was genuine, and required Kent's execution, strongly suggests that he was confident that the ex-king was still alive then, and that Edward III believed him.
27. This text has been transcribed from the version in Cuttino and Lyman, 'Where is Edward II?', pp. 526–7, this being their translation of the corrected Latin original given by them on pp. 537–8 of the same article.
28. Tout, 'Captivity and Death', p. 103.
29. Cuttino and Lyman, 'Where is Edward II?', pp. 530–1.
30. Cuttino and Lyman, 'Where is Edward II?', p. 531.
31. Cuttino and Lyman, 'Where is Edward II?', p. 531.
32. Haines, 'Afterlife', p. 80.
33. Haines, 'Afterlife', pp. 72–4. His assumption about the viewing of the corpse is based on a more basic assumption that the exhibition of the corpse revealed the face. As regards the burial of the heart, there were several precedents for bringing back the heart and bones of dead members of the English aristocracy from Italy. One such heart – that of Henry of Almaine, a cousin of both Roger and Edward II, killed at Viterbo in 1271 – lay in a silver vase near the shrine of St Edward in Westminster Abbey, near the spot where Roger was knighted. Thus it is quite possible that the heart placed below Isabella's tomb in 1358 was that of Edward II, brought back from Italy by Edward III, and not the one she was given in 1327. An alternative possibility is that Edward III purposefully buried the false heart under Isabella's tomb against her wishes, partly to dispose of it (it might still have graced an altar) and partly as a silent witness to the charade of Edward II's death.
34. *English Historical Documents 1327–1485*, p. 497. Haines states that, because Fieschi would have expected a clerk to translate a Latin document for Edward III, he would not have written 'Edward [II]'s English (French?)' in a local Italian form. Edward II's first language was French, not English, and in any case he would have been able to tell Fieschi that his son could read Latin as well. As a papal notary, Fieschi may well have known from Edward's contacts with Avignon that Edward was literate. As a result, Haines's suggestion that Fieschi was not the author of the letter is difficult to accept. See Haines, 'Afterlife', p. 67. For the relationship between Fieschi and Edward III, see Cuttino and Lyman, 'Where is Edward II?', p. 544.
35. Haines, 'Afterlife', p. 68.
36. Haines, 'Afterlife', pp. 65–6.
37. Haines, 'Afterlife', p. 65. It was probably compiled by Arnaud de Verdale, not

Gaucelm de Deaux. In a footnote (p. 80, n. 4) he quotes Theodore Bent who states in a piece in *Notes and Queries*, 6th series, ii, p. 381, that Arnaud (Bishop of Maguelonne, 1339–52) 'had a passion for collecting documents from all parts of the world'.

38. The possibility that a chronicle error led to this mistake and thus indicates a forgery has been considered. This is mainly because the longer *Brut* states Kent died in 1329, which would result in a one and a half year stay. However, this also states that Kent was executed in October, making Edward II's stay at Corfe appear to be two years. No chronicle so far looked at has this chronological error. See Brie (ed.), *The Brut*, ii, p. 267.

39. Haines, 'Afterlife', p. 69.

40. Deveril's implication in the plot of the Earl of Kent, and the order to him to arrest Robert le Bore on 2 May 1330 and to imprison him in Corfe Castle indicate that he was castellan then. There is no indication that he was known to Edward, and so Edward might have been convinced by a false name. Alternatively the castellan may genuinely have been a 'Thomas' in 1327, before Deveril's appointment. Lack of any official records on the subject means we cannot say when Deveril was appointed. He was rewarded in August 1330 with lands worth £20 per year. See *CPR 1327–1330*, pp. 549, 551.

41. If it had been an impromptu communication for Edward's interest, one would have expected some information about how the king had been found, and how his identity was proved.

42. *CCR 1323–1327*, p. 686.

43. One Percival Rycius of Genoa, merchant, was on 27 July 1329 prosecuting to have the return of goods lost in the dromond or the value thereof. See *CCR 1327–1330*, p. 562.

44. Haines states that there was a relationship, though he does not say what it was. See Haines, 'Afterlife', p. 68.

45. *CPR 1334–1338*, p. 489.

46. On 2 May 1336, two months before Edward III replied to the Genoese administration, Joan was granted her petition that her Irish lands should be restored to her, which had been confiscated by the king owing to 'alleged trespasses by her'. Not only were the lands restored, she was also compensated for the income lost. Since she promptly granted them to Geoffrey Mortimer, who had been arrested along with Roger, it is unlikely that the confiscation of the lands had had anything to do with Geoffrey. There is a very slight possibility that it was connected with William de Ockley, he being at one point a member of her household, as stated in the main text. Alternatively Edward may have believed that his father was being harboured on the Mortimer estates in Ireland still, and forgave Joan only when he learnt his father was in Italy. It is not possible to be certain.

47. Cuttino dismissed it because he could not fit it in with his chronology, in which he wished to place Edward at Koblenz on his way to Italy; Haines presumes that William was an impersonator, and was a prisoner, although there is no good evidence to assume this. See Cuttino and Lyman, 'Where is Edward II?', p. 530; Haines, 'Afterlife', p. 74.

48. Edward was crowned Vicar of the Holy Roman Empire on 5 September 1338 at Koblenz.

49. There is no doubt that the two entries relating to William the Welshman's guardian refer to the same man. In the first he is Francisco Lumbard and in the second Francekino Forcet. Both of these are Italian forms of the Christian name, he is not referred to as 'Francis'. The second is merely his Italian diminutive. In the first reference his surname refers to his place of origin, which was used while the royal clerk did not know him so well. See Cuttino and Lyman, 'Where is Edward II?', p. 530. Although the royal account first calls Francisco Lombard a king's sergeant-at-arms, this is probably in order to establish his status. He does not appear elsewhere as a member of the English royal household.

50. The meeting at Koblenz must have taken place in early September; the king then returned to Antwerp by the end of the month. William the Welshman was at Antwerp as his custodian was paid 13s 6d for his expenses for three weeks in December at Antwerp on 18 October. If William the Welshman was not with the king, he did not follow very far behind.

51. The principal objections to William the Welshman being Edward II, given the likelihood that Edward survived Berkeley Castle, are that the man was 'in custody' and that his expenses in Antwerp amounted to so little. This sounds very much like a political prisoner, as Chaplais suggests. However both objections are easily answered: Edward was in the custody of the Genoese, or more particularly Nicholinus de Fieschi. Indeed the testimonial to Nicholinus's good services the day after Edward III's coronation may relate to his production of William the Welshman. In other words, Edward II's status had not changed very much; he was still in custody, brought from Lombardy by Nicholinus de Fieschi. As for the small amount of money for his expenses, Manuele de Fieschi explains this with his reference to the fact that Edward had become a holy man, and lived in a hermitage. He seems to have taken the habit of a monk in Ireland not just to leave Ireland incognito but as a matter of faith. One mark was easily enough for a hermit to live on for three weeks in December, even in Antwerp.

52. *CPR 1338–1340*, p. 190.

53. *CCR 1341–1343*, pp. 83, 182. In addition to his salary on this journey, all his expenses were paid, amounting to more than £86.

54. Thompson (ed.), *Murimuth*, p. 135.

55. Gransden, *Historical Writing*, ii, p. 43.

56. Haines, 'Afterlife', p. 75.

Afterword

1. That Isabella chose to be buried in this dress is suggested on the strength of it being kept for more than fifty years. See Blackley, 'Isabella and the Cult of the Dead', p. 26.

Itinerary of Sir Roger Mortimer, 1306–30

1306

May 22 Westminster [Strachey *et al* (eds), *Monasticon*, vi, i, p. 351]

October [early] *Scotland* (with the king's army) [*CCR 1303–1307*, p. 481–2].

1307

November 26 Langley [*CCR 1307–1313*, p. 46]

December 15 *Protection, going overseas with the king* [*CPR 1307–1313*, p. 28 (not stated which RM)]

1308

February 25 Westminster Abbey [*CCR 1307–1313*, p. 53]

March 1 Westminster? [*CCR 1307–1313*, p. 52]

14 Westminster [*CCR 1307–1313*, p. 55]

16 Westminster [*CPR 1307–1313*, p. 52]

17 Westminster [*CPR 1307–1313*, p. 56]

April 27 Windsor? [*CPR 1307–1313*, p. 70]

October 28 Arrival in *Ireland* [Gilbert (ed.), *Chart. St Mary's*, ii, p. 337]

1309

April 12 Dublin [Curtis, *Ormond Deeds*, no. 438]

August 6 Stamford [*Complete Peerage*, ix, p. 434]

26 Westminster [PRO, C53/96 (no.33)]

28 Westminster [PRO, C53/96 (no.32)]

October 29 Knaresborough [PRO, C53/96 (no.23); *CCR 1307–1313*, p. 197]

December 12 Westminster [PRO, C53/96 (no.22)]

27 Westminster [PRO, C53/96 (no.18)]

1310

February 25 Westminster? [*CCR 1307–1313*, p. 246]

July 18 Wigmore [BL Harley 1240, f42v]

August 31 Conway [BL Harley 1240, f54v]

September	16 Arrival in *Ireland* [Gilbert (ed.), *Chart. St Mary's*, ii, p. 339]
October	1 *Ireland*, with Joan [*CPR 1307–1313*, pp. 282–3]

1311

April	23 Trim [Gilbert (ed.), *Chart. St Mary's*, i, p. 278]
September	29 Trim [Gilbert (ed.), *Chart. St Mary's*, i, p. 278]

1312

April	22 Dublin? [Wood, *Muniments*, p. 332]
May	26 Dublin [Wood *et al.* (eds), *Justiciary Rolls*, p. 238]

1313

Feb/March	? *Gascony* [*CCR 1307–1313*, p. 522]
April	2 Westminster? [*CCR 1307–1313*, p. 522]
	17 Westminster? [*CCR 1307–1313*, pp. 525–6]
May	1 Westminster [PRO, C53/99 (no.8)]
	16 Westminster [PRO, C53/99 (no.5)]
October	29 Westminster [PRO, C53/100 (no.48)]
November	2 Westminster? [PRO, C53/100 (no.39; not stated which RM)]
	9 Westminster? [PRO, (53/100 (no. 35; not stated which RM)]
	26 Westminster [*CCR 1313–1318*, p. 82]

1314

June	17 Wigmore? [BL Harley 1240, f58v]
	23–24 Bannockburn? [Clarke *et al* (eds), *Foedera*, iii, p. 239; Palgrave (ed.), *Parl. Writs*, ii, pp. 421–2; Macpherson *et al* (eds), *Rotuliae Scotiae*, i, 119b, 122a; Gransden, *Historical Writing*, p. 9]
July	22 York? [*CPR 1313–1317*, p. 161]
	29 York? [*CFR 1307–19*, p. 205]
September	16 York [PRO, C53/101 (nos 48, 50); PRO C53/114 (no.19)]
October	1 York [PRO, C53/101 (no. 43)]

1315

February	2 Westminster? [PRO, C53/101 (no. 33; not stated which RM)]
	10 Westminster [PRO, C53/101 (no. 25)]
	25 Westminster? [*CCR 1313–1318*, p. 213]
March	12 Westminster [PRO, C53/101 (no. 18)]

	14 Westminster [PRO, C53/101 (no. 17)]
April	26 Protection during forthcoming stay in *Ireland* [*CPR 1313–1317*, p. 277]
	28 Westminster? [*CPR 1313–1317*, p. 276]
December	6 Kells [Otway-Ruthven, *Medieval Ireland*, p. 228]

1316

January	17 *England* [Palgrave (ed.), *Parl. Writs*, iv, p. 1203]
February	6 Lincoln [PRO, C53/102 (nos 36, 37)]
March	18 Ystradfellte [Griffiths, *Conquerors and Conquered*, p. 88]
April	21 Westminster [PRO, C53/102 (no. 17)]
May	6 Westminster [PRO, C53/102 (nos 14, 19)]
	10 Westminster [PRO, C53/102 (no. 10)]
	12 Westminster [PRO, C53/102 (nos 16, 9, 6)]
	14 Westminster [PRO, C53/102 (no. 12)]
	16 Westminster [PRO, C53/102 (no. 7)]
	17 Westminster [PRO, C53/102 (no. 11)]
	29 Wigmore [BL Harley 1240, f41r]
June	27 Kinlet in Ernwood [PRO DL 27/93; BL Harley 1240, f114]
July	19–26 Bristol [Phillips, *Aymer de Valence*, p. 103]
August	17 Wigmore? [BL Harley 1240, f40r]
	23 Wigmore? [BL Harley 1240, f56v]
November	8 Newburgh [*CFR 1307–1319*, p. 310; PRO, C53/103 (no. 45)]
	10 York [PRO, C53/103 (no. 44)]
	12 York [PRO, C53/103 (no. 42)]
	20 York [PRO, C53/103 (no. 41)]
	22 York [PRO, C53/103 (no. 40)]
	23 York [*CCR 1313–1318*, p. 441]
December	9 Clipstone? [*CPR 1313–1317*, p. 574]
	18 Clipstone? [*CPR 1313–1317*, pp. 574–5]
	30 Clipstone? [*CPR 1313–1317*, p. 610]

1317

January	6 Clipstone? [*CPR 1313–1318*, p. 606]
	24 Dublin [Gilbert (ed.), *Chart. St Mary's*, ii, pp. 407–8]
April	7 Landed at Youghal [*Complete Peerage*, ix, p. 435]
	23 *Ireland* [*CCR 1313–1317*, p. 404]
May	(11 Naas)* [*Rot. Pat. & Claus. Hib.*, p. 22]
	22 Trim [Otway-Ruthven, *Medieval Ireland*, p. 234]
	24 *Ireland* [*CCR 1313–1318*, p. 469]

June	3 [*First battle with the de Lacys in Meath*]
	4 [*Second battle with the de Lacys in Meath*]
	7 *Ireland* [Gilbert (ed.), *Hist. & Mun. Docs Ireland*, p. 402]
	10 *Ireland* [*CCR 1313–1318*, p. 476]
July	18 Dublin [Gilbert (ed.), *Chart. St Mary's*, ii, p. 410]
	20 Dublin? [Gilbert (ed.), *Chart. St Mary's*, ii, p. 356]
	24 Dublin [*Rot. Pat. & Claus. Hib.*, p. 21]
	26 Dublin [*CPR 1327–1330*, p. 453]
August	(17 Dublin?) [*Rot. Pat. & Claus. Hib.*, p. 24]
	20 Dublin [*Rot. Pat. & Claus. Hib.*, p. 21]
	(22 Dublin?) [*Rot. Pat. & Claus. Hib.*, p. 24]
September	5 Loughsewdy [*Rot. Pat. & Claus. Hib.*, p. 24]
	(6 Drogheda?) [*Rot. Pat. & Claus. Hib.*, p. 25]
	8 Dublin [Gilbert (ed.), *Hist. & Mun. Docs Ireland*, p. 403]
	11 Okinselagh ('Glynsely'). [Gilbert (ed.), *Chart. St Mary's*, ii, p. 356]
	(23 Dublin?) [*Rot. Pat. & Claus. Hib.*, p. 22]
October	(2 Trim?) [*Rot. Pat. & Claus. Hib.*, p. 23]
	(8 Dublin?) [*Rot. Pat. & Claus. Hib.*, p. 24]
	(9 Dublin?) [*Rot. Pat. & Claus. Hib.*, p. 24]
	(16 Dublin?) [*Rot. Pat. & Claus. Hib.*, p. 24]
	(18 Dublin?) [*Rot. Pat. & Claus. Hib.*, p. 21]
	(22 Dublin?) [*Rot. Pat. & Claus. Hib.*, p. 27]
	(23 Dublin?) [*Rot. Pat. & Claus. Hib.*, p. 24]
November	(1 Dublin?) [*Rot. Pat. & Claus. Hib.*, p. 25]
	(16 'Castle Olethon'?) [*Rot. Pat. & Claus. Hib.*, p. 22]
	(28 Cork?) [*Rot. Pat. & Claus. Hib.*, p. 22]
	(29 Cork?) [*Rot. Pat. & Claus. Hib.*, p. 24]
December	1 Cork? [*CPR 1327–1330*, p. 345]
	(2 Cork?) [*Rot. Pat. & Claus. Hib.*, p. 25]
	(5 Cork?) [*Rot. Pat. & Claus. Hib.*, p. 22]
	7 Cork? [*CPR 1317–1321*, p. 210; *Rot. Pat. & Claus. Hib.*, p. 24]
	(8 Cork?) [*Rot. Pat. & Claus. Hib.*, p. 24]
	(12 Cork?) [*Rot. Pat. & Claus. Hib.*, pp. 22, 25]
	(18 Cork?) [*Rot. Pat. & Claus. Hib.*, p. 22]
	(28 Cork?) [*Rot. Pat. & Claus. Hib.*, pp. 22, 25]

1318

January	(6 Cork?) [*Rot. Pat. & Claus. Hib.*, p. 22]
	20 Cork [*CPR 1327–1330*, p. 541. NB *Rot. Pat. & Claus. Hib.*,

p. 23, places the administration at Clonmel on this day, so the Clonmel entries in that publication for 16, 18 and 23 probably do not relate to Roger but to Butler, the Justiciar, and thus have been omitted. Similarly references to the administration at Thomastown on 28 January and 2–3 February, and at Kilkenny on 7 February, have been omitted since Roger was at Dublin on 1 and 19 February.]

February   1 Dublin [*Rot. Pat. & Claus. Hib.*, p. 21; *CPR 1327–1330*, p. 345]

(15 Dublin?) [*Rot. Pat. & Claus. Hib.*, p. 26]

19 Dublin [Gilbert (ed.), *Chart. St Mary's*, ii, p. 357]

(27 Dublin?) [*Rot. Pat. & Claus. Hib.*, p. 25]

(28 Dublin?) [*Rot. Pat. & Claus. Hib.*, p. 25]

March   1 Dublin [*CPR 1327–1330*, p. 345]

9 Dublin [*CPR 1321–1324*, p. 331]

(11 Dublin?) [*Rot. Pat. & Claus. Hib.*, p. 25]

(12 Drogheda?) [*Rot. Pat. & Claus. Hib.*, p. 25]

(18 Drogheda?) [*Rot. Pat. & Claus. Hib.*, p. 26]

20 Drogheda [Gilbert (ed.), *Chart. St Mary's*, i, p. 263]

(24 Drogheda?) [*Rot. Pat. & Claus. Hib.*, p. 25]

(29 Drogheda?) [*Rot. Pat. & Claus. Hib.*, p. 23]

(30 Drogheda?) [*Rot. Pat. & Claus. Hib.*, p. 23]

April   (3 Drogheda?) [*Rot. Pat. & Claus. Hib.*, pp. 23, 26]

(15 Dublin?) [*Rot. Pat. & Claus. Hib.*, p. 26]

May   2 *Ireland* [*CPR 1317–1321*, p. 141]

5 Roger recalled to *England* [Richardson and Sayles, *Administration*, p. 84]

July   20 Northampton [PRO C53/105 (nos 88 and 81)]

26 Northampton [PRO C53/105 (no. 85)]

29 Northampton [Phillips, *Aymer de Valence*, p. 170]

30 Northampton [PRO C53/105 (no. 87)]

August   1 Northampton [Phillips, *Aymer de Valence*, p. 170]

9 Leake [PRO C53/105 (no. 83)]

10 Leake [PRO C53/105 (nos 77, 80)]

September   24 York [PRO C53/105 (no. 78)]

25 York [PRO C53/105 (no. 79)]

November   20 York [PRO C53/105 (no. 49)]

30 York [PRO C53/105 (no. 47)]

December   6 York? [Tout, *Place of Edward II*, p. 118]

28 Wigmore [Brakspear, 'Wigmore Abbey', p. 42]

1319

March	15 York [PRO C53/105 (nos 24, 27)]
	17 York? [*CPR 1317–1321*, p. 318]
	26 York [PRO C53/105 (no. 25)]
April	18 York? [*CPR 1317–1321*, p. 325]
May	8 Shrewsbury [BL Harley 1240, f56v]
June	12 Arrived in *Ireland* [Connolly (ed.), *Irish Exch. Payments*, p. 266]
July	14 Dublin [*Rot. Pat. & Claus. Hib.*, p. 26]
	(20 Callan?) [*Rot. Pat. & Claus. Hib.*, p. 26]
August	(13. Cashell?) [*Rot. Pat. & Claus. Hib.*, p. 26]
	(20. Dublin?) [*Rot. Pat. & Claus. Hib.*, p. 27]
September	20 Dublin [*Rot. Pat. & Claus. Hib.*, p. 27]
October	5 Dublin [Gilbert (ed.), *Hist. & Mun. Docs Ireland*, p. 386]
	(23 Athboy?) [*Rot. Pat. & Claus. Hib.*, p. 27]
November	(16 Ross?) [*Rot. Pat. & Claus. Hib.*, p. 27]
December	(2 Cork?) [*Rot. Pat. & Claus. Hib.*, p. 27]
	(3 Cork?) [*Rot. Pat. & Claus. Hib.*, p. 27]
	(8 Cork?) [*Rot. Pat. & Claus. Hib.*, p. 27]

1320

February	(10 Waterford?) [*Rot. Pat. & Claus. Hib.*, p. 27]
March	16 *Ireland* [*Rot. Pat. & Claus. Hib.*, p. 28]
	(27 Drogheda?) [*Rot. Pat. & Claus. Hib.*, p. 27]
	30 Dublin [Clarke, 'Irish Parliaments in the Reign of Edward II', p. 57]
April	22 Dublin [Gilbert (ed.), *Hist. & Mun. Docs Ireland*, p. 350]
	25 Dublin [Gilbert (ed.), *Hist. & Mun. Docs Ireland*, p. 347]
	26 Dublin [Gilbert (ed.), *Hist. & Mun. Docs Ireland*, p. 334]
May	(4 Dublin?) [*Rot. Pat. & Claus. Hib.*, p. 28]
	(6 Dublin?) [*Rot. Pat. & Claus. Hib.*, p. 27]
	(16 Dublin?) [*Rot. Pat. & Claus. Hib.*, p. 27]
	12 Dublin [Gilbert (ed.), *Hist. & Mun. Docs Ireland*, p. 461]
June	14 Athlone [*Rot. Pat. & Claus. Hib.*, p. 28; Otway-Ruthven, *Medieval Ireland*, p. 240]
	18 *Ireland* [*CPR 1317–1321*, p. 456]
August	5 Kilkenny [*Rot. Pat. & Claus. Hib.*, p. 28]
September	10 Dublin [*Rot. Pat. & Claus. Hib.*, p. 28]
	27 Left *Ireland* [Connolly (ed.), *Irish Exchequer Payments*, p. 266]
November	9 Stratfield Mortimer [BL Harley 1240, f6ov]
	16 Westminster? [*CPR 1317–1321*, p. 523]

1321

January	31 Stratfield Mortimer [BL Harley 1240, f6ov]
February	11 Wigmore [Phillips, *Aymer de Valence*, p. 201]
March	7 Wigmore [*CCR 1318–1323*, p. 359]
May	? Clun [Strachey *et al.* (eds), *Monasticon*, vi, i, p. 352]
June	11 Vastern Manor, in Wootton Bassett? [*CCR 1318–1323*, p. 543]
July	22 St Albans [Phillips, *Aymer de Valence*, p. 209]
	29 London. [Phillips, *Aymer de Valence*, p. 209]
August	20 Westminster? [*CPR 1321–1324*, p. 15; BL Harley 1240, f45r]
October	27 Kingston-on-Thames [Phillips, *Aymer de Valence*, p. 217]
November	29 Pontefract [Phillips, *Aymer de Valence*, p. 217]

1322

January	5 Bridgnorth [*DNB*; Phillips, *Aymer de Valence*, 221]
	13 or 14 Betton Strange [*CPR 1321–1324*, p. 47]
	22 Shrewsbury [Denholm-Young (ed.), *Vita*, p. 119]
February	13 Tower of London [Childs and Taylor (ed.), *Anonimalle Chronicle*, p. 107]
February–December	Tower of London

1323

January–July	Tower of London
August	1 Escape from the Tower to Portchester, then to *France* [Stones, 'The Dates of Roger Mortimer's Escape from the Tower of London', pp. 97–8]
September	*Picardy?* [*CCR 1323–1327*, p. 140]
December	*Hainault?* [Chaplais, *St-Sardos*, p. 2]

1324

September	*Hainault* [Chaplais, *St-Sardos*, p. 72]

1325

December	? Paris [Doherty, 'Isabella', pp. 126–7]

1326

January–May	*France?* [based on Edward's letters in *CCR 1323–1327*, pp. 576–81]
May	11 Paris [*CCR 1323–1327*, p. 576]
July	23–4 *Zeeland* (Low Countries) [Doherty, 'Isabella', p. 144]

August   27 Mons [Doherty, 'Isabella', p. 146]
September   21 Brill [Doherty, 'Isabella', p. 150]
              24 Walton, Suffolk [Doherty, 'Isabella', p. 154]
              29 Bury St Edmunds [Harding, 'Isabella and Mortimer', p. 7]
              ? Cambridge [Doherty, 'Isabella', p. 154]
October   ? Barnwell Priory [Doherty, 'Isabella', pp. 154–5]
              6 Baldock [Doherty, 'Isabella', p. 155; Harding, 'Isabella and Mortimer', p. 9]
              ? Dunstable [Doherty, 'Isabella', p. 155]
              ? Oxford [Doherty, 'Isabella', p. 158]
              ? Osney Abbey [Doherty, 'Isabella', p. 158]
              14 Wallingford [Doherty, 'Isabella', p. 159]
              15 Wallingford [Harding, 'Isabella and Mortimer', p. 11]
              ? Gloucester [Harding, 'Isabella and Mortimer', p. 15]
              18 Bristol [Doherty, 'Isabella', p. 161]
November   ? Pembridge [Eyton, *Shropshire*, xi, p. 329]
              24 Hereford [Doherty, 'Isabella', p. 166]
              (25–6 Hereford)** [Doherty, 'Isabella', p. 179]
              (27 Newent) [Doherty, 'Isabella', p. 179]
              (28 Gloucester) [Doherty, 'Isabella', pp. 179–80]
              30 Cirencester [Evans, 'The Family of Mortimer', p. 244]
December   (1 Lichfield) [Doherty, 'Isabella', p. 180]
              (2 Witney) [Doherty, 'Isabella', p. 180]
              (3–21 Woodstock) [Doherty, 'Isabella', p. 180]
              25–31 Wallingford [Doherty, 'Isabella', pp. 180, 182]

1327
January   4 London and Westminster [Harding, 'Isabella and Mortimer', p. 34]
              7 Westminster [Harding, 'Isabella and Mortimer', p. 34]
              28 Westminster [*CCR 1327–1330*, p. 98]
February   1 Westminster [*CCR 1327–1330*, p. 100]
              14 Westminster [PRO C53/114 (no. 73)]
              15 Westminster [PRO C53/114 (no. 90)]
              21 Westminster [BL Harley 1240, f36v]
              24 Westminster [*CPR 1327–1330*, p. 14]
              26 Westminster [PRO C53/114 (nos 81, 84)]
              27 Westminster [PRO C53/114 (nos 82, 85)]
              28 Westminster [*CCR 1327–1330*, p. 98]
March   2 Westminster [PRO C53/114 (no. 78)]

	6 Westminster [PRO C53/114 (no. 76)]
May	8 Nottingham [PRO C53/114 (no. 52)]
	10 Nottingham [PRO C53/114 (no. 54)]
	11 Nottingham [PRO C53/114 (no. 59)]
	12 Nottingham [PRO C53/114 (no. 56)]
	13 Nottingham [PRO C53/114 (nos 55, 57)]
	14 Nottingham [PRO C53/114 (no. 58)]
	28 York [PRO C53/114 (no. 49)]
June	1 York [PRO C53/114 (nos 38, 41, 47, 51)]
	3 York [PRO C53/114 (nos 39, 40, 50)]
	7 York [PRO C53/114 (no. 46)]
	9 York? [*CPR 1327–1330*, p. 125]
	14 York [PRO C53/114 (no. 67)]
	16 York [PRO C53/114 (no. 45)]
	20 York [PRO C53/114 (no. 34)]
	23 York [PRO C53/114 (no. 44)]
	24 York [PRO C53/114 (nos 33, 35)]
	26 York [PRO C53/114 (nos 36, 43)]
	28 York [PRO C53/114 (no. 30)]
	29 York [PRO C53/114 (no. 37)]
	30 York [PRO C53/114 (nos 29, 31, 32)]
July	2 York [PRO C53/114 (nos 28, 42)]
	15 Durham [PRO C53/114 (no. 27)]
	24 Haydon? [BL Harley 1240, f36v–38r]
	26 Haltwhistle? [*CPR 1327–1330*, p 139]
August	8 Durham [*Cat. Anc. Deeds*, iii, A5570]
	14 York? [*CPR 1327–1330*, p. 145]
	15 York [PRO C53/114 (no. 21)]
	16 York [PRO C53/114 (nos 22, 23)]
	22 York? [*CPR 1327–1330*, p. 159]
	26 Doncaster [PRO C53/114 (no. 20)]
	31 Nottingham? [*CFR 1327–1337*, p. 63]
September	2 Nottingham? [*CPR 1327–1330*, p. 163]
	3 Nottingham? [*CPR 1327–1330*, p. 166]
	14 Abergavenny [Tout, 'Captivity and Death', pp. 109–10]
October	4 Nottingham [PRO C53/114 (no. 15)]
	20 Nottingham [PRO C53/114 (no. 14)]
	22 Nottingham [PRO C53/114 (no. 12)]
December	7 Leicester [PRO C53/114 (nos 9, 10)]
	25 Worcester [PRO C53/114 (nos 2, 6)]
	26 Worcester [PRO C53/114 (no. 4)]

27 Worcester? [*CPR 1327–1330*, pp. 200. 203]
28 Worcester? [*CPR 1327–1330*, p. 196)]
29 Droitwich? [*CPR 1327–1330*, p. 226]

1328

January   1 Lichfield [PRO C53/114 (no. 5)]
6 Nottingham? [*CPR 1327–1330*, p. 201]
7 Nottingham [PRO C53/114 (nos 1, 3)]
18 Rothwell? [*CPR 1327–1330*, p. 203]

February   1 Knaresborough [PRO C53/115 (no. 98)]
4 York [PRO C53/115 (no. 87)]
6 York [PRO C53/115 (no. 96)]
8 York [PRO C53/115 (no. 95)]
9 York? [*CPR 1327–1330*, p. 231]
10 York [PRO C53/115 (no. 94)]
21 York [PRO C53/115 (no. 90)]
22 York [PRO C53/115 (nos 75, 89)]
23 York [PRO C53/115 (no. 81)]
29 York [PRO C53/115 (no. 79)]

March   1 York [PRO C53/115 (no. 83); *CCR 1327–1330*, p. 371]
2 York? [*CCR 1327–1330*, p. 369]
3 York [PRO C53/115 (nos 72, 78, 85)]

April   21 Oundle [PRO C53/115 (no. 69)]
28 Northampton? [*CPR 1327–1330*, p. 260]
29 Northampton? [*CFR 1327–1337*, p. 88]

May   3 Northampton [PRO C53/115 (no. 68)]
7 Northampton [PRO C53/115 (no. 67)]
8 Northampton? [*CPR 1327–1330*, p. 263]
9 Northampton? [*CFR 1327–1337*, p. 91]
10 Northampton [PRO C53/115 (nos 55, 61)]
11 Northampton [PRO C53/115 (nos 48, 59)]
12 Northampton [*CCR 1327–1330*, p. 387]
13 Northampton [PRO C53/115 (nos 52, 54)]
14 Northampton [PRO C53/115 (no. 51)]
20 Northampton [PRO C53/115 (no. 50)]
31 Hereford [*Murimuth*, p. 57, in conjunction with the TS 'Itinerary of Edward III and His Household' in the reading room of the PRO]

June   (2–3 Ludlow) [location of the privy seal according to the TS 'Itinerary of Edward III and His Household' in the reading room of the PRO]

July	17 Berwick [Skeat (ed.), *The Bruce*, ii, p. 498]
	25. Pontefract [*CCR 1327–1330*, p. 399]
August	4 York [PRO C53/115 (no. 44)]
	5 York? [*CPR 1327–1330*, p. 309; *CFR 1327–1337*, p. 98]
	6 York [PRO C53/115 (no. 40)]
	7 York [PRO C53/115 (nos 41, 42)]
	8 York [PRO C53/115 (no. 39)]
	9 York [PRO C53/115 (no. 43)]
	12 York [PRO C53/115 (no. 37)]
	20 Pontefract [PRO C53/115 (no. 35)]
	26 Clipstone? [*CPR 1327–1330*, p. 351]
	30 Clipstone [Harding, 'Isabella and Mortimer', p. 162, n. 2]
September	2 Nottingham vicinity [Harding, 'Isabella and Mortimer', p. 162, n. 2]
	16 Wisbech [PRO C53/115 (no. 12)]
October	4 Gloucester [PRO C53/115 (no. 33)]
	16 Salisbury [PRO C53/115 (no. 31)]
	18 Salisbury [PRO C53/115 (no. 32)]
	20 Salisbury [PRO C53/115 (no. 24)]
	21 Salisbury [PRO C53/115 (no. 29)]
	23 Salisbury [PRO C53/115 (no. 30)]
	25 Salisbury [PRO C53/115 (no. 25)]
	26 Salisbury [PRO C53/115 (no. 28)]
	30 Salisbury [PRO C53/115 (no. 26)]
	31 Salisbury [*Complete Peerage*, ix, p. 439, in conjunction with PRO C53/115 (no. 26), in which he is not called Earl of March]
November	3 Salisbury [PRO C53/115 (no. 11)]
	4 Salisbury? [*CPR 1327–1330*, p. 327]
	14 Windsor [PRO C53/115 (no. 18)]
	19 Windsor [PRO C53/115 (no. 15)]
	18 Windsor [PRO C53/115 (no. 7)]
	20 Windsor [PRO C53/115 (no. 13)]
	23 Windsor [PRO C53/115 (no. 14)]
	25 Westminster? [BL Harley 1240, f64r; PRO C53/115 (no. 8)]
	27 Westminster [PRO C53/115 (no. 5)]
	28 Westminster [PRO C53/115 (no. 9)]
	29 Westminster [PRO C53/115 (nos 3, 4)]
December	12 Gloucester? [*CPR 1327–1330*, p. 342]
	15 Gloucester [BL Harley 1240, f49v]

20 Gloucester [PRO C53/115 (no. 10)]
28–31 With the king, travelling to and at Warwick [Fryde, *Tyranny and Fall*, p. 223, in conjunction with the unpublished typescript in the reading room of the PRO, 'Itinerary of Edward III and His Household']

1329

January
1 Warwick [see 28–31 December 1328]
2 Coventry [see 28–31 December 1328]
4 Leicester [*Complete Peerage*, ix, p. 439]
5 Hinckley [PRO C53/115 (no. 2)]
6–12 Leicester [see 28–31 December 1328; also PRO C53/115 (no. 1) for 7 January]
14–15 Northampton [see 28–31 December 1328; also *CCR 1327–1330*, p. 425, for 15 January]
17 Oundle [see 28–31 December 1328]
18 Newnham [*CCR 1327–1330*, p. 425]
26 St Albans [PRO C53/116 (no. 44)]
29 Windsor [PRO C53/116 (no. 43)]
31 Windsor [PRO E101/384/1 f15r]

February
3 Windsor [PRO C53/116 (no. 42)]
9 Westminster? [*CCR 1327–1330*, p. 529]

March
1 Eltham [PRO C53/116 (no. 52)]
4 Eltham [PRO C53/116 (no. 40)]
9 Roger and Joan both in *England* [*CPR 1327–1330*, p. 367]
15 'Wycombe' (West or High) [PRO C53/116 (no. 48)]
19 Woodstock [PRO C53/116 (no. 41)]
22 Woodstock [PRO C53/116 (no. 47)]

April
12 Wallingford [PRO C53/116 (no. 46)]
28 Windsor? [*CFR 1327–1337*, p. 132]

May
15 Eltham [PRO C53/116 (no. 38)]
20 Canterbury [PRO C53/116 (no. 39)]
22 Canterbury [PRO C53/116 (no. 45)]
25 Dover [PRO E101/384/1 f17v]
26 Roger and Joan both in *England* [*CPR 1327–1330*, p. 395]
31 Canterbury [*CCR 1327–1330*, p. 547]

June
15 Canterbury? [*CPR 1327–1330*, p. 398]
16 Canterbury [PRO C53/116 (no. 37)]
20 Windsor [PRO E101/384/1, f18v]

July
7 Chichester [PRO C53/116 (no. 36)]
22 Windsor [PRO C53/116 (no. 34)]

	27 Windsor [*CCR 1327–1330*, p. 563]
	28 Windsor [PRO C53/116 (no. 31)]
August	15 Gloucester [PRO C53/116 (no. 15)]
	16 Gloucester [PRO C53/116 (no. 26)]
	18 Gloucester [PRO C53/116 (nos 14, 24, 25, 32)]
	26 Gloucester [PRO C53/116 (no. 30)]
	27 Gloucester [PRO C53/116 (no. 28)]
	28 Gloucester [PRO C53/116 (no. 29)]
	30 Gloucester [PRO C53/116 (no. 27)]
September	2 Gloucester [BL Harley 1240, f71v]
	5 Wigmore [PRO E101/384/1, f18r]
	6 Wigmore [PRO E101/384/1, f16v]
October	6 Worcester [PRO C53/116 (no. 23)]
	16 Dunstable [PRO C53/116 (nos 16, 17)]
	18 Dunstable [PRO C53/116 (no. 19)]
	20 Dunstable [PRO C53/116 (no. 22)]
	30 Kenilworth [PRO C53/116 (nos 10, 20)]
November	10 Kenilworth [PRO C53/116 (no. 21)]
	17 Kenilworth [PRO C53/116 (no. 13)]
	21 Kenilworth? [*CFR 1327–1337*, p. 155]
	24 Kenilworth [PRO C53/116 (no. 18)]
December	3 Kenilworth [PRO C53/116 (nos 7, 12)]
	5 Ludlow [BL Harley 1240, f41v]
	8 Clun [Eyton, *Shropshire*, x, p. 116]
	12 Kenilworth [PRO C53/116 (no. 11)]
	18 Kenilworth [PRO C53/116 (no. 8)]
	23 Kenilworth [PRO C53/116 (no. 6)]
	26 Kenilworth [PRO C53/116 (no. 4)]
	30 Kenilworth [*Cat. Anc. Deeds*, iii, A5782]

1330

January	1 Kenilworth [PRO C53/116 (no. 5)]
	26 Eltham [PRO C53/117 (no. 102)]
	27 Eltham [PRO C53/117 (no. 104)]
	30 Eltham [PRO C53/117 (no. 105)]
February	8 Tower of London [PRO C53/116 (no. 99)]
	10 Tower of London? [*CPR 1327–1330*, pp. 498–9]
	16 Tower of London [PRO C53/116 (no. 2); C53/117 (nos 90, 95)]
	22 Windsor [PRO C53/117 (nos 101, 103)]
March	10 Winchester? [*CPR 1327–1330*, p. 492]

16 Winchester [PRO C53/117 (no. 97)]
18 Winchester [PRO C53/117 (no. 85)]
20 Winchester [PRO C53/117 (no. 72)]
22 Winchester [PRO C53/117 (no. 89B)]
28 Osney [PRO C53/117 (no. 42)]
29 Woodstock [PRO C53/117 (no. 89A)]
31 Woodstock [PRO C53/117 (nos 87, 88)]

April   1 Woodstock [PRO C53/117 (no. 63)]
12 Woodstock [PRO C53/117 (no. 68)]
16 Woodstock [PRO C53/117 (no. 96)]
20 Woodstock [BL Harley 1240, f47v–f48r]
21 Woodstock [PRO C53/117 (no. 94)]
25 Woodstock [BL Harley 1240, f49v–f50r]
27 Woodstock [PRO C53/117 (nos 92, 93)]
30 Woodstock [PRO C53/117 (no. 82)]

May   1 Woodstock [PRO C53/117 (no. 83)]
2 Woodstock [PRO C53/117 (no. 70)]
4 Woodstock [PRO C53/117 (no. 100)]
19 Woodstock [PRO C53/117 (no. 84)]
25 Woodstock [PRO C53/117 (no. 77)]

June   8 Woodstock [PRO C53/117 (no. 69)]
11 Woodstock [PRO C53/117 (no. 76)]
18 Woodstock [PRO C53/117 (no. 66)]
20 Gloucester? [*CPR 1327–1330*, p. 535]
23 Gloucester? [*CPR 1327–1330*, p. 535]

July   10 Osney [PRO C53/117 (no. 73)]
12 Osney [BL Harley 1240, f43r; PRO C53/117 (no. 64)]
15 Woodstock [PRO C53/117 (no. 57)]
16 Woodstock [PRO C53/117 (no. 59)]
17 Woodstock [PRO C53/117 (nos 38, 39)]
22 Woodstock [PRO C53/117 (no. 60)]
23 Woodstock [PRO C53/117 (nos 53, 58)]
24 Woodstock [PRO C53/117 (no. 52)]
29 Northampton [PRO C53/117 (no. 55)]

August   1 Northampton [PRO C53/117 (nos 45, 54)]
2 Northampton [PRO C53/117 (no. 56)]
6 Kings Cliffe [PRO C53/117 (no. 47)]
10 Stamford [PRO C53/117 (no. 51)]
14 Bourne [PRO C53/117 (no. 46)]
24 Lincoln? [*CPR 1327–1330*, p. 550]

September   1 Clipstone [PRO C53/117 (no. 44)]

2 Nottingham [PRO C53/117 (no. 48)]
6 Nottingham [PRO C53/117 (no. 50)]
8 Nottingham [PRO C53/117 (no. 49)]
11 Nottingham [PRO C53/117 (no. 41)]
13 Nottingham [PRO C53/117 (nos 35, 40, 43)]
15 Nottingham [PRO C53/117 (no. 29)]
16 Nottingham [PRO C53/117 (no. 34)]
22 Clipstone [BL Harley 1240, f44v]

October   18 Nottingham [Blom (ed.), *Calendar of Papal Registers*, ii, p. 498]
22–26 Leicester [Thompson (ed.), *Galfridi le Baker*, p. 46, in conjunction with TS of 'Itinerary of Edward III and His Household' in the reading room of the PRO]
27 Lutterworth [Thompson (ed.), *Galfridi le Baker*, p. 46, in conjunction with TS of 'Itinerary of Edward III and His Household' in the reading room of the PRO]

November   26 Tower of London [Thompson (ed.), *Galfridi le Baker*, p. 46, in conjunction with TS of 'Itinerary of Edward III and His Household' in the reading room of the PRO]
29 Tyburn [Thompson (ed.), *Murimuth*, p. 62]

---

* Those dates given in brackets in the period 1317–20 refer to locations at which the Irish government is known to have operated when Roger was the king's representative in charge, either as King's Lieutenant or Justiciar. The itinerary is therefore not that of Roger himself but of the administrative system which followed him around. As Edmund Butler continued to act as Justiciar during Roger's period of Lieutenancy (1317–18), and certainly did exercise royal authority, dates given here need to be treated with great caution.

** Those dates given in brackets at the end of 1326 refer to locations at which the queen can be placed; Roger is presumed at this time to have been with her most, if not all, of the first five months after the invasion. Roger's visit to Pembridge seems to be the one exception.

Children of Sir Roger and Lady Mortimer

It is easy to list the names of the children of the marriage of Roger and Joan but much harder to establish their order and dates of birth. With twelve children surviving to adulthood, it is quite possible that Joan's confinements included a multiple birth. There is no evidence of twins, however, except in the tenuous connection that two of the daughters, Agnes and Beatrice, were certainly married at the same time, and Catherine's and Joan's marriages were probably also simultaneous.

1. **Edmund**, the son and heir of Roger and Joan, was probably born in late 1302 or early 1303. The earliest likely date is nine months after the marriage of Roger and Joan, who were fourteen and fifteen years old respectively at the time of the marriage. However, the Wigmore Abbey Annals in John Rylands Library does not note his birth, and it is therefore possible that he was born after Margaret, as late as 1305. Since he was married in 1316, at which time he had had his own seal made, he was most probably of sufficient age to inherit, and since Roger himself was married at fourteen, and this was also the age at which the Counts of La Marche (ancestors of Joan de Geneville) came of age, the probability is that he was born in 1302–3. He married the three-year-old Elizabeth, daughter of Bartholomew de Badlesmere, at Ernwood in Kinlet, Shropshire, on 27 July 1316, and had by her two sons, Roger, born in 1327, and John, who died young. Edmund was imprisoned at Windsor Castle during his father's exile, along with his brother Roger and the sons of the Earl of Hereford, and moved to the Tower on 1 October 1326. According to the Wigmore chronicler, he was a clever young man. He was knighted in 1327 at the coronation, but was arrested along with his father in 1330. He did not inherit his father's titles, as these were all forfeited by the sentence of treason, but he soon regained the king's favour, and was summoned to Parliament in his own name. The *Inquisitions Post Mortem* on his estate shows that Wigmore and a number of core Mortimer estates on the Marches were restored to him in 1331. He died in December 1331 or January 1332. His widow later married the Earl of Northampton.

2. **Margaret** was born on 2 May 1304 (John Rylands Lib., Latin MS 215). According to the marriage agreement in the Black Book of Wigmore (BL Harley MS 1240), she married Thomas de Berkeley, the heir of Maurice, Lord Berkeley, in May 1319. After Roger's submission in 1322 she was arrested, and in 1324 she was sent to Sholdham Priory. Her marriage to Berkeley was confirmed, and her offspring declared legitimate by the Pope in 1329. According to the *Complete Peerage*, her eldest surviving son was born in 1330. She died in 1337, supposedly under the age of thirty, and was buried in St Austine's Abbey, Bristol (now Bristol Cathedral).

3. **Roger**, the second son, was born about 1305–6. This date is suggested because it was in 1321 that he was married to Joan, the daughter of Edmund Butler of Ireland, at which time he would have been fifteen. In the same year Roger and Joan decided to settle all their Irish lands on him, and to create a separate Mortimer line through him there. He was arrested and imprisoned at Windsor in 1322, moved to the Tower on 1 October 1326, and released on Roger's return in 1326. In 1327 he was knighted, and, his wife Joan having died without bearing children, his father proposed that he should marry the young widow of the Earl of Pembroke. The right of the marriage was granted him on 3 September 1327 (*CPR 1327–1330*, p. 166). He seems to have died before 27 August 1328, on which day his Irish inheritance was settled on his youngest brother, John.

4. **Maud**. The reason for suggesting Maud as Roger's second daughter is that she was the first married, before 13 April 1319 (according to the *Complete Peerage*). Since Roger's method of betrothing his daughters was to obtain permission for 'one of his daughters' to marry, he may simply have chosen the next in line. Either way, on the above date she appears as the wife of John de Charlton the younger. If twelve at the time of marriage, then she was born about 1307. She was not arrested in 1324 as by then John de Charlton the elder had made his peace with the king. Her first surviving son born in 1334. She was still alive in 1345.

5. **Geoffrey**, the third son, was probably born in 1308 or 1309. He was his mother's mother's heir, and thus inherited a number of de Lusignan estates in France, notably the lordships of Couhé (his seat), Peyrat, Pontarion, Salles and Genté on her death in 1323. As he was in France at the time of Roger's arrest, and yet was able to inherit in 1323 without having to prove his age (and therefore, under the Lusignan rule, at least fourteen) one can suggest that he was serving as a yeoman in the household of a French relation, most probably that of the de Fiennes family in

Picardy, to which Roger went on his escape in 1323. This guaranteed Roger an income in exile. He returned with Roger in 1326, was knighted at the coronation in 1327, and became a firm supporter of his father, taking an active role at court by August 1329, and being trusted with witnessing royal charters in 1330. He was arrested with his father in October 1330, but allowed to go free and enjoy his French inheritance. He there married Joan de Lezay and had a family, and died between 1372 and 1376. See G.W. Watson, 'Geoffrey de Mortimer and His Descendants', *Genealogist*, NS 22 (1906), p. 1.

6. **John**, the fourth son. The fact that he was knighted by his father in Ireland in 1317, a full ten years before his three elder brothers, might suggest that John should be placed earlier in the list of Mortimer children. However, the explanation is probably that he was the only one of the Mortimer boys to travel with Roger to Ireland, and the only one available when Roger received the right to make knights as the king's representative there in 1317–18. The reason he was with Roger and Joan was that he was young enough not to have been placed in another household, and thus no older than about seven. He seems to have come of age in the period during which his father was in exile, as at first only his two eldest brothers were imprisoned at Windsor, but in 1324 he joined them in captivity, being imprisoned in Odiham Castle. On 1 October 1326 he and his brothers were transferred to the Tower. He was probably born in or about 1310. In August 1328 he was granted castles in Ireland, and seems shortly afterwards to have had the Irish estates of his brother Roger settled on him. He did not live to enjoy his inheritance, being killed shortly afterwards in a tournament at Shrewsbury.

7. **Joan**. The reason for placing Joan at this point in the order of children is that she is named as one of the girls arrested in 1324 and imprisoned at Sempringham Priory. At this time only the elder daughters of Roger and Joan were imprisoned, with the exception of Maud, whose husband had been accepted back into the king's favour. Joan is the second named of the three girls mentioned, the eldest being Margaret, and it is thus suspected she was the second or third eldest, and was born at some point between 1308 and 1313. According to the *Complete Peerage* she was married before June 1330 to James Audley, who was born in January 1313. However their eldest surviving son, Nicholas, was betrothed in the period March 1329–March 1331, so the wedding probably took place before July 1328. Although Murimuth states that the double Mortimer wedding at Hereford in 1328 was between Roger's daughters and the heirs of the earldoms of

Norfolk and Pembroke, it is more likely that these latter marriages took place after Roger's elevation to the earldom of March, and after his other, older heirs in wardship had been married to his daughters. In addition, both the Audley and Beauchamp wards received their lands in the first half of 1329. Thus it is suggested that Murimuth (writing in 1337) has confused the Mortimer double wedding at Hereford with another Mortimer wedding, namely that of Joan and Lord Audley, probably at Hereford on or about 31 May 1328, which was possibly also a double wedding with Catherine and Thomas de Beauchamp, a bridegroom of a similar age. Since Roger had been Audley's guardian since December 1316 (according to the *CPR*), this right being renewed in 1326, the marriage was only delayed by the hiatus in his career which suspended the marriage fortunes of all his unmarried children. In view of her sister Isabella also being old enough to be imprisoned in 1324, Joan was probably slightly older than her husband, being born in 1311 or 1312, when Roger and Joan were in Ireland. She died between 1337 and 1351.

8. **Isabella**. Of the twelve children Isabella is the only one not recorded in the *Complete Peerage*. This is because she was not noticed by Dugdale in his *Baronage*, having been ignored by the fourteenth-century Wigmore chronicler. The reason for her being ignored is that she did not make a noteworthy marriage. She is only certainly known through the entries relating to her imprisonment in the Close Rolls, in which she was ordered to be sent to Chicksands Priory. The fact she was old enough to be imprisoned in 1324, and yet of an age comparable with her sister Joan, suggests that she was born in the period 1310–13, and if born separately from her siblings, probably towards the end of this period. It is doubtful that she was the Isabella de Mortimer who is recorded in the Patent Rolls as holding the manor of Wychbold for life on 2 September 1327, and who was pardoned a £10 fine at Roger's request. This pardon being made to her in conjunction with Richard Talbot suggests she was Isabella de Mortimer of Richard's Castle. A similar fine was imposed on Blanche and her husband.

9. **Catherine**. In an early edition of *Notes and Queries* she was described as the eldest daughter, but the fact of her neither being married nor arrested in 1324 suggests she was too young at the time. She was married after October 1326 to Thomas de Beauchamp, Earl of Warwick. Roger had sought and received papal permission for one of his daughters to marry the Earl of Warwick's heir, in 1319. Since her husband was born in 1314, this permission was probably only being sought on account of the consanguinity between the two families, and no actual marriage at this stage was

planned. It is suspected that she was born in about 1314. If there were two Mortimer double weddings at Hereford, one in 1328 and another in 1329, Catherine would have been in the first pair. Like Joan she married a ward of Roger's, and both prospective bridegrooms were about the same age, born in 1313 and 1314 respectively. However, Roger granted these two wards their lands at different times in the first half of 1329, and this might more closely reflect their wedding dates. Thus there is reason to suppose that Catherine was married before February 1329, possibly as part of a double wedding on 31 May 1328. Catherine's second surviving son was born before March 1339. She wrote a will on 4 August 1369 and died shortly afterwards, being buried in St Mary's Warwick in an alabaster tomb, which still bears her effigy and that of her husband.

10 and 11. **Agnes and Beatrice**. Agnes is said in the *Complete Peerage* to have been the third daughter, but there seems to be no sound evidence for this. Both she and Beatrice were said by Murimuth to have been married in late May or early June 1328 in the presence of Roger, Isabella and the king at Hereford. However, it is unlikely that they were married to two such eminent heirs before Roger himself was an earl. It has been suggested by Doherty in his thesis on Isabella (p. 285) that the double wedding of Agnes to Laurence de Hastings, Earl of Pembroke, and Beatrice to Edward, son and heir of Thomas of Brotherton, Earl of Norfolk, took place at Hereford in the summer of 1329, and, as he points out, the privy seal was indeed at Hereford from 8 to 13 September 1329. This was just after a royal visit to Wigmore, to which the court had gone from Gloucester. According to his theory, the court accompanied Roger to Wigmore on 5–7 September 1329 to fetch his two brides, and to take them to Hereford for the wedding. This is unlikely. Avesbury suggests the Round Table tournament which almost certainly accompanied their nuptials was at Wigmore, and this is a more likely venue. Agnes bore her only surviving son in August 1347, but lost her husband the following year, and was married secondly to John Hakelut. Her will is dated 10 October 1367 and she died 25 July 1368, being buried in London at the Minoresses without Aldgate (since destroyed). Beatrice married Thomas, Lord Braose, after her first husband's death, in or before 1334. Her eldest surviving son was by her second marriage, born in 1339, and she died in 1383, the last surviving of Roger's children. It is likely that Agnes and Beatrice were born some time in the period 1315–21.

12. **Blanche**. She is presumed to be the youngest of the Mortimer daughters, but as with Catherine, Agnes and Beatrice, she could have been born

at any point between 1314 and 1322. The name was a de Geneville family name, Blanche being the name of one of Joan's sisters. Blanche Mortimer married Piers de Grandison before 10 June 1320 and died in 1347. Her husband must have been born between 1286 and 1291, about the same age as Roger, and because the de Grandisons were not particularly powerful, being minor Herefordshire lords by comparison with the Mortimers, it is possible that she was married before Roger's fall from grace in 1321. However she bore no children, although her husband was clearly of age. The earliest certain date is that she was married before 10 June 1330, before which they had received the manor of Much Marcle from Margaret Mortimer, Roger's mother. If this was a dowry, it is likely that they were married not long before this. We have no evidence as to when Blanche was born; it was probably after 1315 as she was not arrested in 1322, although de Grandison was a contrariant. She died in 1347, and was buried in the church at Much Marcle, Herefordshire, where her tomb with its effigy is still extant.

SELECT BIBLIOGRAPHY

1. Unpublished primary sources

British Library (BL)

Harleian MS 1240 (Black Book of Wigmore)

Add. MS 6041 (fourteenth-century list of Mortimer muniments)

Egerton Charters 8723 (list of Mortimer muniments taken to the Tower, 1322)

Cottonian MSS Charters II 26/27 (letter from Roger Mortimer to Edward II, c. 1317–21)

Cotton MSS Nero A iv (Ludlow Annals)

Hereford Cathedral Library

Documents concerning the rebellion of Roger Mortimer, 1321–2 (calendared in the National Register of Archives list, NRA 6186)

John Rylands Library, University of Manchester

Latin MS 215 (Wigmore Abbey Annals, c. 1096–1307, transcribed in B.P. Evans's thesis noted below)

Public Record Office (PRO)

C53/93–117 (witness lists 1304–5–1330–31)

C71/7, C71/10 (Scotch Rolls 1314, 1318)

DL27/93 (Marriage allocation of Edmund Mortimer, 1316)

E101/370/19, E101/371/8/97 (Ordinaries of Roger Mortimer's household, c. 1304–5)

E101/384/1 (Wardrobe Book, 3 Edward III)

2. Published primary sources: record and official publications

Appendix to the 35th Report of the Deputy Keeper of the Public Records (1874)

W.W. Blom (ed.), *Calendar of Entries in the Papal Registers Relating to Great Britain and Ireland*, vol. ii (1895)

Calendar of the Charter Rolls Preserved in the Public Record Office, 1226–1516 (6 vols, 1903–27), vols 2–4

Calendar of the Close Rolls Preserved in the Public Record Office, Edward I, Edward II & Edward III (21 vols, 1892–1913)

Calendar of the Fine Rolls Preserved in the Public Record Office, Edward I, Edward II & Edward III 1327–1347 (5 vols, 1911–15)

Calendar of Inquisitions Post Mortem and Other Analogous Documents Preserved in the Public Record Office, Edward I, Edward II & Edward III (13 vols, 1906–52)

Calendar of the Patent Rolls Preserved in the Public Record Office, Edward I, Edward II & Edward III (25 vols, 1891–1916)

Calendar of Various Chancery Rolls: Supplementary Close Rolls, Welsh Rolls, Scutage Rolls, preserved in the Public Record Office 1277–1326 (1912)

Pierre Chaplais (ed.), *The War of Saint-Sardos*, Camden, 3rd series, 87 (1954)

Adam Clarke, J. Caley, J. Bayley, F. Holbrooke, J.W. Clarke (eds), *Foedera, conventiones, litterae, etc., or Rymer's Foedera 1066–1383* (6 vols, 1816), vols ii–iii

Philomena Connolly (ed.), *Irish Exchequer Payments* (Irish MSS Commission, Dublin, 1998)

Edmund Curtis (ed.), *Calendar of Ormond Deeds 1172–1350* (Dublin, 1932)

J.T. Gilbert (ed.), *Historic and Municipal Documents of Ireland, A.D. 1172–1320. From the Archives of the City of Dublin, etc*, Rolls series, 53 (1870)

Lambert B. Larking, 'Inventory of the Effects of Roger Mortimer at Wigmore Castle and Abbey, Herefordshire', *Archaeological Journal*, xv (1858), 354–62

D. Macpherson, J. Caley, W. Illingworth (eds), *Rotuli Scotiae in turri Londinensi et in domo Capitulari Westmonasteriensi asservati* (2 vols, 1814–19)

James Mills (ed.), *Calendar of the Justiciary Rolls: or, Proceedings in the Court of the Justiciar of Ireland Preserved in the Public Record Office of Ireland 1305–1307* (Dublin, 1914)

Francis Palgrave (ed.), *The Parliamentary writs and writs of military summons: together with the records and muniments relating to the suit and service due and performed to the King's high court of Parliament and the councils of the realm, or affording evidence of attendance given at Parliament and councils* (4 vols, 1827)

J.R.S. Phillips, *Documents on the Early Stages of the Bruce Invasion of Ireland, 1315–1316*, Proceedings of the Royal Irish Academy, vol. 79, C, no. 11 (Dublin, 1979)

Yves Renouard (ed.), *Gascon Rolls Preserved in the Public Record Office 1307–1317* (1962)

J. Strachey, John Pridden, Edward Upham (eds), *Rotuli parliamentorum: ut et petitiones, et placita in Parliamento (1278–1503): together with an index to the Rolls of Parliament, comprising the petitions, pleas and proceedings of Parliament . . . A.D. 1278–A.D. 1503* (8 vols, 1767–1832)

Rotulorum Patentium et Clausorum Cancellarie Hiberniae Calendarium, vol. 1, part 1 (1828)

John Stow, *A Survey of the Cities of London and Westminster, and the Borough of Southwark* (2 vols, 1754)

A.H. Thomas (ed.), *Calendar of Plea and Memoranda Rolls* preserved among the archives of the Corporation of the City of London at the Guildhall Rolls A1a–A9: AD 1323–1364 (Cambridge, 1926)

Herbert Wood, *The Muniments of Edmund de Mortimer, Third Earl of March, Concerning his Liberty of Trim*, Proceedings of the Royal Irish Academy, vol. 40, C, no. 7 (Dublin, 1932)

Herbert Wood, Albert E. Langman, Margaret Griffith (eds), *Calendar of the Justiciary Rolls, or Proceedings in the Court of the Justiciar of Ireland, I to VII* years of Edward II, Irish Record Office (Dublin, 1956)

3. Published primary sources: chronicles and annals

Annals of Ulster, vol. ii (1893)

G.J. Aungier (ed.), *French Chronicle of London*, Camden Society, Old series, 28 (1844)

E.A. Bond (ed.), *Chronicon Monasterii de Melsa* (1867)

F.W.D. Brie (ed.), *The Brut*, Early English Text Society (Oxford, 1906–8)

W.R. Childs, J. Taylor (eds), *The Anonimalle Chronicle, 1307–1334, from Brotherton Collection MS 29*, Yorkshire Archaeological Society Record Series, 147 (1991)

N. Denholm-Young (ed.), *Vita Edwardi Secundi* (1957)

John T. Gilbert (ed.), *Chartularies of St Mary's Abbey, Dublin: With the Register of its House at Dunbrody and Annals of Ireland* (2 vols, 1884)

H.C. Hamilton (ed.), *Chronicon Domini Walteri de Hemingburgh*, vol. ii, English Historical Society (1849)

William Henry Hart (ed.), *Historiae et Cartularium Monasterii Gloucestriae*, vol. 1, Rolls series, 33 (1863)

William Hennessy (ed.), *Annals of Loch Cé*, Rolls series, 54 (2 vols, 1871)

G.L. Haskins, 'A Chronicle of the Civil Wars of Edward II', *Speculum*, 14, 1 (1939), 73–81

John Joliffe (ed.), *Froissart's Chronicles* (1968).

H.R. Luard (ed.), *Annales Monastici*, Rolls series, 36 (5 vols, 1864–9)

H.R. Luard (ed.), *Flores Historiarum* (1890)

J.R. Lumby (ed.), *Polychronicon Ranulphi Higden*, vol. viii (1882)

J.R. Lumby (ed.), *Chronicon Henrici Knighton, vel Cnitthon, monachi Leycestrensis*, Rolls series, 92 (2 vols, 1889–95)

Sir Herbert Maxwell (ed.), *Scalacronica: The Reigns of Edward I, Edward II and Edward III as Recorded by Sir Thomas Gray . . .* (Glasgow, 1907)

S.A. Moore (ed.), 'Documents Relating to the Death and Burial of King Edward II', *Archaeologia*, 50 (1887), 215–26

John O'Donovan, *Annals of the Kingdom of Ireland by the Four Masters*, vol. iii (Dublin, 1854)

H.T. Riley (ed.), *Chronica Monasterii S. Albani*, pt 1: *Thomae Walsingham Historia Anglicana*, Rolls series, 28/1 (1865)

H.T. Riley (ed.), *Chronica Monasterii S. Albani*, pt 2: *Willelmi Rishanger quondam monachi S. Albani et quorundam anonymorum Chronica et Annales regnantibus Henrico Tertio et Edwardo Primo . . . 1259–1307*, Rolls series, 28/2 (1865)

H.T. Riley (ed.), *Chronica Monasterii S. Albani*, pt 3: *Johannis de Trokelowe et Henrici de Blaneforde . . .* Rolls series, 28/3 (1866)

R.A. Roberts (ed.), *Edward II, the Lords Ordainers, and Piers Gaveston's Jewels and Horses, 1312–1313*, Camden 3rd series, 41 (1929)

Harry Rothwell (ed.), *Chronicle of Walter of Guisborough*, Camden Society, 3rd series, 89 (1957)

Walter Skeat (ed.), John Barbour, *The Bruce*, Early English Text Society (3 vols, 1870–7)

J. Stevenson (ed.), *The Chronicle of Lanercost* (Edinburgh, 1839)

William Stubbs (ed.), *Chronicles illustrative of the reigns of Edward I and Edward II*: vol. 1: *Annales Londonienses and Annales Paulini*; vol. 2: *Commendatio lamentabilis in transitu magni regis Edwardi, Gesta Edwardi de Carnarvon auctore canonico Bridlingtoniensi, Monachi cujusdam Malmesberiensis vita Edward II, Vita et mors Edward II conscripta a Thoma de la Moore*, Rolls series, 76 (1882–3)

J. Tait (ed.), *Chronica Johannis de Reading and Anonymi Cantuarensis* (Manchester, 1914)

E. Maunde Thompson (ed.), *Chronicon Angliae ab anno domini 1328 usque ad annum 1388*, Rolls series, 64 (1874)

E. Maunde Thompson (ed.), *Chronicon Galfridi le Baker de Swynebroke* (Oxford, 1889)

E. Maunde Thompson (ed.), *Adae Murimuth, Continuatio Chronicarum*, Rolls series, 93 (1889)

Thomas Wright (ed.), *Political Songs of England*, Camden Society, Old series, 14 (1839)

Thomas Wright (ed.), *The Chronicle of Pierre de Langtoft in French Verse*, Rolls series, 47 (2 vols, 1866–8)

4. Unpublished secondary sources

P.C. Doherty, 'Isabella, Queen of England, 1296–1330', D.Phil. thesis (University of Oxford, 1978)

B.P. Evans, 'The Family of Mortimer' Ph.D. thesis (University of Wales, 1937)

D.A. Harding, 'The Regime of Isabella and Mortimer, 1326–1330', M.Phil. thesis (University of Durham, 1985)

Anonymous, unpublished typescript in the reading room of the PRO, 'The Itinerary of Edward III and His Household', covering years 1327–34 (n.d.)

5. Published secondary sources: articles in journals and separately authored analyses

'Two Effigies in Montgomery Church', *Archaeologia Cambrensis*, lxxx (1925), 76–9.

'Wigmore and Neighbourhood', *Transactions of the Woolhope Naturalists Field Club* (1906), 300–6

D.G. Bayliss, 'The Lordship of Wigmore in the Fourteenth Century', *Transactions of the Woolhope Naturalists Field Club*, 36, 1 (1959), 42–8

F.D. Blackley, 'Isabella of France, Queen of England (1308–1358), and the Late Medieval Cult of the Dead', *Canadian Journal of History*, 15, 1 (1980), 23–47

F.D. Blackley, G. Hermansen (eds), 'A Household Book of Isabella of England 1311–12', *Historical Papers* (1969), 140–51

F.D. Blackley, 'Isabella and the Bishop of Exeter', in T.A. Sandquist, M.R. Powicke (eds), *Essays in Medieval History Presented to Bertie Wilkinson* (Toronto, 1969), 220–35

E.A.R. Brown, 'Diplomacy, Adultery and Domestic Politics at the Court of Philip the Fair: Queen Isabelle's Mission to France in 1314', in J.S. Hamilton (ed.), *Documenting the Past: Essays in Medieval History Presented to George Peddy Cuttino* (Woodbridge, 1989)

E.A.R. Brown, 'The Marriage of Edward II of England and Isabelle of France: A Postscript', *Speculum*, 64 (1989), 373–9

R. Butler, 'The Last of the Brimpsfield Giffards and the Rising of 1321–22', *Transactions of the Bristol and Gloucestershire Archaeological Society*, 76 (1957), 75–97

Maude V. Clarke, 'Irish Parliaments in the Reign of Edward II', *Transactions of the Royal Historical Society*, 4th series, 9 (1926), 29–62

Maude V. Clarke, 'Committees of Estates and the Deposition of Edward II', in J.G. Edwards, V.H. Galbraith, E.F. Jacob (eds), *Historical Essays in Honour of James Tait* (Manchester, 1933), 27–45

Charles George Crump, 'The Arrest of Roger Mortimer and Queen Isabel', *English Historical Review*, 26 (1911), 331–2

G.P. Cuttino, T.W. Lyman, 'Where is Edward II?', *Speculum*, 53, 3 (1978), 522–3

J.C. Davies, 'The Despenser War in Glamorgan', *Transactions of the Royal Historical Society*, 3rd series, 9 (1915), 21–64

James Davies, 'Wigmore Castle and the Mortimers', *The Woolhope Club* (1881–2), 22–7

J.C. Dickinson, P.T. Ricketts (eds), 'The Anglo-Norman Chronicle of Wigmore Abbey', *Transactions of the Woolhope Naturalists Field Club*, 39, 3 (1969), 413–46

P.C. Doherty, 'The Date of the Birth of Isabella, Queen of England (1308–1358)', *Bulletin of the Institute of Historical Research*, 48 (1975), 246–8

Kathleen Edwards, 'The Political Importance of the English Bishops During the Reign of Edward II', *English Historical Review*, 59 (1944), 311–47

Kathleen Edwards, 'The Personal and Political Activities of the English Episcopate During the Reign of Edward II', *Bulletin of the Institute of Historical Research*, 16 (1938), 117–19

Kathleen Edwards, 'The Social Origins and Provenance of the English Bishops During the Reign of Edward II', *Transactions of the Royal Historical Society*, 5th series, 9 (1959), 51–79

J.G. Edwards, 'Sir Gruffydd Lloyd', *English Historical Review*, 30 (1915), 593–7

Robin Frame, 'The Bruces in Ireland, 1315–18', *Irish Historical Studies*, xix, 73 (1974), 3–37

E.B. Fryde, 'The Deposits of Hugh Despenser the Younger with Italian Bankers', *Economic History Review*, 2nd series, 3, 3 (1951), 344–62

Natalie Fryde, 'John Stratford, Bishop of Winchester and the Crown, 1323–1330', *Bulletin of the Institute of Historical Research*, 44 (1971), 153–61

Natalie Fryde, 'Welsh Troops in the Scottish Campaign of 1322', *Bulletin of the Board of Celtic Studies*, 26, 1 (1974), 82–9

E.A. Fuller (ed.), 'The Tallage of Edward II, December 16 1312, and the Bristol Rebellion', *Transactions of the Bristol and Gloucestershire Archaeological Society*, 19 (1894–5), 171–278

M.E. Giffin, 'Cadwaladr, Arthur and Brutus in the Wigmore Manuscript', *Speculum*, 16, 1 (1941), 109–20

M.E. Giffin, 'A Wigmore Manuscript at the University of Chicago', *National Library of Wales Journal*, 7 (1952), 316–25

J.L. Grassi, 'William Airmyn and the Bishopric of Norwich', *English Historical Review*, 70 (1955), 550–61

R.M. Haines, 'Adam Orleton and the Diocese of Winchester', *Journal of Ecclesiastical History* 23 (1972), 1–30

R.M. Haines, 'The afterlife of Edward of Carnarvon', *Transactions of the Bristol and Gloucester Archaeological Society*, 114 (1996), 65–86

G.L. Haskins, 'The Doncaster Petition of 1321', *English Historical Review*, 53 (1938), 478–85

G.A. Holmes, 'A Protest Against the Despensers, 1326', *Speculum*, 30 (1955), 207–12

G.A. Holmes, 'The Judgement on the Younger Despenser, 1326', *English Historical Review*, 70 (1955), 261–7

G.A. Holmes, 'The Rebellion of the Earl of Lancaster, 1328–9', *Bulletin of the Institute of Historical Research*, 28 (1955), 84–9

W.H. St John Hope, 'On the Funeral Effigies of the Kings and Queens of England', *Archaeologia*, 60 (1907), 517–70.

R.S. Hoyt, 'The Coronation Oath of 1308', *English Historical Review*, 71 (1956), 353–83

A. Hughes, 'The Politics of Music in the Coronation Service of Edward II, 1308', *Journal of Musicology*, 6 (1988), 150–68

Joseph Hunter, 'Measures Taken for the Apprehension of Sir Thomas de Gurney, One of the Murderers of Edward II', *Archaeologia*, 27 (1838), 274–97

Joseph Hunter, 'The Mission of Queen Isabella to the Court of France', *Archaeologia*, 36 (1855), 242–57

Hilda Johnstone, 'The Eccentricities of Edward II', *English Historical Review*, 48 (1933), 264–7

Hilda Johnstone, 'Isabella, the She-wolf of France', *History*, 21 (1936), 208–18

M. Keen, 'Treason Trials Under the Law of Arms', in *Transactions of the Royal Historical Society*, 5th series, 12 (1962), 85–104

G. Lambrick, 'Abingdon and the Riots of 1327', *Oxoniensia*, 29 (1966), 129–41

May McKisack, 'Edward III and the Historians', *History*, 45 (1960), 1–15

Sophia Menache, 'Isabelle of France, Queen of England – a Reconsideration', *Journal of Medieval History*, 10 (1984), 107–24

Ranald Nicholson, 'A Sequel to Edward Bruce's Invasion of Ireland', *Scottish Historical Review*, 42 (1963), 30–40

J.R.S. Phillips, 'The "Middle Party" and the Negotiating of the Treaty of Leake, August 1318: a Reinterpretation', *Bulletin of the Institute of Historical Research*, 46 (1973), 11–27

J.R.S. Phillips, 'The Mission of John de Hothum to Ireland, 1315–1316', in James Lydon (ed.), *England and Ireland in the Later Middle Ages: Essays in Honour of Jocelyn Otway-Ruthven* (Dublin, 1981), 62–85

J.R.S. Phillips, 'Edward II and the Prophets', in W.M. Ormrod (ed.), *England in the Fourteenth Century* (1985), 189–201

Sir Maurice Powicke, 'The English Commons in Scotland in 1322 and the Deposition of Edward II', *Speculum*, 35 (1960), 1–15

Derek Pratt, 'The Marcher Lordship of Chirk, 1329–1330', *Transactions of the Denbighshire Historical Society*, 39 (1990), 5–41

Michael Prestwich, 'A New Version of the Ordinances of 1311', *Bulletin of the Institute of Historical Research*, 57 (1984), 189–203

Michael Prestwich, 'The Charges Against the Despensers, 1321', *Bulletin of the Institute of Historical Research*, 58 (1985), 95–100

J.H. Round, 'The Landing of Queen Isabella', *English Historical Review*, 14 (1899), 104–5.

Nigel Saul, 'The Despensers and the Downfall of Edward II', *English Historical Review*, 99 (1984), 1–33

G.O. Sayles, 'The Formal Judgements on the Traitors of 1322', *Speculum*, 16 (1941), 57–63

Caroline Shenton, 'Edward III and the Coup of 1330', in J.S. Bothwell (ed.), *The Age of Edward III* (York, 2001), 1–34

J.B. Smith, 'Edward II and the Allegiance of Wales', *Welsh History Review*, 8 (1976), 137–71

E.L.G. Stones, 'The Dates of Roger Mortimer's Escape from the Tower of London', *English Historical Review*, 66 (1951), 97–8

E.L.G. Stones, 'The Anglo-Scottish Negotiations of 1327', *Scottish Historical Review*, 30 (1951), 49–54

C. Swynnerton, 'Certain Chattels of Roger Mortimer of Wigmore', *Notes and Queries*, 11th series, x, 126–7

F.J. Tanquerey, 'The Conspiracy of Thomas Dunheved, 1327', *English Historical Review*, 31 (1916), 119–24

John Taylor, 'The French *Brut* and the Reign of Edward II', *English Historical Review*, 72 (1957), 423–37

John Taylor, 'The Judgement on Hugh Despenser the Younger', *Medievalia et Humanistica*, xii (1958), 70–7

A. Tomkinson, 'Retinues at the Tournament of Dunstable, 1309', *English Historical Review*, 74 (1959), 70–89

Thomas Frederick Tout, 'The Captivity and Death of Edward of Carnarvon', *Bulletin of the John Rylands Library*, vol. 6 (1921), 69–113

G.A. Usher, 'The Career of a Political Bishop: Adam de Orleton (c. 1279–1345), *Transactions of the Royal Historical Society*, 5th series, 22 (1972), 33–47

C. Valente, 'The Deposition and Abdication of Edward II', *English Historical Review*, 113 (1998), 852–81

G.W. Watson, 'Geoffrey de Mortimer and His Descendants', *Genealogist* NS, 22 (1906), 1–16.

S.L. Waugh, 'The Profits of Violence: the Minor Gentry in the Rebellion of 1321–22 in Gloucestershire and Herefordshire', *Speculum*, 52 (1977), 843–69

S.L. Waugh, 'For King, Country and Patron: the Despensers and Local Administration, 1321–22', *Journal of British Studies*, 22 (1983), 23–58

Bertie Wilkinson, 'The Coronation Oath of Edward II and the Statute of York', *Speculum*, 19, 4 (1944), 445–69

Bertie Wilkinson, 'The Negotiations Preceding the "Treaty" of Leake, August 1318', in R.W. Hunt, W.A. Pantin, R.W. Southern (eds), *Studies in Medieval History Presented to Frederick Maurice Powicke* (Oxford, 1948), 333–53

Bertie Wilkinson, 'The Sherburn Indenture and the Attack on the Despensers, 1321', *English Historical Review*, 63 (1948), 1–28

6. Published secondary sources: monographs and collections of essays

Olive Armstrong, *Edward Bruce's Invasion of Ireland* (1923)

Joshua Barnes, *The History of that Most Victorious Monarch Edward III* (Cambridge, 1688)

G.W.S. Barrow, *Robert Bruce and the Community of the Realm of Scotland* (3rd edn, Edinburgh, 1988)

Caroline Bingham, *The Life and Times of Edward II* (1973)

T.H. Bound, *History of Wigmore* (1876)

M. Buck, *Politics, Finance and the Church in the Age of Edward II: Walter Stapeldon, Treasurer of England* (Cambridge, 1983)

Pierre Chaplais, *Piers Gaveston, Edward II's Adoptive Brother* (Oxford, 1994)

W.R. Childs and J. Taylor (eds), *Politics and Crisis in Fourteenth-century England* (Gloucester, 1990)

G.E. Cokayne, revised by V. Gibbs, H.A. Doubleday, D. Warrand and Lord Howard de Walden (eds), *The Complete Peerage of England, Scotland, Ireland, Great Britain and the United Kingdom extant, extinct or dormant* (14 vols, 1910–98)

James Conway Davies, *The Baronial Opposition to Edward II* (Cambridge, 1918)

Art Cosgrove (ed.), *A New History of Ireland: ii Medieval Ireland* (Oxford, 1987)

R.R. Davies, *Lordship and Society in the March of Wales 1282–1400* (Oxford, 1978)

G.R.C. Davis, *Magna Carta* (1st pub. 1963, 6th reprint 1989)

Sir William Dugdale, *The Baronage of England*, vol. i (1661)

Sir William Dugdale (ed. J. Caley, H. Ellis, B. Bandinel), *Monasticon* (6 vols in 9, 1817–30)

A.B. Emden, *A Biographical Register of the University of Oxford to AD 1500* (3 vols, Oxford, 1957–9)

R.W. Eyton, *Antiquities of Shropshire* (12 vols, 1854–60)

Michael Faraday, *Ludlow 1085–1660* (Chichester, 1991)

Robin Frame, *English Lordship in Ireland 1318–1361* (Oxford, 1982)

Natalie Fryde, *The Tyranny and Fall of Edward II 1321–1326* (Cambridge, 1979)

Antonia Gransden, *Historical Writing in England ii: 1307 to the Early Sixteenth Century* (1982)

Ralph Griffiths, *The Principality of Wales in the Later Middle Ages: the Structure and Personnel of Government*. i. *South Wales 1277–1536* (Cardiff, 1972)

Ralph Griffiths, *Conquerors and Conquered in Medieval Wales* (Stroud, 1994)

R.M. Haines, *The Church and Politics in Fourteenth-Century England: the Career of Adam Orleton, c. 1275–1345* (1978)

Elizabeth Hallam, *The Itinerary of Edward II and His Household, 1307–1328*. List and Index Society Publications, 211 (1984)

Elizabeth Hallam, *English Royal Marriages: the French marriages of Edward I and Edward II; facsimiles* (1981)

J.S. Hamilton, *Piers Gaveston, Earl of Cornwall, 1307–1312* (1988)

G.A. Holmes, *The Estates of the Higher Nobility in Fourteenth-Century England* (Cambridge, 1957)

Harold Hutchison, *Edward II, the Pliant King* (1971)

Hilda Johnstone, *Edward of Carnarvon* (Manchester, 1946)

Maurice Keen, *The Later Middle Ages* (1973)

Maurice Keen, *Chivalry* (1984)

J.F. Lydon, *The Lordship of Ireland in the Middle Ages* (Dublin, 1972)

J.R. Maddicott, *Thomas of Lancaster* (Oxford, 1970)

K.B. McFarlane, *The Nobility of Later Medieval England* (Oxford, 1973)

May McKisack, *The Fourteenth Century* (Oxford, 1959)

Kate Mertes, *The English Noble Household, 1250–1600* (Oxford, 1988)

Robert W. Mitchell, *English Medieval Rolls of Arms*, vol. i, *1244–1334* (1983)

L. Moir, *Historic Ludlow Castle and Those Associated with It* (Ludlow, 1950)

John E. Morris, *The Welsh Wars of Edward I* (Oxford, 1901)

Ranald Nicholson, *Scotland: the Later Middle Ages* (Edinburgh, 1974)

G.H. Orpen, *Ireland Under the Normans, 1216–1333*, vols iii and iv (1920)

A.J. Otway-Ruthven, *A History of Medieval Ireland* (1968; reprint, New York, 1993)

Michael Packe, *King Edward III* (1983)

J.R.S. Phillips, *Aymer de Valence* (Oxford, 1972)

Sir Maurice Powicke, *The Thirteenth Century* (2nd edn, 1962)

Michael Prestwich, *The Three Edwards: War and State in England, 1272–1377* (1980)

T.B. Pugh (ed.), *County History of Glamorgan*, vol. iii: *the Middle Ages* (Cardiff, 1971)

William Rees, *South Wales and the Border in the Fourteenth Century* (Southampton, 1932)

H.G. Richardson, G.O. Sayles, *The Administration of Ireland 1172–1327* (Dublin, 1963)

Royal Commission on Historical Monuments (England), *An Inventory of the Historical Monuments in Herefordshire / Royal Commission on Historical Monuments England*, vol. iii: *North-West* (1934)

L.F. Salzman, *Edward I* (1968)

William Seymour, *Battles in Britain and their Political Background, 1066–1547* (1975)

W.A. Shaw (ed.), *Knights of England* (2 vols, 1906)

Sir John Smyth, *The Lives of the Berkeleys* (3 vols, Gloucester, 1883–5)

Leslie Stephen, Sir Sidney Lee (eds) *Dictionary of National Biography* (1885–1912)

P.D. Sweetman, *Archaeological Excavations at Trim Castle, Co. Meath, 1971–74*, Proceedings of the Royal Irish Academy, 78, C, 6 (1978), 127–98

John Taylor, *English Historical Literature in the Fourteenth Century* (Oxford, 1987)

John Taylor, *The Universal Chronicle of Ranulph Higden* (Oxford, 1966)

Thomas Frederick Tout, *Chapters in English Administrative History* (Manchester, 6 vols, 1923)

Thomas Frederick Tout, *The Place of Edward II in English History* (2nd edn, Manchester, 1936)

Juliet Vale, *Edward III and Chivalry* (1982)

Lord Howard de Walden, *Some Feudal Lords and Their Seals* (1904)

GENEALOGICAL TABLES

1. The Mortimer family, *c.* 1200–1330, showing Roger's connections with the royal family, the Princes of Wales, and the Earls of Arundel
2. The Earls of Pembroke and the Counts of La Marche, showing Roger's connections with Robert Bruce and the Earls of Pembroke and Gloucester, and his wife's connections with the royal family, the Earls of Pembroke and Warwick and the Counts of La Marche
3. The de Fiennes family, showing Roger's connections with the royal family, the Counts of Hainault and the Earls of Hereford through his mother
4. The de Braose and de Lacy families, showing Roger's and his wife's connections with these families and the Earls of Warwick and the de Verdon family
5. The English royal family
6. The French royal family

Table 1: THE MORTIMER FAMILY, c. 1200–1330

showing Roger's connections with the royal family, the Princes of Wales, and the Earls of Arundel

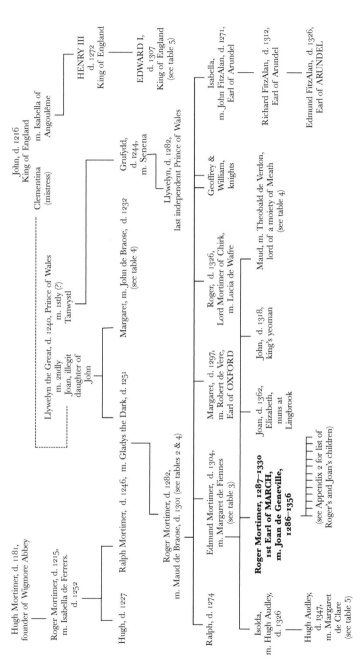

Table 2: THE EARLS OF PEMBROKE AND THE COUNTS OF LA MARCHE

showing Roger's connections with Robert Bruce and the Earls of Pembroke and Gloucester
and his wife's connections with the royal family, the Earls of Pembroke and Warwick and the Counts of La Marche

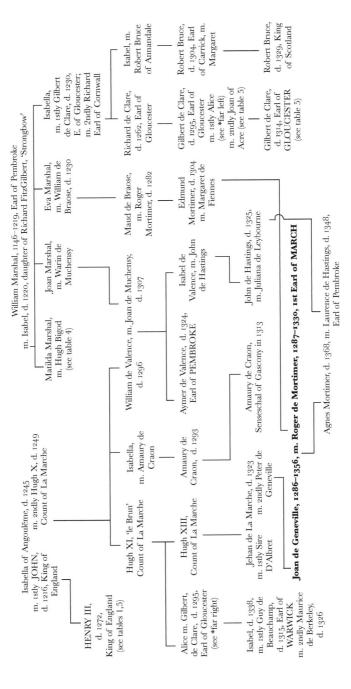

Table 3: THE DE FIENNES FAMILY

showing Roger's connections with the royal family, the Counts of Hainault and the Earls of Hereford through his mother

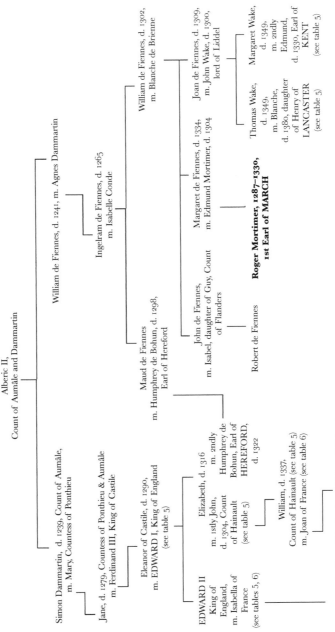

Table 4: THE DE BRAOSE AND DE LACY FAMILIES

showing Roger's and his wife's connections with these families and the Earls of Warwick and the de Verdon family. (N.B. Walter and Hugh de Lacy of Rathwire, Roger's tenants and enemies in 1315–7, were probably descended from Robert, a younger brother of Hugh de Lacy, the lord of Meath, who died in 1186)

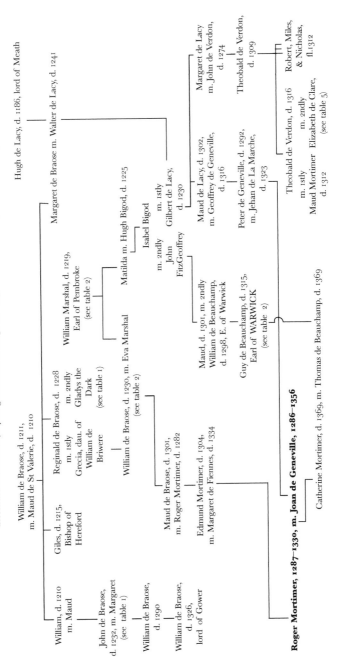

Table 5: THE ENGLISH ROYAL FAMILY

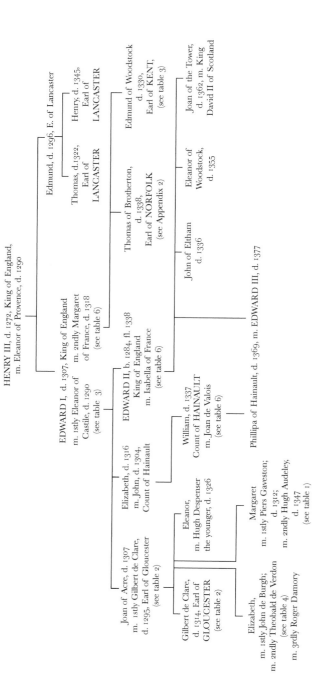

HENRY III, d. 1272, King of England,
m. Eleanor of Provence, d. 1290

EDWARD I, d. 1307, King of England
m. 1stly Eleanor of Castile, d. 1290
(see table 3)
m. 2ndly Margaret of France, d. 1318
(see table 6)

Edmund, d. 1296, E. of Lancaster

Thomas, d.1322, Earl of LANCASTER

Henry, d. 1345, Earl of LANCASTER

Joan of Acre, d. 1307
m. 1stly Gilbert de Clare, d. 1295, Earl of Gloucester
(see table 2)

Elizabeth, d. 1316
m. John, d. 1304, Count of Hainault

EDWARD II, b. 1284, fl. 1338, King of England
m. Isabella of France
(see table 6)

Thomas of Brotherton, d. 1338, Earl of NORFOLK
(see Appendix 2)

Edmund of Woodstock d. 1330, Earl of KENT,
(see table 3)

Gilbert de Clare, d. 1314, Earl of GLOUCESTER
(see table 2)

Eleanor, m. Hugh Despenser the younger, d. 1326

William, d. 1337 Count of HAINAULT
m. Joan de Valois
(see table 6)

John of Eltham d. 1336

Eleanor of Woodstock, d. 1355

Joan of the Tower, d. 1362, m. King David II of Scotland

Elizabeth,
m. 1stly John de Burgh;
m. 2ndly Theobald de Verdon
(see table 4)
m. 3rdly Roger Damory

Margaret
m. 1stly Piers Gaveston; d. 1312;
m. 2ndly Hugh Audeley, d. 1347
(see table 1)

Phillipa of Hainault, d. 1369, m. EDWARD III, d. 1377

Table 6: THE FRENCH ROYAL FAMILY

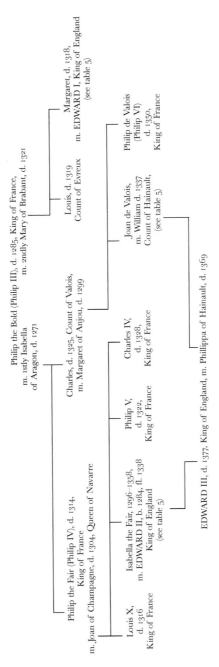

Philip the Bold (Philip III), d. 1285, King of France,
m. 1stly Isabella
of Aragon, d. 1271
m. 2ndly Mary of Brabant, d. 1321

Philip the Fair (Philip IV), d. 1314,
King of France
m. Joan of Champagne, d. 1304, Queen of Navarre

Charles, d. 1325, Count of Valois,
m. Margaret of Anjou, d. 1299

Louis, d. 1319
Count of Evreux

Margaret, d. 1318,
m. EDWARD I, King of England
(see table 5)

Louis X,
d. 1316
King of France

Philip V,
d. 1322,
King of France

Charles IV,
d. 1328,
King of France

Isabella the Fair, 1296–1358, fl. 1338
m. EDWARD II, b. 1284, d. 1338
King of England
(see table 5)

Joan de Valois,
m. William d. 1337
Count of Hainault,
(see table 5)

Philip de Valois
(Philip VI)
d. 1350,
King of France

EDWARD III, d. 1377, King of England, m. Phillippa of Hainault, d. 1369

Index

Croft, Hugh de (d. 1317): 44, 82, 85, 278 (n. 18)

Cromwell, John de (d. 1335?), Lord Cromwell (1308), Steward of the Royal Household (1314–16): 49, 104, 147, 202

Culpeper, Thomas (d. 1321): 113

Culpeper, Walter (d. 1321): 112–113

Cumberland: 123

Cusack, John de: 89, 96

Cusack, Walter de: 81

Cuttino, George Peddy, historian: 253–254, 260

Dalry, Scotland: 26

Dalswinton Castle, Scotland: 54

Damory, Elizabeth (c. 1295–1360), Lady Damory (1317): 127

Damory, Roger (d. 1322), Lord Damory (1317): 33, 79, 90–92, 94–95, 97, 99–101, 103–105, 110, 124, 126

Daniel, John (d. 1326): 160

Darcy, John (d. 1347), Justiciar of Ireland (1323): 175

Darlington, Co. Durham: 177

Dee, River, N. Wales: 13

Dee, River, Ireland: 70

Denbigh, Wales: 171

Derbyshire: 234

Desmond, Ireland: 88

Despenser family: 16

Despenser, Eleanor (1292–1337), Lady Despenser (1314): 135, 171, 200

Despenser, Hugh (c. 1223–1265), Lord Despenser: 8, 65

Despenser, Hugh (1261–1326), Lord Despenser (1295), Earl of Winchester (1322): 1, 33, 103, 107–111, 114, 123–124, 128–129, 137, 143, 156, 159–161, 163

Despenser, Hugh (d. 1326), Lord Despenser (1314): 1–2, 97, 199, 231–232, 239, 259, 273 (n. 23)
– at coronation of Edward II: 38
– rise to prominence, 1314–1320: 65, 87, 90, 95, 99
– role in negotiating Treaty of Leake, 1318: 91–92
– antagonism of Roger and other Marcher lords: 99–104
– war with Marcher lords: 105–110, 114, 266
– banishment: 109–111, 113
– return to England: 123
– government 1322–1326: 121, 124, 126–127, 131, 137–139
– acquisitiveness: 127, 172, 201
– unwelcome in France: 136, 143, 283 (n. 10)
– attempts to prevent Edward leaving England: 142
– ordered to leave court by Pope: 148
– tries to bribe French to kill Isabella: 148
– Lord Mortimer of Chirk dies in his custody: 149
– compared with Roger as a strategist: 153
– price of £2,000 set on his head by Roger and Isabella: 154
– compared with snake in Garden of Eden: 155
– takes flight with king: 153–157, 251
– arrest, judgement and execution: 159–164
– forfeited estates: 171, 173, 202, 228, 234

Deveril, John: 229–230, 258, 262

Devon: 21

Deuddwr, Wales: 78